W9-BYG-323

BAKING

BAKING

JAMES PETERSON

TEN SPEED PRESS
BERKELEY

Copyright © 2009 by James Peterson
Photographs copyright © 2009 by James Peterson

All rights reserved.
Published in the United States by Ten Speed Press, an imprint of the
Crown Publishing Group, a division of Random House, Inc., New York.
www.crownpublishing.com
www.tenspeed.com

Ten Speed Press and the Ten Speed Press colophon are registered
trademarks of Random House, Inc.

Library of Congress Cataloging-in-Publication Data
on file with the publisher.

ISBN 978-1-58008-991-3

Printed in China

Design by Nancy Austin and Katy Brown

10 9 8 7 6 5 4 3 2 1

First Edition

For Paul Geltner

ACKNOWLEDGMENTS

I'd like to thank my consultant, Christopher Ciresi, for his guidance, good advice, and for being a wealth of information. I'd also like to thank Zahra Badakhshan, whose hands appear many times in this book. There are a daunting number of people who have taken the book from manuscript form into its final form. I'd like to thank Lorena Jones for first acquiring the book and then, of course, my editor Clancy Drake, who has spent months laboring tirelessly over the manuscript and galleys getting them in shape. Much appreciation goes to Leslie Evans, my copy editor, for her amazing attention to detail, as well as to proofreader Linda Bouchard and indexer Ken Della Penta. Needless to say, this book was enormously complex to design, a design accomplished so beautifully by Nancy Austin and Katy Brown, with assistance from Chloe Rawlins and Colleen Cain. Thanks also go to Hal Hershey for production management and to Sara Golski for her help with corrections and just about anything editorial. I'd also like to thank publicity director Debra Matsumoto and my publicist, Kristin Casemore.

Then there are always those people who, while not working directly on the book, in one form or another keep me in one piece. I'd like to thank my agents, Elise and Arnold Goodman, for their hard work and persistence, and Zelik Mintz for being there and standing by me. I'd also like to thank Sarah Leuze and Joel Hoffman for their commitment and professionalism.

vii

CONTENTS

INTRODUCTION • xi

ASSUMPTIONS • xiii

Cakes • 1

Pies, Tarts, and Pastries • 125

Cookies • 245

Breads, Quick Breads, and Bread-Based Desserts • 281

Custards, Soufflés, Fruit Curds, and Mousses • 351

INDEX • 370

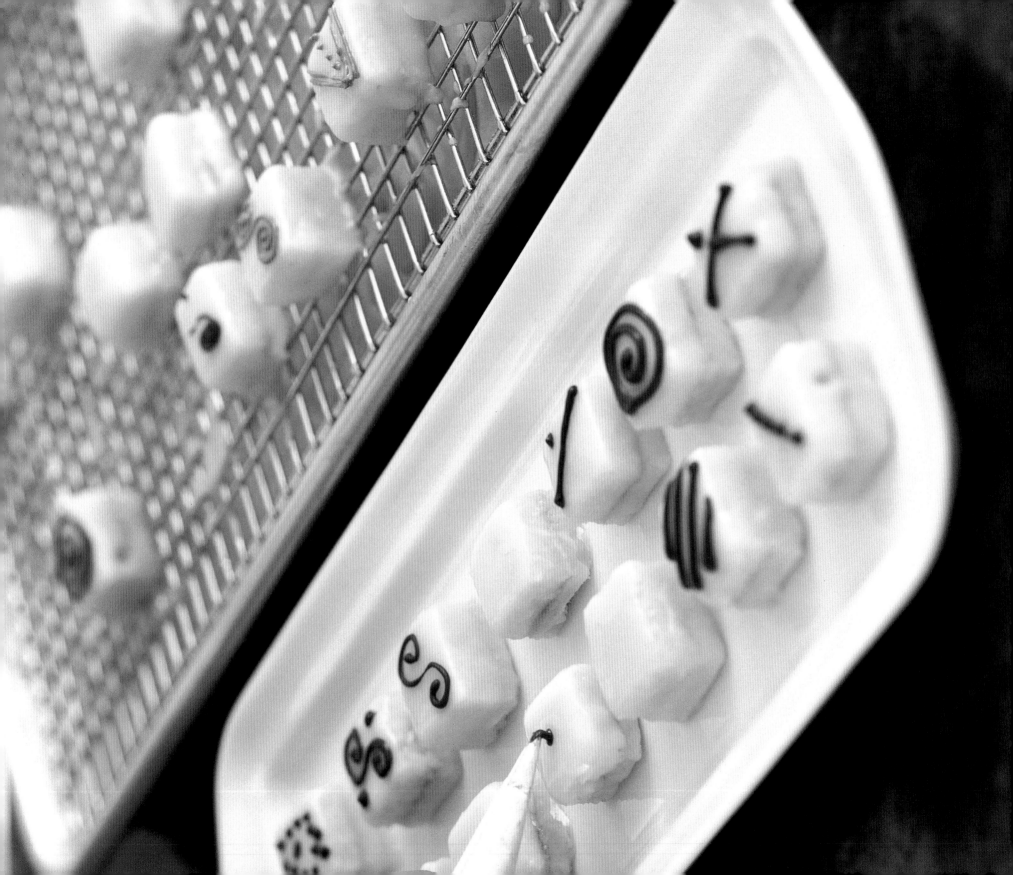

INTRODUCTION

I'm not a natural baker. Whereas when confronted with a stew or roast, I seem to know just what to do, when it comes to baking I need exact measurements and exact directions. And even with instructions in hand I manage to get flour all over the kitchen floor and chocolate on a whole sinkful of dishes. But I do savor the joys of baking: its precision, its particular (and sometimes peculiar) exigencies, and the pleasure of presenting a finished product to my guests or family. As I have progressed as a baker over the last four decades, I've gotten a lot of oohs and aahs, which is always extremely gratifying.

There is no shortage of excellent baking books available. I was motivated to add to the number because it has long seemed to me that most baking books never really explain the rudiments of the art in a way that would allow the reader to build on knowledge gradually acquired. What I hope to bring to the table is an approach that will truly teach you to think like a baker.

This book was years in the making. As with my other highly illustrated step-by-step books, recipe testing and photography went hand in hand—only this time, I worked with a full-time baking consultant "on set." It seemed wise given my proclivities (or lack thereof).

Baking is organized and written in such a way as to enable you to understand the principles and techniques at play in a given classic recipe, and then to apply what you learn to baking projects that aren't even included in the book. This means that most of the chapters are organized in a modular fashion. The chapter on cakes, for example, starts with basic recipes for the six different kinds of cakes, then moves on to recipes for frostings, fillings, and glazes. Next come an array of instructions for assembling cakes, such as raspberry buttercream layer cake (page 74), each of which results in a delicious and beautifully decorated cake and also serves as an example of techniques that can be used successfully with myriad other recipes (in the case of the raspberry buttercream layer cake, the main technique illustrated is how to

assemble a layer cake without using a cake stand). Or, to take a principle from the chapter on pies, tarts, and pastries, once you realize that pastry dough comes in only five basic varieties, it becomes much easier to master the techniques required to execute a fully decorated pastry.

Often the difference between an ordinary cake and a fantastic one involves only a simple trick or two. In each chapter and recipe, I have tried to take every opportunity to teach good technique, whether in headnotes and recipe methods or in the many sidebars with stand-alone tips and techniques. *Baking* describes what can go wrong and how best to avoid common pitfalls such as over- or under-beating, but also how to use little bits of extra knowledge to get great results rather than merely good ones. Thus, *Baking* is for both novices and experienced bakers seeking to improve the quality of their cakes, tarts, cookies, or breads and make them look as good as the wares in the windows of Fauchon, the famous patisserie in Paris and New York.

Key to this book's focus on teaching and technique is its abundant photography—more than 1,500 images that show the most important parts of virtually every technique and recipe described in the text. This step-by-step color photography is indispensable for teaching certain techniques that are next to impossible to explain fully with words. Being able to see how a recipe's ingredients come together in stages throughout the process of baking reinforces good technique and gives the reader confidence, and a greater ability to get it just right the very first time.

The art of baking has an implicit logic that lends itself well to such an approach to teaching and learning. The behavior of certain ingredients in combination can be predicted and categorized—in sweet baking, we're usually concerned with the big four: flour, butter, eggs, and sugar; when making breads, the interactions of water, yeast, and flour matter most. In keeping with the book's philosophy of providing a solid foundation in baking technique, *Baking* contains many classic recipes in the French tradition, adapted for use in American kitchens. It's also a reflection of my own discovery of baking and progress as a baker, starting in my years in France, through my experiments and learning in my own restaurant and those of other chefs, and comprehending also my decades as a food writer and cooking teacher.

Before you embark on a baking project from this book, I suggest you skim through the rest of the chapter to familiarize yourself with the basic issues and techniques (if you are a less experienced baker) or the tricks of the trade and possibilities for variation (if you are a more experienced baker). It is my hope that *Baking* will provide a firm foundation in baking fundamentals so you can create perfectly executed classics, feel comfortable diverging from the basic recipes, improvise creations of your own, and dive confidently into any baking recipe you feel inspired to try.

ASSUMPTIONS

In general, when I cook, I don't believe in observing a lot of rules—though I do have strong ideas about what works best and tastes best. In baking, this sort of anarchy in the kitchen doesn't fly; so while I can often choose one flavoring or filling over another, like all other bakers I for the most part adhere to fairly strict rules, which are written into the recipes you'll find in this book. This section contains some comments on ingredients and equipment that are standard in my recipes.

INGREDIENTS

Baking powder and baking soda Though both are used as leaveners, don't confuse baking soda with baking powder. Baking powder contains an acid that causes the bicarbonate of soda to release carbon dioxide. To activate, baking soda needs acid from another source such as from chocolate or lemon.

Use "double acting" baking powder (this shouldn't be a problem, as this is probably the only kind you will find at the store). Don't keep baking powder or baking soda for more than a year.

Butter Butter is unsalted. If you only have salted butter, just cut down on the salt in the recipe. But do avoid salted butter in very buttery preparations such as buttercream.

Corn syrup Unless otherwise noted, corn syrup is light.

Cream All the cream called for in this book is either "whipping" cream or "heavy" cream, with butterfat content between 36 and 40 percent, never "light" cream, which has only about 18 to 30 percent butterfat. For the most part, crème fraîche will work as a substitute for heavy cream, but don't use sour cream unless called for; it has less butterfat.

Eggs All eggs are large. Brown or white makes no difference.

Flour All the recipes were tested using King Arthur brand all-purpose flour and Swans Down cake flour. After years of playing with different flours, I've found that King Arthur brand, which is fairly high in gluten, will absorb more liquid than softer flours, especially those from the South. If your favorite all-purpose flour is a softer (and thus less absorbent) one, you may not need to use cake flour when it's called for in the recipe—instead, go ahead and use your softer all-purpose flour on its own.

Fruit Most of the fruit called for is fresh, but frozen fruit is great for purees. Make sure to buy individually frozen fruit that comes in a bag, not fruit in syrup that comes in a can.

Nuts Nuts can turn rancid, even in the freezer. The best strategy is to roast them as soon as you get them; this will help their flavor and add to their shelf life. Spread them on a sheet pan and roast in a 350°F oven for 15 minutes. Stir around once during the roasting. Once you have roasted them, store nuts in the freezer.

Nut oils Most nut oils are already rancid before you open the can or bottle. To avoid this, buy nut oils that have been made with roasted nuts, specifically Le Blanc brand. Store nut oils in the freezer.

Salt Regular fine salt or fine sea salt will do in all these recipes.

Spirits Spirits used in baking are there to provide flavor, so, buy the best spirits you dare.

Eaux de vie, such as kirsch or *framboise*, should be French, German, or Swiss. Bourbon should be "straight," not "blended." Rum should be dark rum, preferably pot-stilled, from Martinique. Cognac should say "Cognac" on the bottle and not just "brandy." (However, you don't need to buy an old rare Cognac; a young fruity one will do.) When you add

Marble Marble is beloved of pastry bakers, since its cool, smooth surface helps keep buttery dough from warming while it's being worked. If you decide to buy a marble, buy the largest one you can lift and store. Scraps from a marble yard are a good source.

Molds and ramekins Baking molds and ramekins are used for tarts and tartlets, babas and savarins, brioche, madeleines, custards, soufflés, and more. For tarts, cookies, and cakes, non-stick or silicone molds are best. If you're stuck with traditional molds—especially if you are making madeleines or financiers, which love to stick—butter them, butter them again, and then flour them. When buying baking molds, keep in mind that some miniature tartlets require two molds per tartlet (see page 147).

Porcelain ramekins come in handy for custards and soufflés. It's ideal to have two sizes—5- or 6-ounce and 8-ounce; the recipes in this book call for 5- or 6-ounce ramekins, which are perfect for single-serving custards and soufflés. **Crème brûlée dishes**, which are shallow porcelain dishes with fluted edges, look dramatic at table. If you don't have them, use regular porcelain ramekins, or try making crème brûlée in a baking dish and then bringing the dish to the table to serve.

Ovens Most baking is done on the middle rack of the oven. Placing a pizza stone on the bottom of your oven will help it maintain an even temperature. A convection oven is a great help in baking, as it cooks rapidly and evenly. Puff pastry does especially well in a convection oven. The recipes in this book were developed and tested using a conventional oven. If you have a convection oven, lower the temperature by 50 degrees.

Parchment paper Almost indispensable in baking, parchment paper is now available at most supermarkets. If you can't find it, substitute waxed paper (which will leave traces of harmless wax on foods), but not aluminum foil, which will leave specks of metal and may tear.

Pastry bags and tips Buy large pastry bags so you can pipe plenty of mixture, such as the batter for a large cake. Buy an assortment of pastry bag tips, both fluted and plain.

spirits to mixtures such as simple syrup, make sure that the mixture is cool, or the flavor and aroma of the spirits will volatilize and evaporate.

Sugar Sugar is granulated unless otherwise called for.

Vanilla Be sure to use real vanilla extract. Use real vanilla beans for infusing in custards and batters.

Vegetable oil Make sure vegetable oil is fresh, as it can go rancid in a few months. Canola or sunflower oil make good choices for baking.

EQUIPMENT

Bread pans Bread pans come in various sizes and are usually made of aluminum or some other inexpensive metal. In this book, I have used four sizes: miniature 2-cup pans, standard 4- or 6-cup pans, and a large 2-quart pan.

Cake pans I usually call for standard round cake pans of 9 inches (actually 9½ inches), though sometimes I specify 8-inch or 10-inch pans (these are also standard sizes). Keep in mind that cakes shrink, such that a cake baked in a 9½-inch pan will end up being 9 inches. **Sheet pans** are of a standard size, called a "half sheet pan" in the industry. They measure approximately 13 by 17 inches with 1-inch-high sides.

Cake racks Cake racks are essential tools for cooling cakes and cookies. Buy at least one large cake rack (the size of a sheet pan) for flipping out sheet cakes. Round cake racks are convenient for individual round cakes.

Copper bowls Egg whites rise better when beaten in copper. This leaves two choices—a copper bowl designed for beating by hand (make sure you buy a big one so there's plenty of room to whisk) or a copper insert for your stand mixer. Be sure to clean the copper thoroughly with salt and vinegar before you use it each time. Make sure there is no trace of fat adhering to the bowl.

Food processor A food processor is indispensable for grinding nuts and for pureeing solid mixtures. It is also useful for making most dough.

Pastry scrapers and bench scrapers Bench scrapers (also called pastry scrapers and dough cutters) are typically metal, though some are made of plastic. They are versatile tools that can be used to scrape together ingredients on a work surface, transfer ingredients from work surface to a bowl or pan, and cut dough without wrecking its structure, among other things. Some plastic pastry scrapers have one straight and one rounded edge. This allows you to use them on both the work surface and inside bowls for folding mixtures.

Pastry cutters These old fashioned gadgets—essentially a series of stiff wires attached to a handle—are handy for cutting cubes of cold butter into flour when you're working in a bowl. When working directly on the work surface, use a pastry scraper. When you are mixing dough in a stand mixer or food processor, the machine does the work.

Pie and tart pans While pie and tart pans come in innumerable sizes, the most common pie pan, and the one used in this book, is 11 inches in diameter from top edge to top edge, leaving about 9 inches of diameter in the middle. Tart pans are harder to standardize. Assume a recipe uses a 9-inch tart pan, unless otherwise specified—this book is filled with tarts made in irregular sizes. A less expensive alternative to a tart pan is a tart ring, which is simply a metal ring that you set on a sheet pan. The sheet pan provides the base for the tart.

Plastic wrap Plastic wrap is another kitchen essential, good for wrapping cakes or pastries destined for the freezer, or for covering and protecting all sorts of mixtures and finished desserts.

Pots and pans In general, pots and pans should be heavy, so they cook evenly. In baking, it's generally best to avoid aluminum pans, which can turn preparations with egg yolk gray and react with acidic ingredients.

Rolling pins If you have a single rolling pin in your kitchen, make it a large wooden pin. I use the traditional French type of pin, which is a large cylinder with no handles. If you feel comfortable with them, rolling pins with handles work well, too. Avoid the Italian pins, which taper at the ends.

Rubber spatulas These are indispensable for folding mixtures, cleaning out bowls and pans, and transferring small amounts of mixtures. While traditionally made of rubber, flexible spatulas nowadays are made of silicone, which lasts longer and won't burn.

Stand mixer Perhaps the most useful item in the baker's kitchen, a stand mixer is great for making pastries, combining all manner of mixtures, beating egg whites, and kneading bread dough. Some stand mixers will even accommodate a copper bowl insert, which is handy for beating egg whites. Most stand mixers come with three attachments: a dough hook, a paddle blade, and a whisk. Each of these is designed with a different stiffness in mind for whatever's being combined. Usually, it is obvious which is appropriate for the task at hand. For example, unless otherwise noted in the recipe, the dough hook attachment should be used when making bread.

If you plan on making a lot of bread, you may want to buy a heavy-duty, professional grade stand mixer; otherwise a stand mixer designed for the home kitchen is sufficient.

Note that directions for whipping (such as egg whites or cream) include times for a stand mixer, unless otherwise noted. For example, to beat 4 egg whites to stiff peaks in a stand mixer will take 1 minute of beating on medium speed and then 1 minute more on high speed. Whipping with a hand-held mixer or by hand will take longer, so rely on doneness cues given in the recipe to know when you've whipped long enough.

CAKES

Basic Cakes

Basic French Sponge Cake (Genoise) · 8
Moist Sponge Cake · 10
Chocolate Sponge Cake · 12
Chocolate Soufflé Cakes · 12
Fine-Crumb European Sponge
 Cake (Biscuit) · 14
Butter-Enriched Sponge Cake · 16
Sour Cream Sponge Cake · 18
Almond Flour Sponge Cake · 20
Almond Paste Sponge Cake · 22
Angel Food Cake · 24
Pound Cake · 25
German Chocolate Cake · 26
Fluffy Light Butter Cake · 28
Cream and Butter Sheet Cake · 29
Devil's Food Cake · 30
Vanilla Butter Cake · 31
Carrot Cake · 32
Chiffon Cake · 34
Babas and Savarins · 36
French Meringue Layer Cake · 38
Hazelnut Meringue (Dacquoise) · 40
Chocolate Meringue Logs · 41
Cheesecake · 42

Frostings, Fillings, and Glazes

Professional-Style Buttercream · 45
Italian Meringue Buttercream · 46
Quick and Easy Orange Buttercream · 46
Dark Chocolate Ganache · 50
Creamy Chocolate Frosting
 (Crème d'Or) · 52
Dark Chocolate Glaze · 53
White Chocolate Glaze · 55
Vanilla Custard Sauce
 (Crème Anglaise) · 54
Strawberry Bavarian Cream · 56
Classic Crème Mousseline · 57
Fruit Crème Mousseline · 58
Seven-Minute Frosting · 59
Italian Meringue · 60
Lemon Glaze · 61
Stabilized Whipped Cream · 62
Chestnut Cream Cake Filling · 64
Rolled Fondant · 67
Royal Icing · 67
Royal Icing for Cookies · 67

Assembled Cakes

Devil's Food Cake with Ganache,
 Chocolate Buttercream, and
 Chocolate Curls · 71
Chocolate Hazelnut Cake with Chocolate
 Filling and Hazelnut Buttercream · 72
Raspberry Buttercream Layer Cake · 74
Orange Buttercream Layer Cake · 77
Strawberry and White Chocolate
 Mousse Ladyfinger Cake · 78
Dark Chocolate Mousse Cake · 80
Mango Crème Mousseline Cake · 81
Chocolate Cherry Cake with
 White Chocolate Glaze · 84
Classic Strawberry-Marzipan
 Cake (Fraisier) · 86
Whipped Cream–Covered
 Chocolate Chestnut Cake · 90
Strawberry Bavarian Cake · 92
Individual Chocolate Meringue Cakes · 94
Chocolate Mousse Dome Cake · 96
Peach Crème Mousseline Cake · 99
Miniature Cake Petits Fours · 102
Rolled Pistachio Buttercream Cake · 104
Apricot Jelly Roll · 106
Bûche de Noël · 108
Marzipan · 109

Methods and Techniques

BAKING CAKES

Ensuring a Cake Rises Evenly • 5

Preparing and Filling Cake Pans
and Molds • 6

Coating Ramekins with Cocoa Powder • 6

Piping Cake Batter with a Pastry Bag • 7

Beating Whole Eggs • 8

Making a Basic French Sponge Cake
(Genoise) • 9

Warming Eggs • 10

Making a Moist Sponge Cake • 11

Making a Chocolate Sponge Cake • 12

Making Chocolate Soufflé Cakes • 13

Making a Fine-Crumb European
Sponge Cake (Biscuit) • 15

Folding with Flour • 16

Making a Butter-Enriched Sponge Cake • 17

Making and Using Layers • 18

Making a Sour Cream Sponge Cake • 19

Making an Almond Flour Sponge Cake • 21

Making an Almond Paste Sponge Cake • 23

Making an Angel Food Cake • 24

Making and Glazing a Pound Cake • 26

Making a German Chocolate Cake • 27

Making a Fluffy Light Butter Cake • 28

Making a Cream and Butter Sheet Cake • 29

Making a Devil's Food Cake • 30

Making a Dump Cake (Vanilla
Butter Cake) • 31

Making Carrot Cakes • 33

Making a Chiffon Cake • 35

Making Babas and Savarins • 37

**Using a Pastry Bag to Make
Meringue Disks • 38**

Making a French Meringue Layer Cake • 39

Making a Hazelnut Meringue
(Dacquoise) • 40

Making Chocolate Meringue Logs • 41

Making a Cheesecake • 43

FROSTING, FILLING, AND GLAZING CAKES

Storing Frostings, Fillings, and Glazes • 44

Making Professional-Style Buttercream • 45

**Judging How Much Buttercream
Is Enough • 46**

**Cooking Sugar Syrup to the
Soft Ball Stage • 47**

Flavoring Buttercream • 48

Reconstituting Congealed or
Separated Buttercream • 49

Making Ganache • 51

Making Whipped Ganache • 51

Malking Creamy Chocolate Frosting • 52

Coating a Cake with Hot Icing • 52

Glazing a Chiffon Cake • 34

**Judging When a Crème
Anglaise Is Done • 55**

Making a Vanilla Custard Sauce
(Crème Anglaise) • 55

Making Strawberry Bavarian Cream • 56

Flavoring Crème Mousseline • 57

Making Fruit Crème Mousseline • 58

Making Egg White–Based Frosting
(Seven-Minute Frosting) • 59

Icing a Cake with a Spoon (Chestnut Cake
with Seven-Minute Frosting) • 59

Making Italian Meringue • 60

Fruit Glazes • 61

Whipped Cream • 62

Using Stabilized Whipped Cream • 63

Making Rolled Fondant • 66

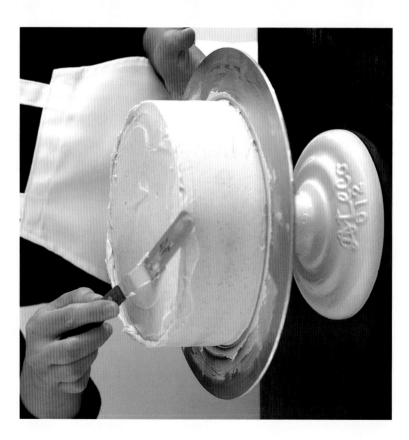

ASSEMBLING CAKES

Judging Amounts of Frosting, Glaze, and Simple Syrup Needed for Layer Cakes • 69

Assembling a Layer Cake on a Cake Stand (Devil's Food Cake) • 70

Assembling a Cake with Layers of Dacquoise and Cake (Chocolate Hazelnut Cake) • 72

Assembling a Layer Cake without Using a Cake Stand (Raspberry Buttercream Layer Cake) • 75

Assembling a Rectangular Layer Cake (Orange Buttercream Layer Cake) • 76

Assembling a Cake in a Cake Ring (Strawberry and White Chocolate Mousse Ladyfinger Cake) • 79

Assembling a Cake in a Springform Pan (Dark Chocolate Mousse Cake) • 80

Assembling a Cake with a Translucent Mirror (Mango Crème Mousseline Cake) • 82

Making a Caramel Cage • 83

Assembling a Four-Layer Cake in a Ring (Chocolate Cherry Cake with White Chocolate Glaze) • 84

Assembling a Layer Cake with Two Fillings (Whipped Cream–Covered Chocolate Chestnut Cake) • 91

Assembling a Bavarian Cake • 93

Assembling a Square Cake with Marzipan Topping (Classic Strawberry-Marzipan Cake/Fraisier) • 88

Filling and Glazing Individual Chocolate Meringue Cakes • 94

Assembling a Cake with Slices of Rolled Cake (Chocolate Mousse Dome Cake) • 97

Assembling a Cake with Layered Squares (Peach Crème Mousseline Cake) • 98

Making a Sheet Cake • 101

Making Miniature Cake Petits Fours • 103

Making a Rolled Cake (Pistachio Buttercream Cake) • 105

Making a Jelly Roll • 106

Assembling a Bûche de Noël • 108

DECORATING CAKES

Filling and Using a Pastry Bag • 64

Hulling and Slicing Strawberries • 86

Making and Using a Paper Cone • 87

Making Meringue Mushrooms • 109

Rolling Out Marzipan and Using It to Ice a Cake • 110

Reconstituting Dried-Out Marzipan and Coloring Marzipan • 110

Making Marzipan Roses • 111

Making Marzipan Leaves and Berries • 111

Covering a Cake with Rolled Fondant • 112

Decorating a Cake with a Rolled Fondant Strip and Fondant Polka Dots • 113

Wrapping a Cake with a Wide Chocolate Strip • 114

Decorating a Cake with Meringue Logs • 115

Decorating a Cake with a Paper Cone • 115

Decorating the Sides of a Cake with Ladyfingers • 115

Decorating a Cake with Chopped or Shaved Nuts or Cake Crumbs • 115

Decorating a Cake with Fresh Flowers • 116

Decorating a Cake with a Gelatin Mirror • 116

Decorating a Cake with Cat's Tongue Cookies • 116

Decorating a Cake with Fresh Fruit • 116

Decorating a Cake with Layered Cake Squares • 117

Decorating a Cake with a Caramel Cage • 117

Decorating a Cake with Cocoa Powder • 117

Decorating a Cake with Buttercream • 117

Decorating a Cake with Slices of Rolled Cake • 117

Decorating a Cake with Chocolate Curls • 118

Decorating a Cake with Confectioners' Sugar • 118

Decorating a Cake Using a Serrated Knife • 118

While it seems there are hundreds of different kinds of cakes, there are really only six: sponge cakes, butter cakes, oil-based cakes (such as carrot cake and chiffon cake), yeasted cakes (including babas and savarins), meringue-based cakes, and custard cakes (cheesecake, for example). Once you know how to make one of each type, you'll know how to make them all.

Four basic ingredients make virtually all cakes and pastries what they are: flour, eggs, sugar, and butter. Cakes can be made with other ingredients, such as flavorings (nuts, chocolate, fruits) and leavenings (baking powder and baking soda), but the amazing variety is the result of manipulating the four basic ingredients in different ways.

Flour is the most essential ingredient for practically all cakes because it becomes firm when hot so that air stays trapped in the cake even after it has cooled. Virtually no cake can exist without eggs; they set at a lower temperature than flour so your cake doesn't fall until it is getting hot enough to set the flour, and they trap air, which keeps the cake light. Most cakes are sweetened with sugar or something closely related, such as honey. Other than sweetening the cake, sugar helps keep a cake tender; when beaten with butter, it helps entrap air. Butter isn't used in all cakes, but when it is, it imparts an ineffable flavor and finesse and keeps the flour from getting tough.

CAKE SIZES AND SHAPES

Most of us associate cakes with the classic tall round layer cakes we've feasted on at birthday parties. Less festive, but easier because they require no assembly, are flat sheet cakes. To make a round layer cake, you can cut one cake into two or three or even more layers using a serrated knife (see page 70)—slicing more than two layers takes a little practice—and put filling in between, or you can bake two layer cakes and cut each of these in half or in thirds. Most of the cake recipes given here are for one, or sometimes two, 9-inch round layer cakes—the size cake pan found in most home kitchens—typically 1 to 1½ inches thick.

The amount of batter for two 9-inch round layer cakes are the same as for a sheet cake baked in a classic 13 by 17-inch sheet pan with 1-inch-high sides. (There are slight variations in brands of sheet pans, but anything within an inch of these dimensions will work. Cakes sometimes rise over the edge of the sheet pan, which is fine.) If you're making a square or rectangular cake, just cut a sheet cake into the size you want and slice into layers. You can also roll some very moist sheet cakes (see page 104).

European-style cakes are usually smaller, both shorter and with a smaller diameter, than American cakes—6-inch cakes that serve four are common. A recipe for one 9-inch cake can be used to make two 6-inch cakes.

Some very elegant cakes with lots of layers are made by piping disks of cake batter onto parchment paper–lined sheet pans or into round cake pans (see page 7). These disks can be made very thin—with a ¼-inch plain tip or smaller—and come in handy when you need thin layers that would be impossible to obtain by slicing a cake crosswise.

This cakes section is divided into four parts: making basic cakes (such as butter cakes and foam cakes); making frostings, fillings, and glazes (such as buttercream); assembling cakes; and decorating cakes. Each finished cake is designed to teach more than one recipe or technique that can be used for many more cakes than just the one shown, and when the fillings and assembly techniques are mixed and matched, you can improvise many dozens of cakes by using different cakes, frostings, glazes, and fillings.

While cake recipes have to be pretty exact and don't give a lot of leeway for improvisation, the fillings do. They can be flavored in many different ways with fruits, spices, coffee, chocolate, and spirits, and they can even be combined. If you make cakes a lot and find yourself with leftover frostings or fillings, save them in the freezer. You can combine them at some point as long as the flavors make sense. In other words, if you have a little leftover lemon curd, a bit of mango crème mousseline, maybe some vanilla pastry cream, or some kirsch-flavored buttercream, these can all be beaten together.

Again, virtually all cakes are of only six kinds, which are presented here in a logical way. Sponge cakes are divided into three basic kinds: those made with whole eggs, those made with separated whites and yolks, and those made with whites only. Butter cakes are also divided into three kinds: the classic kind, of which pound cake is the most fundamental; those that are basically sponge cakes but with lots of melted butter or cream added; and high-ratio cakes, developed in the 1930s (see sidebar, page 22). Next are oil-based cakes, such as carrot cake; yeasted cakes, such as babas and savarins; meringues, made with egg whites and sometimes nuts or chocolate; followed by custard cakes, cheesecake being the prime example.

The next section describes frostings, fillings, and glazes and starts with two kinds of buttercream, a professional version and an easy homespun version; followed by two kinds of frosting made with chocolate and cream; white and dark chocolate glazes; white and dark chocolate mousses, which make excellent fillings; fruit mousses; Bavarian creams, which can be flavored with virtually anything; crème mousseline, which is much like buttercream but is stabilized with pastry cream; fruit curds; egg white–based frostings and fillings; stabilized whipped cream, which can be used as a lighter frosting or filling; and a fondant that can be rolled and used to cover a cake.

The following section, devoted to the assembly of finished cakes, shows how to use the cakes and fillings given in the earlier sections. Each cake is designed to teach a technique that's useful for far more cakes than just the cake shown. For example, the chocolate hazelnut cake (page 72) is designed to show you how to use a cake stand and what I call the "free form" technique. The raspberry buttercream layer cake (page 74) shows how to assemble a cake without a cake stand. The orange buttercream cake (page 77) is a lesson in how to make a rectangular cake and how to flavor a buttercream with orange. The dark chocolate mousse cake (page 80) is an example of how to use mousse as a filling and how to make a perfectly even, professional-looking cake by constructing it in a springform pan. The strawberry and white chocolate mousse cake (page 78) demonstrates how to make a cake with a filling that starts out with a liquid and how to decorate a cake with rows of ladyfingers. The mango mousseline cake (page 81) shows how to make a buttery frosting with virtually any fruit and how to make miniature cookies for decoration. An elaborate strawberry cake (page 86) is an example of how to decorate the sides of a square cake with fruit and how to use marzipan to give a polished look, very easily, to a finished cake.

One method, more popular in Europe than in the United States, is to brush cake layers with a light sugar syrup that's been flavored with a little coffee, vanilla, liqueur, fruit brandy, whiskey, Cognac, or rum. The advantage to this is that the cake is always moist, even if it started out stale. If you make cakes in this way, you can save up the basic cakes, tightly wrapped, in the freezer, and then just assemble them at the last minute. If you're ambitious, you might want to make several kinds of cakes, maybe with contrasting flavors and colors and textures, so that when you assemble a cake you can use a variety of different layers. Fillings are a little trickier to store than cakes because they are emulsions, usually of cream or butter, which can separate when frozen and thawed. Most of the time, a separated filling such as a buttercream can be warmed slightly—just put it in a metal bowl and stir it with a whisk over a low flame for 30 seconds—and then beaten, first with a paddle attachment and then with a whisk.

But there's never a need to waste a filling, even one that won't cooperate when you try to beat it back to life. If you have hopelessly broken buttercream or ganache, for example, beat it into a little batch of pastry cream to make a crème mousseline.

Another European trick that's an easy way to make perfectly even and smooth cakes that look truly professional is to assemble your cakes in a springform pan or in a cake ring with a cardboard bottom. This allows you to use liquid ingredients such as Bavarian creams and also keeps the sides of the cake perfectly even.

When you've assembled your cake, either a simple cake with one kind of cake layer and one kind of filling or a complex cake with assorted fillings and layers, there are many choices, some very simple, for giving it a professional look. One of the easiest is simply to press cake crumbs or chopped nuts against the sides. More complicated are such things as meringue logs, wide chocolate strips, rounds of rolled cake on the outside of a dome cake, strips of ladyfingers wrapped around the cake, shiny colored mirrors made from fruit purees for the tops of the cakes, decoration with royal icing, sheets of marzipan or fondant simply rolled over the cake— all can be used to give any cake a dramatic impact.

Ensuring a Cake Rises Evenly

Because the outside rim of a cake is heated first, it can cook before the center, causing the edges of the cake to rise less and hold their shape, while the center, which cooks more evenly and slowly, rises to form a dome. To prevent this, wrap a wet towel around the cake pan. This technique slows down the cooking of the outside edge and results in a cake that is perfectly flat on top.

PREPARING AND FILLING CAKE PANS AND MOLDS

There is nothing more frustrating than laboring over a cake and then having it stick to the pan. Most of us butter and flour cake pans to prevent sticking, and most of the time this works. But to be absolutely certain the cake comes out of the pan with its surface perfectly smooth, butter the inside of the pan, cover the pan bottom with a round of buttered parchment paper, and then flour the inside of the pan and the paper. Don't cut the round of paper any larger than the pan; if it extends up the sides around the edges it will make a rough edge on the cake. On the other hand, it's fine if the parchment paper is slightly smaller than the cake pan. To butter and flour a cake pan, brush the inside of the pan with room-temperature butter, put a handful of flour in the pan, and rotate it until the bottom and sides are coated with flour. Invert the pan and tap it against the work surface to shake out any excess flour.

To butter the molds: Use room-temperature butter, which will provide a thicker coat than melted butter. If you need an especially thick coating of butter, such as when making madeleines, place the butter-coated molds in the refrigerator for a few minutes and then coat them again.

COATING RAMEKINS WITH COCOA POWDER

To coat a ramekin with flour or cocoa powder, butter it and fill it with sifted cocoa powder or flour and rotate so that the ramekin's sides are coated. Pour any excess cocoa powder or flour into the next ramekin.

PREPARING AND FILLING CAKE PANS AND MOLDS

1. Place a cake pan on a sheet of parchment paper and draw a circle around it. Cut out the circle to make a round of parchment paper.

2. Thoroughly brush the cake pan with room-temperature butter and press the parchment paper into the pan—the butter holds the parchment paper in place.

3. Brush the parchment paper with butter. Put flour in the pan and rotate the pan until it is thoroughly coated. Invert the pan and tap it to shake off any excess flour.

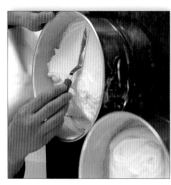

4. An offset spatula is an ideal tool for smoothing the top of the cake batter.

To coat buttered molds with flour or cocoa powder: put the flour or cocoa powder in one of the molds and rotate it so that it leaves a light coating on the bottom and sides. Transfer the excess to the next mold by inverting the powder-coated mold and giving it a good tap to loosen any excess powder.

To fill a cake pan: Most cake batters are easily spread in cake pans with an offset spatula, a very handy gadget that a lot of home cooks don't have. Scoop smooth cake batter into parchment paper–lined and floured cake pans. Smooth off the top of each pan with an offset spatula. If you don't have an offset spatula, spread the batter with a rubber spatula or pipe it into the pan with a pastry bag fitted with a ³⁄₄-inch plain tip.

PIPING CAKE BATTER WITH A PASTRY BAG

It is sometimes convenient to fill a pastry bag with cake batter and then pipe it onto a sheet of parchment paper or into a pan before baking it—for example, when making ladyfingers (see page 15) or cakes with very thin layers (see page 81). Starting with piped layers is often easier than trying to slice a cake into thin layers with a knife. Virtually any batter, provided it isn't too runny, can be used in this way.

Here are some useful tips to keep in mind when piping batter:

The thickness of what you're piping is always somewhat greater than the size of the tip—in other words, a ¹⁄₄-inch tip will pipe out a layer about ¹⁄₃ inch thick.

Draw rings or rectangles on parchment paper to guide your piping (see page 15), turning the parchment paper over before you pipe so that the batter does not touch the ink or pencil lead.

As you're piping disks for cake layers, especially if you're using a very small tip, you'll probably end up with gaps in the disks where the pastry bag wasn't positioned exactly where it needed to be. Don't worry—just smooth over the disks with an offset spatula before you bake them.

Usually, a recipe for a cake that is about 1¹⁄₂ inches thick when baked will make three ¹⁄₃-inch-thick disks of batter, instead of four as you might expect.

Piped layers about ¹⁄₃ inch thick will bake in 12 minutes in a 375°F oven; 10 minutes in a 400°F oven for thinner, ¹⁄₄-inch layers. See the photos on page 15.

SPONGE CAKES

Sponge cakes are cakes made by beating whole eggs, separated eggs, or just egg whites with sugar and then folding the beaten mixture with butter or flavorful ingredients such as chocolate. Last, flour and/or other dry ingredients are folded with the egg mixture. If the cake is based on beaten egg whites instead of whole eggs, the beaten egg yolks are also folded into the mixture. One of the best-known sponge cakes, called *biscuit* (pronounced bees-kwee), is made by beating egg yolks and egg whites separately, each with sugar, and then folding the two mixtures together while sifting flour over them. American sponge cakes are made in the same way as biscuit except that they usually contain slightly more egg. A whole-egg sponge cake, called a *genoise*, is made by beating whole eggs with sugar until the eggs quadruple in volume and then sifting the flour over them while folding it in. Most recipes also call for folding in a small amount of melted butter. Both of these cakes, while light and airy, tend to be dry. Because of this, European bakers brush each layer liberally with simple syrup flavored with some kind of fruit brandy, rum, or coffee while stacking them; the cake ends up moist, almost wet. One advantage of this method is that you can moisten cakes that are a little stale (whether from being held too long or from being frozen), so you can bake cakes ahead of time, wrap them in plastic, and freeze them. Both kinds of sponge cakes are leavened only with the air beaten into the eggs. They contain no baking powder or baking soda.

There are many sponge-cake variations—some of which are used for rolled cakes—made by folding various ingredients, such as melted butter, hot cream or milk, or sour cream, with the beaten eggs. Some sponge cakes also contain almond flour or almond paste. A sponge cake made with almond flour or almond paste is flexible, moist, and perfect for rolling because almonds contain no gluten.

Sponge cakes are flavored in several ways. They are made into chocolate cakes by substituting cocoa powder for some of the flour that is folded into the beaten eggs or egg whites, or by folding melted chocolate—sometimes melted with butter—into the egg mixture before folding in the flour.

Sponge Cakes Made with Whole Eggs

Whole-egg sponge cakes are made by beating whole eggs with sugar until the mixture triples or quadruples in volume, and then folding the mixture with sifted flour and sometimes melted butter, *beurre noisette* (brown butter, see page 196), or melted chocolate.

Basic French Sponge Cake (Genoise)

This is a purist's cake because it contains no leavening—it's lightened with air alone—and has a delicate egg flavor and a light texture that make it seem to fall apart in the mouth.

To make this classic French sponge cake, you need to beat whole eggs with sugar until they become very pale and are tripled or quadrupled in volume. Because eggs whip up more quickly when they are not ice cold, warm them in a bowl of warm water before cracking them, or use a hand whisk to beat them with the sugar in a bowl placed over a saucepan of barely simmering water until they feel warm to the back of a finger. Beat the egg-sugar mixture until you can lift the whisk and move it back and forth through the batter and the ribbon holds its shape for at least 5 seconds. If you overbeat the eggs, the cake may be dry or, worse, it may fall in the oven. If the eggs are not beaten sufficiently, the cake will be heavy.

Because genoise is often somewhat dry, many bakers—especially French ones—brush each layer generously with flavored simple syrup, making the cake very moist, even wet. The syrup can be flavored with coffee, vanilla, liqueurs such as Grand Marnier, fruit brandies such as kirsch, whiskey, Cognac, or rum.

This recipe makes 1 layer, which is easily sliced cross-wise into 2 layers; with practice it can be sliced into as many as 4. The cake can be used for any round layer cake. It can be filled with mousseline (page 57), buttercream (page 45), classic chocolate mousse (page 366), white chocolate mousse (page 367), fruit Bavarian (page 56), stabilized whipped cream (page 62), or whipped ganache (page 51). It can be glazed or frosted with these same fillings and/or it can be covered with marzipan (page 110) or rolled fondant (page 67).

MAKES 1 ROUND LAYER CAKE (9 BY 1 INCH)

Butter and flour for the cake pan

3 eggs

1/4 cup plus 2 tablespoons sugar

1/2 cup plus 2 tablespoons cake flour

3 tablespoons butter, melted (optional)

Preheat the oven to 350°F. Butter and flour a 9-inch round cake pan, or line the bottom with a round of parchment paper.

Combine the eggs and sugar in a bowl. Unless the egg mixture already feels warm, put the bowl over a saucepan of barely simmering water and whisk until warm and frothy. Beat on high speed with a stand mixer fitted with the whisk attachment for 4 minutes, with a handheld mixer for 20 minutes, or by hand using a bowl and balloon whisk for 12 minutes, or until the ribbon stage: when the beater is lifted, the mixture falls in a wide band onto the surface, forming a figure eight that stays for 5 seconds before dissolving.

Carefully transfer the egg mixture to a large bowl. Fold in the flour by sifting it over the beaten eggs and folding with a rubber spatula. In a smaller bowl, fold together the melted butter and about one-fifth of the egg mixture. Fold the butter-egg mixture into the egg mixture in the larger bowl.

Transfer the batter to the prepared pan and gently smooth the top with an offset spatula. Bake for about 25 minutes, or until the cake bounces back to the touch and a toothpick inserted into the center comes out clean.

Let cool for 5 minutes in the cake pan and then turn out onto a cake rack.

Beating Whole Eggs

Because whole eggs take longer to beat than egg whites, it is best to beat them using a good-quality stand mixer. You can beat them by hand, but you must use a large balloon whisk and a large deep bowl or you'll exhaust yourself—beating 3 eggs takes about 12 minutes. You must also be a little ambidextrous (this just takes a little practice), or have a friend you can switch off with. The slowest method of all is to use a handheld mixer, which takes about 20 minutes on high speed to beat 3 eggs. Beating times for all methods increase proportionately with the number of eggs.

1. Unless the egg mixture already feels warm, put the bowl over a saucepan of barely simmering water and whisk with a hand whisk until warm and frothy.

2. Beat the mixture until a ribbon forms when you lift the whisk attachment and move it back and forth over the batter. The batter should also form a ribbon at least 2 inches long between the end of the whisk and the top of the batter and should form a figure eight that stays for at least 5 seconds on the surface of the beaten eggs.

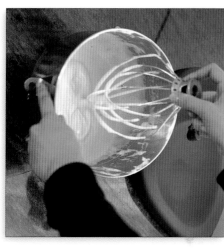

3. Transfer the beaten eggs to a wider bowl—to make folding easier—and sift over the flour while folding.

4. If you are using the melted butter, stir about one-fifth of the cake batter into the butter until smooth and then fold this mixture back into the batter.

5. Gently transfer the batter to a parchment paper–lined or buttered and floured cake pan.

Moist Sponge Cake

This sponge cake has all the flavor and texture of genoise, but none of the dryness that genoise so often has. It is made just like a classic genoise, except that hot milk or cream and melted butter are folded into the beaten eggs at the same time as the flour, imparting extra moistness that makes it perfect for rolling. When baked in a 13 by 17-inch sheet pan, this moist cake is only about ³/₈ inch thick, just what you want when making a rolled cake. If you bake this cake as a round cake—in a 9-inch cake pan—you can frost and decorate it in the same way as a genoise (see page 8).

MAKES 1 SHEET CAKE (13 BY 17 BY ³/₈ INCH),
OR 1 ROUND LAYER CAKE (9 BY 1 INCH)

Butter and flour for the round cake pan, if using

1 teaspoon vanilla extract

¹/₄ cup milk or heavy cream

3 tablespoons butter

3 whole eggs, warmed (see sidebar, below)

3 egg yolks, warmed (see sidebar, below)

³/₄ cup plus 2 tablespoons sugar

³/₄ cup cake flour

Warming Eggs

Because eggs froth up better when warm, many recipes call for eggs that have been allowed to come to room temperature or have been warmed even more. To warm eggs quickly, just put them, whole in the shell, in a bowl of hot water from the tap and let them sit for 5 minutes.

If making a sheet cake, preheat the oven to 400°F and line a 13 by 17-inch sheet pan with parchment paper. If making a round cake, preheat the oven to 350°F and butter and flour a 9-inch round cake pan.

Combine the vanilla, milk, and butter in a small saucepan, bring to a simmer, and cook just long enough to melt the butter. Remove from the heat and set aside.

Using a stand mixer, beat the eggs, egg yolks, and sugar on high speed for about 5 minutes, or until the ribbon stage: when the beater is lifted, the mixture falls in a wide band onto the surface, forming a figure eight that stays for 5 seconds before dissolving.

Carefully transfer the beaten egg mixture to a large bowl to make it easier to fold. Pour the milk-butter mixture down the side of the bowl all at once and fold it in with a rubber spatula quickly but gently. Sift the flour over the bowl and fold it into the egg mixture, one-third at a time, making sure the last batch is incorporated before adding more. Be sure to scrape the spatula along the bottom of the bowl—flour tends to settle there.

Pour the mixture into the prepared pan. If you are making a sheet cake, smooth and spread the mixture with an offset spatula and use your thumb to make a moat around the cake to keep the batter from sticking to the sides of the pan. Bake a sheet cake for about 12 minutes and a round cake for about 25 minutes, or until firm to the touch.

Let the cake cool for 10 minutes and then turn it out onto a cooling rack. If you are making a sheet cake, gently pull the parchment paper away from the surface of the cake.

1. Whisk the eggs, egg yolks, and sugar on high speed for about 5 minutes, or until the egg mixture forms a ribbon.

2. Transfer the egg mixture to a wide bowl. Pour the milk mixture down one side of the bowl and fold it quickly but gently with the egg mixture.

3. To make a sheet cake, pour the batter onto a parchment paper–lined sheet pan. Spread the batter with an offset spatula.

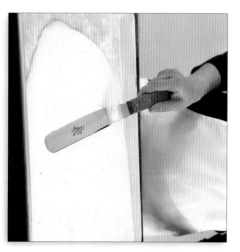

4. Make a small moat around the edge of the cake with your thumb.

5. When the cake is baked, let it cool for 10 minutes, then invert onto a cooling rack and gently pull away the parchment paper.

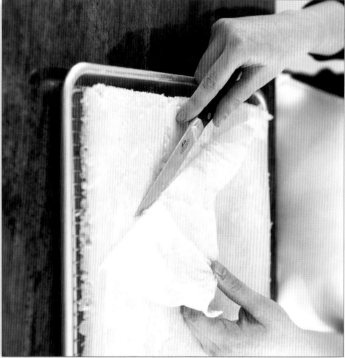

Chocolate Sponge Cake

In most recipes for chocolate sponge cake, some of the flour is simply replaced with cocoa powder. The result is rather tame and a bit dry. The method shown here is similar, but the resulting cake is moister than a classic genoise and has a deep chocolate flavor. Bittersweet chocolate is melted with water, then the mixture is stirred until smooth and folded with beaten whole eggs, in the same fashion as classic genoise (page 8). Fill with crème d'or (page 52), whipped ganache (page 51), seven-minute frosting (page 59), or chocolate buttercream (page 48). Glaze with ganache (page 50).

MAKES 2 ROUND LAYER CAKES (9 BY 1½ INCHES)

Butter and flour for the cake pans
8 ounces bittersweet chocolate
1 cup cold water
8 eggs, warmed (see sidebar, page 10)
1 cup sugar
1½ cups cake flour

Preheat the oven to 350°F. Butter and flour two 9 by 1½-inch round cake pans.

Combine the chocolate and water in a small saucepan and heat the mixture over low heat while stirring with a wooden spoon for about 5 minutes, or until the mixture thickens to the consistency of smooth pudding. Remove from the heat.

Combine the eggs and sugar and beat on high speed with a stand mixer for about 12 minutes or with a handheld mixer for about 20 minutes, or until quadrupled in volume and the mixture falls in a ribbon stage: when the beater is lifted, the mixture falls in a wide band onto the surface, forming a figure eight that stays for 5 seconds before dissolving. Using a rubber spatula, fold the chocolate mixture with the eggs while sifting the flour over the mixture. Alternate between adding flour—about one-fourth at a time—and folding until the flour is no longer visible.

Pour the batter into the prepared pans. Bake for about 25 minutes, or until a toothpick inserted in the center comes out clean.

Detach the cakes from the sides of the pans by running a metal spatula or small knife around the edges. After the cakes have cooled for 10 minutes, turn them out onto a cake rack. Serve, preferably while still warm, passing whipped cream or chantilly cream at the table.

MAKING A CHOCOLATE SPONGE CAKE

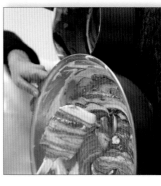

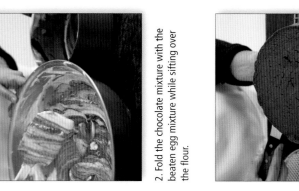

2. Fold the chocolate mixture with the beaten egg mixture while sifting over the flour.

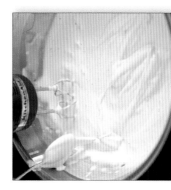

1. Combine the eggs and sugar and beat on high speed until quadrupled in volume.

3. Detach the cake from the sides of the pan by running a metal spatula or small knife along the sides.

4. After the cake has cooled for 10 minutes, transfer it to a cake rack.

Chocolate Soufflé Cakes

These cakes are cakelike on the outside and hot and creamy on the inside—eating one is like eating warm cake with hot melting mousse on top. The soufflé cakes are made in the same way as genoise, except that melted chocolate and butter are folded with the beaten eggs while the flour is being folded in. They are best when the outside is cakelike and the inside molten. To get this effect, freeze the soufflés in their individual ramekins for at least a couple of hours before baking.

The unbaked cakes can be frozen, well covered, weeks before you need them. Just pull them out of the freezer and bake when you want to serve them. You can serve them in their ramekins or you can unmold them onto plates.

MAKES 6 SERVINGS

Room-temperature butter and unsweetened cocoa powder for the ramekins
½ cup butter
8 ounces bittersweet chocolate, coarsely chopped
4 eggs, at room temperature
⅓ cup granulated sugar
3 tablespoons flour
Confectioners' sugar for sprinkling

Brush six 5- or 6-ounce ramekins with room-temperature butter. Sift cocoa powder over a sheet of parchment paper, pour the powder into one of the ramekins, and turn it until the inside is coated. Pour the excess cocoa powder into the next ramekin and repeat until all have been coated (see photo, page 6).

Combine the butter and chocolate in a heatproof bowl set over a saucepan of simmering water. Stir with a whisk or silicone spatula until smooth and melted. Remove from the heat.

Combine the eggs and granulated sugar and beat on high speed with a stand mixer for about 5 minutes or with a hand-held mixer for about 25 minutes, or until the ribbon stage: when the beater is lifted, the mixture falls in a wide band onto the surface, forming a figure eight that stays for 5 seconds before dissolving.

Pour the egg mixture over the chocolate mixture and fold with a rubber spatula while sifting the flour over the mixture. Alternate between adding flour—about one-fourth at a time—and folding until the flour is no longer visible.

Transfer the mixture to the prepared ramekins and smooth the tops. Cover with plastic wrap and freeze for at least 2 hours.

Preheat the oven to 425°F. Bake the soufflé cakes for 17 to 20 minutes, until risen almost by half.

Sprinkle with confectioners' sugar and serve. If you want to unmold the soufflé cakes, run a knife around the inside edge of the ramekins. Turn the soufflé cakes over onto plates, lift off the ramekins, and sprinkle with confectioners' sugar. Serve warm.

1. Melt the butter and chocolate over a saucepan of barely simmering water. Stir with a whisk or silicone spatula until smooth.

2. Beat the eggs and granulated sugar to the ribbon stage, then pour the beaten eggs over the chocolate mixture.

3. Fold together the chocolate and egg mixtures while sifting over flour.

4. Pour the soufflé mixture into the molds. Then cover the soufflés with plastic wrap and freeze for at least 2 hours. Bake until half risen.

5. To unmold the soufflé cakes, run a knife around the inside edge, then invert them onto plates and lift off the molds.

6. The finished soufflé cake can be served in its mold, with confectioners' sugar sprinkled on top.

Sponge Cakes Made with Separated Eggs

American sponge cakes and European sponge cakes, called *biscuit*, are made with separated eggs. Some recipes call for beating the yolks with sugar to aerate them, but usually it's the whites that entrap the most air. While biscuit batter is best known as the basis for ladyfingers, it can be baked as a regular layer cake or sheet cake. When a more moist and flexible cake is needed—such as for rolled cakes—melted butter is folded in with the beaten whites and yolks. When folding the whites and yolks together, don't make the mistake of completely folding them before you start to sift the flour over the mixture or you'll overwork it and make it heavy.

Fine-Crumb European Sponge Cake (Biscuit)

. . . .

This basic biscuit cake batter is used to make both ladyfingers and layer cakes. It has a very fine crumb and is excellent for making a cake that will be cut into very thin layers—a 1-inch-thick cake can be sliced into 4 layers with a little practice!

There are two ways you can make thin layer cakes: You can slice a layer crosswise using a serrated knife—which can be awkward, especially if the cake is fragile—or you can pipe the cake batter into disks with a pastry bag. You can make these piped disks any thickness you like by choosing the appropriate-size plain tip and then piping out the batter in a spiral, working from the center and moving out. To keep track of the size of the disks, draw circles on parchment paper and turn the parchment paper over so you can see the circles without the ink or pencil touching the batter. Thin, piped layer cakes cook in about 12 minutes. If the layers are very thin—about 1/4 inch—bake them in a 400°F oven instead of the usual 350°F for about 10 minutes, so they cook quickly without time to dry out. Turn it over onto the work surface, wait 5 minutes, and peel away the parchment paper. Fill with buttercream, whipped ganache, classic or fruit mousseline, or chocolate mousse.

MAKES 1 ROUND LAYER CAKE (9 BY 1 INCH), 2 ROUND CAKE DISKS (9 BY 1/3 INCH), 3 LADYFINGER STRIPS (4 BY 14 INCHES), OR 50 LADYFINGERS

Butter and flour for the round cake pan, if using

4 eggs, separated

Pinch of cream of tartar, unless using a copper bowl

1/2 cup plus 1 tablespoon granulated sugar

1 teaspoon vanilla extract

3/4 cup cake flour

Confectioners' sugar for sifting

Preheat the oven to 350°F for a round cake or 375°F for disks or ladyfingers. Butter and flour a 9 by 1-inch round cake pan, if using.

Combine the egg whites with the cream of tartar (if using) and beat in a stand mixer fitted with the whisk attachment on medium-high speed for about 4 minutes, or until medium peaks form. Add the granulated sugar and beat on high speed for about 1 minute more, or until stiff peaks form.

While the egg whites are beating, whisk together the egg yolks and vanilla in a bowl for about 1 minute, or until smooth. Transfer the egg yolk mixture to a large bowl. Pour the egg white mixture over it and fold in with a rubber spatula while sifting the flour over the mixture. Alternate between adding flour—about one-fourth at a time—and folding until the flour is no longer visible.

If you are making a round cake, transfer the mixture to the prepared cake pan and bake until the cake bounces back to the touch when you press on it, about 30 minutes.

If you are making ladyfingers, fit a pastry bag with a 1/4-inch plain tip (see Note). Draw 2 parallel lines on a sheet of parchment paper to serve as guides. The distance between the lines should equal the desired length of the ladyfingers. Turn over the parchment paper. Pipe the ladyfingers perpendicular to the lines.

If you are using the ladyfingers to decorate the edge of a cake (see page 78), pipe them so they touch; otherwise, leave about 1/4 inch between them. Sift confectioners' sugar over them and bake for about 12 minutes, or until firm to the touch.

If you are making disks, fit a pastry bag with a 1/4-inch tip. Draw 2 circles the desired size of the disks on parchment paper and turn over the parchment paper. Fill the bag with the batter and pipe out the disks, starting in the center and working outward in a spiral. Bake for about 12 minutes, or until firm to the touch. Allow to cool for 5 minutes and peel away from the parchment paper.

Note: You can use a larger tip if you want to make thicker ladyfingers—they will end up just slightly thicker than the tip you use.

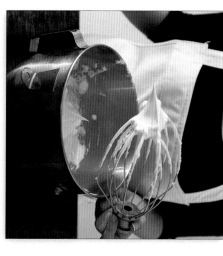

1. Beat egg whites to stiff peaks with granulated sugar added during the beating.

2. Whisk egg yolks with vanilla extract, then fold them in with the whites.

3. Sift the flour over the egg white–yolk mixture.

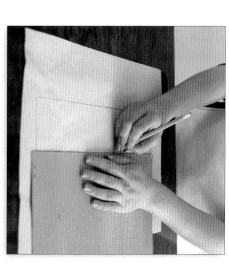

4. Draw two parallel lines on a sheet of parchment paper. The distance between the lines should equal the length of the ladyfingers. Or draw a circle.

5. Pipe in rows. Here, the ladyfingers are left touching in a row because they're going to be used on the side of a cake.

6. Sprinkle with confectioners' sugar.

7. To pipe a disk, start in the center of the circle and spiral outward.

8. Bake until golden brown.

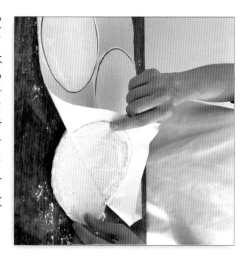

9. Let cool for 5 minutes, then invert and peel the parchment away from the ladyfingers or disks.

Butter-Enriched Sponge Cake

· · · · · · · · · · · · · · · · · ·

This cake is sometimes used instead of hot milk sponge cake to make rolled cakes because it has a rich buttery flavor and a finer crumb. It's also flexible and rolls easily. The oven temperature is higher for sheet cakes than it is for layer cakes, because a higher temperature ensures that the cake will cook before it has time to dry out.

MAKES 2 SHEET CAKES (13 BY 17 BY 1/2 INCH)

8 eggs, separated

Pinch of cream of tartar, unless using a copper bowl

1 cup plus 2 tablespoons granulated sugar

1/2 cup plus 2 tablespoons butter, melted

1 1/2 cups cake flour

Confectioners' sugar for sprinkling

Folding with Flour

In an ideal world, we'd all have three arms so that we could fold together beaten mixtures while sprinkling over dry ingredients such as flour or sugar. Unless you have a friend who will sift over the dry ingredients while you fold, work in stages by sifting over about one-fourth of the dry ingredients, folding completely, sifting over another fourth, folding again, and so on until all of the flour or sugar has been added.

Preheat the oven to 400°F. Line two 13 by 17-inch sheet pans with parchment paper.

In a stand mixer fitted with the whisk attachment, beat the egg whites and cream of tartar (if using) on medium-high speed for about 2 minutes, or until medium peaks form. Add 3/4 cup of the granulated sugar in a stream, and beat on high for 1 minute longer, or until stiff peaks form.

While the egg whites are beating, in a bowl large enough to fold together the finished cake batter, whisk the egg yolks with the rest of the granulated sugar for about 1 minute, until they are slightly pale.

With a rubber spatula, begin folding together the egg white and yolk mixtures. Place one-quarter of the mixture in a small bowl and fold in the melted butter. Fold the butter mixture back into the egg mixture while sifting over the flour, about one-quarter at a time. Alternate between adding the flour—about one-fourth at a time—and folding until the flour is no longer visible.

With an offset spatula, spread the batter evenly in the prepared pans. Use your thumb to make moats around the cakes to keep the batter from sticking to the sides of the pans. Bake for about 12 minutes, or until the tops of the cakes are firm to the touch. If the cakes seem to be cooking unevenly after 6 minutes, rotate the pans.

While the cakes are baking, sprinkle 2 sheets of parchment paper at least as large as the sheet pans with confectioners' sugar.

Remove the cakes from the oven and flip out the cakes onto the sheets of prepared parchment paper by setting the cakes right next to the parchment. Immediately peel away the cooked parchment paper from the bottoms of the cakes. Let cool, then trim off any dried-out edges. To learn how to roll the cake, see page 105.

1. Beat the egg whites to medium peaks; add ¾ cup of the granulated sugar and beat to stiff peaks. Beat the yolks for about 1 minute, or until slightly pale. Add the beaten yolks to the beaten whites and fold together.

2. Combine one-quarter of the egg mixture with the melted butter in a small bowl. Return this mixture to the rest of the egg mixture in the bowl.

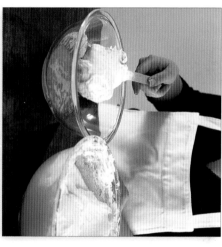

3. Sift over one-quarter of the flour, fold, sift over another one-quarter, and fold. Continue until you use all of the flour.

4. Spread the mixture onto parchment paper–lined sheet pans. Use an offset spatula to spread the cake batter in an even layer on the sheet pans.

5. Use your thumb to make moats around the cakes to keep the cake mixture from sticking to the sides of the sheet pans. Bake until the tops are firm to the touch.

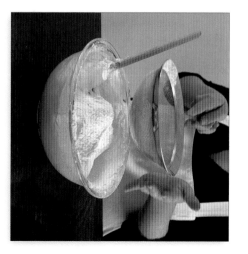

6. Sprinkle 2 sheets of parchment paper with confectioners' sugar. Turn over the sheet pans with the cakes onto the sheets of parchment paper and immediately peel away the cooked parchment paper.

7. Trim off any dried-out edges of the sheet cakes.

Sour Cream Sponge Cake

When a cake is made of very fine layers and iced, the effect is striking because the texture of fine delicate cake and rich smooth filling merge together into a very specific combination of light silkiness. This delicate Austrian cake is best known as a layer in the classic torte dobos. This cake batter is almost identical to the classic separated-egg sponge cake (biscuit), except that sour cream or crème fraîche is folded in with the beaten whites and yolks as flour is being sifted over the mixture, which makes the cake more moist and flexible.

Because a dobos is made with as many as 9 thin layers of cake, the batter is often piped into thin disks on parchment paper–lined sheet pans instead of being spread out in cake pans in the usual way. Fill this cake with mousseline, fruit-flavored mousse, or whipped ganache.

Making and Using Layers

The effect of very thin layers, separated with thin layers of frosting, is dramatic, satisfying, and elegant to look at. The usual way to go about it is to make layer cakes, let them cool, and then cut them crosswise with a long serrated knife. Ideally, the knife should be longer than the diameter of the cake and you should use a gentle sawing motion with very little force. Don't give up if you cut one of the layers unevenly or the layers even end up in pieces—just arrange them on the cake as best you can. When the cake's assembled, no one will see that the layers are broken. You can also start out by making thin sheet cakes—the batter for a 9-inch layer cake also makes a sheet cake 13 by 17 by 3/8 inch—and cutting out rounds, or you can put the batter in a pastry bag and pipe rings on sheets of parchment paper—just draw the circles first and turn the paper upside down so the batter doesn't touch the ink or graphite.

Butter and flour for the round cake pan, if using

6 egg yolks, warmed (see sidebar, page 10)

1/2 cup plus 2 tablespoons granulated sugar

1/4 cup plus 2 tablespoons sour cream or crème fraîche

5 egg whites

Pinch of cream of tartar, unless using a copper bowl

3/4 cup cake flour

Confectioners' sugar, if making disks

If you are piping disks, preheat the oven to 375°F, draw rounds on parchment paper, turn the paper over, and use it to line a sheet pan. If you have an 8-inch cake ring, use that as a guide to draw the circles. If you are making a round cake, preheat the oven to 350°F and butter and flour a 9-inch round cake pan.

Combine the egg yolks, the 1/2 cup granulated sugar, and 1 tablespoon of the sour cream and beat in a stand mixer on high speed for about 8 minutes, or until pale and fluffy and quadrupled in volume. Fold in the remaining sour cream.

Beat the egg whites with the cream of tartar (if using) in a stand mixer fitted with the whisk attachment on medium-high speed for about 2 minutes, or until medium peaks form. Add the remaining granulated sugar, and beat on high speed for about 2 minutes more, or until stiff peaks form.

Carefully transfer the egg yolk mixture to a large bowl. Add about one-quarter of the egg white mixture to lighten the mixture, then fold in the remaining egg white mixture with a rubber spatula while sifting the flour over the mixture. Alternate between adding flour—about one-fourth at a time—and folding until the flour is no longer visible.

If making disks, fill a pastry bag fitted with a 1/4-inch tip and pipe the batter onto the parchment paper in rings, then sprinkle them with confectioners' sugar. Bake for about 15 minutes, or until the disks are pale brown and firm to the touch. Allow to cool for 5 minutes, then peel away the parchment paper from the disks.

If making a round layer cake, spread the batter in the prepared cake pan. Bake for about 25 minutes, or until firm to the touch. Allow to cool for 5 minutes.

1. Use a round cake ring to draw circles on a sheet of parchment paper. Turn the parchment paper over so you can see the rings through it.

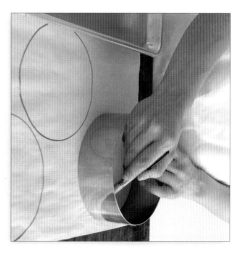

2. Beat the egg yolks with ½ cup of the granulated sugar and 1 tablespoon of the sour cream, until quadrupled in volume. Transfer to a bowl and fold in the rest of the sour cream.

3. Beat the egg whites to medium peaks and add the rest of the granulated sugar. Beat to stiff peaks. Fold in about one-fourth of the egg white mixture with the egg yolk mixture. Fold in the rest of the egg white mixture while sifting over flour.

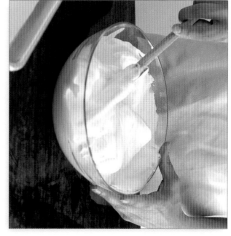

4. Alternate between adding flour—about one-fourth at a time—and folding until the flour is no longer visible.

5. Fill a pastry bag with a ¼-inch tip and pipe the batter onto the parchment paper in rings.

6. Sprinkle over confectioners' sugar. Bake until pale brown and firm to the touch, about 15 minutes. Allow to cool for 5 minutes and peel away the parchment paper.

Almond Flour Sponge Cake

· ·

This cake contains whole eggs plus additional egg whites. The whole eggs are required to provide body—the cake contains very little flour and needs something to hold it together—while the whites add airiness. The steps for making the cake are also somewhat unusual because the flour is mixed with the eggs at the beginning. The almond flour gives the cake a nutty complexity and a dense crumb, which makes it easy to slice into as many as four layers. You can use this cake in the same way as any sponge cake (it may be rolled, for example) and include as many frostings or icings as you like between the layers. To make four layers, you can bake two layer cakes and slice them in half, or you can bake two thin sheet cakes and cut out two rounds from each one. Fill with mousseline, Bavarian cream, or whipped ganache.

MAKES 2 SHEET CAKES (13 BY 17 BY ³/₈ INCH),
1 SHEET CAKE (13 BY 17 BY ³/₄ INCH),
OR 2 ROUND LAYER CAKES (9 BY 1 INCH)

Butter and flour for the round cake pans, if using

1¹/₂ cups almond flour

¹/₂ cup plus 1 tablespoon cake flour

³/₄ cup granulated sugar

4 eggs

6 egg whites

Pinch of cream of tartar, unless using a copper bowl

Confectioners' sugar, if making a sheet cake

If you are making round cakes, preheat the oven to 350°F and butter and flour two 9-inch round cake pans. If you are making sheet cakes, preheat the oven to 375°F and line two 13 by 17-inch sheet pans with parchment.

Combine the almond flour, cake flour, and ¹/₂ cup of the granulated sugar in a food processor. With the motor running, add the eggs, 2 at a time, until the mixture is smooth. Transfer the mixture to a bowl large enough to hold all the batter.

Beat the egg whites with the cream of tartar (if using) on medium-high speed in a stand mixer fitted with the whisk attachment for about 2 minutes or with a handheld mixer for about 3 minutes, or until medium peaks form. Add the remaining granulated sugar, and beat on high speed for 1 to 5 minutes longer (depending on what kind of mixer you are using), until stiff peaks form.

Mix one-fourth of the egg white mixture into the almond mixture until smooth, to lighten the mixture. Using a rubber spatula, fold this mixture with the remaining egg white mixture.

Transfer the batter to the cake pans or sheet pans. If you are using sheet pans, spread the batter with an offset spatula and run your thumb around the edges to make a small moat to keep the edges of the cakes from sticking to the pans.

Bake round cakes for about 25 minutes, or until they bounce back to the touch. Bake sheet cakes for about 15 minutes, or until firm and they bounce back to the touch.

If you are baking sheet cakes, sprinkle 2 sheets of parchment paper as large as the sheet pan with confectioners' sugar. Run a knife around the edges of the cakes to make it easier to get them out of the sheet pans. Quickly flip out the cakes over the parchment paper as soon as they come out of the oven by placing the cakes right next to the parchment. Peel away the cooked parchment from the bottoms of the cakes. Cut the cakes into rounds or rectangles and layer them with the same fillings you'd use for a sponge cake.

If you are baking round cakes, let them cool for 5 minutes in the cake pans and then turn out onto cake racks.

1. Combine the almond flour, cake flour, and ½ cup of the granulated sugar in a food processor and process to combine. Add the eggs, 2 at a time, and process until smooth.

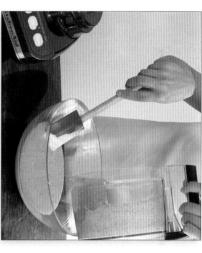

2. Transfer the almond mixture to a bowl large enough to hold all the batter.

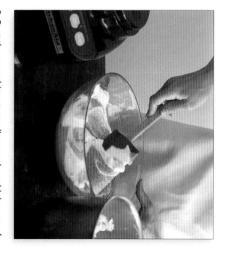

3. Beat the egg whites to medium peaks, add the rest of the granulated sugar, and beat to stiff peaks. Fold about one-fourth of the beaten egg whites into the almond mixture and stir until smooth. Then fold in the rest of the beaten egg whites.

4. If you are making sheet cakes, use an offset spatula to spread the cake mixture over parchment paper–lined sheet pans. Run your thumb around the edges of the cake, forming a small moat. This makes the cake easier to get out of the sheet pan once baked.

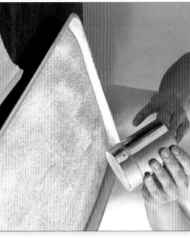

5. Bake for about 15 minutes, or until the cake springs back to the touch. When the cake is done, sprinkle it with confectioners' sugar.

6. Run a knife around the edge of the cake to make it easier to get out of the sheet pan.

7. Sprinkle a sheet of parchment paper with confectioners' sugar to prevent the cake from sticking. Turn the cake onto the coated parchment paper.

8. Immediately pull away the parchment paper that was baked with the cake.

Almond Paste Sponge Cake

Almond paste sponge cake is similar to almond flour sponge cake (page 20), but has an even more intense almond flavor. The techniques used to make it are straightforward: Almond paste is beaten with egg yolks and sugar, and then the mixture is folded with beaten egg whites. Because the cake is somewhat dense, it works better as a thin sheet cake than it does as a layer cake, and it can be used to make petits fours (page 102) or rolled cakes (see page 106).

MAKES 1 SHEET CAKE (13 BY 17 BY 3/8 INCH)

1/2 cup almond paste

6 egg yolks

1 teaspoon vanilla extract

1/2 cup granulated sugar

1 tablespoon grated lemon or orange zest (see page 194)

5 egg whites

Pinch of cream of tartar, unless using a copper bowl

2/3 cup cake flour

Confectioners' sugar for sprinkling

Preheat the oven to 375°F. Line a 13 by 17-inch sheet pan with parchment paper.

In a stand mixer with the paddle attachment, beat the almond paste on medium-high speed for about 1 minute, or until it softens. Beat in the egg yolks, one by one, and continue beating for about 1 minute, or until the mixture is smooth. Add the vanilla and 1/4 cup of the granulated sugar and continue beating on medium-high speed for about 12 minutes, or until the mixture turns pale yellow. Add the zest.

Beat the egg whites and cream of tartar (if using) on medium-high speed for about 2 minutes, or until soft peaks form. Add the remaining granulated sugar, and continue beating for about 2 minutes, until medium peaks form.

Mix about one-fourth of the egg white mixture with the almond mixture to lighten it. Fold in the rest of the egg white mixture with a rubber spatula, while sifting the flour over the mixture. Alternate between adding flour—about one-fourth at a time—and folding until the flour is no longer visible.

Spread the batter in the sheet pan with an offset spatula and run your thumb around the edge of the cake, making a moat (this will keep the batter from sticking to the sides of the pan). Sprinkle the cake with confectioners' sugar. Bake for about 17 minutes, or until firm to the touch.

While the cake is baking, sprinkle a sheet of parchment paper as large as the sheet pan with confectioners' sugar.

When the cake is done, flip it onto the parchment paper and immediately peel away the cooked parchment paper from the bottom of the cake by holding it flat against the cake as you peel. Sprinkle what is now the top of the cake with confectioners' sugar. Cut the cake into rounds or rectangles for layering.

1. Beat the almond paste in a stand mixer fitted with the paddle attachment for 1 minute to soften it and make it easier to work with.

2. Add the egg yolks, vanilla, and 1/4 cup of the granulated sugar and beat for about 12 minutes, or until very pale, as shown here. Add flavoring, such as grated orange zest.

3. Beat the egg whites with a pinch of cream of tartar (if using) to soft peaks, add the rest of the granulated sugar, and beat to medium peaks.

4. Combine the almond mixture with the egg whites by first folding about one-fourth of the egg whites with the almond mixture to lighten it.

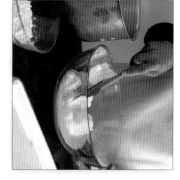

5. When the egg whites and almond mixture are evenly combined, fold in the rest of the egg whites and sift over the flour while folding.

6. Line a sheet pan with parchment paper—there is no need for buttering or flouring—and spread the mixture evenly on top. Use your thumb to make a moat around the cake to keep the batter from sticking to the sides of the pans (see photo page 101). Sprinkle the cake with confectioners' sugar before baking.

7. While the cake is baking, sprinkle a sheet of parchment paper with confectioners' sugar. When the cake is finished baking, cut around the sides of the sheet pan to help detach the cake.

8. Sprinkle the cake with confectioners' sugar to keep it from sticking when you turn it over onto the sugared parchment paper.

9. Lift the cake up and flip it over onto the sugared parchment paper.

10. Immediately peel off the parchment paper from the bottom of the cake—don't wait or the parchment paper will stick. Sprinkle what is now the top of the cake with confectioners' sugar.

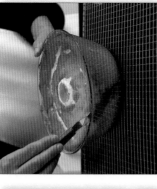

1. Beat the egg whites with cream of tartar (unless using a copper bowl) to medium peaks. Add sugar and continue beating to between medium and stiff peaks.

2. Fold with sifted flour and lemon juice. Spoon the batter into an ungreased tube pan and smooth the surface with the back of a spoon.

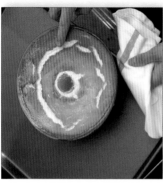

3. Bake for about 45 minutes, or until the cake springs back to the touch. Let the cake rest, upside down on a bottle, for 45 minutes (see page 35) before you unmold it.

4. Cut along the inside of the pan with a small metal spatula or thin knife to release the cake.

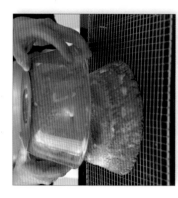

5. Invert the cake onto a cake rack and lift off the cake pan.

Sponge Cakes Made with Eggs Whites Only

While many sponge cakes contain beaten egg whites, most also contain egg yolks or whole eggs. And while there are cakelike mixtures, such as meringue and dacquoise, made of egg whites, these aren't sponge cakes. Angel food cake, the only sponge cake made with egg whites alone, is essentially meringue with flour folded in.

Angel Food Cake

Angel food cake, which is sponge cake made only with egg whites (no yolks), must be baked in an ungreased tube pan. It can be made with a handheld mixer, but a stand mixer makes it easier.

MAKES ONE 9-INCH TUBE CAKE

15 egg whites (2 cups)
Pinch of cream of tartar, unless using a copper bowl
1 cup sugar
1 tablespoon lemon juice
1¼ cups cake flour

Preheat the oven to 350°F.

Beat the egg whites and the cream of tartar (if using) with a stand mixer fitted with the whisk attachment on medium-high speed for about 3 minutes or with a handheld mixer on high speed for about 8 minutes, or until medium peaks form. Add the sugar in a steady stream and beat for about 2 minutes more in a stand mixer or 5 minutes more with a handheld mixer, or until medium to stiff peaks form. Don't overdo it—it's better to underbeat the egg whites slightly than to overbeat them.

Sprinkle the lemon juice over the egg white mixture and sift over the flour. Alternate between adding flour—about one-fourth at a time—and folding until the flour is no longer visible.

Carefully transfer the batter to the ungreased tube pan. Bake for 40 to 45 minutes, until a paring knife or skewer comes out clean and the top of the cake feels firm and springs back to the touch.

Turn the tube pan upside down and set over the neck of a bottle to cool (see page 35) for 45 minutes. To remove the cake from the tube pan, roll it on its side and slide a knife or small spatula around the inside of the tube pan against the outside wall and around the tube in the middle. Invert the cake onto a cake rack and lift off the cake pan.

Butter cakes are made by whipping air into room-temperature butter and sugar and then adding eggs and flour, or by adding melted butter to beaten eggs and sugar. So-called high-ratio cakes are made by combining butter with the dry ingredients and then adding the liquid ingredients.

Most butter cakes are made in much the same way as pound cake, by creaming room-temperature butter with granulated or superfine sugar to work air into the butter. Next, eggs are added, one by one, until they form a creamy emulsion with the butter and sugar. Last, flour is added and worked into the butter mixture as quickly as possible so the butter isn't overworked. Many butter cakes are made in the same way, with variations at different stages. Among the most common of these variations are cakes in which baking powder is mixed with the flour before the flour is folded into the butter mixture. If an acidic ingredient is being included in the cake, say sour cream or brown sugar, some baking soda may be needed for balance since baking powder is a mixture of baking soda and an acid. The acid in these ingredients causes the baking soda to release carbon dioxide, which leavens the cake.

When liquids such as milk and sour cream are combined with the butter-egg mixture, more gluten is activated and the cake can hold more butter. The result is a cake with all the buttery flavor of pound cake but with a more airy texture. In some butter cake recipes, the eggs are separated and the yolks are mixed with the butter-sugar mixture. The whites are beaten, usually with some sugar, and folded into the batter for extra lightness. One cake that uses all of these leavening ingredients and techniques is a 1-2-3-4 cake or fluffy light butter cake (page 28).

Some butter cakes are made like whole-egg sponge cakes (whole eggs are beaten with the sugar) except that they contain far more butter and sometimes heavy cream. These cakes are among the lightest and most delicate of all cakes.

High-ratio cakes, also called dump cakes, are a relatively recent invention—you'll never see recipes for them that predate the 1940s—and are put together in a different order. To make a high-ratio cake, combine the sliced butter and a small amount of liquid, usually milk, with the dry ingredients before adding the eggs and the rest of the liquid called for in the recipe (see sidebar, page 22).

Butter cakes are flavored by adding melted chocolate to the butter-sugar-egg combination or by folding melted chocolate or cocoa powder into the batter at the end. Butter cakes are also flavored with simple ingredients such as spices, poppy seeds, chopped nuts, lemon or orange zest, and vanilla

or other extracts beaten with the eggs and butter. Remember also that layer cakes can be flavored with simple syrup.

Some of the richest and lightest textured cakes—very similar to madeleines (page 260)—are made by combining melted butter (sometimes mixed with cream or milk) with beaten whole eggs and sugar, before adding the dry ingredients. If you want a luxurious cake, with a tight crumb, consider one of these.

Pound Cake

. . . .

Traditional pound cake is made by combining equal parts by weight of butter, eggs, sugar, and flour; it contains no leavening such as baking powder and, as a result, can be rather dense, but in a satisfying, buttery kind of way. Any airiness that traditional pound cakes do have is a result of beating the butter and sugar for a long time—until the mixture has the consistency of sour cream—and then continuing the beating while adding the eggs. Flour is added at the end and worked as little as possible to avoid making the cake tough. This pound cake is especially moist and buttery because milk is added as well as extra butter. All-purpose flour is used instead of cake flour because you need the extra gluten to absorb the milk and extra butter. If you would like to glaze the cake, try the lemon glaze on page 61.

MAKES 1 LOAF CAKE (5 BY 9 INCHES)

Butter and flour for the loaf pan

1¼ cups plus 2 tablespoons butter, sliced, at cool room temperature

1⅓ cups sugar

¼ teaspoon salt

5 eggs

¼ cup plus 2 tablespoons milk

1 teaspoon vanilla extract

2 teaspoons grated lemon zest (see page 194), optional

1 tablespoon grated orange zest (see page 194), optional

1½ cups all-purpose flour

Butter a 5 by 9-inch loaf pan and put a rectangle of parchment paper on the bottom. Flour the sides of the pan. Preheat the oven to 350°F.

In a stand mixer with the paddle attachment, beat the butter, sugar, and salt on high speed for about 8 minutes, or until fluffy. Don't be tempted to shorten the beating time or your cake will be heavy. Scrape the sides of the bowl with a rubber spatula every minute or so.

Pound Cake, continued

In a bowl, beat the eggs, milk, and vanilla. With the mixer on medium speed, add the egg-milk mixture to the butter mixture, one-third at a time. Wait until each addition is thoroughly incorporated before adding more.

The mixture will have the consistency of sour cream or small curd cottage cheese, depending on the temperature. Add the zests to the batter and beat for 30 seconds more.

Turn off the mixer and add all the flour. Beat on low speed for about 5 seconds, or just long enough to mix in the flour with no leftover lumps. Scrape the sides of the bowl with a rubber spatula, then mix for 5 minutes more.

Scrape the batter into the prepared loaf pan. Don't smooth over the surface of the batter or it may lose some of its airiness—it will settle as it bakes.

Bake for about 1 hour and 15 minutes, or until a toothpick or knife inserted in the center comes out clean. Let cool for 15 minutes before turning out of the pan. Serve sliced. The cake keeps for several days tightly wrapped in plastic.

1. Combine the butter, sugar, and salt in the bowl of a stand mixer with the paddle attachment. Work the butter and sugar together on high speed for about 8 minutes, or until fluffy and creamy.

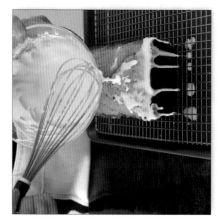

2. Beat the eggs with the milk and vanilla with the mixer on medium speed. Add this mixture, one-third at a time, to the butter mixture. Wait until each addition is thoroughly incorporated before adding more. Beat the batter until it looks like sour cream or, if the room is cold, small curd cottage cheese.

3. Add the zests to the batter and beat in. Add the flour and beat the mixture just long enough to get rid of the lumps. Transfer the batter to a buttered loaf pan. Don't smooth over the surface of the batter or it may lose some of its airiness—it will settle as it bakes.

4. Bake until a knife stuck into the middle of the cake comes out with no batter attached, but a crumb or two is okay.

5. If you like, drizzle lemon glaze over the room-temperature pound cake. Let it drip down the sides for a rustic homespun effect.

German Chocolate Cake

Some American versions of this cake contain coconut and walnuts, but this version is so rich and chocolaty that these additions aren't really needed. This cake is traditionally served with a coconut and pecan filling; I suggest instead chocolate or vanilla buttercream. While the finished cake is nothing like a pound cake, the steps are very similar. Butter is beaten with sugar and egg yolks. A mixture of melted chocolate and sour cream is then added to the egg yolk mixture. The egg whites are beaten with sugar to stiff peaks. The egg yolk mixture is then folded into the whites while a mixture of flour, baking powder, and baking soda is sifted over it.

MAKES 2 ROUND LAYER CAKES (9 BY 1½ INCHES)

Butter and flour for the cake pans

¾ **cup heavy cream**

6 ounces bittersweet chocolate, coarsely chopped

½ **cup sour cream**

2 teaspoons vanilla extract

1½ **cups cake flour, sifted**

2 teaspoons baking powder

1 teaspoon baking soda

½ **teaspoon salt**

1 cup sugar

1 cup butter, sliced, at room temperature

4 eggs, separated

Pinch of cream of tartar, unless using a copper bowl

BAKING

Preheat the oven to 350°F. Butter and flour two 9-inch round cake pans.

Place the cream in a small saucepan and bring it to a simmer over medium heat. Pour it over the chocolate in a bowl large enough to hold all the finished cake batter. Let sit for about 5 minutes, or until all the chocolate has melted, then whisk the mixture until there are no lumps. Stir in the sour cream and vanilla.

In a bowl, whisk together the flour, baking powder, baking soda, and salt.

In a stand mixer fitted with the paddle attachment, beat 3/4 cup of the sugar with the butter for about 2 minutes. Switch to the whisk attachment and beat for 5 minutes more, or until soft and creamy. Beat in the egg yolks, one by one. Beat in the chocolate mixture until well combined.

Transfer the chocolate–egg yolk mixture back to the large bowl. Sift the dry ingredients over the mixture and fold with a rubber spatula just until there are no lumps.

In a stand mixer fitted with the whisk attachment, beat the egg whites and the cream of tartar (if using) at medium-high speed for about 2 minutes, until medium peaks form. Add the remaining sugar, then beat for about 3 minutes more, or until stiff peaks form. Whisk one-fourth of the egg white mixture into the chocolate mixture to lighten it and then fold in the rest of the white mixture, just long enough so you no longer see streaks of egg white.

Transfer the batter to the prepared cake pans and smooth the tops with an offset spatula. Bake the cakes for about 35 minutes, or until they bounce back to the touch or a toothpick inserted in the center comes out clean. Let cool for 5 minutes in the cake pans and then turn out onto cake racks.

1. Pour the simmering cream over the chocolate and let sit for 5 minutes. Stir the chocolate mixture until smooth, then stir in the sour cream and the vanilla.

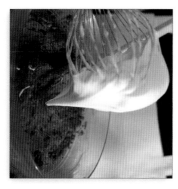

2. Whisk together the dry ingredients except the sugar.

3. Combine 3/4 cup of the sugar with the butter in a bowl. Cream the butter and sugar by hand with a whisk, with a handheld mixer, or in a stand mixer with the whisk attachment.

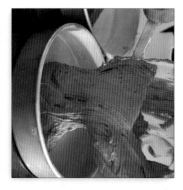

4. Beat in the egg yolks one by one. Beat in the chocolate mixture until smooth.

5. Sift over the dry ingredients and fold until there are no lumps.

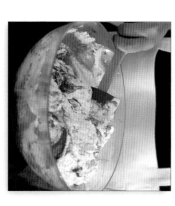

6. Beat the egg whites with the cream of tartar (if using) to medium peaks, add the remaining sugar, and beat for 1 minute more. Whisk about one-fourth of the egg whites into the chocolate mixture.

7. Fold the rest of the egg whites into the chocolate mixture. Transfer the batter to 2 buttered and floured cake pans. Smooth the tops of the cakes with an offset spatula.

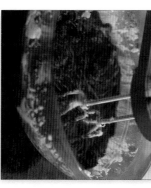

8. Bake until the cake bounces back to the touch or a toothpick inserted in the center comes out clean.

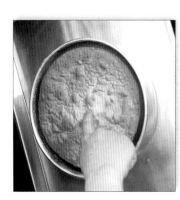

1. Cream the butter and the 3/4 cup sugar with a heavy wooden spoon. When the mixture is creamy and easy to work, switch to a whisk. Whisk in the egg yolks, one at a time.

2. Use the whisk to stir in the milk and vanilla. Then use a whisk to stir in the dry ingredients, 1/2 cup at a time, just enough to incorporate them.

3. Beat the egg whites with the cream of tartar (if using) to soft peaks, add the remaining sugar, and beat to medium peaks. Whisk about one-fourth of the egg whites into the butter mixture.

4. Fold in the rest of the egg whites. Fill the cake pans and use a rubber spatula to smooth the tops.

5. Bake until the cake bounces back to the touch or a knife or toothpick poked through the top comes out clean.

Fluffy Light Butter Cake

This yellow cake has the same ingredients as pound cake but is lighter because it contains milk and baking powder. Because of its lightness, it is the perfect foil for a rich frosting such as you might use for a sponge cake like a genoise (see page 8).

MAKES 2 ROUND LAYER CAKES (9 BY 1 INCH), OR 1 ROUND LAYER CAKE (9 BY 2 INCHES)

Butter and flour for the cake pans

1 1/4 cups cake flour

1 3/4 teaspoons baking powder

1/4 teaspoon salt

3/4 cup butter, at room temperature

3/4 cup plus 3 tablespoons sugar

3 eggs, separated

2/3 cup milk

1 teaspoon vanilla extract

Pinch of cream of tartar, unless using a copper bowl

Preheat the oven to 350°F. Butter and flour one or two 9-inch cake pans.

In a bowl, sift together the flour, baking powder, and salt and whisk to combine.

Cream the butter and the 3/4 cup sugar using a heavy wooden spoon, a handheld mixer, or a stand mixer fitted with the paddle attachment. When the butter softens, switch to a whisk. Continue whisking, for about 5 minutes. Whisk in the egg yolks, one at a time, until the mixture is smooth. Whisk in the milk and vanilla, then the flour mixture, 1/2 cup at a time. Don't overwork. Transfer the egg mixture to a large bowl to make folding easier.

Beat the egg whites and cream of tartar (if using) for about 2 minutes, until soft peaks form, then beat in the remaining sugar for about 2 minutes, until medium peaks form.

Whisk one-fourth of the egg white mixture into the butter mixture to lighten it. Fold in the rest of the egg white mixture with a rubber spatula. Spread the batter in the cake pans. Bake 1-inch-thick cakes for about 30 minutes or a 2-inch-thick cake for about 40 minutes, or until the cakes bounce back to the touch or until a knife or toothpick inserted in the centers comes out clean. Let cool for 5 minutes in the cake pans and then turn out onto a cake rack.

28

BAKING

Cream and Butter Sheet Cake

Because it has a delicate texture and buttery flavor, don't use too much frosting or too strongly flavored a frosting on this cake, or its flavor may not come through. Consider frosting this cake with a delicate buttercream flavored with kirsch, raspberry brandy (eau de vie de framboise), Cognac, or poire William (see page 48). Here are directions to make a sheet cake, but you can also make a 9-inch round layer cake.

MAKES 1 SHEET CAKE (13 BY 17 BY 1/2 INCH)

1¹/₂ cups cake flour

1 teaspoon baking powder

4 eggs, warmed

1 cup granulated sugar

¹/₂ cup heavy cream

Zest of 1 lemon, or 1 teaspoon vanilla extract

¹/₂ cup butter, melted

Confectioners' sugar for sprinkling

Preheat the oven to 375°F. Line a 13 by 17-inch sheet pan with parchment paper.

In a bowl, whisk together the flour and baking powder and sift them.

In a second bowl, combine the eggs and granulated sugar and beat on high speed with a stand mixer fitted with the whisk attachment for about 3 minutes or with a handheld mixer for 10 minutes, or until pale and almost tripled in volume. Stir in the cream and zest.

Whisk the butter into the egg mixture. Gently stir the dry ingredients into the egg mixture with a whisk, just long enough to eliminate lumps.

Spread the batter in the prepared sheet pan with an offset spatula. Bake for about 15 minutes, or until firm to the touch.

Take a sheet of parchment paper the same size as the sheet pan and sprinkle it with confectioners' sugar. Remove the cake from the oven and quickly flip it out over the parchment paper. Immediately peel away the cooked parchment paper from the bottom of the cake. Sprinkle the top of the cake—what was the bottom—with confectioners' sugar.

VARIATION

To make one 9-inch round layer cake, butter and flour a 9-inch cake pan and preheat the oven to 350°F. Spread the cake batter into the prepared pan, and bake for 25 minutes, until firm to the touch. Let it rest for 10 minutes, run a knife around the edges to detach it, and turn it out onto a cake rack to cool. Slice into layers and frost with buttercream or mousseline.

MAKING A CREAM AND BUTTER SHEET CAKE

1. Zest the lemon.

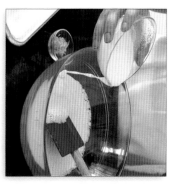

2. Beat the eggs with the granulated sugar until smooth and pale. Stir in the heavy cream and lemon zest or other flavoring such as vanilla.

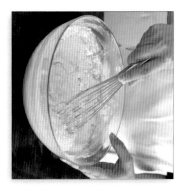

3. Fold in the melted butter. Add the dry ingredients and whisk until the mixture is smooth and there are no lumps.

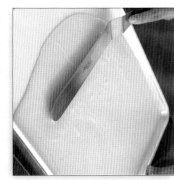

4. Spread the mixture evenly over a parchment paper–lined sheet pan with an offset spatula. Bake.

5. Turn out the sheet cake onto a sheet of parchment paper sprinkled with confectioners' sugar or onto a work surface. Peel back the parchment paper while the cake is still hot—the paper may stick to a cold cake.

2. Combine the chocolate, butter, and sour cream in a heatproof bowl. Place the bowl over a saucepan of barely simmering water. Stir until smooth. Remove from the heat as soon as the chocolate has melted.

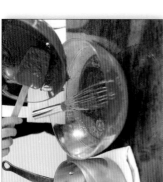

1. Use a chef's knife to coarsely chop the chocolate.

3. Whisk together the eggs and sugar. Stir the chocolate mixture into the egg mixture. Sift over the dry ingredients while stirring gently.

4. Transfer the batter to one or two buttered and floured cake pans and bake.

5. If you don't have a cake rack, you can unmold the cake on parchment paper that has been sprinkled with confectioners' sugar to prevent sticking.

Devil's Food Cake

This rich, deeply flavored cake can be frosted with chocolate frosting, such as buttercream or whipped ganache, to reinforce the chocolate effect, or a contrasting frosting, such as a kirsch-flavored buttercream, white chocolate mousse, white chocolate whipped ganache, or mousseline, to balance the chocolate.

MAKES 2 ROUND LAYER CAKES (9 BY 1 INCH)
OR 1 ROUND LAYER CAKE (9 BY 2 INCHES)

Butter and flour for the cake pans

1 cup cake flour

1½ teaspoons baking soda

1 teaspoon baking powder

¼ teaspoon salt

½ cup butter, sliced, at room temperature

6 ounces bittersweet chocolate, chopped

1 cup sour cream

¾ cup sugar

3 eggs

Preheat the oven to 350°F. Butter and flour one or two 9-inch cake pans.

In a bowl, stir together the flour, baking soda, baking powder, and salt.

Combine the butter, chocolate, and sour cream in a heatproof bowl and place the bowl over a saucepan of simmering water. Stir until smooth; remove from the heat as soon as the chocolate has melted.

In a large bowl, whisk together the sugar and eggs until smooth. Stir the chocolate mixture into the egg mixture. Sift the dry ingredients over the chocolate-egg mixture while folding with a rubber spatula.

Pour the mixture into the prepared pans. Bake 1-inch-thick cakes for about 25 minutes or a 2-inch-thick cake for about 40 minutes, or until the cakes spring back to the touch or a toothpick inserted in the center comes out clean. Let the cakes cool for 5 minutes and turn them out onto a cake rack. Frost as suggested above.

Vanilla Butter Cake

This rich buttery cake is an example of a dump cake (see sidebar) in that it contains a high ratio of sugar to flour. It's best frosted with something relatively light such as stabilized whipped cream or white chocolate ganache.

MAKES 2 ROUND LAYER CAKES (9 BY 1 INCH),
OR 1 ROUND LAYER CAKE (9 BY 2 INCHES)

Butter and flour for the cake pans

2¹/₂ cups sugar

1¹/₂ cups cake flour

¹/₂ teaspoon salt

1 tablespoon plus 1 teaspoon baking powder

2 eggs

3 egg yolks

1¹/₂ cups milk

2 teaspoons vanilla extract

³/₄ cup plus 2 tablespoons butter, sliced

Preheat the oven to 350°F. Butter and flour one or two 9-inch cake pans.

In a bowl, whisk together the flour, sugar, salt, and baking powder.

In a second bowl, whisk together the eggs, egg yolks, ¹/₂ cup of the milk, and the vanilla.

Add the remaining milk and the butter to the dry ingredients. Using a stand mixer fitted with the paddle attachment or a wooden spoon, mix for about 2 minutes, or until well combined. Add one-fourth of the egg mixture. Work until smooth, then work in half of the remaining egg mixture. Add the last of the egg mixture and mix until smooth.

Transfer the batter to the prepared cake pans and smooth the tops with an offset spatula. Bake 1-inch-thick cakes for about 25 minutes or a 2-inch-thick cake for about 35 minutes, or until firm to the touch or a toothpick inserted in the center comes out clean. Let cool for 5 minutes in the cake pans and then turn out onto cake racks.

Dump Cakes

Dump cakes are also called "high-ratio" cakes because they contain a higher than usual proportion of sugar to flour. They are called dump cakes because they are made by combining room-temperature butter and a small amount of liquid—milk or cream—with the dry ingredients for about 2 minutes, or just long enough to distribute the ingredients. The rest of the liquids, including beaten egg, are "dumped" in last and the mixture is beaten just long enough to eliminate lumps. The result is light and buttery. If you want to know if a recipe uses the high-ratio method shown here, notice when the butter is added. If it is added at the beginning, with the dry ingredients, it is probably a recipe for a high-ratio cake.

1. Combine the dry ingredients with a hand whisk or the paddle attachment on a stand mixer. Separately, whisk together the eggs, egg yolks, ¹/₂ cup of the milk, and the vanilla.

2. Add the butter and the remaining milk to the dry ingredients and work together with the paddle attachment on an electric mixer or with a wooden spoon for about 2 minutes, until the wet ingredients and the butter disappear.

3. When the butter and milk are well combined, add the egg mixture, one-fourth at a time, waiting until the mixture is smooth before adding more egg mixture.

4. Scoop the batter out into one or two buttered and floured cake pans. Smooth off the top of each cake(s) with an offset spatula. Bake until the cake(s) bounce back to the touch or until a toothpick inserted in the center comes out clean.

OIL-BASED CAKES

Cakes made with oil have the advantage of staying moist even when cool, whereas cakes made with butter seem heavier when chilled because the butter hardens. When oil is used to bake a cake, it is usually whisked with whole eggs. The egg-oil mixture is then gently stirred with dry ingredients (usually flour, sugar, baking powder, and salt) and any other ingredients, such as carrots, bananas, or pineapple, that are added for texture and flavor.

Carrot Cake

Carrot cake is especially moist because it is made with oil. Oil, unlike butter, remains liquid at room temperature, so the cake stays moist even when cool. This recipe contains walnuts, which give the cake a delightful crunch, and pineapple, which adds flavor and contrast.

The carrots are best when grated on a box grater. Some graters have tiny punch-outs instead of teeth for the finest grate. When grating the carrots, avoid these and use the smallest teeth. The frosting will go together faster if the ingredients are at room temperature. This recipe is adapted from a very traditional version in Joy of Cooking.

MAKES TWO ¹/₂-QUART LOAF CAKES (2 BY 3 BY 5 INCHES), OR ONE 1-QUART LOAF CAKE (5 BY 7 BY 3 INCHES)

Cake

Butter and flour for the pans

2 to 3 medium carrots, peeled

²/₃ cup flour

¹/₂ cup granulated sugar

1 teaspoon baking soda

³/₄ teaspoon baking powder

¹/₂ teaspoon ground cinnamon

¹/₄ teaspoon ground cloves

¹/₄ teaspoon grated nutmeg

¹/₄ teaspoon ground allspice

¹/₄ teaspoon salt

¹/₃ cup vegetable oil, or a combination of hazelnut or walnut oil and vegetable oil

2 eggs

1 cup chopped walnuts

¹/₂ cup drained chopped pineapple

One 8-ounce package cream cheese, at room temperature

¹/₄ cup plus 2 tablespoons butter, at room temperature

1 teaspoon vanilla extract

1³/₄ cups confectioners' sugar

Preheat the oven to 350°F. Butter and flour the loaf pans.

To make the cake, cut the carrots into 3- or 4-inch sections and grate them, preferably by hand with a box grater. Hold the carrot sections straight up and down against the grater and grate down to the core. Give the section a quarter turn and grate, again down to the core. Continue in this way until you have only the woody core, which you can throw out. If you are using a food processor, use the finest grater attachment. You should end up with 1 cup finely grated carrots.

In a bowl, whisk together the flour, granulated sugar, baking soda, baking powder, cinnamon, cloves, nutmeg, allspice, and salt, then sift into a large bowl.

In a bowl, whisk together the oil and eggs and stir into the dry ingredients with a rubber spatula. Stir in the walnuts, pineapple, and carrots.

Transfer the batter to the prepared loaf pans and bake for 30 to 55 minutes, or until a toothpick inserted in the center comes out clean. Let cool for 5 minutes before taking the loaves out of the pans. Let the loaves cool on cake racks for 1 hour.

To make the frosting, combine the cream cheese, butter, vanilla, and sugar in the bowl of a stand mixer fitted with the paddle attachment and beat on medium speed for about 10 minutes, or until smooth.

Spread the tops of the loaves with the frosting. Serve in slices.

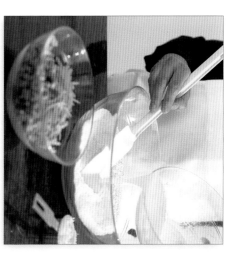

1. Combine all the dry ingredients with a whisk and then sift them. Whisk together the eggs and oil. Use a rubber spatula to stir the egg mixture gently into the dry ingredients. Stir the walnuts, pineapple, and carrots into the egg mixture.

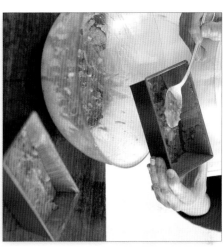

2. Spoon the batter into buttered and floured loaf pans.

3. Bake the loaves until a skewer, toothpick, or paring knife comes out clean. Let cool for 5 minutes before taking the loaves out of the pans, then let cool on a cake rack for 1 hour.

4. Spread the tops of the loaves with cream cheese frosting.

the egg yolk mixture and stir until well combined. Fold this mixture into the egg white mixture with a rubber spatula.

Transfer the batter to an ungreased 10-inch tube pan with a removable bottom. Bake for about 45 minutes, or until the cake bounces back to the touch. Turn the tube pan upside down and set over the neck of a bottle to cool (see opposite page) for 45 minutes.

Glazing a Chiffon Cake

Set the cake on a cake rack over a sheet pan so you can recoup any glaze that drips off the cake. Prepare a glaze (page 53) and spread it over the top of the cake with a long metal spatula. (An offset spatula is somewhat easier to work with.) Spread the glaze over the top of the cake, working out from the center, so the glaze drips down the sides. Spread the glaze around the sides of the cake.

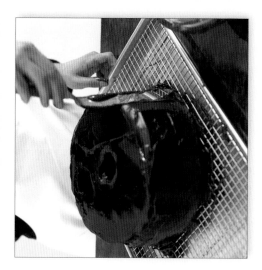

Chiffon Cake

Basic chiffon cakes are made by beating together egg yolks, oil, and water or other liquid (orange juice is used here) before they are combined with beaten egg whites and the dry ingredients. The combination of oil, beaten egg whites, and flour makes a cake much like angel food but even moister. You can substitute hazelnut oil for some of the vegetable oil to give this cake a deeply nuanced flavor, but this is expensive and by no means essential. You can make chiffon cakes with cake flour, but all-purpose flour gives them a somewhat deeper flavor. The other chiffon cake peculiarity is baking in an ungreased tube pan, so the cake clings to the sides instead of falling as it might in a greased pan. Despite the claims of most recipes, chiffon cake does stick to the pan, but because it is in a tube pan with a removable bottom, it is easy to get the cake out of the pan and sticking isn't much of a problem.

MAKES ONE 10-INCH TUBE CAKE

1³/₄ cups all-purpose flour, or 2¹/₄ cups cake flour

1 tablespoon baking powder

1 teaspoon salt

1¹/₂ cups sugar

5 egg yolks

¹/₂ cup orange juice or water

¹/₂ cup vegetable oil, or ¹/₄ cup hazelnut or walnut oil combined with ¹/₄ cup vegetable oil

8 egg whites

1 teaspoon vanilla extract

¹/₂ teaspoon cream of tartar, unless using a copper bowl

2²/₃ cups dark chocolate glaze (page 53)

Preheat the oven to 350°F.

In a bowl, whisk together the flour, baking powder, salt, and 1 cup of the sugar. In another bowl, stir together the egg yolks, orange juice, and oil.

Beat the egg whites, vanilla, and cream of tartar (if using) on high speed with a stand mixer for about 2 minutes or with a handheld mixer for about 8 minutes, or until medium peaks form. Add the remaining sugar and beat for 1 to 2 minutes more, or until stiff peaks form.

Sift the dry ingredients over the egg white mixture, about one-fourth at a time, folding with a rubber spatula after each addition until all the dry ingredients are incorporated. Place about one-fourth of the egg white mixture in the bowl with

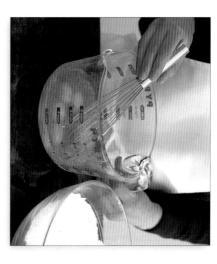

1. Sift together the dry ingredients except ½ cup of the sugar. Beat together the yolks, orange juice, and oil, just long enough to combine them and break up the egg yolks.

2. Add the vanilla and cream of tartar (if using) to the egg whites and beat to medium peaks. Add the remaining sugar and beat to stiff peaks. Sift the dry ingredients over the egg whites while folding.

3. Fold together the egg yolk mixture with the egg white mixture. Pour the batter into an ungreased tube pan with a removable bottom and bake for 45 minutes.

4. The cake is ready when it springs back to the touch.

5. As soon as the cake comes out of the oven, stick an empty wine bottle in the center hole and turn over the whole contraption. Let the cake rest, upside down, for 45 minutes.

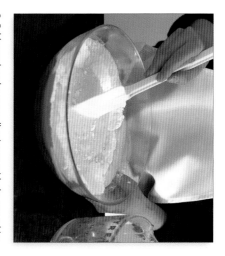

6. Give the cake, still upside down, a little shake while you hold it over a cake rack. If the cake doesn't come loose, slide a small metal spatula around the sides of the cake, between the cake and the tube pan, and try again.

7. Roll the cake on its side to detach it from the base and the tube in the center. If it won't come away from the base, slide a thin knife between the cake and the base to detach the cake.

8. Turn the cake upside down and lift off the bottom of the tube pan.

YEAST CAKES

A yeast cake is essentially a kind of light bread that is sweetened at the end with flavored simple syrup. If you like, it's worth experimenting with a homemade starter (see pages 306, 307, and 313) instead of using a straight yeast method (shown here). The starter adds depth of flavor to the cake.

Babas and Savarins

. . . .

If you like the flavor of spirits, babas and savarins are the perfect way to make the most of hard spirits such as rum (the most traditional), whiskey, Cognac, kirsch, or other fruit brandies such as eau de vie de framboise (dry raspberry brandy). Technically, yeast cakes are breads, but babas and savarins, although they are unsweetened, are so cakelike in effect that they seem to belong in this chapter. Babas and savarins are French yeast breads made with the same light dough but in different shapes. Babas are baked in dariole molds—fez-shaped molds that look a little like cocktail jiggers— while savarins are baked in doughnut-shaped molds. Babas are meant for individual servings, but savarins are traditionally baked in larger molds meant to serve 6 or 8 or so. I, however, like to make miniature savarins for individual servings.

If you are setting out to buy savarin or baba molds, try to buy nonstick or even silicone as the dough tends to stick. Once baked, both babas and savarins are soaked in simple syrup flavored with spirits.

MAKES 10 BABAS, OR 20 MINIATURE SAVARINS

Butter for the molds
1 1/3 cups flour
1/2 teaspoon salt
2 eggs
1 teaspoon active dry yeast
1 tablespoon sugar
1/2 cup warm water
1/4 cup plus 2 tablespoons butter, melted

Simple syrup
3/4 cup sugar
3/4 cup hot water
3 tablespoons or more dark rum, whiskey, Cognac, kirsch, or other fruit brandies

Whipped cream
1 cup heavy cream
1 tablespoon confectioners' sugar
1 teaspoon vanilla extract

Butter ten 4-ounce baba molds or 20 miniature savarin molds.

In a stand mixer fitted with the paddle attachment, thoroughly combine the flour and salt so the salt doesn't touch the yeast. Add the eggs, yeast, sugar, and water. Beat the dough for about 8 minutes on medium speed. At first, the dough will adhere to the sides of the bowl and form strings between the paddle and the walls of the bowl. Continue beating until the dough pulls away from the sides and clings to the paddle attachment. Use a rubber spatula to scrape the inside of the bowl so all the dough gets incorporated. Add the butter and continue beating for 3 to 5 minutes, until the butter disappears. Transfer the dough to a bowl and cover it with plastic wrap; the plastic should touch the dough's surface to prevent a crust from forming but not be tucked under the dough or it will keep it from rising. Put the dough in a slightly warm place (but no warmer than 80°F or the butter will melt and ooze out of the dough) for about 1 1/2 hours or in the refrigerator overnight, or until the dough has about doubled in size.

Press down on the dough with your fist to flatten it. If making babas, fill the molds halfway with dough; if making miniature savarins, about three-quarters up. Dip your fingers in cold water to make the dough easier to work with and to prevent it from sticking to your fingers. Cover the molds loosely with plastic wrap and let rise in a warm place for about 30 minutes, or until the dough comes almost to the top of the baba molds or slightly over the rim of the savarin molds.

Preheat the oven to 350°F.

Bake for about 30 minutes for babas and 20 minutes for savarins, or until the dough is golden brown and has risen up out of the molds. Take one of the cakes out of its mold and lift it; it should feel light. Let the rest of the cakes cool in their molds for 5 minutes before turning them out.

While the cakes are baking, make the syrup. In a bowl, combine the sugar and water and stir until the sugar is completely dissolved. Let the syrup cool to just slightly warm, or chill it over a bowl of ice water, and add the rum.

1. Combine the salt with the flour. Add the eggs, yeast, sugar, and water. Work the dough in a stand mixer with the paddle attachment until the dough pulls away from the sides of the bowl. Add the butter and work until no butter is visible.

2. Put the dough in a bowl and cover with plastic wrap. Make sure the plastic wrap touches the surface of the dough to prevent a crust from forming. Avoid wrapping the dough in such a way that it can't rise. Leave in a warm place for about 90 minutes or overnight in the refrigerator, until doubled in volume.

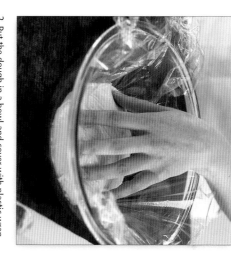

3. Brush the inside of the baba and/or savarin molds with room-temperature butter.

4. Fill the baba molds about halfway up. Fill the savarin molds with just enough dough to come three-fourths of the way up the sides. Let rise, and bake.

5. Prepare a simple syrup. Push the babas and savarins down into the flavored syrup. Gently squeeze each baba and miniature savarin while they're submerged in the syrup several times, until no more bubbles come up when you squeeze.

6. Serve plain or with whipped cream.

Pour the syrup into a bowl. Press each of the babas or savarins down into the syrup for about 1 minute, or until they are well soaked. Gently squeeze each baba or savarin several times while they're submerged in the syrup, until no more bubbles come up when you squeeze.

To make the whipped cream, whip the cream, confectioners' sugar, and vanilla extract to stiff peaks and pipe or spoon it into the middle of the savarins. If you've made babas, slice them in half vertically and pipe or spoon the whipped cream over the insides. The babas and savarins can also be served plain.

Meringue is a frothy mixture of sugar and beaten egg white. When baked, it becomes crispy and extremely light and starts to dissolve the instant it touches your tongue. There are three kinds of meringue: French, Swiss, and Italian. Familiar crunchy French meringue is piped or spooned into various shapes and slowly baked. It is sometimes piped into round disks that are then used as cake layers. Swiss meringue is almost identical to French meringue, except that it is heated while being beaten, it's sweeter, and it's harder. It's used to make decorations such as the little mushrooms on a *bûche de noël*. Italian meringue is soft and fluffy and is used as an icing or as the basis for other mixtures such as frozen fruit mousse.

Nut-flavored meringues are made by folding ground nuts such as almonds or hazelnuts and some kind of starch into raw French meringue. The best known is *dacquoise*, made by adding flour or cornstarch, ground nuts, and sometimes milk to beaten egg whites for French meringue before shaping and baking.

Using a Pastry Bag to Make Meringue Disks

Disks of crisp meringue make wonderful cake layers because their crunchiness contrasts beautifully with the delicate texture of most cakes. You can adjust the thickness of the meringue layers by using different diameter tips with your pastry bag. Keep in mind that thinner disks should be used in cakes that have lighter fillings; if the meringue is too thick and hard, the filling will ooze out when you try to cut or slice the cake.

Trace circles on a sheet of parchment paper. Put a small dollop of meringue in each corner of a sheet pan and lay the parchment paper in the pan. The meringue dollops will keep it in place. Select a plain tip with an opening about the size of the desired thickness of the meringue circles. Start piping meringue at the center of each circle and gradually work out in a spiral pattern until you have filled the circle. To end the piping, quickly pull back the tip, reversing its direction. See photos, opposite.

French Meringue Layer Cake

Meringue's fragile, brittle, and instant melt-in-the-mouth texture makes up for its lack of flavor. Meringue is never served alone but is juxtaposed with cakes, frostings, ice cream, or other mixtures to provide a bit of crunch. French meringue is made by beating sugar with egg whites until the mixture is very stiff. On a humid day, confectioners' sugar is folded into the mixture to keep it crunchy once baked. Here we make meringue disks for a cake.

Circles of crisp meringue make wonderful cake layers because their crunchiness contrasts beautifully with the delicate texture of most cakes and frostings. You can make a cake with just meringue disks and frosting such as whipped chocolate ganache, or for greater drama, alternate meringue disks with layers made from a soft cake. You can adjust the thickness of the meringue layers by using different diameter tips with the pastry bag when you pipe out the rounds. Keep in mind that thinner rounds should be used in cakes that have lighter fillings; if the meringue is too thick and hard, the filling will ooze out when you try to cut or slice the cake.

Meringue is ideally baked very slowly so that it dries out rather than actually cooks. If the oven is too hot or the meringue left in too long, it will turn ivory or even brown and the bright snowy white effect will be lost. A convection oven is great for making meringue because the moving air accelerates the drying.

MAKES 2 ROUND CAKE DISKS (9½ BY ¼ INCH), OR 12 ROUND CAKE DISKS (3½ BY ¼ INCH)

5 egg whites
Small pinch of cream of tartar, unless using a copper bowl
³/₄ cup granulated sugar
1 cup and 2 tablespoons confectioners' sugar, if it is very humid

In a stand mixer fitted with the whisk attachment, beat the egg whites and cream of tartar (if using) on medium-high speed for about 2 minutes, or until soft peaks form. Add the granulated sugar, and beat for 4 minutes longer, or until stiff peaks form. For meringue that is impervious to humidity, fold in the confectioners' sugar.

Preheat the oven to 300°F. Draw circles on a sheet of parchment paper, put a dollop of meringue in each corner of a sheet pan to hold the paper in place, and place the paper over on the sheet pan.

Select a tip about the same size as the desired thickness of the rounds and fill the pastry bag with the meringue. Starting

MAKING A FRENCH MERINGUE LAYER CAKE

at the center of each circle, pipe the meringue, gradually working out in a spiral pattern, until you have filled the circle. To end the piping, quickly pull back the tip, reversing its direction.

Put the meringue in the oven and turn down the oven to 225°F. If you have a convection oven, turn it down to 200°F and put on the convection. Bake for 2 to 4 hours, depending on the humidity, until hard and no longer sticky to the touch.

Note: If you need the meringue to hold its shape for more than a couple of days (for decorations, for example), fold in the confectioners' sugar as you would on a very humid day.

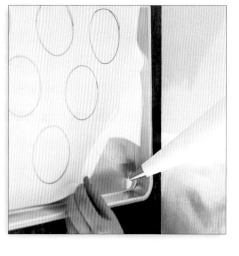

2. Draw rounds on a sheet of parchment paper, turn the paper over, and put a dollop of meringue in each corner to hold the paper in place.

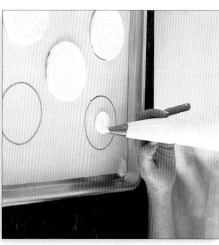

3. Select a tip about the same size as the desired thickness of the rounds. Start from the center of each circle and gradually work out in a spiral pattern. To end the piping, quickly pull back the tip, reversing its direction. Bake.

1. Beat the egg whites and cream of tartar (if using) to soft peaks. Add the granulated sugar and beat to stiff peaks—the whites should stick straight out from the end of the whisk.

Hazelnut Meringue (Dacquoise)

While rounds of French meringue make wonderful layers in cakes such as the meringue cakes on page 38, meringue is brittle and doesn't have a lot of flavor. For a meringue with an intriguing nutty flavor, fold a mixture of sugar, ground hazelnuts or almonds, and a small amount of flour with uncooked French meringue. Pipe this mixture into disks on a parchment paper–lined sheet pan—buttered tart rings hold the mixture in place, but you can also pipe it directly onto the parchment paper. Bake slowly like meringue.

MAKES ENOUGH FOR 3 ROUND MERINGUE DISKS (9 BY ¼ INCH)

1½ cups hazelnuts or blanched almonds

1¼ cups sugar

3 tablespoons cake flour

Butter for the tart rings

8 egg whites

Pinch of cream of tartar, unless using a copper bowl

Preheat the oven to 350°F. Place the nuts on a baking sheet and toast them for about 15 minutes, or until you can smell their aroma. Remove and set aside to cool. Turn down the oven to 275°F.

In a food processor, grind the nuts with ½ cup of the sugar and the flour for about 1 minute, or until the nuts turn into a fine powder. Take care not to process them until they become oily.

Butter three 9-inch tart rings and set them on parchment paper–lined sheet pans. If you don't have 9-inch tart rings, draw circles on the parchment paper and turn it over on the sheet pan.

In a stand mixer fitted with the whisk attachment, beat the egg whites and cream of tartar (if using) on high speed for about 4 minutes, or until stiff peaks form. Then beat in the remaining sugar. Continue beating for about 1 minute more, or until the egg whites are stiff and shiny. Transfer the egg white mixture to a large bowl and fold in the nut mixture with a rubber spatula.

Fit a pastry bag with a ⅓-inch plain tip and fill it with the meringue. Starting at the center of each tart ring or circle, pipe the meringue, gradually working out in a spiral pattern, until you have filled the ring or circle. To end the piping, quickly pull back the tip, reversing its direction. Smooth the tops of the disks with an offset spatula.

Bake for about 90 minutes, or until the disks are hard, crisp, and pale brown and the center is firm to the touch. If at any point the *dacquoise* starts to look too brown, turn down the oven to 200°F. Let cool.

If you've used tart rings, slide a knife around the inside of the rings and pull the rings off. Peel away the parchment paper.

Use *dacquoise* disks in cakes as you would rounds of other cakes, which works best if you construct your cake in a ring or springform pan.

MAKING A HAZELNUT MERINGUE (DACQUOISE)

1. Beat the egg whites and cream of tartar (if using) to stiff peaks, add the rest of the sugar, and beat for 1 minute more until shiny. Fold with the ground hazelnut mixture.

2. Pipe the mixture into buttered tart rings set on parchment paper–lined sheet pans; if you are piping free form, draw circles on a sheet of parchment paper and turn it over on a sheet pan. (See page 64 for how to fill and use a pastry bag.)

3. Smooth the tops of the disks with an offset spatula.

4. Bake until hard and crisp and pale brown.

Chocolate Meringue Logs

In addition to being flavored with nuts, meringue can also be flavored with cocoa and used in the same way—as plain flavored with cocoa and used in the same way—as plain a cake—as plain meringue. Here, chocolate meringue is piped into logs for decorating the sides of a cake. It can be baked at a slightly higher temperature than plain meringue since discoloration isn't an issue.

MAKES ENOUGH FOR THE SIDES OF 1 LAYER CAKE (9 INCHES ROUND)

1/2 cup unsweetened cocoa powder

1/2 cup confectioners' sugar

6 egg whites

Pinch of cream of tartar, unless using a copper bowl

1/2 cup granulated sugar

Preheat the oven to 300°F. Line a 13 by 17-inch sheet pan with parchment paper.

In a bowl, whisk together the cocoa powder and confectioners' sugar.

In a stand mixer fitted with the whisk attachment, beat the egg whites and cream of tartar (if using) on medium-high speed for about 2 minutes, or until medium peaks form. Add the granulated sugar and beat for about 1 minute more, or until the egg whites are stiff and shiny. Transfer the egg white mixture to a large bowl. Sift the confectioners' sugar mixture over the egg whites, while folding with a rubber spatula.

Fit a pastry bag with a 1/3-inch tip and fill it with the chocolate meringue. Lift the parchment paper from the sheet pan, pipe a tiny dollop of meringue into each corner of the sheet pan to hold the parchment paper down, then replace the parchment paper. Pipe the meringue in strips that run from one side of the sheet pan to the other, so that you end up with 12-inch logs.

Bake for about 1 hour, or until dry to the touch and when you lift up a piece it feels light.

MAKING CHOCOLATE MERINGUE LOGS

1. Fold the cocoa-sugar mixture into the beaten egg white mixture.

2. Pipe a tiny dollop of the meringue in each corner of a sheet pan to hold the parchment paper in place during baking.

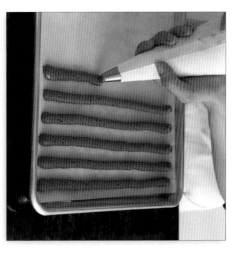

3. Pipe the meringue out in long strips. Bake until crisp.

CUSTARD CAKES

Cheesecake, with its eggy filling, is the quintessential custard cake. All cheesecakes are custards held together with eggs, egg whites, or egg yolks. The differences in the texture and flavor of the filling are dictated by the use of cream cheese (dense and creamy) or ricotta or other fresh cheese (relatively light). The consistency is also affected by whether you use egg yolks, egg whites, or whole eggs. Egg yolks provide a creamy melting texture, while egg whites make a cheesecake more custardlike.

Cheesecake

Very little can go seriously wrong with a cheesecake, and even when struck with that most common of woes—cracking—a cheesecake is still perfectly edible. The secret to preventing cracking is to make sure the cream cheese, eggs, and sour cream are at room temperature and to bake the cheesecake in a water bath so that it cooks evenly and never gets too hot. If, despite all your efforts, your cheesecake cracks, spread a thin layer of sour cream over the top before serving.

Cheesecakes are easily flavored by adding cocoa, strong coffee, spices, vanilla, or fruit purees. You can also serve cheesecake with a sauce. Pureed and strained frozen raspberries are especially good because their tart acidity sets off the sweetness of the cheesecake.

Many cheesecake recipes call for a graham cracker crust, but this isn't always worth the bother because the cheesecake filling releases a small amount of liquid as it bakes, making the bottom crust soggy. One solution is to coat only the sides of the cheesecake with graham cracker crumbs after it has baked. This step, too, is optional.

MAKES 1 CHEESECAKE (8 TO 10 INCHES ROUND)

Butter for the pan

Two 8-ounce packages cream cheese, at room temperature

³/4 cup sugar

3 eggs, at room temperature

1 egg yolk, at room temperature

1¹/2 cups sour cream, at room temperature

1¹/2 teaspoons vanilla extract

1 teaspoon lemon juice

¹/4 teaspoon salt

10 graham crackers (optional)

Preheat the oven to 350°F. Brush an 8- to 10-inch springform pan with butter.

In a stand mixer with the paddle attachment, beat the cream cheese with the sugar on medium speed for about 5 minutes, or until smooth. On low to medium speed, add the eggs and egg yolk, one by one. Don't add another egg until the one before it is completely incorporated. Mix in the sour cream, vanilla, lemon juice, and salt, mixing for about 30 seconds, or just long enough to combine the ingredients.

Pour the batter into the prepared springform pan, wrap the pan in aluminum foil, and place it in a baking pan or roasting pan at least as deep as the springform pan. Fill the baking pan with the hottest water from the tap until the water comes halfway up the sides of the springform pan. Place in the oven and bake for about 90 minutes, or until only a 1-inch-diameter bull's-eye in the center of the cake moves when you jiggle the pan.

Put the graham crackers in a resealable plastic bag and crush them with your fingers or a rolling pin. If you want them very fine, work them through a strainer after crushing. Or, puree the graham crackers in a food processor.

Remove the cake from the springform pan, but leave it on the base. Hold it up with one hand while using the other to pat the sides with the graham cracker crumbs. Allow to cool. If cracks appear, they can be disguised by covering the top of the cheesecake with a layer of sour cream.

VARIATIONS

The cheesecake may be flavored with spices, 2 tablespoons (or more to taste) cocoa, 1 tablespoon strong coffee, 1 tablespoon vanilla, or ¹/2 cup fruit puree. If you are adding more than ¹/3 cup liquid flavoring to the cheesecake, you should adjust the amount of egg, egg white, or egg yolk in the recipe. Add 1 whole egg per ³/4 cup extra liquid, 1 egg white per ¹/3 cup extra liquid, or 1 egg yolk per ¹/2 cup extra liquid.

1. Pour the cheesecake batter into the prepared pan.

2. Wrap aluminum foil around the springform pan to prevent the water from seeping in or the batter from seeping out.

3. Put the pan in a container with high sides such as a roasting pan and pour in enough hot tap water to come halfway up the sides.

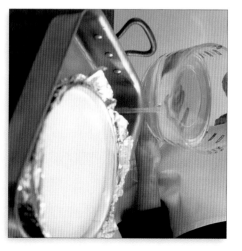

4. Bake for about 90 minutes, or until the center of the cake moves just a little when jiggled.

5. Take the cake out of the springform pan but leave it on the base. Hold it up with one hand while using the other to pat the sides with graham cracker crumbs.

FROSTINGS, FILLINGS, AND GLAZES

Once you've baked your cake, you can cover it or layer it with various frostings, fillings, and glazes. A glaze is usually a thin coating applied hot to the outside of a cake, while a frosting is thicker and richer and is spread in between the layers and sometimes also on the outside. The most commonly used frostings and fillings are buttercream, mousseline (pastry cream with butter beaten in), and whipped chocolate ganache. Other fillings aren't really frostings but are preparations such as chocolate mousse, Bavarian creams, fruits, jam, or whipped cream that are used to cover and layer cakes. Most of us are in the habit of using only one filling for our cakes, but a cake can be made more dramatic by using two or more.

Storing Frostings, Fillings, and Glazes

Buttercream, crème mousseline, and chocolate mousses can be frozen for up to several months if tightly covered. Fillings that have been aerated with whipped cream (such as creamy chocolate frosting or *crème d'or*, whipped ganache, or Bavarian creams), however, don't freeze well and loose their airiness when they thaw. If you want to make a Bavarian cream in advance, it's best to freeze the crème anglaise and then thaw it and fold it with whipped cream just before you use it.

Buttercream

Few of us can resist the temptation of a cake covered with a rich buttercream frosting. When well made, buttercream still has the flavor of butter—never make it with shortening—in addition to whatever it's been flavored with. Essentially sweetened and flavored butter, buttercream is made in various ways. By far the simplest, and the version favored by most home cooks, is made by beating butter with confectioners' sugar and flavoring. The only drawback to homestyle buttercream is the very subtle gritty texture imparted by the cornstarch contained in confectioners' sugar, but this is subtle enough that most people don't notice it.

The most popular professional version is made by beating hot sugar syrup into egg yolks, a process that cooks the yolks without curdling them. Butter is then beaten into the sweetened egg yolks. A lighter version is made in much the same way except that egg whites are used instead of yolks. The hot sugar syrup turns the whites into an Italian meringue. After the meringue is cooled, butter is beaten in.

Whichever buttercream you make, beat it thoroughly before you use it. It should have the consistency of sour cream and should have no little holes in it when you examine a little of it on the side of a spatula. The holes come out with continued beating and leave the buttercream, and the finished cake, glossy and smooth. Keep in mind also that because buttercream hardens when chilled, cakes made with buttercream should be allowed to warm to near room temperature before they are served or the frosting will be hard.

Buttercream flavorings seem to be limitless—see page 48 for a few ideas.

Professional-Style Buttercream

....

To make professional-style buttercream, based on egg yolks, whisk hot sugar syrup, cooked to the softball stage, into the beaten egg yolks. Continue beating this mixture—called a "bombe" mixture—until cool and then beat in the cold butter.

A stand mixer works best for egg yolk–based buttercream because the egg yolks require a lot of beating to get them to quadruple in volume and to stabilize them before adding the syrup. A handheld mixer will also work, but you'll need to at least double the beating time.

Here the eggs are warmed slightly, so when the soft-ball stage sugar syrup is added, the yolks don't cool it and cause it to harden into little pellets.

MAKES 5¹/₂ CUPS, ENOUGH FOR A 3- OR 4-LAYER 9-INCH CAKE

2 cups sugar

²/₃ cup water plus more as needed

8 egg yolks, slightly warmed (see Note)

1¹/₂ cups (1¹/₄ pounds) cold butter, cut into cubes

Flavoring (see page 48)

Put the sugar and water in a heavy-bottomed saucepan and bring to a simmer over medium heat.

While the syrup is cooking, in a stand mixer fitted with the whisk attachment, beat the yolks on high speed for about 8 minutes, or until they have quadrupled in volume and are very pale.

While the egg yolks are beating, check the syrup with a thermometer or with a spoon (see page 47). If the syrup is ready before the egg yolks, add 1 tablespoon of water to the syrup and keep simmering.

When the syrup and yolks are ready, turn the mixer to high speed and pour the syrup into the yolks between the whisk and the sides of the bowl. It is important to keep the syrup from touching the whisk or the bowl because it will harden into little globules, which will break off into the buttercream. (Don't worry, a few are unavoidable.) Continue beating the egg yolk–sugar mixture until it is just slightly warmer than room temperature (hold your hand on the bottom of the mixer bowl; ideally, it should feel neither hot nor cold).

Turn down the mixer speed to medium and add the butter cubes, a small handful at a time. Wait until each batch is absorbed before adding more. Beat for about 10 minutes, or until smooth and fluffy. Beat in the flavoring until fully incorporated. Spread the buttercream on a cake (see page 70).

Note: To heat the egg yolks slightly, put the eggs in a bowl of hot water for 5 to 10 minutes before you crack and separate them.

1. Beat the egg yolks on high speed in a stand mixer until pale and quadrupled in volume. With the mixer still on high speed, pour the soft-ball stage sugar syrup into the bowl, between the sides of the bowl and the moving whisk. Beat until the mixture is just slightly warmer than room temperature.

2. Turn down the mixer speed to medium and add the cold butter, cut into cubes, a small handful at a time. Wait until each batch of butter is absorbed before adding more.

3. The finished buttercream is smooth and fluffy.

Quick and Easy Orange Buttercream

Professional-style buttercreams, made with a bombe (hot sugar syrup beaten into egg yolks, see page 45) or Italian meringue (hot sugar syrup beaten into egg whites, see page 60), have the advantage of being satiny smooth. But because both of these require using soft ball–stage sugar, a step many of us don't want to fuss with, homemade-style buttercream, made simply by beating butter with confectioners' sugar, offers a tempting alternative. Homemade-style buttercream sometimes leaves a very subtle roughness in the mouth that is not noticeable to most people. To eliminate most of this texture, beat the buttercream thoroughly—at least five minutes in a stand mixer—until it has the consistency of sour cream. It gets firmer once it is on the cake and chills somewhat. An orange flavoring is great for buttercream that you want to use to frost delicate white and yellow butter cakes and sponge cakes.

MAKES 5½ CUPS, ENOUGH FOR A 3- OR 4-LAYER 9-INCH CAKE OR 2 SHEET CAKES

> **1½ pounds butter, sliced, at room temperature**
>
> **2½ cups confectioners' sugar**
>
> **2 tablespoons grated orange zest (see page 194), or 2 teaspoons or more orange oil**

Using a stand mixer fitted with the paddle attachment or a handheld mixer on high speed or a wooden spoon (see Note), beat the butter for 5 to 10 minutes, until smooth and easy to work. Add the sugar and zest and beat until smooth, starting on low so the sugar doesn't fly around and then turning the mixer to high. Switch to the whisk attachment or hand whisk and beat for about 5 minutes, or until the butter has the consistency of sour cream.

Note: If using a handheld mixer or a wooden spoon, make sure the butter is at or almost at room temperature (65°F to 67°F) so it is easier to work.

Italian Meringue Buttercream

Egg white–based buttercream, made by beating butter into Italian meringue, is made in almost the exact same way as egg yolk–based buttercream, except that soft ball–stage sugar syrup is poured into beaten egg whites instead of beaten egg yolks. Most professional chefs prefer buttercream made with egg yolks—probably because of its rich unctuousness—but when a perfectly white buttercream is called for, as on a wedding cake, the pale yellow egg yolk–based buttercream won't work. You can make the buttercream in the same bowl in which you made the meringue. The finished buttercream has a silky smooth texture and a delicate buttery flavor.

MAKES 5½ CUPS, ENOUGH FOR A 3- OR 4-LAYER 9-INCH CAKE

> **4 cups Italian meringue (page 60)**
>
> **1½ cups butter, cubed or sliced**

After you make the Italian meringue, simply add the butter, a handful at a time, to the meringue and beat on medium to high speed with either a stand mixer or a handheld mixer until the butter disappears. Wait until each batch of butter is worked in before adding more. To flavor the buttercream, see page 48.

Judging How Much Buttercream Is Enough

If you're making a round layer cake, count on 1 cup of buttercream per layer (including the top) for a ⅓-inch-thick layer of frosting and about 1½ cups frosting for the sides. So, a four-layer cake requires a total of 5½ cups of frosting—1 cup for each layer and 1½ cups for the sides. A single layer 13 by 17-inch sheet cake will require about 2 cups.

Cooking Sugar Syrup to the Soft Ball Stage

When sugar and water are boiled together, the sugar becomes more concentrated. To make 1 cup of syrup and bring it to the soft ball stage, combine 1 cup of sugar, 2 tablespoons of corn syrup, and 1/2 cup of water in a heavy-bottomed saucepan. Stir the mixture to dissolve the sugar. Bring the syrup to a simmer and brush down the sides, using a brush dipped in cold water, to prevent crystals from forming. As the bubbles in the simmering syrup get larger, start testing for the soft ball stage. To so this, use a spoon to put a small amount of the hot syrup into some ice water, then pinch the syrup between your thumb and forefinger.

You will notice the syrup going through stages. Early in the process, the sugar will dissolve in the water, so continue boiling. Next, it will form a thread between your two fingers, so wait and test again. Eventually, it will become thick enough to roll into a soft ball with the consistency of chewed gum. If the sugar hardens completely when you stick it in the water, you've cooked the syrup too much—it has reached hard crack stage. In that case, add a few tablespoons of water to the hot syrup and start testing again. You also can use a thermometer to know when the syrup has reached the softball stage; it should measure 238°F.

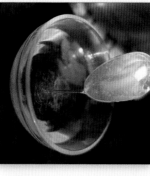

1. Test for the soft ball stage by dripping a little syrup in ice water.

2. The soft ball stage.

3. The hard crack stage.

4. Testing syrup with a thermometer; soft ball stage is 238°F.

Flavoring Buttercream

You can flavor buttercream with virtually anything: ground spices such as cinnamon or ginger, coffee, chocolate, spirits such as kirsch or Cognac, or vanilla or almond extract. Most of these flavorings should be added to taste, a very little bit at a time. Liquid ingredients must be used very sparingly because if you add too much, you'll make the buttercream too runny—avoid adding more than 1 tablespoon liquid per 1 cup of buttercream. If you want more flavor from a liquid ingredient such as brandy, add it to a simple syrup and brush it onto the cake layers instead of adding it all to the buttercream. All the flavorings listed below should be added to finished buttercream; beat the flavoring in until it's thoroughly incorporated and the buttercream is light and fluffy. This usually takes about one minute in a stand mixer equipped with the whisk attachment on high speed.

Chocolate Buttercream: Add 2 ounces melted bittersweet chocolate or 1 ounce melted bitter unsweetened chocolate per 1 cup of buttercream. Chocolate makes buttercream firmer, because it hardens when cool; bittersweet and unsweetened chocolate also make buttercream less sweet.

Vanilla Buttercream: Add 1/2 teaspoon vanilla extract per 1 cup of buttercream.

Hazelnut, Pistachio, or Almond Buttercream: Use 1/4 cup nut paste per 1 cup of buttercream. If oil is floating on the top of the container of nut paste, mix it in the can until smooth like peanut butter. If the paste is very stiff and hard to work, transfer it to a bowl and mix it with a heavy-duty wooden spoon or with the paddle attachment of a stand mixer until smooth. Use the paddle attachment of a stand mixer on medium speed to combine the nut paste with the buttercream for about 4 minutes, or until the mixture lightens, then switch to the whisk attachment and beat on high speed for about another 5 minutes, or until the buttercream is airy and smooth.

Chestnut Buttercream: Add 3 tablespoons chestnut puree per 1 cup of buttercream, or more to taste.

Citrus Buttercream: Add 1 teaspoon grated zest or 1/2 teaspoon citrus oil or 2 teaspoons citrus extract per 1 cup of buttercream, or more to taste.

Coffee Buttercream: For good coffee flavor, add 2 to 4 teaspoons of a strong brew such as espresso or make extrastrong instant coffee (ideally labeled "dark," "French," or "Italian" roast). Or combine 1 to 2 teaspoons instant coffee with 2 to 4 teaspoons water, and beat this mixture into 1 cup of buttercream.

Buttercream Flavored with Spices: Add 1/2 teaspoon ground cinnamon or 1/4 teaspoon ground cloves per 1 cup of buttercream, or to taste.

Buttercream Flavored with Spirits: Add 1 teaspoon spirits per 1 cup of buttercream, or more to taste. This proportion applies to all spirits: fruit brandies; rum; bourbon or Irish whiskey; grappa or marc; Cognac or Armagnac. Spirits must be full flavored or you'll need to use too much. Use dry, clear unsweetened fruit brandies such as kirsch (cherry flavor), *framboise* (raspberry flavor), *mirabelle* (plum flavor), or *poire William* (pear flavor). Buy Swiss or French—not American—kirsch or *framboise* or other *eaux de vie;* dark rum from Martinique, Jamaica, or Haiti; and authentic Cognac, not just brandy. Don't hesitate to buy the least expensive bottle of Cognac because the word "Cognac" guarantees a full flavor.

Reconstituting Congealed or Separated Buttercream

Because buttercream is an emulsion like cream or mayonnaise, it sometimes separates while you are beating it. This is especially true if you are beating cold buttercream you've saved in the refrigerator or freezer.

If buttercream separates and starts to look grainy after you've added all the butter and flavoring, beat a little longer—5 minutes or so—to see if it comes together on its own. If it still won't smooth out, put the bowl over a very low flame (provided the bowl is metal) or over a saucepan of simmering water for about 20 seconds and beat again

for 5 minutes. You may have to do this once or twice to get it to work.

Here, congealed buttercream left over from another cake is worked over the gentle heat of barely simmering water in a saucepan until a small amount of melted buttercream forms in the bottom of the bowl. It is then beaten with the paddle attachment to soften it and then with the whisk attachment until it's light, fluffy, and perfectly smooth, with no holes.

RECONSTITUTING CONGEALED OR SEPARATED BUTTERCREAM

1. Put the chopped pieces of buttercream in the metal bowl of a stand mixer and place the bowl over a low flame or simmering water for about 20 seconds, or until you see a little melted buttercream collect in the bottom of the bowl.

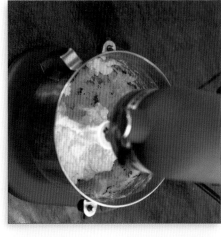

2. Work the buttercream with the paddle attachment until it is smooth. Switch to the whisk attachment and beat for 5 minutes more.

3. Check the consistency of the buttercream by spreading a small amount on a spatula. The buttercream should be perfectly smooth, with no little holes.

Chocolate and Cream or
Butter Frostings and Glazes

Glazes are usually shiny, relatively dense, and very rich coatings for the outsides of cakes. They are applied in thinner layers than frosting. Frostings and other fillings, while often very rich, are lighter than glazes and are applied in thicker layers on the inside of cakes and sometimes on the outside as well. While melted chocolate can be used alone as a cake glaze, most chocolate glazes contain cream and/or butter to soften the glaze once it sets.

Ganache, the most popular glaze, is made by combining melted bittersweet chocolate and heavy cream and stirring the mixture until smooth. The hot ganache can be poured over cakes and left to set, or it can be used as a hot sauce for ice cream or profiteroles. You can change the texture and flavor of ganache by adding more or less chocolate to the cream or by whisking in butter, which will make the glaze stiffer when it sets. Ganache is easy to flavor with a small amount of strong coffee, liqueurs, or spirits such as whiskey, brandy, or grappa.

Crème d'or is made by folding melted chocolate into whipped cream.

Chocolate butter glaze is simple to make: Just melt together equal parts butter and chocolate with a little corn syrup. The corn syrup helps the glaze keep its sheen after it has been applied to a cake.

Dark Chocolate Ganache

When it's hot, ganache has the consistency of rich chocolate sauce; when cold, it sets into a firm glaze. For this reason, ganache can be used both as a sauce and as a glaze for cakes. Recipes vary—the ratio of cream to chocolate differs—and some include butter so the ganache sets up more firmly when cold. To imagine the taste and texture of ganache made with butter, think of a hot fudge sundae in which the chocolate has hardened on the cold ice cream. A classic ganache, made with equal parts cream and chocolate, will still harden, but not as dramatically as it does when made with butter. When ganache is whipped, it becomes fluffy and pale and makes a perfect frosting. One approach for icing a cake is to use whipped ganache between the layers and unwhipped ganache for the top and sides. Here is the classic recipe, calling for equal parts heavy cream and bittersweet chocolate. For a white chocolate version, see the variation opposite.

MAKES 1¾ CUPS, OR 2 CUPS WHEN WHIPPED, ENOUGH FOR 2 LAYERS

8 ounces bittersweet chocolate, chopped

1 cup heavy cream

Place the chocolate in a heatproof bowl.

Bring the cream to a simmer and pour it over the chocolate. Let the mixture sit for about 10 minutes, or long enough to melt the chocolate. Stir the ganache with a rubber spatula for 1 minute and then switch to a whisk and stir until smooth and the consistency of sour cream. If you are using the ganache to ice a cake, let it cool for 4 or 5 minutes before you use it (or set it over an ice water bath to cool quickly), so it thickens and adheres better to the cake. If you are using it as a sauce, use it right away.

For a lighter frosting, beat or whip the ganache until it is light and fluffy.

VARIATIONS

If you want a lighter frosting, use a stand mixer or a handheld mixer to whip the ganache until it is light and fluffy. To judge this, notice that early during the beating, the ganache has the consistency of cream cheese. When it is ready after anywhere from 2 to 10 minutes in a stand mixer—the time depends on the chocolate and the exact temperature—it should have the consistency of sour cream.

White chocolate ganache is made in the same way as dark chocolate ganache except that white chocolate is used instead of bittersweet dark chocolate. Make sure the ganache is cool before whipping it or it will break and never get fluffy. Put a bowl of just-made ganache in a bowl of ice water, to cool, if necessary. Whip only until it's fluffy—if you overbeat it, the cream will turn to butter. The amount of time it takes to whip white chocolate ganache depends on the brand of chocolate and the temperature of the ingredients, and can range from 30 seconds to 4 minutes.

MAKING GANACHE

Pour simmering cream over the chocolate.

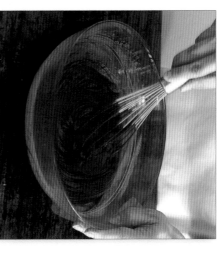

Stir until smooth and cover with plastic wrap or use right away.

MAKING WHIPPED GANACHE

To whip ganache (white chocolate ganache is shown here), put the bowl of just-made ganache in a bowl of ice water to cool it.

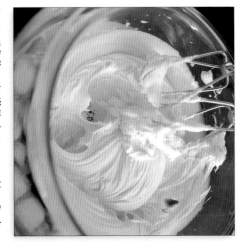

Beat until fluffy and stiff, like beaten egg whites. Don't overbeat, or you'll get white chocolate butter.

CAKES   51

1. Melt the chocolate and beat the cream and vanilla to soft peaks. Pour the melted chocolate down the side of the bowl into the whipped cream.

2. Fold together until you don't see any cream.

Creamy Chocolate Frosting (Crème d'Or)

Except for a little vanilla, this frosting contains the same ingredients (chocolate and cream) in the same proportions as ganache, but it is prepared differently—the chocolate is melted by itself and then folded with whipped cream. Because crème d'or is made with whipped cream, it should be folded just long enough to incorporate the chocolate or the cream will turn to butter. Crème d'or is lighter and more like whipped cream than whipped ganache.

MAKES 2 CUPS, ENOUGH FOR 2 LAYERS

8 ounces bittersweet chocolate, coarsely chopped

1 cup heavy cream

1 teaspoon vanilla extract

Melt the chocolate in a bowl set over a saucepan of simmering water. Take care not to let any moisture touch the chocolate, or it will seize. When most of the chocolate has melted, remove from the heat and stir until perfectly smooth. If the chocolate doesn't completely melt, put the bowl back over the simmering water for 1 to 2 minutes while scraping the sides of the bowl with a rubber spatula.

Put the cream and vanilla in a bowl large enough to hold the finished frosting or the bowl of a stand mixer and place it in the freezer for 5 minutes. Then, beat the cream to soft peaks (the cream droops off the end of the whisk).

If you are making the frosting by hand, pour the melted chocolate down the side of the bowl containing the whipped cream and use a rubber spatula to fold the mixture together until completely homogeneous. If you are making it in a stand mixer, turn the mixer speed to low when the cream reaches soft peaks and pour the chocolate over the whipped cream while beating. Keep the frosting refrigerated until you are ready to use it. If it gets too warm, it can melt and lose its airiness.

Coating a Cake with Hot Icing

Before coating a cake with hot icing, the cake should be sealed in one of two ways: First by coating the cake with half of the icing, refrigerating the cake until the icing hardens, and then covering with a second coat; or, by "crumb" coating the cake with a thin layer of frosting such as buttercream (use the same frosting that is in the cake), chilling the cake until the coating hardens, and then pouring over the hot glaze. Place the cake on a cake rack set on a sheet pan so you can reuse the glaze that runs off the cake. Allow the glaze to harden before serving.

Dark Chocolate Glaze

Some bakers prefer this rich glaze, made by melting together chocolate and butter, to ganache and crème d'or, because it is very firm when it sets and it keeps its sheen. Usually this glaze contains a little corn syrup to stabilize it and keep it from taking on a matte appearance when cold. You can also make a hybrid glaze by including butter in a standard ganache—the butter makes it richer and firmer when cold. If you're using this glaze after it is no longer pourable, put the bowl over a low flame (if the bowl is metal) or over a saucepan of simmering water while working the glaze with a whisk until it has a consistency you can pour.

MAKES 1¹/₃ CUPS, ENOUGH TO COVER THE TOP
AND SIDES OF A 9-INCH ROUND CAKE

8 ounces bittersweet chocolate, chopped
1 tablespoon corn syrup
¹/₂ cup butter, cubed or sliced

Melt the chocolate with the corn syrup and butter in a heatproof bowl set over a saucepan of simmering water. Stir with a rubber spatula until smooth.

White Chocolate Glaze

This glaze is very firm and rich once set because it is pure white chocolate, except for a small amount of cream. Use this glaze on the top and sides of a cake to create a thin hard coating. This recipe makes just enough to cover the top of a 9-inch round cake, so double the amount to glaze the sides as well. If you want to use a white chocolate filling between layers, use whipped white chocolate ganache (page 51) or white chocolate mousse (page 367).

MAKES 1 CUP, ENOUGH TO COVER THE TOP
OF A 9-INCH ROUND CAKE

8 ounces white chocolate, chopped
¹/₄ cup heavy cream

Combine the chocolate and cream in a heatproof bowl set over a bowl of simmering water. Stir with a rubber spatula just long enough to melt the chocolate, then remove from the heat. Stir until the mixture is smooth. Use right away.

Crème Anglaise and Bavarian Creams

Chocolate mousse is stiff because chocolate hardens when it's cold. Fruit mousses, on the other hand, have to be made stiff, usually with gelatin. Fruit mousses can be served alone, but they are especially well suited for layering in cakes.

Professional pastry chefs use a variety of methods to make fruit mousses and may base their mousses on combinations of bombe mixture (page 60), pastry cream (page 54) combined with gelatin and the appropriate fruit puree. Curds, such as citrus curds (page 364) or passion fruit curd (page 364), also make marvelous mousses when folded with whipped cream and dissolved gelatin. While mousses made using each of these methods have subtle differences in texture, the best and easiest to make are Bavarian creams.

Bavarian creams are among the most delicious fruit mousses because they're light and airy, yet rich and creamy. A Bavarian cream is made by folding whipped cream into a flavored crème anglaise (crème anglaise is a kind of liquid custard) containing gelatin. The secret to a successful Bavarian cream is using whipped cream beaten to soft peaks and the correct amount of gelatin. Overbeaten or underbeaten whipped cream will make a Bavarian cream dry or heavy. Too much gelatin makes a Bavarian cream rubbery; too little, and the Bavarian cream never sets. Provided you serve the Bavarian cream cold, a teaspoon of powdered gelatin per 1 cup of liquid (including the cream before beating) is usually right. Virtually any fruit can be pureed, strained, and substituted for the strawberries used here, but beware of tropical fruits such as mangos, papayas, and pineapples, which contain enzymes that break down gelatin. A puree of tropical fruit must be brought to a boil to break down its enzymes before you can use it with gelatin.

To make a classic Bavarian cream, you must first make a custard sauce, a crème anglaise.

Vanilla Custard Sauce (Crème Anglaise)

To make most Bavarian creams, you first need to make a liquid custard called a "crème anglaise." Custards are made by slowly cooking liquid or semiliquid mixtures that have been combined with eggs, egg whites, or egg yolks until the mixture sets. Crème anglaise has the same ingredients as crème brûlée (an example of a sweet custard) except that milk is used instead of cream. But crème anglaise is cooked in a saucepan while stirring so it thickens but doesn't set completely.

Because crème anglaise is thickened with egg yolks alone, with no starch to stabilize them as there is in pastry cream, don't overheat it or it will curdle. Until you gain confidence, cook the crème anglaise over low to medium heat in a nonaluminum (aluminum turns it gray) heavy-bottomed saucepan, but don't bother with a double boiler which is hard to control. While stirring, reach into the corners of the saucepan with the wooden spoon or spatula so the egg yolks don't hide there and curdle. Knowing when the crème anglaise is done is the only tricky part. The classic method is to dip a wooden spoon into it and then make a line on the spoon with your finger. If, when you hold the spatula sideways, the line stays there, the crème anglaise is ready. However, there is always the danger of the crème anglaise curdling while you're staring at the spoon and the line on the spoon is sometimes hard to see. Many cooks find it easier simply to look at the surface of the custard sauce while stirring it over the heat. At the start, the sauce generates lots of tiny ripples; when it is ready, these ripples turn into larger waves. When you're first learning, you might want to use a thermometer (the crème anglaise is ready at 180°F), but this too can be fraught with peril because the difference of a few degrees can be critical.

Classic recipes may contain as few as 8 egg yolks or as many as 20 per quart of milk.

MAKES 1 QUART

1 vanilla bean, or 2 teaspoons vanilla extract

3 cups milk

8 egg yolks

3/4 cup sugar

If using a vanilla bean, split it in half lengthwise. Place the milk and vanilla bean (if using) in a small nonreactive saucepan over low to medium heat, and bring to a simmer.

While the milk is heating, stir together the egg yolks, vanilla extract if using, and sugar until the mixture is pale, about 4 minutes. Ladle about half of the hot milk into the yolk mixture while stirring constantly. Pour the mixture back into the saucepan with the rest of the milk, stirring until well combined.

Put the saucepan back over low to medium heat and stir with a wooden spoon. Reach into the corners as you stir or the mixture may curdle there. When the tiny ripples turn to larger smooth waves or a line stays on the back of the spoon (see sidebar below), take the mixture off the heat and continue stirring for 2 minutes, so the heat retained in the saucepan doesn't overcook the custard.

If you've used the vanilla bean, remove it from the custard and scrape the tiny seeds out of both halves into the crème anglaise.

Cover the crème anglaise, let it cool for an hour, and then refrigerate; or set the saucepan in a bowl of ice water and stir until cold. Strain the crème anglaise with a medium- or coarse-mesh strainer. (A fine-mesh strainer will strain out the vanilla seeds.) Cover with plastic wrap touching its surface to prevent a film from forming on top.

Judging When a Crème Anglaise Is Done

Because crème anglaise contains no starch to stabilize the egg yolks, it will curdle if allowed to boil. On the other hand, if it's not heated to a high enough temperature (180°F), it won't thicken and take on the right silky consistency. The traditional method for judging doneness is to dip a wooden spoon into the hot crème anglaise and then make a line with a finger along the length of the flat part of the spoon. While holding the spoon sideways, the line should hold its shape when the crème anglaise is done. The problem with this method is that it's hard to judge whether the line is moving or not and half the time the crème anglaise will curdle while you're staring at the line. Either use an instant-read thermometer or learn to judge the doneness by looking at the surface of the crème anglaise while you're stirring it over the heat. Don't expect it to thicken dramatically—the thickening is subtle—but notice the fine little ripples that form as you stir it. As it cooks these small ripples will disappear and be replaced with thicker, creamy waves.

MAKING A VANILLA CUSTARD SAUCE (CRÈME ANGLAISE)

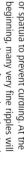

1. Use a small paring knife to split a vanilla bean almost in half lengthwise and simmer in a saucepan with the milk.

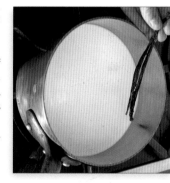

2. Once the hot milk and the egg mixture are combined, stir constantly and thoroughly with a wooden spoon or spatula to prevent curdling. At the beginning, many very fine ripples will appear on the surface; when the ripples become larger and fewer, remove from the heat but keep stirring for at least 1 minute.

3. Make a line on the back of the spoon with your finger—if the sauce is done, the line should stay in place (see sidebar, left).

4. Remove the vanilla bean and scrape along the inside of each of the halves with a paring knife to gather up the tiny seeds. Put the seeds back in the sauce.

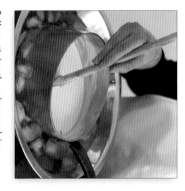

5. Keep stirring the crème anglaise as it chills. If you're in a hurry, set the saucepan in a bowl of ice water.

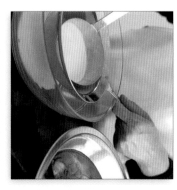

6. Strain the sauce with a medium- or coarse-mesh strainer. A fine-mesh strainer strains out the vanilla seeds.

Strawberry Bavarian Cream

Once you've made one Bavarian cream, you can make them all: just substitute different fruit purees, chocolate, coffee, or even exotic ingredients such as spices. Bavarian creams made with berries are especially impressive because they barely hold together and melt on your tongue with a burst of fruit flavor. They're rich and creamy but airy at the same time.

You can make virtually any fruit Bavarian cream by following this recipe but substituting different fruits for the strawberries. (If you're using tropical fruit puree, it must be brought to a boil first or the enzymes it contains will break down the gelatin and your Bavarian will never set.) Because the amount of gelatin in this recipe is less than in most gelled desserts, be sure to serve the Bavarian cold. If it must be served at room temperature, double the amount of gelatin, but be ready to put it in serving dishes or use it in a cake as soon as you make it, before it has time to set.

Another advantage to fruit Bavarians is that you can make them with frozen fruit since the texture of the fruit isn't important. When buying frozen fruit, be sure to buy unsweetened. If you can find only fruit with sugar, cut the sugar in the crème anglaise by half and then add sugar to taste to the fruit mixture before you fold in the whipped cream.

MAKES 6½ CUPS, ENOUGH FOR A 4-LAYER 9-INCH ROUND CAKE

1½ pounds fresh strawberries, stemmed, or one 20-ounce package frozen unsweetened strawberries, thawed

2 tablespoons (2 packets) powdered unflavored gelatin

¼ cup plus 2 tablespoons cold water

2 cups crème anglaise, warmed (page 54)

2 cups heavy cream

1 teaspoon vanilla extract

2 tablespoons sugar

Ladyfingers for lining the mold, optional (page 14)

Puree the strawberries in a food processor. Use the backside of a ladle to push the puree through a strainer into a large bowl. If you want the strained puree to be perfectly smooth, strain it first through a coarse-mesh strainer and then through a fine-mesh strainer. Put the gelatin and water in a small bowl and let sit for about 10 minutes, or until it swells, or blooms, and absorbs the water. Stir the softened gelatin with a fork to get rid of any lumps.

In a bowl, stir the gelatin into the crème anglaise and continue stirring until it completely dissolves.

Combine the heavy cream with the vanilla and sugar and beat to soft peaks; refrigerate until needed.

Stir the crème anglaise into the strawberry puree. If the mixture feels cool to the touch, work quickly so the gelatin doesn't set before you add the cream. (If the mixture starts to set, place the bowl over a saucepan of simmering water and stir the mixture to warm it and melt the gelatin.) If the mixture is too warm, it will melt the whipped cream, so stir it with a whisk until it feels neither hot nor cold. Fold the whipped cream into the strawberry mixture with a rubber spatula. If you can't get rid of little pieces of cream by folding, stir with a whisk just long enough to thoroughly combine the mixture.

If you're serving the Bavarian cream as a dessert, pour it immediately into eight to ten 5- or 6-ounce glasses or ramekins, or in a ladyfinger-lined mold (see page 78), and place in the refrigerator until set. If you're using it in a cake, see page 92.

MAKING STRAWBERRY BAVARIAN CREAM

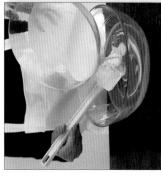

1. Combine the gelatin with cold water. Let it sit until it swells, or blooms, and absorbs the water.

2. Stir the softened gelatin into the warm crème anglaise and stir until the gelatin dissolves. Stir the crème anglaise into the cold strawberry puree.

3. Fold the whipped cream into the crème anglaise–strawberry puree mixture. Whisk for 30 seconds or so to get rid of any bits of whipped cream that aren't completely folded in. The Bavarian cream is now ready to use.

Crème Mousselines

Although their names are similar, don't confuse mousselines with mousses. While in the strictest sense a mousseline is any preparation that's been lightened with whipped cream, pastry chefs use "crème mousseline" to mean pastry cream that's been beaten until light with butter. Crème mousselines are richer than most mousses because they contain a large amount of butter but are a little less rich and less sweet than buttercream. Because of their smooth, unctuous consistency, and because they are neither too sweet nor too rich, they can be used as thick (or thin) filling layers in cakes.

Flavoring Crème Mousseline

Crème mousseline can be flavored with fruit by replacing the milk in the pastry cream with strained fruit puree, or the crème mousseline can be made in the classic way—with pastry cream made from milk—and then flavored. For 2 cups pastry cream, you can use one of the following:

2 tablespoons dry fruit brandy such as kirsch, dark rum, or Cognac

4 teaspoons instant coffee dissolved in

   2 tablespoons water

8 ounces melted bittersweet chocolate

2 additional teaspoons vanilla extract

2 tablespoons grated orange zest (see page 194)

1 tablespoon grated lemon zest (see page 194)

Classic Crème Mousseline

. . . .

A classic crème mousseline is made by beating ½ cup but-ter into 1 cup pastry cream. It can be flavored with fruit by adding fruit puree or fruit brandies, or you can make a fruit mousseline by making the pastry cream with strained fruit puree instead of milk.

MAKES 4½ CUPS, ENOUGH FOR A 3-LAYER 9-INCH ROUND CAKE

2 cups milk

1 teaspoon vanilla extract

½ cup sugar

1 egg

3 egg yolks

5 tablespoons cornstarch

1½ cups cold butter, cubed

Flavoring (see sidebar at left)

In a saucepan, bring the milk and vanilla to a simmer. In a bowl large enough to also hold the hot milk, whisk together the sugar, egg, and egg yolks for about 1 minute, or until smooth and pale. Whisk in the cornstarch until smooth. Ladle about half of the hot milk into the egg mixture, while stirring constantly with a whisk. Pour this mixture back into the saucepan, place the saucepan over medium heat, and stir with a whisk until the mixture bubbles and thickens. Place the hot pastry cream in a bowl, cover it with plastic wrap, and let it cool. If you are in a hurry, beat the pastry cream in a stand mixer with a nonreactive paddle attachment until it reaches room temperature.

With the mixer's whisk attachment, beat the pastry cream on medium speed. Add the cubes of butter, about one-third at a time, waiting until each addition is absorbed before adding the next. Add the flavoring, starting with the smallest recommended amount, to taste. Beat on high speed for 3 to 5 minutes, until light and fluffy.

Use immediately or store in the refrigerator, tightly covered, for up to 3 days or freeze for up to 2 months. When mousseline has been stored, you may need to whip it for a few minutes to re-aerate it before using it in a cake.

the mixture bubbles and thickens. Place the hot pastry cream in a bowl, cover it with plastic wrap, and let it cool. If you are in a hurry, beat the pastry cream in a stand mixer with a nonreactive (nonaluminum) paddle attachment until it reaches room temperature.

With the mixer's whisk attachment, beat the pastry cream on medium speed. Add the butter slices, about one-third at a time, waiting until each addition is absorbed before adding the next. Beat on high speed for 3 to 5 minutes, until light and fluffy.

Use immediately or store in the refrigerator, tightly covered, for up to 3 days or freeze for up to 3 months. When mousseline has been stored, you may need to whip it for a few minutes to re-aerate it before using it in a cake.

Fruit Curds

Fruit curds are made by thickening fruit juices or purees with eggs or egg yolks and sometimes starch. They can be used as light tangy alternatives, or additions to more traditional cake fillings such as buttercream or crème mousseline. Fruit curds can be beaten with cold butter to create a mixture that's very much like a crème mousseline; beaten with buttercream or crème mousseline (1 part fruit curd to 2 parts buttercream or crème mousseline) to create a richer but still tangy filling; folded with whipped cream (gelatin can be added if the mixture needs to sit awhile); or combined with *beurre noisette* (page 196), which stiffens them and gives them a butterscotch flavor.

Curds are simple to make: Just combine sugar, eggs, strained fruit puree or juice, and butter and whisk in a bowl set over a saucepan of simmering water until it thickens. You can use as little or as much butter as you like—from none to about 4 tablespoons per egg.

Recipes for lemon curd (page 364), passion fruit curd (page 364), and passion fruit mousse (page 365) can be found in Chapter 5.

Egg White–Based Frostings and Fillings

When egg whites are heated and beaten with sugar, they fluff up and take on an irresistible silky texture. Depending on the exact method, egg whites and sugar beaten in this way become either seven-minute frosting (opposite) or Italian meringue (page 60). There is very little difference between the two, and either can be used to frost a cake or combined with butter to make buttercream.

Fruit Crème Mousseline

To make a fruit crème mousseline, make pastry cream using strained fruit puree or fruit juice instead of the milk. You can freeze any fruit crème mousseline you don't use for up to 2 months.

MAKES 4½ CUPS, ENOUGH FOR A 3-LAYER 9-INCH ROUND CAKE

2 cups fruit puree, such as raspberry, strawberry, peach, passion fruit, or mango

⅔ cup sugar

1 egg

3 egg yolks

5 tablespoons cornstarch

1½ cups butter, sliced or cubed

Bring the fruit puree to a gentle simmer in a small, nonreactive saucepan.

Whisk together the sugar, egg, and egg yolks for about 1 minute, or until smooth and pale. Whisk in the cornstarch until smooth. Pour about half of the hot fruit puree into the egg mixture. Pour this mixture back into the saucepan, place the saucepan over medium heat, and stir with a whisk until

MAKING FRUIT CRÈME MOUSSELINE

2. Pour the mixture back into the saucepan. Stir the mixture with a whisk until it bubbles and thickens.

1. Whisk together the sugar, egg, egg yolks, and cornstarch in a heatproof bowl until smooth. Pour half of the hot fruit puree into the bowl while whisking.

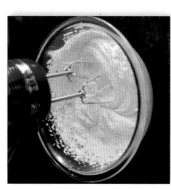

3. Transfer the mixture to a bowl, cover, and let cool. Beat in butter slices, one-third at a time, until smooth. Continue beating until pale, creamy, and fluffy.

MAKING EGG WHITE–BASED FROSTING (SEVEN-MINUTE FROSTING)

1. Combine the egg whites, sugar, corn syrup, and vanilla extract in a bowl.

2. Put the bowl over a saucepan of simmering water—don't let the water touch the bottom of the bowl—and stir with a whisk. Lift the bowl off the saucepan and quickly touch the bottom of the bowl; the mixture is hot enough when you can't hold your hand against the bottom of the bowl.

3. Beat on high speed with a stand mixer for about 10 minutes or a handheld mixer for about 20 minutes, or until the mixture is very stiff.

Seven-Minute Frosting

This frosting is made by heating egg whites with sugar and corn syrup and then beating the mixture. It is nearly identical to Italian meringue in appearance and flavor, but unlike Italian meringue, it doesn't require soft ball-stage sugar syrup.

MAKES 4 CUPS, ENOUGH TO COVER AND FILL THREE 9-INCH ROUND CAKE LAYERS

4 egg whites

1 cup sugar

2 tablespoons light corn syrup

1 teaspoon vanilla extract

Combine the egg whites, sugar, corn syrup, and vanilla extract in a bowl and place the bowl over a saucepan of simmering water. Stir with a whisk until the bottom of the bowl is too hot to hold your hand against when you lift it out of the saucepan.

Beat on high speed with a stand mixer for about 10 minutes or with a handheld mixer for about 20 minutes, or until the mixture is very stiff. Use to frost cakes.

ICING A CAKE WITH A SPOON (CHESTNUT CAKE WITH SEVEN-MINUTE FROSTING)

1. Spread the frosting over the top of the cake. You can use a spoon or an offset spatula at this stage.

2. Spread the frosting over the top so it starts to run over the sides. Ice the sides of the cake. A cake stand comes in handy here.

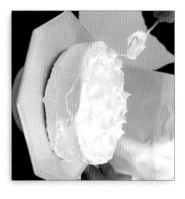

3. To create a dynamic effect, place the back of a spoon against the frosting and quickly lift to form swirls.

4. Bake in a 400°F oven until the tips of the swirls brown (optional).

CAKES

59

Italian Meringue

Italian meringue is almost identical to that gooey white frosting we see fluffed on chocolate cakes. When used as a frosting, it's made slightly differently (see page 46) but traditionally it is made by beating soft ball–stage sugar syrup into egg whites.

MAKES 4 CUPS, ENOUGH TO COVER AND FILL THREE 9-INCH ROUND CAKE LAYERS

1³/4 cups sugar

¹/2 cup water or more as needed

6 egg whites, slightly warmed

Pinch of cream of tartar, unless using a copper bowl

Put 1¹/2 cups of the sugar and the water in a small saucepan and bring to a boil.

Beat the egg whites and the cream of tartar (if using) with a stand mixer on medium speed or a handheld mixer on high speed for 1 minute. Switch to high speed and beat with a stand mixer for about 5 minutes or with a handheld mixer for about 10 minutes, or until the egg whites reach stiff peaks. Add the remaining sugar and beat for 1 minute more.

Test the sugar syrup with a thermometer or the back of a spoon until it reaches the soft ball stage (see page 47). If the syrup is ready before the egg whites are stiff, add a tablespoon of water, then start testing again; if the egg whites are stiff before the syrup is ready, turn the mixer to low speed—don't stop beating.

With the mixer on high speed, pour the syrup in a steady stream between the whisk and the bowl. Beat the egg whites for about 7 minutes, or until very stiff and the bottom of the bowl feels barely warm.

Italian meringue can be combined with other mixtures such as buttercream, fruit purees, ganache, whipped cream, crème mousseline, and fruit curds, with or without gelatin to create different textures.

MAKING ITALIAN MERINGUE

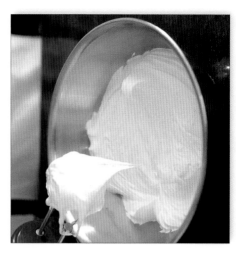

3. Finished Italian meringue.

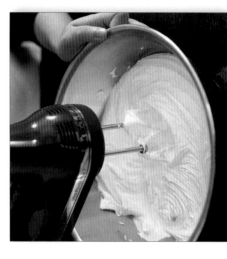

2. Beat until cool and very stiff.

1. Beat the egg whites on high speed to medium peaks, add the remaining sugar, and beat to stiff peaks. Pour the soft ball–stage syrup into the egg whites, with the mixer on high speed. Don't let the syrup touch either the whisk or the sides of the bowl.

Lemon Glaze

This simple glaze gives a sweet and tangy note to loaf cakes such as pound cake and carrot cake.

MAKES ABOUT $1/2$ CUP, ENOUGH TO GLAZE ONE POUND CAKE

1$1/3$ cups confectioners' sugar

3 tablespoons lemon juice

2 tablespoons heavy cream, or more as needed

Combine the sugar and lemon juice in a small bowl and stir with a whisk until smooth. Whisk in cream, 1 tablespoon at a time, until the glaze is smooth and falls in a thin stream when you lift the whisk.

Drizzle the glaze over the room-temperature pound cake set on a cake rack on a sheet pan. Let the icing drip down the sides for a rustic, homespun effect.

Fruit Glazes

Fruit preserves make lovely, delicate coatings and fillings for cakes. They can be spread or brushed inside a rolled cake, giving it a little tang without making the cake too rich. When made into glazes by being strained and heated with water, they're used to finish pastries such as fruit tarts.

To make about 1 cup of smooth glaze (enough for one 13 by 17-inch sheet cake), start with one 12- or 13-ounce jar of apricot jam or other jam or preserves. If you want a perfectly smooth glaze, use a small ladle to push the jam through a strainer to eliminate any pulp. If the jam is too stiff to strain, heat it in a saucepan or in the microwave before straining. Beat the jam with a whisk to make it easier to spread. If you want a very thin coating, you can dilute the jam with a tablespoon or two of water, kirsch, or other flavorful liquid.

Spread the cream in or on a cake with an offset spatula or pipe it, with a 1/2-inch or larger plain tip, in straight lines on top of a cake (see opposite page).

Whipped Cream

Whipped cream is marvelous stuff—simple to make, versatile, and the obvious accompaniment to any number of desserts. It is also used as a component in a variety of cake and tart fillings.

One problem with whipped cream is its tendency to release liquid as it sits; if used as a cake filling, the cake is soon soggy. Whipped cream can be stabilized by hanging it in a kitchen towel, ends tied together, overnight in a cool place, which causes it to release much of its liquid. Cooks refer to this as "squeezing." But even "squeezed" whipped cream continues to release a small amount of liquid, so if you use it to fill a cake, the cake should be eaten within a day or two.

Another alternative is to stabilize whipped cream by dissolving gelatin in some of the cream and stirring the mixture into the remaining cream while beating, just as the cream reaches medium peaks.

Cream must be kept cold for it to whip properly. If it is allowed to warm, it will turn directly into butter as it is being beaten. To avoid this, first put the heavy cream into a bowl and put the bowl and whisk in the freezer for 5 minutes. If the kitchen is very hot, beat the cream over a bowl of ice.

Cream expands when it is whipped—1 cup heavy cream makes 2 cups whipped cream. To sweeten cream, add granulated or superfine sugar before beating—confectioners' sugar has a slightly gritty texture because it contains cornstarch. How much sugar to use is a matter of taste. Two tablespoons sugar per 1 cup of cream suits most people; others find it not sweet enough.

Whipped cream is simply heavy cream that's been whipped until fluffy and firm. When sweetened and flavored with vanilla, whipped cream is called Chantilly cream. To make Chantilly cream, make stabilized whipped cream, but leave out the gelatin.

Stabilized Whipped Cream

Because it is less sweet and less rich than most frostings, stabilized whipped cream makes a wonderful filling or icing for a cake. The cream allows the flavor of the cake to come through in a way that buttercream, for instance, does not. Gelatin keeps the cream from softening and losing its texture.

A couple of caveats: When you dissolve the gelatin in the cream, don't let the mixture get too hot—it just needs to be really warm to dissolve the gelatin—or you'll heat up the rest of the cream when you pour it in. For this same reason, make sure the cream is very cold before you beat it. Stabilized cream works best with whipped cream beaten to medium peaks. Beat the cream almost all the way to where you want it before adding the gelatin—the gelatin stops the emulsifying process so the cream stops getting stiffer.

If you have leftover stabilized cream in the refrigerator, or it seems to set in the bowl as you're using it, give it a couple of good whisks with a hand whisk; it should look like regular whipped cream again.

MAKES 4 CUPS, ENOUGH FOR A 4-LAYER 9-INCH ROUND CAKE

2 teaspoons (2/3 packet) powdered unflavored gelatin

2 tablespoons water

2 cups heavy cream or crème fraîche

4 tablespoons sugar or more, to taste

2 teaspoons vanilla extract (optional)

Put the gelatin and water in a small bowl and let sit for about 10 minutes, or until it swells, or blooms, and absorbs the water. Stir the softened gelatin with a fork to get rid of any lumps.

Add 1/4 cup plus 2 tablespoons of the cream to the gelatin mixture and put the bowl over a saucepan of simmering water. Stir the mixture with a rubber spatula—a rubber spatula allows you to pull the gelatin away from the sides of the bowl—until it is smooth, then take the saucepan off the heat. Don't heat it any more than is needed to dissolve the gelatin.

Combine the remaining cream with the sugar and vanilla and beat to medium peaks. Turn the mixer to low speed and pour in the gelatin mixture in a steady stream, avoiding the whisk and sides of the bowl. If you're making the stabilized whipped cream by hand, stir the gelatin mixture into the cream with a whisk. Continue beating the cream just long enough to incorporate the gelatin.

1. Spread stabilized whipped cream over the top and sides of a cake. Using a cake stand allows the cake to be rotated easily.

2. Continue spreading the cream over the top and sides of the cake until smooth and even.

3. Pipe the whipped cream in ropes across the cake using a plain tip.

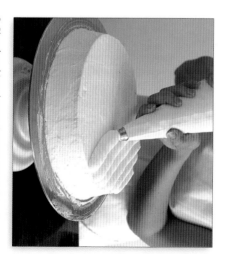

4. Hold a spatula along the sides of the cake while rotating the cake to smooth off the ends of the ropes.

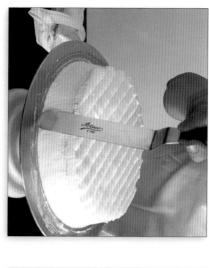

5. Decorate the edge of the base with chopped chocolate or chopped nuts by holding them in your hand and gently pressing them against the bottom edge of the cake.

Filling and Using a Pastry Bag

Amateur bakers immediately assume that any dessert requiring a pastry bag is too difficult and just, well, too "professional." While it's true that much of the elaborate decorations accomplished with a pastry bag takes some practice, a pastry bag makes certain very basic tasks a lot easier.

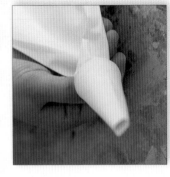

1. If the pastry bag is new, slide a tip inside to judge the size of the bag's opening.

2. Cut the end off with a pair of scissors so the tip will stick through about ½ inch. Start by cutting just a little bit; if you cut too much, the bag is ruined, so test the hole with the tip until the cut is just the right size.

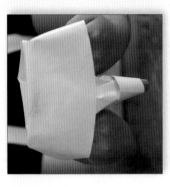

4. Push the twist into the back of the tip. This keeps filling from flowing out the tip while you're filling the bag.

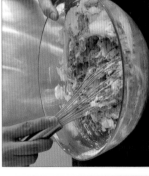

3. Push the tip into the end of the bag and twist the bag slightly just behind the tip.

5. Fold down the top of the bag to make a sleeve so you can hold the bag with one hand while adding filling with the other.

6. Scrape the spatula along the rim of the sleeve to detach the filling. Don't fill the bag more than two-thirds or it will be hard to handle.

Chestnut Cream Cake Filling

You can make chestnut cream filling by combining sweetened chestnut puree (crème de marrons) with whipped cream. Use stabilized whipped cream if the cake is not being served until the next day.

High-quality chestnut puree is available in a can. The Clement Faugier brand (which is consistently excellent) comes unsweetened as "chestnut puree" or sweetened as "crème de marrons." Use the sweetened version alone as a cake filling or combine it with stabilized whipped cream.

MAKES 2½ CUPS FILLING, ENOUGH FOR TWO 9-INCH ROUND CAKE LAYERS

One 7-ounce can sweetened chestnut puree

1 to 2 tablespoons dark rum or Cognac, or more to taste (optional)

1 cup heavy cream, or 2 cups stabilized whipped cream (page 62)

Beat the chestnut puree with a whisk until smooth and stir in the rum to smooth it and make it easier to combine with the cream.

Beat the cream to medium peaks. Mix about one-fourth of the cream into the chestnut mixture to lighten it, then fold in the rest with a rubber spatula or whisk.

Spread it over the layers of a cake.

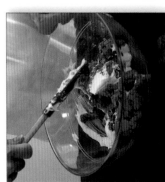

1. Work the sweetened chestnut puree with dark rum until the mixture is smooth. Fold one-fourth of the whipped cream in with the flavored chestnut puree.

2. Incorporate the rest of the whipped cream.

7. Unfold the sleeve, and close the end of the bag by bringing the two corners together like an accordion.

8. Slide the folded part of the bag between your thumb and forefinger until the filling is taut. Make sure the bag is taut with filling, not flaccid, or you won't be able to control the flow while you're piping.

9. Twist the end of the bag to hold in the filling.

10. With the bag pointed upward, squeeze the bag to push out any air pockets.

11. Control the flow of the filling by squeezing the bag with one hand—use the same hand to pinch the bag between thumb and forefinger to keep the filling in—and pointing the tip with the other.

12. If you will be decorating using the pastry bag, and you are not very experienced using it, practice different effects before you start.

13. To pipe wavelike edges as shown here, hold the pastry bag at an angle almost parallel with the cake or surface and squeeze while lifting. Continue in this way, lifting and lowering the bag slightly as you pipe.

14. To make round and separate rosettes, hold the bag vertical to the surface you are decorating, about ¹/₂ inch away from the surface. After squeezing out each rosette, move the tip in a counterclockwise direction and quickly lift it away.

1. Combine the gelatin and water and allow to expand or "bloom." Place over a pan of simmering water and stir until dissolved.

2. Add the glycerin and corn syrup to the gelatin, still over the pan of simmering water, and stir to dissolve.

3. Pour the gelatin mixture in a circle over a bowl of confectioners' sugar. Don't pour the liquid in one spot only, or it will congeal before it combines with the sugar. Stir until the liquid is well combined.

4. Knead the mixture with two hands in the bowl—if it doesn't come together with the mixer, knead it by hand—until it comes together into a single mass.

5. Knead the fondant on the work surface until smooth and homogeneous, scraping it up as needed with a pastry scraper. Press the fondant into a disk with the heel of your hand. Wrap in plastic and refrigerate until needed.

Rolled Fondant

There are two kinds of fondant: liquid fondant, which is the shiny glaze you see on the tops of napoleons and éclairs, and rolled fondant. Essentially confectioners' sugar held together with gelatin and smoothed out with corn syrup and a little shortening or glycerin, rolled fondant can be rolled out into sheets much like pie crust and used to decorate luxurious cakes—it is often used on wedding cakes. A sheet of rolled fondant is easy to make and gives a professional look to any cake.

A ball of rolled fondant will keep for up to 24 hours in the refrigerator, but it must be kept moist by wrapping it first in plastic wrap, then a damp towel, and then in a second sheet of plastic wrap. It will keep longer if it is already rolled out and placed on a cake, where it doesn't matter if it dries out. Glycerin can be purchased at any drugstore—it keeps the fondant moist and malleable.

**MAKES ENOUGH TO COVER 2 ROUND LAYER CAKES
(9 BY 3 INCHES)**

1 tablespoon (1 packet) powdered unflavored gelatin

1/4 cup water

3/4 cup light corn syrup

1 tablespoon plus 2 teaspoons glycerin

7 3/4 cups confectioners' sugar plus more for rolling

Put the gelatin and water in a small bowl and let sit for about 10 minutes, or until it swells, or blooms, and absorbs the water. Stir the softened gelatin with a fork to get rid of any lumps.

Place the bowl over a saucepan of simmering water and stir to dissolve the gelatin. Pour the corn syrup and glycerin over the gelatin and continue to stir until the mixture is perfectly clear.

Put the confectioners' sugar in a large bowl and pour the gelatin mixture in a circle over it. Don't pour the liquid in one spot or it will congeal before it combines with the sugar. Combine with a rubber spatula or with a stand mixer fitted with the paddle attachment (make sure the paddle is plastic coated).

When the mixture pulls together so that it's a cohesive mass that barely sticks to your hands, sprinkle a work surface with confectioners' sugar and turn out the fondant onto it. Coat your hands with confectioners' sugar and knead the fondant for about 10 minutes, or until smooth and pliable.

If you're not using the fondant right away, wrap it in plastic wrap, then a damp towel, and then again with plastic wrap, and place it in the refrigerator for up to 24 hours. To roll and use on a cake, see page 112.

Royal Icing

A simple mixture of raw egg whites and confectioners' sugar, royal icing is mostly used for decoration. It works especially well in a paper cone because of its tendency to form ribbons that give it a fluid natural appearance on cakes when you wave the cone over the cake. With a little practice, the easiest way to write on a cake is with royal icing in a paper cone. Professional pastry chefs make elaborate designs with it.

MAKES ABOUT 1/4 CUP, ENOUGH FOR DECORATING ONE CAKE

1 egg white

1 cup confectioners' sugar, or more as needed

Combine the egg white and confectioners' sugar and mix with a whisk until smooth and thick enough that the whisk leaves light trails on the top of the icing.

VARIATION

ROYAL ICING FOR COOKIES: To make enough royal icing for 60 cookies, quadruple the above recipe and add food coloring and 1 teaspoon of lemon oil or other flavoring. If you like, you can substitute 6 tablespoons of heavy cream for the egg whites.

Work the mixture with a whisk until smooth and thick enough that the whisk leaves light trails on the top of the icing.

ASSEMBLED CAKES

Once you're familiar with basic cakes, frostings, fillings, and glazes, it is a simple matter to put the cakes together. The simplest cakes, sheet cakes, are simply flat sheets of cake spread with some kind of frosting, such as buttercream. Rolled cakes start out as thin sheet cakes—you just bake the cake in a sheet pan—but are then coated with filling and rolled up. Only slightly more elaborate are layer cakes, which can be round, square, or rectangular. Because of their height, layer cakes also require some decoration on the sides.

Layer Cakes

Except perhaps for rolled cakes, layer cakes are the most dramatic and require the most skill to put together. There are, however, several approaches used by professional bakers that you can use also that make it much easier to assemble elegant and impressive cakes. Here, I've divided cake assembly into two basic methods—by hand or in a mold. To assemble a cake by hand means to finish the cake either by holding it in one hand while applying frosting with the other, or by setting the cake on a revolving cake stand. Raspberry buttercream layer cake is an example of assembling a cake by holding it in one hand (page 74); devil's food cake with ganache, chocolate buttercream, and chocolate curls (page 71) and chocolate hazelnut cake with chocolate filling and hazelnut buttercream (page 72) show how to assemble a cake by using a cake stand.

The second basic method, assembling a cake in a mold, relies on a springform pan or a cake ring to hold the cake's shape and make the sides perfectly even. This technique is the easiest way to make consistently professional-looking cakes. Dark chocolate mousse cake is an example of assembling a cake using a springform pan (page 80); strawberry and white chocolate mousse ladyfinger cake demonstrates using a cake ring (page 78).

Most layer cakes include layers of frosting about $1/4$ inch thick (amounts below are for that thickness), but some cakes may contain much thicker layers of lighter fillings such as Bavarian cream. For these, double or triple the amount per layer, to come up with $1/2$- and $3/4$-inch-thick layers respectively. These are somewhat rough estimates that will vary depending on the exact thickness of the frosting. Keep in mind also that cakes that are glazed, say with liquid ganache, are sometimes first coated with a thin layer of buttercream so the surface of the cake is perfectly smooth and won't absorb any glaze and so the glaze adheres evenly. This crumb coating is usually about half as thick as a regular coating. The amount of glaze you'll need depends on how much the cake itself absorbs. Cake layers that have been brushed generously with simple syrup and cakes that have been crumb coated will absorb less icing and slightly less frosting. Some bakers like to apply glaze in two stages. The first stage seals the cake, especially when the cake is then refrigerated so the glaze hardens. The second coating, often poured over the cake instead of being spread, leaves the cake perfectly smooth and shiny. When using chocolate glaze to ice a cake, start by applying a thin layer of glaze on the top and sides to seal the cake and keep it from absorbing the final layer of glaze and giving it an uneven look.

When assembling a layer cake, you can make the layers any thickness you like, by slicing a cake crosswise using a serrated knife. American cakes are typically much higher than European cakes because American cakes usually comprise 2 to 4 layers, each 1 to 2 inches thick. European cakes may include the same number or even more layers than an American cake, but the layers are thinner, usually from $1/4$ to $1/2$ inch thick. European cakes are also more likely to have flavored simple syrup brushed on each layer, while American cakes typically do not.

To construct an American cake, use two cake layers, each 1 to $1^1/2$ inches thick. You can stack the cakes on top of each other to make 2 layers, or you can cut each cake in half so you have 4 layers. To construct a European cake, cut a 1- to $1^1/2$-inch-thick cake into 2 to 4 layers and stack these, with layers of filling in between. You can make a hybrid cake by cutting 2 cakes into 4 layers each and then stack them so you have a cake with thin layers like a European cake but high like an American cake.

Sometimes it can be hard to cut a cake into thin layers because the cake crumbles or you just need more practice. Because the layers are hidden within the cake, don't worry if they tear—just assemble the broken pieces, like a jigsaw puzzle, on the cake. You can also make thin layers by piping the cake batter into disks with a pastry bag. This way, you can make the layers as thin as you like. Most bakers pipe these disks on a sheet of parchment paper on a sheet pan, but you can make the disks more even by baking them in parchment paper–lined cake pans.

Judging Amounts of Frosting, Glaze, and Simple Syrup Needed for Layer Cakes

Here are the amounts needed for brushing with simple syrup, and frosting and glazing cakes. Keep in mind that these amounts are just enough to cover the layers, top, and sides of the cake. When constructing your cake in a cake ring or springform pan, there is sometimes a gap between the edge of the cake and the sides of the ring; this is especially likely if you construct the cake in the same springform pan you used to bake the cake, because the cake will have shrunk about 1/2 inch, leaving a 1/4-inch gap around the cake. You can leave the gap there and smooth off the sides of the cake after you take the cake out of the mold, or you can fill in the gap with extra frosting or filling. If you decide to fill in the gap, count on 1/2 cup extra frosting for 1 inch of height for a cake baked in a 9-inch cake pan.

If you're setting out to assemble a layer cake and perhaps even have more than one kind of filling and flavored sugar syrup for brushing on the cake layers, it's helpful to know how much filling and syrup you need for each layer, for the sides, and for the top.

Frosting needed for a 4-layer round cake 9 by 2 inches: You'll need 5 1/3 to 7 1/3 cups of frosting depending on how thick you make the layers:

• 1 to 1 1/2 cups frosting per layer and top (so a 4-layer cake will require 4 to 6 cups of frosting just for the layers and top)

• 2/3 cup frosting per 1 inch of height (for just the sides) (so a 2-inch-high cake will require 1 1/3 cups of frosting for the sides)

Glaze needed for a 4-layer round cake 9 by 2 inches: Glazes are usually poured over cakes while still liquid and then allowed to harden on the cake. Because of this, they form thinner layers than frosting and less is required to cover the cake. A typical 4-layer 9-inch cake will require about 2 1/4 cups of glaze to cover the top and sides of the assembled cake.

Syrup needed for a 4-layer round cake 9 by 2 inches: Not all cakes require syrup, but if you want a very moist cake, or you want to use cake that's gotten somewhat dry from long storage, brushing each layer with flavored simple syrup will bring the cake back to life. In either case, count on 1 to 1 1/3 cups syrup.

Frosting needed for a sheet cake 13 by 17 inches: The exact amount of frosting needed to cover a sheet cake depends on how thick you want the layer, but 4 to 5 cups of frosting is usually right for a 1/4-inch-thick layer.

Glaze needed for a sheet cake 13 by 17 inches: Because glazes are liquid when warm and get absorbed by the cake, it's usually necessary to add them in two stages, letting the first layer of glaze harden and form a seal before pouring over the second coating. Count on 2 1/2 to 3 cups per layer, added half at a time.

Syrup needed for a sheet cake 13 by 17 inches: Brush with 1 to 1 1/2 cups.

Assembling a Layer Cake on a Cake Stand

In the following pages, I show cakes finished by hand without the help of any kind of mold such as a cake ring or springform pan. The trick to making a cake with a perfectly smooth top and sides is to continually switch from the top to the sides and back again as you are frosting; as you smooth the sides, you generate a ridge of extra frosting around the edge of the top, which you should then spread over the top; as you smooth the top, the same thing happens—a ridge of frosting forms around the edge of the top—so that you need to spread the excess frosting on the sides. Continue alternating in this way until the cake is perfectly smooth. It may take a while.

4. Smooth off the sides of the cake with a metal spatula and remove excess frosting to expose the cardboard that surrounds the base of the cake. Refrigerate for 15 minutes.

3. Dollop whipped ganache on each layer and spread in an even layer. Use a metal spatula to keep smoothing over the extra ganache that oozes out between each layer.

8. Hold a bench scraper straight up and down on the side of the cake and rotate the cake to smooth off the sides.

7. Use a spatula to scrape up buttercream that accumulates around the edges of the cake. Use this buttercream to ice the sides of the cake.

2. Place a round of cardboard on the cake stand and set the first cake layer on top. Brush with flavored syrup (optional).

6. Continue smoothing the buttercream around the top and sides of the cake.

11. To make large chocolate curls, peel them off the chunk of chocolate with a vegetable peeler.

1. Use a serrated knife to cut 2 devil's food layer cakes into 2 layers each so you have 4 layers.

5. Dollop the top of the cake with the buttercream and spread it over the top of the cake. Allow the excess buttercream to form around the edges of the cake, providing you with frosting for the sides.

9. Spread the buttercream that accumulates along the top rim of the cake to smooth off the top. Continue doing this, alternating between top and sides, until the cake is perfectly smooth.

10. To make small chocolate curls, slice the back side of a pastry tip along the chunk of chocolate while pressing firmly.

BAKING

Devil's Food Cake with Ganache, Chocolate Buttercream, and Chocolate Curls

Here is an elaborate cake assembled on a cake stand. Whipped chocolate ganache is used between the cake layers and chocolate buttercream to frost the top and sides. Buttercream is best for the top and sides because it is smoother and shinier than whipped ganache. You can also fill the cake with buttercream, but that makes it extremely rich. I decorate the finished cake with chocolate curls.

Buy or cut a round of cardboard about 1/2 inch in diameter more than the cake to set the cake on. This leaves a 1/4-inch border around the cake; allowing room for the frosting makes it easy to move the cake from the cake stand when it is finished.

MAKES ONE 4-LAYER 9-INCH ROUND CAKE

2 round devil's food layer cakes 9 by 1 inch (page 30)

4 cups chocolate buttercream (page 48)

1½ cups simple syrup (page 36) flavored with instant coffee, rum, Cognac, or bourbon (optional)

4 cups whipped ganache (page 51)

Block of bittersweet ganache for chocolate curls (optional)

Have ready a 9-inch cardboard round. Using a serrated knife, cut each of the layer cakes in half crosswise, for a total of 4 layers. Reserve one of the bottom halves for the top of the cake. The smooth surface will make it easier to spread the buttercream.

Put a dollop of buttercream on the cardboard round to hold the cake in place. Place one of the cake layers on the cardboard, put it on a cake stand if using, brush with the syrup, and spread with about one-fourth of the ganache, using a metal offset or regular spatula. Add a second cake layer, brush with syrup, and spread with one-third of the remaining ganache. Put on the third layer, brush with syrup, and spread with the remaining ganache. If you have ganache left over, save it to crumb coat the cake before spreading on the buttercream (see page 68).

Use the reserved bottom layer, turned over, as the top layer. As you layer the cake, keep smoothing the ganache that oozes out between each layer. This makes it easier to put on the buttercream frosting.

Spread any leftover ganache on the sides and top of the cake to crumb coat it and refrigerate the cake for 15 minutes to harden the ganache.

Dollop the buttercream on top of the cake and spread it evenly. With a spatula, scrape up buttercream that accumulates around the edges of the cake and use it to ice the sides of the cake. Scrape any excess buttercream off the spatula into a small bowl to avoid getting crumbs in the main batch. If you're using a cake stand, hold a bench scraper or the spatula straight up and down on the side of the cake and rotate the cake to smooth the sides.

Spread the buttercream that accumulates along the top rim of the cake to smooth off the top. Continue doing this, alternating between top and sides, until the cake is perfectly smooth. While you're working, scrape the spatula along the edge of a bowl to eliminate excess frosting and to make it easier to smooth the cake. When you are nearing completion, wipe off the spatula between two sheets of paper towel to keep it clean and smooth.

To make small chocolate curls, scrape the wide end of a pastry bag tip against a block of chocolate; to make large curls, use a vegetable peeler. If the curls are too brittle and break, heat the block of chocolate for a few seconds in the microwave; if too soft, put it in the refrigerator. Decorate the cake by arranging the chocolate curls over the top.

Chocolate Hazelnut Cake with Chocolate Filling and Hazelnut Buttercream

This elaborate cake shows you how to use two kinds of cake layers, a moist chocolate sponge cake, cut into layers, and disks of dacquoise, along with two kinds of fillings, whipped chocolate ganache and hazelnut buttercream, to assemble a finished cake. You can simplify the recipe by doubling the amounts of one component—cake or filling—and eliminating another.

When making such an elaborate cake, a cake stand is helpful in two ways. First, it allows you to place the cake closer to eye level than the usual work surface. Second, the top revolves so you can turn the cake while spreading icing or frosting on the sides. This technique makes it much easier to smooth the icing with a metal spatula or a bench scraper. When building the cake, dollop the frosting on each layer with a rubber spatula and then spread the frosting with a metal spatula, or pipe the frosting in a spiral shape onto each layer with a pastry bag.

1 round chocolate sponge cake 9 by 1½ inches (page 12) or other cake

7 cups hazelnut buttercream (page 48)

1½ cups simple syrup (page 36), flavored with instant coffee, rum, Cognac, or bourbon (optional)

Two 9-inch dacquoise disks (page 40)

2 cups whipped ganache (page 51)

2 cups hot ganache (page 50)

Decoration

½ cup heavy cream

1 tablespoon sugar

Hazelnuts

Block of bittersweet chocolate for chocolate curls (optional)

ASSEMBLING A CAKE WITH LAYERS OF DACQUOISE AND CAKE (CHOCOLATE HAZELNUT CAKE)

1. Cut the chocolate cake into 2 layers. Place the first layer on a round of cardboard. Brush the cake with flavored simple syrup (optional).

2. Fill a pastry bag fitted with a ⅓-inch plain tip with buttercream. Pipe the buttercream in a spiral onto the cake.

3. Place a *dacquoise* disk on top of the buttercream.

4. Spoon the whipped ganache onto the cake. Spread it with an offset or regular metal spatula.

5. Place a second *dacquoise* disk on the cake.

6. Pipe another layer of buttercream on top of the *dacquoise* disk.

7. Place the second cake layer on top of the buttercream and brush it with flavored simple syrup (optional).

8. Spread the top of the cake with buttercream, using an offset or regular metal spatula.

Have ready a 9-inch cardboard round or a 9½-inch springform pan (to allow room to apply frosting to the sides). Cut the layer cake in half crosswise, using a serrated knife. Reserve the bottom layer for the top layer of the cake. The smooth surface will make it easier to spread the buttercream.

Put a dollop of buttercream on the cardboard round, or the bottom of the springform pan, to hold the cake in place. Place the top layer of the cake on the cardboard or pan bottom and put it on a cake stand, if using. Brush the layer with the simple syrup.

Fit a pastry bag with a ⅓-inch plain tip and fill with the buttercream. Pipe on a layer of the buttercream in a spiral. Press a *dacquoise* disk on top of the buttercream and spread the whipped ganache over it with an offset or regular metal spatula. Press on the second *dacquoise* disk and pipe on another layer of buttercream. Use the reserved bottom layer, turned over, as the top layer and brush it with the remaining syrup.

Spread the rest of the buttercream over the top and sides of the cake. Use a metal spatula on the sides and a bench scraper on the sides. Alternate smoothing the sides and the top until all is smooth. If you're using a cake stand, hold a bench scraper or the spatula straight up and down on the side of the cake and rotate the cake to smooth the sides.

Save any excess buttercream for a second coat. Put the cake in the refrigerator or freezer for 15 minutes to firm up the buttercream coating. If you have extra buttercream, give the cake a second thin coat and chill again for 15 minutes. It is important that the cake be cold when you pour the ganache over it or the ganache will melt the buttercream.

Set the cake on a cake rack set over a clean sheet pan.

Check the temperature of the ganache—it should feel warm to the touch but not too hot or it will melt the buttercream. Use a pitcher or ladle to pour the ganache over the chilled cake until completely covered. Avoid spreading the ganache with a spatula, which would make the ganache coating less even and perfect. Allow the ganache to set for about 30 minutes.

To decorate the cake, whip the cream with the sugar and pipe it, with a fluted tip, in little rosettes around the cake. Place a hazelnut in the center of each of the rosettes. If you like, decorate with chocolate curls (see page 118). Serve in wedges.

9. Mask the sides of the cake with buttercream using a regular metal spatula.

10. Alternate between the top and sides of the cake, smoothing the top with a spatula and the sides with a bench scraper.

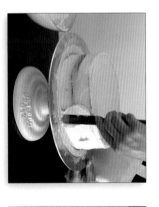

11. Gently rotate the cake stand while holding the spatula or bench scraper in place to create a very smooth effect.

12. Once you've coated the cake with a smooth layer of buttercream, put it in the freezer or refrigerator for 15 minutes to harden the buttercream. If you have leftover buttercream, give the cake another thin coat and chill for 15 minutes more.

13. Set the cake on a cake rack set over a sheet pan. Check the temperature of the ganache—it should feel warm to the touch but not too hot or it will melt the buttercream. Use a pitcher or ladle to pour the warm ganache over the chilled cake until completely covered.

Raspberry Buttercream Layer Cake

This recipe shows in detail how to construct a traditional French sponge cake with buttercream icing without a cake stand.

The cake is constructed on top of a round of cardboard, which makes it easier to transfer the cake to a serving dish and allows you to hold the cake in one hand while applying frosting with the other. Cut a round of cardboard about 1/2 inch in diameter larger than the cake so there is a rim about 1/4 inch wide around the cake to make room for the icing.

This European-style cake with thin layers is only about 3 inches high.

MAKES ONE 3-LAYER 9-INCH ROUND CAKE

1 cup slivered almonds

4 cups plain buttercream (page 45)

3 tablespoons clear raspberry brandy (eau de vie de framboise), kirsch, or raspberry coulis, for flavoring the buttercream (page 48)

1 1/2 cups simple syrup (page 36)

1/2 cup sweet wine, such as Beaumes-de-Venise, or 3 additional tablespoons raspberry brandy, kirsch, or raspberry coulis, for flavoring the syrup

1 round sponge cake, such as a genoise (page 8)

Fresh raspberries for decorating

Toast the almonds in a 350°F oven for about 15 minutes, or until pale brown. Flavor the buttercream with the raspberry brandy (see page 48). You can add more to taste, but don't make the buttercream too runny. Flavor the simple syrup with the sweet wine.

Have ready a 9 1/2-inch cardboard round. Cut the sponge cake crosswise into 3 layers, using a serrated knife. If you want the cake to have a perfectly delicate texture, trim off the crust on the top, bottom, and sides of the cake. Reserve the bottom layer for the top of the cake. The smooth surface will make it easier to spread the buttercream.

Put a dollop of buttercream on the cardboard to hold the cake in place and set the top cake layer on the cardboard. Brush with the flavored syrup and put about 1 cup of buttercream in a mound in the center. Holding the cake with one hand, with the other hand, using a metal offset or regular spatula, spread the buttercream until it completely covers the cake layer. Check the thickness of the buttercream by making indentations with the spatula. The buttercream should be about 1/4 inch thick. Add the second cake layer, brush with the

syrup, and spread with another cup of buttercream. Add the reserved bottom layer, smooth side up, and brush the top with the syrup.

Set aside 1/2 cup of the remaining buttercream for the rosettes and dollop the rest over top of the cake. Spread the buttercream over the top, working from the center outward, so the extra buttercream hangs over the edges. Use this to coat the sides. Scrape any excess buttercream off the spatula into a little bowl to avoid getting crumbs in the main batch. Smooth the sides with a bench scraper or spatula and allow the excess buttercream to form on the top edge. Smooth the top. Repeat, going back and forth between the top and sides, until the frosting is completely smooth. If you wish, freeze the cake for 15 minutes and apply another thin layer of buttercream.

Heat a metal spatula at least as long as the cake is wide by dipping it in hot water or waving over a hot flame. If you've dipped the spatula in water, wipe off the water with a towel. Smooth the cake with the warm spatula.

Here is where the cardboard comes in handy. Hold the cake up and use the other hand to press a thin rim of the toasted almonds all around the sides.

To decorate the cake with simple rosettes, fit a pastry bag with a 1/2-inch fluted tip (see page 64) and fill with the reserved buttercream. Hold the tip about 1/2 inch above the cake and squeeze. When the rosette is formed, move the tip quickly in a counterclockwise direction and quickly lift it away. Place a raspberry in the center of each one. Serve in wedges.

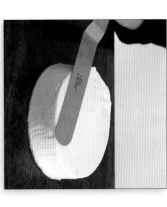

1. If you want the cake to have a perfectly delicate texture, trim off the crust on the top, bottom, and sides of the cake.

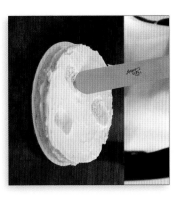

2. Use a serrated knife at least as long as the cake is wide to slice the cake crosswise into 3 equal layers.

3. Cut a round of cardboard about 1/2 inch more in diameter than the cake, so there is a 1/4-inch-wide circle surrounding the cake. Put a dollop of buttercream on the cardboard to hold the cake in place.

4. Put one of the cake layers in the center of the cardboard and brush with the flavored syrup.

5. Spread buttercream on the first and second layers. Check the thickness of the buttercream by making indentations with a metal spatula. The buttercream should be about 1/4 inch thick.

6. Put the final layer (the reserved bottom) on the cake, smooth side up, brush with syrup, and spread with buttercream.

7. Spread the buttercream over the top of the cake, working from the center outward, so that extra buttercream hangs over the edges. You'll use this to coat the sides.

8. Smooth the sides with a bench scraper or spatula and continue to spread buttercream on the sides. Scrape excess buttercream off the spatula into a little bowl to avoid getting crumbs in the main batch.

9. Continue alternating between smoothing off the sides and top of the cake until it is even and completely covered. If you wish, freeze the cake for 15 minutes and apply another thin layer of buttercream.

10. Heat a long metal spatula by dipping it in hot water or waving over a hot flame. Wipe the spatula dry if it's wet and smooth the cake with the warm spatula.

11. Hold the cake up and use your hand to stick a thin rim of toasted almonds all around the sides.

12. Decorate with buttercream rosettes (see page 65). Place a raspberry in the center of each rosette.

1. Use a cardboard template to cut the sheet cake into 3 rectangles.

2. If the sheet cake has a hard crust, trim it off to make the cake more delicate (optional).

3. Stack the cake rectangles on the cardboard rectangle and trim the edges so there's a 1/4-inch cardboard border around the cake.

4. Place the first rectangle on the cardboard and brush with the flavored simple syrup (optional). Syrup should ooze up around your finger when you press on the cake.

5. Seal the rectangle by spreading it with one-third of the apricot glaze (optional).

6. Spread about 1 cup buttercream on the rectangle with an offset spatula. A little bit of extra buttercream should ooze out the sides.

7. Continue layering the cake with syrup, glaze, and buttercream. Add the rest of the buttercream for the top and sides.

8. While frosting the top, allow a generous amount of buttercream to droop over the sides.

9. Continue smoothing the top and sides, taking turns between top and sides, until the cake is perfectly smooth.

10. Slowly pull a serrated knife toward you, with the blade against the top of the cake, while moving the knife gently from side to side, to leave a wavy impression on top of the icing.

11. Pipe buttercream along the edges of the cake (see page 65).

Orange Buttercream Layer Cake

You can make elegant rectangular cakes very simply by cutting a sheet cake into rectangles and stacking them. Because a rectangular cake is very easy to trim around the edges, it is easy to make the cake even and professional looking.

Here, several techniques are used to flavor the cake orange. The buttercream is flavored with orange zest and orange oil and the simple syrup is infused with orange rinds that have first been blanched to eliminate bitterness. Each layer is sealed with apricot glaze, but this is by no means essential. You may also flavor the simple syrup with the orange-flavored liqueur Grand Marnier.

MAKES ONE 3-LAYER 5 BY 11-INCH RECTANGULAR CAKE

2 cups simple syrup (page 36; optional)

2 oranges (optional)

3 tablespoons or more Grand Marnier (optional)

1 sheet cake 13 by 17 by 1/2 inch, such as butter-enriched sponge cake (page 16) or cream and butter sheet cake (page 29)

1 cup apricot glaze (see page 61), optional

6 cups orange buttercream (page 46)

If you are flavoring the syrup with orange zest, use a paring knife to cut the zest from the oranges, leaving as little of the white pith clinging to it as possible. Put the zest in a saucepan with enough water to cover, bring to a boil, and cook for 2 minutes. Drain and repeat.

Put the blanched zest in a saucepan with the simple syrup, bring to a simmer, cover, and let simmer for 15 minutes. Set aside to cool. Add the Grand Marnier to the cool syrup, whether it has been infused with orange zest or not.

Cut a cardboard rectangle 5 1/2 by 11 1/2 inches. Use this as a template to cut 3 rectangles crosswise from the sheet cake. If the rectangles have hard crusts, trim the crusts using a serrated knife. Stack the rectangles on the cardboard and trim all around until the sides and ends are even and there is a 1/4-inch border around the cardboard. Set the trimmed cake layers aside.

Place 1 cake rectangle on the cardboard and brush it with the flavored syrup. Keep brushing until syrup comes up around your finger when you press on the cake. Cover with about one-third of the apricot glaze. Spread about 1 cup buttercream over the glaze with an offset spatula. There should be a little oozing out the sides. Place a second layer on top of the first and repeat the syrup, glaze, and buttercream. Then add the third layer and repeat.

Spread the remaining buttercream over the top and sides of the cake with an offset spatula. Allow a fairly large amount to droop over the sides. Continue smoothing the top and sides, taking turns between top and sides, until the cake is perfectly smooth.

If you like, make a zigzag pattern in the frosting: Hold a serrated knife over the top of the cake on the end farthest from you. With the blade against the top of the cake, slowly pull the knife toward you while moving the knife gently from side to side. Pipe any remaining buttercream around the top and bottom of the cake with a pastry bag fitted with a fluted tip (see page 65).

To make round and separate rosettes, lift the bag up after squeezing out each rosette; for a wavelike effect, move the tip away from you while squeezing. Garnish with flowers, if you like.

Strawberry and White Chocolate Mousse Ladyfinger Cake

· ·

Some cakes are impossible to make without a cake ring or springform pan because the liquid filling needs to be held in place while it sets. Unlike springform pans, which have a base that holds the cake even after the sides of the spring-form pan are taken off, cake rings are just rings. To support the cake and seal it in the ring, you need to cut out a circle of cardboard that fits snugly into the bottom of the ring. It is also a good idea to line the ring with plastic wrap before you put in the cardboard to keep the filling from seeping out around the cardboard. If you're making a cake with an unusual size like the one here, you'll probably need to use a ring—rings come in all sizes—but springform pans are available for most of the more common cake sizes.

To finish this cake, you need two 12-inch strips of lady-fingers. The ladyfingers should be about 1/2 inch longer than your cake ring is high. You will also need at least one thin cake layer—you can use as many as you like but here I use one—as the base for the cake. It is convenient to make biscuit batter (page 14) and use it to pipe out the ladyfingers and a disk for the cake.

MAKES ONE 6½-INCH ROUND CAKE

1 biscuit cake disk 6½ by ½ inch (page 14)

2 strips ladyfingers (page 14), each 3 by 12 inches

1 cup simple syrup (page 36), flavored with Armagnac, Cognac, kirsch, or rum (optional)

3¾ cups white chocolate mousse (page 367)

8 to 10 large strawberries, stemmed (see page 86)

1 tablespoon strawberry glaze (page 61), or strawberry preserves (optional)

Have ready a 6½-inch cake ring. To support the cake disk in the ring, cut out a disk of cardboard that fits snugly inside the cake ring. Take it out of the ring. Trim off ½ inch all around the cake disk so there's room to fit the ends of the ladyfingers next to the cake.

Line the cake ring with a sheet of plastic wrap that's large enough to hang over the outside of the ring. This keeps any filling from leaking out and prevents the ladyfingers from sticking to the ring. Push the cardboard back into the ring so it is flush with the bottom. Put in the cake disk so there's a 1/2-inch space surrounding it and insert the strips of ladyfingers with the base in the space surrounding the cake disk. Make sure the ladyfingers reach all the way down to the bottom of the cake and touch the cardboard. Brush the cake disk and the inside wall of the ladyfingers with the simple syrup.

Ladle in the white chocolate mousse until it comes up to the height of the ring. Refrigerate the cake for at least 5 hours so the mousse can set.

Warm the outside of the ring with a hot, wet towel for about 30 seconds to help loosen the cake from the ring and push the cake up through the ring. Slice the strawberries and fan them around the perimeter of the mousse. Fan a second batch around the center of the mousse. Brush with the hot strawberry glaze or the preserves heated with 2 teaspoons of water.

VARIATION

You can make this cake in a standard 9-inch size. The cake shown here is small and elegant, but its unusual size requires a 6½-inch ring and an odd amount of mousse—1½ recipes. To make the cake in a standard 9-inch size, make a double recipe of biscuit batter and use half to pipe a 9-inch disk and the other half to pipe two 18-inch-long strips of ladyfingers for the sides. Use a triple recipe of white chocolate mousse and about double the other ingredients.

1. Peel the parchment paper away from the cake disk. Cut a round of cardboard just large enough to fit snugly in the cake ring.

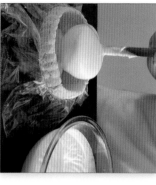

2. Trim the cake disk to the size of the cake ring, then trim around the cake disk with a pair of scissors so that it is 1 inch less in diameter than the cardboard.

3. Line the inside of the cake ring with plastic wrap, cardboard disk, and cake disk. Insert a strip of ladyfingers around the sides of the cake.

5. Lightly brush the cake disk and the insides of the ladyfingers with simple syrup.

6. Ladle in the mousse.

4. Insert another strip of ladyfingers in the cake and trim any excess from the end of one of the strips so that there is no overlap.

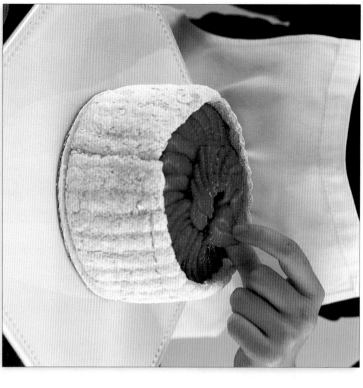

7. Refrigerate the cake, then loosen with a hot wet towel around the cake ring and gently push the cake up and out of the ring.

8. Arrange a ring of strawberries around the edge of the mousse.

9. Arrange the remaining strawberries in a ring going in the opposite direction from the first.

10. Brush the cake with hot glaze or preserves.

Dark Chocolate Mousse Cake

....

To give your cake a professional look, construct it in a springform pan the same size you used to bake the cake—you can wash out and use the one you baked the cake in. Take out the bottom and line the inside of the ring with plastic wrap, in case the bottom doesn't fit perfectly, which would cause the filling to leak if it is very liquid. Put the bottom back in and alternate the cake layers with layers of frosting. When the cake is assembled, chill it for a few hours or overnight, take it out of the mold, and peel away the plastic.

The cake shown here is made from 2 layer cakes, each cut in half crosswise to make 4 layers. The bottom 3 layers are covered with chocolate mousse. The top layer and sides of the cake can be covered with chocolate glaze, ganache, or chocolate buttercream.

MAKES ONE 4-LAYER 9-INCH ROUND CAKE

> **2 round chocolate sponge cakes 9 by 1½ inches (page 12)**
>
> **1½ cups simple syrup (page 36), flavored with coffee, rum, Cognac, or bourbon (optional)**
>
> **3 cups or slightly more chocolate mousse (page 366)**
>
> **3 cups chocolate or coffee buttercream (page 48), dark chocolate glaze (page 53), or ganache (page 50) (optional)**

Using a serrated knife, cut each of the cake layers in half crosswise, for a total of 4 layers. Reserve one of the bottom halves for the top of the cake. The smooth surface will make it easier to spread the buttercream.

Line the bottomless ring of a springform pan—the one you baked the cake in is fine—with plastic wrap and replace the metal bottom. Place 1 cake layer in the pan and brush it with ¼ to ⅓ cup simple syrup. Spread one-third of the mousse over it with an offset spatula, add a second cake layer, brush with syrup, cover with mousse as before, and repeat for the third layer. If the cake layers are fragile, use the bottom of another springform pan or a cardboard ring to support a layer as you move it.

Use the reserved bottom layer, turned over, as the top layer and brush with the syrup. Chill the cake in the springform pan for at least 30 minutes to firm up the mousse.

Run a knife around the inside of the springform pan and snap open and remove the ring and plastic wrap. Smooth the sides of the cake with a metal spatula. If using buttercream, dollop it on top of the cake and spread it evenly. With

a spatula, scrape up buttercream that accumulates around the edges of the cake and use it to frost the sides.

If using chocolate glaze or ganache, set the cake on a cake rack set on a sheet pan and pour just enough of the hot glaze or ganache over it to thinly coat the top and sides to create a first coat. Chill the cake for at least 15 minutes. Pour the remaining glaze over the cake. You may find it helps to hold the cake in one hand—the metal plate from the springform pan supports it—and gently rotate it, angling it here and there, so the glaze coats it evenly. Let cool for 30 minutes or so before serving. See page 73 for pictures of how to glaze.

ASSEMBLING A CAKE IN A SPRINGFORM PAN (DARK CHOCOLATE MOUSSE CAKE)

1. Put the first cake layer into the prepared pan and brush with the flavored simple syrup (optional). Spread over about one-third of the mousse with an offset spatula.

2. Insert a second cake layer. If the cake layers are fragile, use the bottom of another springform pan or a cardboard ring to support the layer as you move it.

3. Brush the second cake layer with the simple syrup and cover with mousse. Put on the third cake layer, brush with syrup, and cover with the rest of the mousse.

4. Take the cake out of the springform pan, add the final cake layer, and cover with frosting or glaze.

Mango Crème Mousseline Cake

Here, a cake ring is used to make a cake that is perfectly even on top and on the sides. The cake is then surrounded with little cat's tongue cookies and the top of the cake is decorated with a translucent mango mirror. The effect is very professional and the method adaptable to any fruit. Most recipes for mirrors call for half apricot preserves (or whatever preserves have the appropriate color) and half strained fruit purée (coulis). The jam provides pectin, which helps the mirror set without making it rubbery, as it would be if it were made with gelatin alone.

You can make the three cake disks called for here out of any of white or yellow cake by piping the batter into disks (see page 40) or by making a round layer cake and slicing it crosswise into thirds. This recipe is for an 8-inch cake, but if you don't have an 8-inch ring, you can make this cake in the standard 9-inch size by increasing the amounts of the simple syrup and mousse by about 50 percent.

MAKES ONE 3-LAYER 8-INCH ROUND CAKE

Three disks of any white or yellow cake, 8 by 1/3 inches

1 cup simple syrup (page 36), flavored with kirsch, rum, or Cognac (optional)

4 1/2 cups mango crème mousseline (page 58)

Mirror

2 teaspoons (2/3 packet) powdered unflavored gelatin

3 tablespoons cold water

1/3 cup strained mango puree

2/3 cup strained apricot preserves

Cookies

1 recipe cat's tongue cookies (page 263), about 1/2 inch longer than the cake ring is high

Line an 8-inch cake ring with plastic wrap and press in a cardboard round the same size as the ring, to support the cake. Trim the cake disks to the size of the cake ring by pressing the cake ring onto one of them and pulling away the excess, then trim off 1/2 inch all around the cake disks so there will be room to fit the end of the cookies and the filling will mask the outside of the cake—creating a perfectly smooth effect. Place one of the cake disks in the ring on top of the cardboard. Brush with the flavored simple syrup and spread over about one-third of the crème mousseline, spreading it all the way to the ring—you want the space between the ring and the cake layers to be filled with crème mousseline. Press on a second cake disk, brush with syrup, and coat with half of the remaining crème mousseline. Press on the third cake disk and brush with syrup. Spread over the remaining crème mousseline so it comes all the way to the top of the ring. Smooth the top with a metal spatula. Chill for at least 1 hour.

To make the mirror, put the gelatin in a small bowl with the water and let sit for about 10 minutes, or until it swells, or blooms, and absorbs the water. Stir the softened gelatin with a fork to get rid of any lumps.

Combine the gelatin mixture with the mango puree and apricot preserves in a small saucepan and bring to a simmer. Remove from the heat and stir until the gelatin dissolves. Let cool until barely warm—hot enough so the gelatin doesn't set but not hot enough to melt the crème mousseline.

Pour the mango mixture over the cake and spread it with an offset or metal spatula. Chill until set, at least 3 hours. Trim off any gelatin that has dripped over the edge of the cake ring.

When the cake is thoroughly chilled, warm the outside of the ring with a hot, wet towel for about 30 seconds to help loosen the cake from the ring and push the cake up through the ring.

Press the cookies onto the sides of the cake. If they don't stick, press a hot spatula against the sides of the cake to melt the crème mousseline slightly and immediately press on a cookie. Serve in wedges.

1. Trim the cake disks to the size of the cake ring. Cut out a round of cardboard just large enough to fit snugly in the cake ring.

2. Cut away another 1/4 inch around the sides of the cake disks.

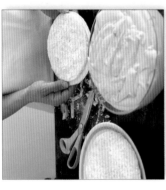

3. Use the first cake disk you cut to size as a template to cut the remaining disks the same size.

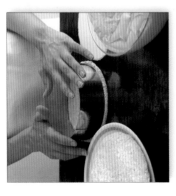

4. Press the cardboard into the ring and place the first cake disk on top of the cardboard. Brush it with flavored syrup (optional) to moisten it.

5. Dollop about one-third of the crème mousseline on top of the first cake disk and spread it evenly all the way to the ring.

6. Place over the second cake disk, brush with flavored syrup, and spread with half of the remaining crème mousseline.

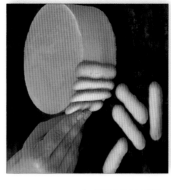

7. Place over the third cake disk and brush with the syrup.

8. Spread the crème mousseline evenly over the top of the cake. Chill for at least 3 hours before taking the cake out of the mold or at least 1 hour before decorating it with a mirror.

9. Prepare the mirror mixture and pour over the chilled cake.

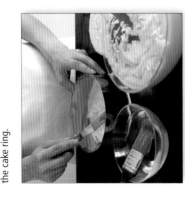

10. Spread the mirror mixture over the top of the cake with an offset spatula. Chill for at least 3 hours more to allow the mirror to set.

11. Unmold the cake by pressing it up through the cake ring. If it's stubborn and doesn't want to come loose, wrap the outside of the ring for 30 seconds with a towel soaked in hot water.

12. Press the cookies, overlapping slightly, against the sides of the cake.

BAKING

Making a Caramel Cage

Small cakes and other desserts look dramatic when covered with a little caramel dome.

1. Rub the outside of a metal bowl with vegetable oil. Prepare the caramel (see page 356).

2. Immediately after dipping the bottom of the caramel pan in water, pour the caramel in thin streams over the bowl and allow to cool for 5 minutes.

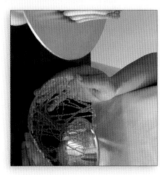

3. Gently nudge the dome off the bowl.

4. If the dome is smaller than the cake, place it on top; if it is large enough, place it over the cake or over individual servings.

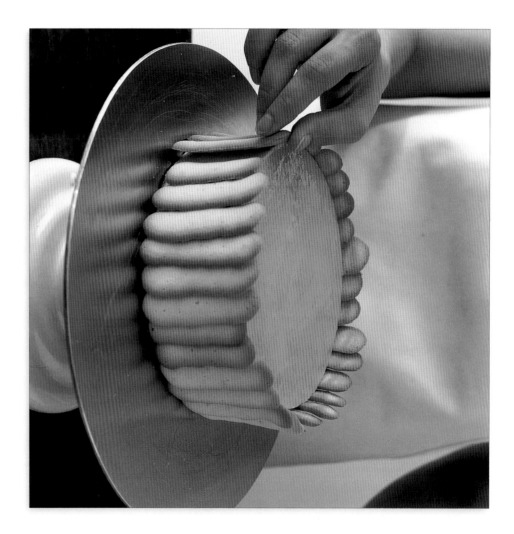

1. Cut out a round of cardboard to fit in the cake ring, or use a springform pan. Line ring or pan with plastic wrap. Press the cardboard into the cake ring so it rests flush with the bottom or put the bottom back in the springform pan.

2. Slice the tops off the cakes, then slice each cake crosswise into 2 layers.

3. Start by placing a cake layer on the cardboard or in the springform pan. Brush the layer with simple syrup (optional).

4. Spread over a layer of stabilized whipped cream, one-third of the cherries, then more whipped cream.

Chocolate Cherry Cake with White Chocolate Glaze

This cake, constructed in a ring but finished by hand, consists of four layers of devil's food cake separated with layers of stabilized whipped cream and frozen or bottled cherries. You can also use fresh cherries, but they must be cooked first with a little sugar and water. To obtain the four layers for this cake, bake two devil's food layer cakes. Slice the tops off the cakes so the cake is perfectly flat when you apply the glaze. Process the tops in a food processor to provide you with the crumbs needed to decorate the sides.

MAKES ONE 4-LAYER 9-INCH ROUND CAKE

2 round devil's food cakes 9 by 1 inch (page 30)

1½ cups simple syrup (page 36), flavored with kirsch (optional)

4 cups stabilized whipped cream (page 62)

One 12-ounce package sweet frozen cherries, thawed, or one 12-ounce bottle, drained

1 cup white chocolate glaze (page 53)

Have ready a 9-inch cake ring or a 9-inch springform pan. If using a cake ring, cut out a cardboard round to fit inside the cake ring, line the ring with plastic wrap, and press in the cardboard. If using a springform pan, take out the bottom, line the empty ring with plastic, and put the bottom back in so the plastic covers the sides on the inside but is on the outside on the bottom.

Cut the tops off the cakes so the cakes are perfectly flat on top. Process the tops to make crumbs. Using a serrated knife, cut each of the cake layers in half crosswise, for a total of 4 layers. Reserve one of the bottom halves for the top of the cake. The smooth surface will make it easier to spread the whipped cream.

Place one of the cake halves in the cake ring or pan and brush it with the syrup. Spread a layer of whipped cream over it, add one-third of the cherries, and spread over a little more whipped cream. Repeat with two more cake halves, then the reserved bottom cake half, turned over, as the top layer. Spread a thin layer of whipped cream over the top of the cake to seal it. Chill for at least 2 hours.

Wrap a hot wet towel around the cake—hold it against the ring for 30 seconds—and push the cake up out of the ring and remove the plastic wrap. Slide the ring back over the cake but don't push it all the way down—let a small part of the ring stay above the top of the cake to hold in the glaze. Pour the glaze on the center of the cake. Rotate the cake so the glaze covers the top evenly. Chill for 30 minutes to set the glaze.

If there is any excess glaze around the outside of the ring, slide a knife around the ring to cut away the excess. Push the cake up through the ring. While holding the cake with one hand, use the other hand to smooth off the sides with additional whipped cream using a metal spatula. Still holding the cake with one hand, gently press cake crumbs against the sides of the cake with the other hand. Serve in wedges.

5. Repeat with another cake layer, more syrup, and more whipped cream. Sprinkle over half of the remaining cherries, more whipped cream, and another cake layer.

6. Spread over whipped cream, the remaining cherries, and more whipped cream.

7. Place the last cake layer. If it sticks up above the ring, cut across it so it is flat and level with the ring.

8. Spread a thin layer of stabilized whipped cream over the top of the cake to seal it. Chill for at least 2 hours.

9. Push the cake up out of the ring and remove the plastic wrap.

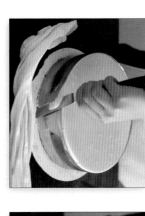

10. Slide the ring back over the cake but don't push it all the way down—let a small part of the ring surround the top of the cake to hold in the glaze.

11. Pour the glaze over the center of the cake.

12. Rotate the cake so the glaze covers the top evenly. Chill for 30 minutes to set the glaze.

13. Slide a knife around the ring to cut away any excess glaze.

14. Push the cake up through the ring.

15. Hold the cake with one hand and use the other hand to smooth off the sides with additional stabilized whipped cream.

16. Gently press cake crumbs against the sides of the cake.

Classic Strawberry-Marzipan Cake (Fraisier)

This is a striking, colorful cake with red strawberries, white cake, and a green marzipan topping. There are lots of steps, and while the marzipan topping is easy to roll out and put on, you can skip it if you like. The top of this cake is finished with a sheet of marzipan—an easy way to make elegant, very even, and professional-looking cakes. Green marzipan is traditional, but any color will do.

A square cake—a lovely change from the usual rounds—makes an elegant impression. This recipe is for one of the great classic French cakes, fraisier, but you can make square cakes using any cake, fillings, or frostings you like. To assemble a square cake, you need a metal cake square or a square springform pan. Here we show an adjustable cake square, but if you plan on baking square cakes mainly of a certain size, a nonadjustable square or springform pan is less expensive and easier to work with. An 8-inch or smaller square is convenient because a 13 by 17-inch sheet cake will give you two 8-inch square cake layers.

The filling for this cake is a classic crème mousseline flavored with kirsch, although in an ideal world, we'd use dry strawberry brandy—eau de vie de fraise—but it's almost impossible to find in the United States. If you already have 3½ cups pastry cream on hand, beat 1¾ cups butter into it to make your crème mousseline. There are several flavoring alternatives to kirsch, including mirabelle, which is French plum brandy, and eau de vie de framboise, which is French raspberry brandy.

Crème mousseline

5½ cups classic crème mousseline (page 57) made using these amounts:

2½ cups milk

2 teaspoons vanilla extract

½ cup plus 2 tablespoons sugar

2 eggs

2 egg yolks

¼ cup plus 2 tablespoons cornstarch

1½ cups plus 4 tablespoons butter, cubed or sliced

3 to 5 tablespoons kirsch, mirabelle, eau de vie de framboise, Cognac, or strained strawberry puree

1 sheet cake 13 by 17 by ½ inch, such as butter-enriched sponge cake (page 16) or cream and butter sheet cake (page 29)

1½ cups simple syrup (page 36), flavored with kirsch, Cognac, or strawberry puree

25 large strawberries, about 1 pound total, stemmed

1 square green marzipan 9 by ⅛ inch (page 109)

Royal icing (page 67), optional

Prepare the classic crème mousseline with the ingredients listed above.

Have ready an 8-inch cake square or an 8-inch square springform pan. Cut out a square of cardboard to fit snugly into the cake square. Cut the sheet cake into two 8½-inch

Hulling and Slicing Strawberries

To remove the stem from a strawberry without wasting any of the fruit, use a paring knife. Insert a paring knife into the top of the strawberry, next to the stem. While holding the knife, rotate the strawberry with the other hand until the stem comes away. Slice the strawberry vertically for decorating.

square layers, using the cardboard as a template. (The cake is cut slightly large so it fits snugly in the mold.) Fit the cardboard into the bottom of the cake square.

Place one of the cake layers in the cake square. Brush with the simple syrup.

Sort through the strawberries to select 15 of similar size; reserve two strawberries for the top. Trim off the bottoms so they stay flat and are the same height. Reserve the bottom pieces to use in the filling. Cut the 15 strawberries vertically in half. Reserve those strawberries you don't use. Arrange the halved strawberries with their pointed tips on top and the flat side facing out and pressed against the side of the cake square. Continue until you've lined all 4 sides of the cake square, which should take about 15 strawberries (slice more if you need to). When the cake square is completely lined with strawberries, use an offset spatula to spread in enough crème mousseline to come almost all the way up to the top of the strawberries. Press the crème mousseline against the strawberries to fill any gaps along the sides of the cake square.

Chop the strawberry bottoms and any leftover strawberries—except the two reserved for the top—and spread these over the crème mousseline. Add more crème mousseline and press down against the strawberries to fill in any gaps between the strawberries along the sides of the cake. You should have about ½ cup crème mousseline remaining for the top of the cake.

Place the other cake layer on top and brush with the syrup. Ideally, there should be about ½ inch of space from the top of the cake to the top of the cake square to provide room for another thin layer of crème mousseline and the marzipan. Spread over the remaining crème mousseline.

Roll the marzipan up onto a rolling pin. Brush off any sugar clinging to the marzipan. Unroll the marzipan over the top of the cake as you would a sheet of pastry. Cut around the cake to trim the marzipan. If you like, decorate with royal icing. Place the two reserved strawberries on top. Chill for 4 hours. Remove the cake square by warming it with a hot, wet towel for 30 seconds and lifting it up off the cake.

Note: To store cakes that you've already cut into, press plastic wrap around any exposed edges and place in the refrigerator.

Making and Using a Paper Cone

1. Fold a square of parchment paper in half on the diagonal. Cut it in two across the fold so you end up with two triangles.

2. Lift one of the pointier tips of one the triangles (marked "A") and curve it under so that the tip of a cone begins to form along the long length (hypotenuse) of the paper triangle.

3. Lift up the opposing pointy tip (marked "C") and curve it around the first cone you formed.

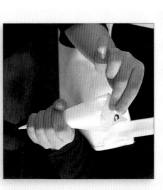

4. Line up all the tips of the triangles and pick up the cone between your thumb and forefinger.

5. Fold the tips down into the cone.

6. Fill the cone and fold one corner down, then fold over the folds. To use, snip off the tip to let the filling flow out.

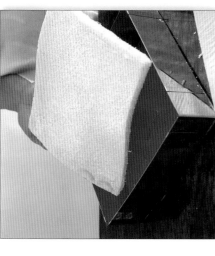

1. Cut out a cardboard square just large enough to fit in the cake square.

2. Cut out two square layers of sheet cake.

3. Put the cardboard in the cake square and gently place a cake layer on the cardboard. Brush the cake with simple syrup.

4. Place the halved strawberries around the sides of the mold, with the flat side facing out.

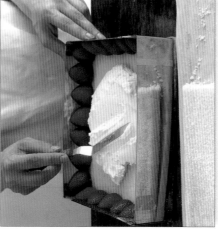

5. Spread the filling almost to the height of the strawberries. Push it firmly against the strawberries so there are no gaps when you unmold the cake.

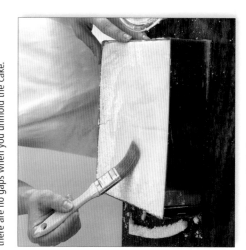

6. Spread chopped strawberries over the filling.

7. Cover the chopped strawberries with more filling.

8. Place the second cake layer on top and brush with simple syrup.

9. Spread the top of the cake with a thin layer of filling to hold the marzipan in place. Run the spatula along the sides of the mold so the filling comes evenly to the edge.

10. Roll out the marzipan on a work surface dusted with confectioners' sugar.

11. Roll the marzipan up onto a rolling pin. Brush off any sugar clinging to the marzipan.

12. Unroll the marzipan over the cake.

13. Cut around the cake mold, detaching extra marzipan.

14. Refrigerate the cake for at least 4 hours. To unmold, warm the outside of the ring and push the cake, with its cardboard base, up through the ring.

15. Decorate with royal icing using a paper cone (see page 87) and the 2 reserved strawberries.

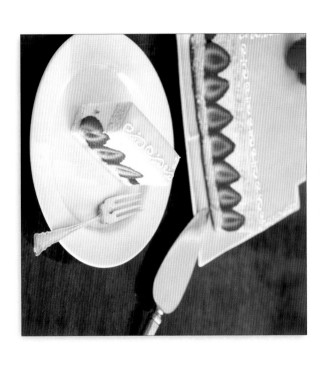

Whipped Cream–Covered Chocolate Chestnut Cake

. . . .

This cake shows how you can create a dramatic effect by using more than one kind of filling in each layer. A ring of stabilized whipped cream is piped around the edges of each of the cake layers and filled the inside of the layers with chestnut filling. When the cake is sliced, the two fillings are visible on the sides. While not an issue here, this method is also useful if you have a somewhat runny filling that needs to firm up in the cake—it is held in place by the ring of stiffer mixture. The cake is decorated with tubes of stabilized whipped cream and chopped chocolate or chocolate meringue logs.

MAKES ONE 4-LAYER 9-INCH ROUND CAKE

2 round chocolate sponge cakes 9 by 1½ inches (page 12)

1½ cups simple syrup (page 36), flavored with coffee, bourbon, rum, or Cognac (optional)

6 cups stabilized whipped cream (page 62)

3 cups chestnut cream cake filling (page 64)

4 ounces bittersweet chocolate, chopped, or enough chocolate meringue logs to cover the sides of the cake (page 41), optional

Have ready a 9-inch cake ring or a 9-inch springform pan. If using a cake ring, cut out a cardboard round to fit inside the cake ring, line the ring with plastic wrap, and press in the cardboard. If using a springform pan, take out the bottom, line the empty ring with plastic, and put the bottom back in so the plastic covers the sides on the inside but is on the outside on the bottom. Using a serrated knife, cut each of the cake layers in half crosswise, for a total of 4 layers. Reserve one of the bottom halves for the top of the cake. The smooth surface will make it easier to spread the buttercream.

Place the first cake layer on the bottom of the ring or pan and brush with the simple syrup. Fit a pastry bag with a ½-inch plain tip, fill with the whipped cream, and pipe a ring of whipped cream around the perimeter of the cake. Spread about 1 cup of the chestnut filling over the layer within the boundaries made by the whipped cream. Continue stacking and layering the cake in this way until you have 3 layers, each with a ring of whipped cream and covered with filling. Use the reserved cake bottom, upside down, for the top of the cake. Make sure there is no chestnut mixture on the sides of the cake.

To take the cake out of a cake ring, wrap a hot, wet towel around the cake ring for 30 seconds and then push the cake up through the ring. Smooth the edges with a metal spatula dipped in hot water and wiped dry. For a cake in a springform pan, release the ring and lift off.

Spread a thin layer of whipped cream over and around the cake. Fit the pastry bag with a ¾-inch plain tip, fill the bag with the remaining whipped cream, and pipe strips across the top of the cake. Smooth the ends with a spatula.

To decorate the cake with chopped chocolate, hold the chocolate in one hand and the cake in the other and press the edge of the cake against the chocolate.

To decorate the cake with meringue logs, break the logs into pieces ranging from ½ inch to 2 inches longer than the cake is high—this creates a more attractive effect than if the logs are all the same size—and press the logs against the sides of the cake. For a professional touch, wrap the cake with a satin ribbon.

1. Slice each layer cake into 2 layers and place the first cake layer on a ring of cardboard.

2. Pipe a ring of stabilized whipped cream along the edges of the cake layer.

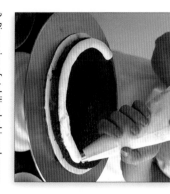

3. Spread 1 cup of the chestnut filling in the center and up to the ring around the cake layer.

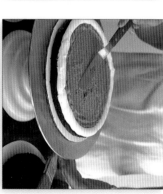

4. Place the second and third cake layers, piping rings of whipped cream and spreading with chestnut filling.

5. Put on the last cake layer—ideally, the bottom of one of the cakes—and spread with whipped cream.

6. Spread the tops and sides with a thin layer of whipped cream.

7. With a ³⁄₄-inch plain pastry tip, pipe strips of whipped cream over the top of the cake.

8. Smooth off the ends of the whipped cream strips with a spatula.

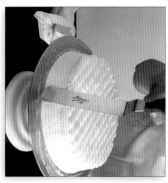

9. Decorate the sides with chopped chocolate . . .

10. . . . or surround the cake with chocolate meringue logs.

Strawberry Bavarian Cake

. . . .

Because Bavarian creams are runny before they set, and you're including one as part of this cake, you have to assemble the cake in something that won't leak. The springform pan is lined with plastic wrap so none of the Bavarian cream mixture can leak out or stick to the pan. The cake layers are made by slicing a 1- to 1½-inch-thick layer cake crosswise into 4 rounds with a long serrated knife. Getting all four layers to come out with no tears can be tricky, but tears don't matter much because the cake layers are so thin no one will notice—just arrange the broken pieces as best you can. You can also just cut the layer cake into 2 or 3 rounds, and add more Bavarian cream between each layer. The sugar syrup brushed on each layer makes the cake especially moist—and it allows you to use a cake that has been frozen or gotten a little stale—but it isn't essential. It is convenient when constructing this cake to add the Bavarian cream with a 1-cup ladle so you can see at a glance how much you're using. The cake is finished with a raspberry mirror.

MAKES ONE 4-LAYER 9-INCH ROUND CAKE

1 layer cake 9 by 1 to 1½ inches, such as genoise (page 8)

1½ cups simple syrup (page 36), flavored with kirsch or other flavoring (optional)

6½ cups strawberry Bavarian cream (page 56)

Mirror

2 teaspoons (²/₃ packet) powdered unflavored gelatin

3 tablespoons cold water

²/₃ cup raspberry jam

¹/₃ cup raspberry puree

1 tablespoon kirsch (optional)

Decoration

1 cup cake crumbs or chopped nuts

Have ready a 9-inch cake ring or a 9-inch springform pan. If using a cake ring, cut out a cardboard round to fit inside the cake ring, line the ring with plastic wrap, and press in the cardboard. If using a springform pan, take out the bottom, line the empty ring with plastic, and put the bottom back in so the plastic covers the sides on the inside but is on the outside on the bottom.

Using a serrated knife, cut the cake layer in half crosswise, and cut each half in half, for a total of 4 layers (see Note). Reserve the bottom half for the top of the cake. The flat surface will make it easier to make a smooth mirror.

Place one cake layer in the springform pan or cake ring, brush it thoroughly with the simple syrup, and ladle in 1½ cups of the Bavarian cream. Put in the second layer, brush with syrup, and add another 1½ cups Bavarian cream. Repeat with the third layer. Use the reserved bottom layer, turned over, as the top layer, brush with syrup, and add the remaining Bavarian cream, about 2 cups. Chill for at least 1 hour.

To make the mirror, put the gelatin and water in a small bowl and let sit for about 10 minutes, or until it swells, or blooms, and absorbs the water. Stir the softened gelatin with a fork to get rid of any lumps. Combine the jam and puree in a small saucepan and heat slightly. Add the gelatin and stir until smooth. Let cool until warm but not hot and add the kirsch. Strain the mirror mixture and pour it over the cold cake to form the mirror. Rotate the cake so the mirror mixture forms an even coating. Place in the refrigerator for at least 4 hours, or until thoroughly chilled and set.

If using a springform pan, remove the cake from the pan. If using a cake ring, warm the outside of the ring with a hot, wet towel for about 30 seconds to help loosen the Bavarian cream from the ring and push the cake up through the ring. Decorate the sides of the cake with cake crumbs. To slice the cake, dip the knife in hot water, wipe it dry, and cut into wedges.

Note: If you can't manage to split the cake into 4 layers, increase the amount of Bavarian cream between each layer so you use it all up.

1. Line the bottom of a springform pan with a sheet of plastic wrap. Place a round of cardboard in the ring and put in the first cake layer. Brush the cake layer with the simple syrup.

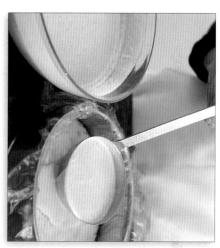

2. Ladle in 1½ cups of the Bavarian cream.

3. Continue assembling, using the rest of the Bavarian cream to finish the top. Chill for at least 1 hour before applying the mirror.

4. Combine the jam and puree in a small saucepan and heat just slightly. Add the softened gelatin and stir until smooth. Let cool until warm but not hot and add the kirsch.

5. Prepare and strain the mirror mixture and pour it over the cold cake.

6. Rotate the cake so the mirror mixture forms an even coating. Chill to set.

7. Take the chilled cake out of the springform pan and decorate its sides with cake crumbs or chopped nuts.

8. To slice the cake, dip a knife in hot water, wipe it dry, and cut the cake into wedges.

FILLING AND GLAZING INDIVIDUAL
CHOCOLATE MERINGUE CAKES

1. Use a pastry bag to pipe a layer of whipped ganache on half of the disks.

2. Place the remaining meringue disks—smooth side facing out—on top of those with the filling.

3. Use any extra whipped ganache to smooth off the sides of the disks.

4. Pour just enough hot ganache over the meringue cakes to coat the top and sides.

5. Smooth the hot ganache over the top and sides of each of the cakes.

6. If you prefer, sift cocoa powder over the top and sides of the cakes instead of the hot ganache.

7. If you've used hot ganache, you can coat the sides of the cakes with chopped nuts.

Individual Chocolate Meringue Cakes

Whipped ganache is sandwiched between two disks of meringue and the individual meringue cakes are glazed with liquid ganache. When coating cakes or other desserts with hot glaze, work over a sheet of parchment paper so that you can reuse any glaze that drips off the cakes. You can also coat the cakes with cocoa powder instead of hot ganache.

MAKES 6 INDIVIDUAL MERINGUE CAKES

1¼ cups whipped chocolate ganache (page 51)

Twelve 3½-inch meringue disks (page 39)

1¾ cups hot ganache (page 50), or 3 tablespoons cocoa powder

1 cup chopped nuts (optional)

Fit a pastry bag with a ¼-inch plain tip, fill with the whipped chocolate ganache, and pipe a layer of the ganache on each of 6 meringue disks. Press the remaining disks on top of the ganache, bottom side up for a smoother surface. Use any extra filling to smooth the sides of the cakes.

Put the cakes on a rack set over a sheet pan. If using hot ganache, pour it over the cakes and spread it while it is still hot with a small offset spatula. Use just enough to coat the top and sides. Save any ganache that drips off the cakes and reuse it. With your hand, press chopped nuts against the sides of the cakes. If you're using cocoa powder, sift it over the tops and sides of the cakes using a strainer.

Chocolate Mousse Dome Cake

. . . .

If you want to create real drama and impress guests, make this cake in the shape of a dome. The dome is covered with slices of rolled cake which is filled with chocolate mousse. You can use any cake you like for the inside layers, but for the rolled layers you need a cake that's flexible and suitable for rolling, such as butter-enriched sponge cake (page 16).

MAKES ONE 9-INCH DOME CAKE

1 round cake layer at least 9 inches in diameter, no more than 1/2 inch thick

1 sheet cake 13 by 17 inches and no more than 1/2 inch thick, suitable for rolling (pages 10, 16, 20, or 22)

1 cup simple syrup (page 36), flavored with kirsch or other flavoring

One 12-ounce jar apricot or other fruit jam, or 3 cups buttercream, crème mousseline, or other filling

2 tablespoons water

6 cups filling, such as chocolate mousse (page 366), Bavarian cream (page 56), or crème d'or (page 52)

Apricot glaze (see page 61) for brushing the outside of the dome (optional)

Whipped cream (page 62) for decorating (optional)

Use a 2 1/2 to 3-quart bowl about 9 inches in diameter— 1/2 inch one way or the other won't matter. Use the bowl as a template to cut the round cake layer to fit the top of the bowl. If the sheet cake is too stiff to roll, brush it lightly with the simple syrup and cover it with a moist towel for 10 minutes.

Heat the jam in a saucepan with the water until hot but not boiling, and strain. Spread the sheet cake with the strained jam. Roll the cake by pinching along the length of one of the short ends and gradually rolling (see page 106 for photos). As you roll, you may find it helpful to lift the parchment paper on your end. Alternate between pressing, squeezing, and rolling. Roll as tightly as you can. When the cake is rolled, tuck the parchment paper under it and push against the roll with the side of your hand, tightening it as much as possible without causing the filling to ooze out the ends.

Line the bowl with plastic wrap. First, sprinkle the bowl with a little water to get the plastic to cling. With a bread knife, slice the rolled cake into 1/2-inch-thick rounds. Don't slice any thicker than this or you may not have enough to cover the bowl. Arrange the rounds in the bowl, starting at the bottom, until you've completely covered the plastic. As you near the edge of the bowl, there may not be room for whole rounds; just trim a little off the sides to make them smaller and finish the cake with these.

Fill the cake-lined bowl with chocolate mousse. Leave room in the bowl for the round cake layer.

Trim the round cake layer so it is just large enough to fit in the bowl, on top of the filling, but inside the rolls so it is not visible when you unmold the cake. Brush with syrup, if desired. Place the cake in the bowl over the filling and inside the layer of cake rolls. Chill for at least 5 hours and turn it out over a serving dish.

Peel away the plastic. If you like, brush with glaze and decorate with whipped cream.

1. Use a bowl to cut out a cake round. Line the inside of the bowl with plastic wrap.

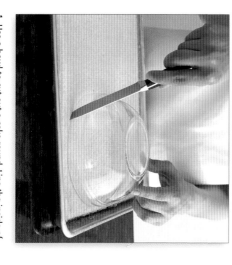

2. Use a bread knife to slice rounds from the rolled cake. Line the inside of the bowl with the rolled cake rounds. Push the rounds together so there are no spaces in between.

3. Fill the lined bowl with the mousse or other filling.

4. Trim the cake round so that it fits on top of the filling and is not visible from the outside. Brush the cake round with flavored syrup (optional).

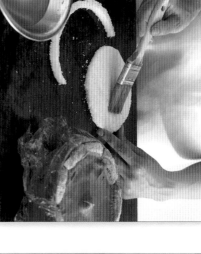

5. Press the cake round in the bowl over the filling. Chill for at least 5 hours.

6. Before serving or decorating, brush the cake with apricot glaze.

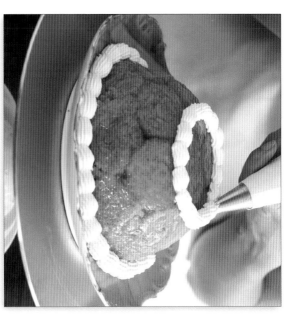

7. Decorate the cake with whipped cream just before serving.

1. Measure a sheet cake so you can cut it crosswise into 4 rectangles all approximately 4 by 11 inches.

2. Spread the top of the rectangle with the jam.

3. Cut the sheet cake into 4 rectangles as measured. Stack the rectangles on top of each other and slice them lengthwise in half so you end up with 2 strips, each approximately 2 by 11 inches. Trim the sides and ends of the strips and slice the strips into 1/2-inch-thick squares.

4. Arrange the cake squares, on their sides, along the inside of a cake ring lined with a cardboard disk and plastic wrap.

5. Place a cake disk, slightly smaller than the cardboard ring, inside the lined cake ring.

6. Brush the cake with the simple syrup and spread over a 1/2-inch layer of crème mousseline.

7. Put in the second cake disk and brush with simple syrup.

8. Fill the cake ring with the rest of the peach crème mousseline and smooth off the top. Chill for at least 3 hours.

9. Wrap a hot, wet towel around the ring to loosen the cake.

10. Push the cake up through the ring.

11. Heat a spatula in hot water or by waving it for a few seconds over a hot flame. Smooth the sides of the cake with the hot spatula.

12. Shortly before serving, arrange skewers or chopsticks on top of the cake. Sprinkle with confectioners' sugar.

Peach Crème Mousseline Cake

In this elegant cake, slices of one cake are used to make the sides for another. You'll need a cake ring or springform pan to hold the cake slices and filling in place. This recipe uses only two cake layers and enough peach crème mousseline to fill up the cake ring, but you can use as many cake layers as you like and stack them with other fillings, such as Bavarian cream or white chocolate mousse. It is most convenient to make two sheet cakes and use one to make the squares for lining the cake and the other to make the circular layers.

MAKES ONE 2-LAYER 9½-INCH ROUND CAKE

1 cup raspberry jam

2 sheet cakes 11 by 16 by ½ inch, such as vanilla butter cake (page 31) or fluffy light butter cake (page 28)

⅔ cup flavored simple syrup (page 36), optional

6 cups peach crème mousseline (page 58)

Confectioners' sugar for sprinkling

Have ready a 9½-inch cake ring or springform pan. If using a cake ring, cut out a cardboard round to fit inside the cake ring, line the ring with plastic wrap, and press in the cardboard. If using a springform pan, take out the bottom, line the empty ring with plastic, and put the bottom back in so the plastic covers the sides on the inside but is on the outside on the bottom.

If desired, heat the jam in a small saucepan, then strain. Spread 1 sheet cake with the jam and cut it crosswise into four rectangles, each 4 by 11 inches. Stack the rectangles so you have 1 cake with 4 layers with jam between each layer and on the top. Slice the cake in two lengthwise so you now have two 2 by 11-inch rectangles. Trim the edges of the rectangles to make them even.

Slice the cake rectangles into ½-inch squares and arrange them, on their sides—so the layers go up and down—along the inside wall of the cake ring or springform pan.

Out of the second sheet cake, cut two cake rounds, just large enough to fit inside the cake-lined ring or pan. Place a cake round in the cake ring or pan and press it against the cardboard so it presses up against the squares of cake and helps hold them in place. Brush it with the simple syrup. Spread over a ½-inch layer of crème mousseline. Put in the second cake round, brush with syrup, and add enough filling to come all the way to the top of the cake ring. Smooth off the top of the cake with a metal spatula dipped in hot water and wiped dry. Chill the cake for at least 3 hours.

To take the cake out of a cake ring, wrap a hot, wet towel around the cake ring for 30 seconds and then push the cake up through the ring. Smooth the edges with a metal spatula dipped in hot water and wiped dry. For a cake in a springform pan, release the ring and lift off.

Shortly before serving, arrange skewers or chopsticks on top of the cake. Sprinkle with confectioners' sugar, then take away the skewers. Serve the finished cake in wedges.

SHEET CAKES

Sheet cakes are used in 3 ways: as simple cakes covered with frosting and served in rectangles; cut into smaller rectangles and stacked to make square or rectangular layer cakes; and rolled up into a rolled cake.

If you're serving a sheet cake as a simple cake covered with frosting, you'll need to bake a cake about 1 inch thick. To make the cake, double a recipe for one 1/2-inch-thick sheet cake and put all the batter into 1 sheet pan. Bake the cake in a 350°F oven for about 25 minutes, or until it springs back to the touch.

To make a rectangular layer cake, cut a sheet cake about 1/2 inch thick into rectangles (3 is usually a good number) (see page 76) and stack them with filling in between.

Any recipe for a traditional round cake can be converted to a sheet cake; just keep in mind that a recipe for a round cake 9 by 1 1/2 inches will make a sheet cake 15 by 17 by 1/2 inch. Sheet cakes 1/2 inch thick bake in about half the time as round cakes—15 minutes instead of 30. They should also be baked at a higher temperature—375°F instead of 350°F—so they cook quickly before they have a chance to dry out.

You can bake sheet cakes in buttered and floured sheet pans, but there is always a risk of the cake sticking and tearing. It is safer to line the sheet pan with parchment paper (preferably) or waxed paper (if you don't mind a trace of wax in your cake). Have ready another sheet of parchment paper the same size as the cake and dust it with confectioners' sugar, which prevents sticking. When the sheet cake comes out of the oven, turn it out immediately onto the prepared parchment paper. As soon as you flip the cake over, peel away the parchment paper that the cake was baked on.

How to Make a Sheet Cake

Spread the cake batter onto a parchment paper–lined 13 by 17-inch sheet pan. There is no need to butter or flour the sheet pan or the paper. Use an offset spatula to spread the cake batter in an even layer. Use your thumb to make a moat around the cake to keep the batter from sticking to the sides of the sheet pan.

Bake at 375°F for about 15 minutes, or until the cake springs back to the touch or a toothpick inserted in the center comes out clean. Check the cake when half of the cooking time is up to see if it is browning evenly; if not, rotate the pan in the oven.

While the cake is baking, sprinkle a sheet of parchment paper at least the same size as the cake with confectioners' sugar to keep the cake from sticking to it.

When the cake is done, turn the cake out onto the sheet of parchment paper and immediately start peeling away the cooked parchment paper from the bottom of the cake. Trim off any dried-out edges from the sheet cake.

To cover a sheet cake with a 1/4-inch-thick layer of frosting, you will need 4 cups of frosting.

1. Spread the cake batter onto parchment paper–lined sheet pans.

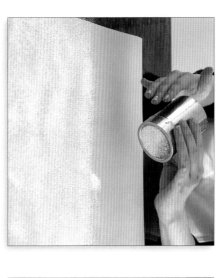

2. Use an offset spatula to spread the cake batter in an even layer on the sheet pan.

3. Use your thumb to make a moat around the cake. Bake until a toothpick comes out clean.

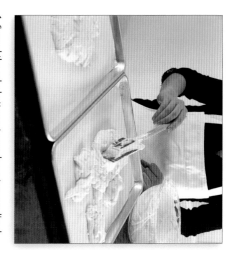

4. While the cake is baking, sprinkle a sheet of parchment paper with confectioners' sugar to keep the cake from sticking to the work surface.

5. When the cake is done, turn the sheet pan over onto the sheet of parchment paper and immediately start peeling away the cooked parchment paper.

6. Trim off any dried-out edges from the sheet cake.

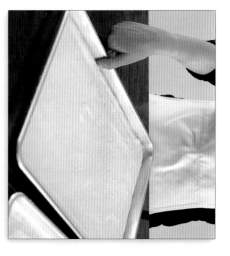

Miniature Cake Petits Fours

A petit four can be virtually any miniature sweet thing—never more than a bite or two—usually served after dinner with coffee. Professional pastry chefs divide petits fours into two types: dry petits fours, which are really just miniature cookies, and fresh petits fours, which are miniature cakes or tarts. The miniature cakes are presented here, and two other fresh petits fours can be found in chapter 2—one kind consists of miniature pastry shells cooked with a fruit filling (see page 203), the other uses prebaked shells as holders for fruit curds, raw fruits, and white and dark chocolate ganache (see page 202).

These luxurious miniature cakes are time consuming to make, but delightful to look at and fun to eat—they're perfect for an elegant party. An almond paste sponge cake is used here, but any sheet cake will do; the finished cake should be about 3/8 inch thick. Fondant is the classic icing for these kinds of petits fours, and apricot glaze is the classic filling. Buttercream is used to seal the tops and sides of the petits fours before they're coated with fondant. Petits fours are iced by dipping them individually in fondant or by pouring the fondant over the petits fours arranged on a cake rack set over a sheet pan. Both methods are shown here. Classic recipes for petits fours call for brushing the cake with simple syrup flavored with some kind of spirit, but this isn't essential.

MAKES 80 PETITS FOURS

Simple syrup (optional)

1/2 cup sugar

1/2 cup hot water

1/4 cup or more kirsch or other spirit

1 cup apricot preserves

2 tablespoons water

1 almond paste sponge cake (page 22)

1/2 cup buttercream (page 45), optional

3 cups liquid fondant (page 163)

Food coloring (optional)

2 tablespoons colored royal icing (page 67), optional

To make the simple syrup, dissolve the sugar in the water and let cool. Flavor to taste with kirsch.

Heat the apricot preserves with the 2 tablespoons water in a saucepan and stir until smooth. Strain and let cool slightly.

Trim any crusty places off the surface of the cake with a serrated knife, then trim it so it measures 10 by 16 inches. Cut it into two 8 by 10-inch rectangles. Brush one of the rectangles liberally with some of the simple syrup. Spread half of the apricot glaze over the rectangle and place the other rectangle on top. Brush the top rectangle with simple syrup and spread over the rest of the apricot glaze. Spread the buttercream in a thin layer over the cake. Cut the cake into 1-inch-wide strips. Transfer the strips to a parchment paper–lined sheet pan and refrigerate for 15 minutes.

If you have any buttercream left, use it to coat the sides of the strips. Cut across the strips to make 1-inch cubes. If necessary, thin the fondant by heating it in a bowl set over a saucepan of simmering water; if it's still too thick, thin it with water, 1 teaspoon at a time. It should flow in a steady stream from a spoon. Color the fondant with food coloring. (Use the tip of a knife dipped in a drop of food coloring for greater control—a whole drop is sometimes too much.)

Coat the petits fours with fondant by dipping them in a bowl of fondant or by pouring the fondant over the petits fours arranged on a cake rack set over a sheet pan. If you're pouring the fondant, reuse the fondant that drips off onto the sheet pan. Let the petits fours sit for 20 minutes for the fondant to harden. If the coating is too thin, you can coat them again.

Use a paper cone (see page 87) to decorate with colored royal icing. The petits fours can be stored in a tightly sealed container for up to 3 days; don't refrigerate.

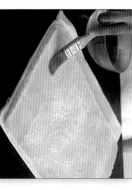

1. Prepare the simple syrup and flavor it with Kirsch. Brush the sheet cake with the flavored syrup.

2. If the cake is crusty in places, use a serrated knife to trim off the crust.

3. Cut the cake into 2 equal rectangles and spread the apricot glaze over one of the rectangles.

4. Gently place the unglazed rectangle over the glazed rectangle. Leave the parchment under the top layer to make it easier to move. Slide out the parchment as you place the top rectangle on the bottom rectangle.

5. Trim the edges so they're even.

6. Brush the top of the cake with the flavored syrup and spread a thin layer of buttercream on top of the cake. (Reserve some buttercream for the sides.)

7. Cut the cake into 1-inch-wide strips. Transfer the strips to a parchment-lined sheet pan and refrigerate for 15 minutes.

8. Spread the sides of the strips with a thin layer of buttercream.

9. Cut the strips into 1-inch cubes and transfer them to a cake rack set over a sheet pan.

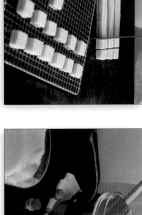

10. Color the fondant, and stir it over the saucepan of hot water until it has the consistency and color you like.

11. Dip the cake cubes one at a time into the fondant.

12. Transfer the petits fours back to the cake rack.

13. If you prefer, pour the fondant over the petits fours on the cake rack.

14. Decorate the petits fours with colored royal icing. Here, cocoa powder was added.

ROLLED CAKES

All rolled cakes start as sheet cakes. They don't require any special skill, but it is important to keep in mind that the sheet cake you use must be moist and flexible enough so it doesn't crack when you try to roll it. While three kinds of sheet cakes (hot milk–cream sponge, biscuit made with melted butter, and almond flour sponge) are especially suited for rolling, you can use any cake you like as long as it is pliable enough to roll. If your cake threatens to crack as you try to roll it, brush it lightly with flavored simple syrup before or during rolling.

Most rolled cakes are made by rolling up the short end of a sheet cake—which gives you a relatively thick roll—instead of rolling the long side, which produces a thinner roll. This second option gives you more slices or thicker slices.

A 12-inch-long rolled cake, made from a sheet cake baked in a traditional 13 by 17-inch sheet pan and rolled from the short end, will be several inches thick. It will serve 8 to 12 people, depending on how thick you slice it—1 to 1½ inches is usually right. Any filling you'd use for a layer cake, such as buttercream or whipped ganache, is delicious in a rolled cake. Stabilized whipped cream, rolled in a chocolate sheet cake—such as a chocolate sponge cake (page 12)—makes a beautiful rolled cake and needs only a quick sprinkling of confectioners' sugar before serving.

Rolled Pistachio Buttercream Cake

Buttercream is easily made flavorful and luxurious by combining it with a nut paste, such as almond, hazelnut (sometimes sold as praline), or pistachio. Check the consistency of the buttercream before you spread it on the cake—if it is too hard, it will tear the cake as you try to spread it. If it feels hard, beat it until it has the consistency of sour cream.

You don't have to use the same flavor buttercream for both the inside and the outside of the rolled cake; try using hazelnut, almond praline, kirsch, or chocolate.

MAKES 1 ROLLED CAKE

1 sheet cake 13 by 17 by ¼ inch, such as a butter-enriched sponge cake (page 16)

1 cup simple syrup (page 36), flavored with rum, Cognac, bourbon, or kirsch (flavoring optional)

2 cups pistachio buttercream (page 48) for filling, at room temperature

3 cups pistachio buttercream or other buttercream, at room temperature, or 1 cup confectioners' sugar, for the outside of the roll

Place the cake on a sheet of parchment paper the same size as the cake. Fold in an edge of the sheet cake to see if it is brittle and cracks. If so, brush the cake with the simple syrup, cover it with a moist towel for 10 minutes, and try again. Spread the cake with the 2 cups buttercream.

Roll the cake by pinching along the length of one of the short ends and gradually rolling. As you roll, you may find it helpful to lift the parchment paper on your end. Alternate between pressing, squeezing, and rolling. Roll as tightly as you can. When the cake is rolled, tuck the parchment paper under it and push against the roll with the side of your hand, tightening it as much as possible without causing the filling to ooze out the ends.

Spread the rolled cake with a layer of buttercream, unless you prefer confectioners' sugar. Confectioners' sugar should be sprinkled over just before serving. Chill for 4 hours in the refrigerator or wrap tightly and freeze for up to a month.

1. Brush the sheet cake with the cold, flavored simple syrup. Use only enough so the liquid penetrates to the other side.

2. Spread the sheet cake with the pistachio buttercream.

3. Start rolling up the sheet cake by pinching a short end into a tight roll.

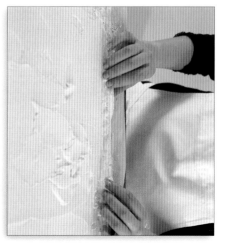

4. Roll up the sheet cake by lifting up the parchment paper on the side facing you and then by rolling with your hands, as tightly as you can. Alternate between pressing, squeezing, and rolling.

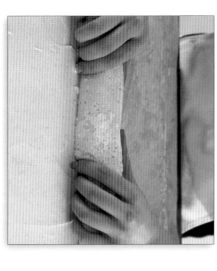

5. When the roll is completed, tuck under the parchment paper and push against the roll with the side of your hand, tightening it as much as possible without causing the filling to ooze out the ends.

Apricot Jelly Roll

Fruit preserves, strained to eliminate pulp, are the traditional fillings for many rolled cakes. To strain jam, heat it in a saucepan with about 2 tablespoons water per 1 cup of jam and stir to make it more liquid and easier to strain. Work it through a fine-mesh strainer. Count on 1 cup of strained jam (glaze) for a 13 by 17-inch sheet cake.

MAKES 1 ROLLED CAKE

Confectioners' sugar for sprinkling

1 sheet cake 13 by 17 inches and no more than ¹/₂ inch thick, such as a butter-enriched sponge cake (page 36)

¹/₂ cup simple syrup (page 16), flavoring optional

One 12-ounce jar apricot preserves

3 tablespoons water

Sprinkle a sheet of parchment paper liberally with confectioners' sugar, and place the sheet cake on it. Brush the cake with the simple syrup.

Heat the preserves in a small saucepan with the water. If there are pieces of pulp in the preserves, strain them. Brush the glaze on the cake.

Roll the cake by pinching along the length of one of the short ends and gradually rolling. As you roll, you may find it helpful to lift the parchment paper on your end. Alternate between pressing, squeezing, and rolling. Roll as tightly as you can. When the cake is rolled, tuck the parchment paper under it and push against the roll with the side of your hand, tightening it as much as possible without causing the glaze to ooze out the ends. Freeze the roll for 30 minutes to firm it up before slicing.

2. Start rolling by pinching the short end of the sheet cake together into a very small rope.

4. Keep checking as you're rolling to make sure the roll is tight. If it isn't, press under and around it with your hands to help shape it.

1. Lightly brush the sheet cake with the simple syrup and spread the cake with the strained jam.

3. Lift up the parchment paper and with a combination of pressing the roll together with your fingers and rolling it in the parchment paper, gradually roll it.

5. When you're done rolling, press against the roll with the parchment paper to help make it firm. Freeze the roll for 30 minutes to help it firm up before slicing.

Bûche de Noël

A bûche de noël, literally a Christmas log, is an elaborate rolled cake decorated with chocolate buttercream to look like a log. It can be as simple or as elaborate as you like. Meringue mushrooms are a classic decoration for this dessert; you can also use marzipan leaves, berries, and stems.

MAKES 1 LOG

1 rolled cake (see page 104 or page 106), without frosting on the outside

4 cups chocolate buttercream (page 48)

Meringue mushrooms (opposite page)

Marzipan leaves, berries, and stems (pages 110 and 111)

Cut the ends off the rolled cake (the log) at an angle and attach them to the sides of the log with buttercream so they look like branches on the side of the log. Coat the log with buttercream, then use a metal spatula to make lengthwise streaks to simulate bark. Arrange the meringue mushrooms on the log. Decorate with marzipan leaves, berries, and stems.

ASSEMBLING A BÛCHE DE NOËL

1. Cut both ends off the rolled cake at a 45-degree angle, approximately.

2. Dollop a mound of the chocolate buttercream near one end of the log and slightly to the side.

3. Place one of the end wedges over the buttercream and apply more buttercream around the base of the end, holding it in place.

4. Repeat with the other end piece at a different position on the log.

5. Use a small offset spatula to apply the rest of the buttercream. Form flat streaks to simulate bark.

6. Arrange the meringue mushrooms on the log.

7. Decorate the log with strands of marzipan (stems) and marzipan leaves and berries.

Making Meringue Mushrooms

Meringue mushrooms are used to decorate a *bûche de noël* (opposite page). To make them, line a sheet pan with parchment paper. Fit a pastry bag with a ¼-inch plain tip and fill the bag with meringue (page 38). Make the mushroom stems by squeezing the pastry bag while lifting straight up so the stem narrows to a point. Make the caps by holding the bag about ¼ inch from the parchment paper and squeezing to make a small, even, slightly mounded round.

Cut a small hole in the underside of the mushroom caps to make a place to insert the narrow end of the stem. Put a tiny bit of buttercream or other filling in the hole and insert the stem. Set aside until the buttercream hardens before using.

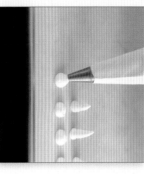

1. Make the stems by squeezing with the pastry bag while lifting straight up so that the stem narrows to a point.

2. Make the caps by holding the bag about ¼ inch from the parchment paper and squeezing to make a small, even, slightly mounded round.

3. Cut a little hole in the underside of the mushroom caps. Put a tiny bit of buttercream or other filling in the hole and insert the stem.

Marzipan

Many of us think that marzipan and almond paste are the same thing, but unlike almond paste, marzipan can be shaped or rolled out with a rolling pin and then used as a covering for a cake. You'll save yourself a lot of work by just buying marzipan instead of almond paste, but if you're stuck with almond paste and need marzipan, here's what to do. Knead the almond paste with corn syrup and powdered sugar until smooth, and color it with food coloring (a drop is usually enough—see page 110). When working with marzipan, be sure to keep the part you aren't using covered with plastic wrap so it doesn't dry out.

MAKES 1½ POUNDS, ENOUGH TO COVER ONE 9-INCH ROUND LAYER CAKE

1 pound almond paste

2 cups confectioners' sugar

1 tablespoon light corn syrup

Knead the almond paste with the sugar and corn syrup for about 20 minutes, or until the mixture is smooth and you can roll it into a small ball with no cracks.

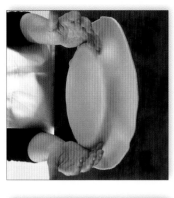

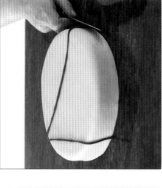

1. Dust the work surface with confectioners' sugar and roll the marzipan out about 1/8-inch thick and large enough to cover the sides as well as the top of the cake.

2. Roll the marzipan up onto the rolling pin and unroll it over the cake.

3. Starting in the middle of the cake and working out, gently push out any air pockets with the flat of your hand.

4. Gently tuck the marzipan around the sides of the cake with the sides of your hands.

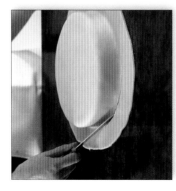

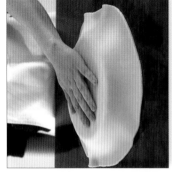

5. Cut around the base of the cake with a sharp paring knife. Err on the side of leaving too much marzipan attached to the cake.

6. Trim the marzipan a second time so that it just covers the sides of the cake.

7. If you like, roll out a thin strand of colored marzipan . . .

8. . . . to decorate the cake.

Reconstituting Dried-Out Marzipan and Coloring Marzipan

Marzipan should be stored in the refrigerator, tightly wrapped with plastic wrap and then in a plastic-covered container, but even if you do everything right, marzipan hardens as it ages. To fix it, knead it with a small amount of corn syrup on a surface dusted with confectioners' sugar.

To color it, put a drop of food coloring on a surface. Touch the drop and then the piece of marzipan with a paring knife so you add the dye a very small amount at a time. Use the heel of your hand to work in the coloring. Use more coloring as necessary. If you are coloring a large amount of marzipan, mix it in a stand mixer using the paddle attachment.

1. Roll the marzipan into a long cylinder. Cover with plastic wrap.

5. Place two of the petals on top of each other and begin to roll, starting from what will be the side of the rose.

1. Roll the marzipan into a long cylinder. Cover with plastic wrap.

2. Cut the cylinder into 7 to 9 segments 3/4 inch long.

2. Cut the cylinder into 7 to 9 segments 3/4 inch long.

6. After rolling from 1/2 to 3/4 inch thick, put in another petal.

3. Roll the segments into little balls. Keep them covered with plastic wrap as you go.

7. Keep rolling, adding petals every 1/2 to 1 inch until you've used all of the petals.

4. Flatten the balls into petals with one end thinner than the other.

8. Use the tip of a knife to separate the petals near the top of the rose for a natural appearance.

9. Cut off the base of the rose so it will stay on a cake. Angle the cut if you want the rose to lean on the cake.

10. Place the finished roses in an egg carton and let dry for 24 hours before using. They will keep for several weeks.

MAKING MARZIPAN LEAVES AND BERRIES

1. To make leaves, use a rolling pin to roll out a 1/16-inch-thick sheet of colored marzipan.

2. Using a leaf-shaped cookie cutter, cut the leaves out of the marzipan.

3. Press on the leaves with a paring knife, forming a line that runs down the middle and smaller lines at an angle.

4. To make berries, roll the marzipan into a 1/8-inch-thick cord and cut into sections. Roll the sections into tiny balls.

DECORATING CAKES

The following pages contain a number of decorating ideas, some of which are illustrated here and some of which appear in fuller form elsewhere in the book.

COVERING A CAKE WITH ROLLED FONDANT

You can use any combination of cake layers and fillings to make a multilayered cake and then cover it with rolled fondant, but a sponge cake such as a genoise (see page 8) is ideal.

Fill, frost, and refrigerate a 9-inch round cake about 3 inches high. Half of the recipe for rolled fondant on page 67 is sufficient for a cake of this size.

DECORATING A CAKE WITH A ROLLED FONDANT STRIP AND FONDANT POLKA DOTS

To decorate a cake as as shown here, first cover it with a sheet of rolled fondant as described below. To make the dots and strip, start with 4 ounces of fondant, divide it into four parts and color each piece. To color fondant, add food coloring a little at a time, kneading it in. When you have the colors as you want them to be, pinch off a small piece of each color and roll out to make the dots; cut them out with the large end of a pastry bag tip. Arrange the dots on top of the fondant-covered cake. Roll the remaining pieces of colored fondant into $1/8$-inch ropes with your hands. Place the ropes next to each other on the work surface, and then roll the ropes together with a rolling pin so they form a multicolored band about $1 1/2$ inches wide and $1/8$ inch thick. Wrap this around the outside base of the cake, cutting the ends so they butt smoothly against each other.

COVERING A CAKE WITH ROLLED FONDANT

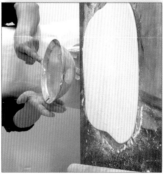

1. Dust the work surface with sifted confectioners' sugar and roll out the fondant about $1/8$ inch thick and large enough to cover the sides as well as the top of the cake.

2. Sprinkle confectioners' sugar over the surface of the fondant sheet.

3. Roll the fondant up on the rolling pin. As you're rolling, brush any excess sugar off the fondant so it doesn't end up on the cake.

4. Unroll the fondant over the cake.

5. Gently massage the top of the fondant, starting in the middle of the cake and working toward the outside, to work out any air bubbles.

6. Cut the fondant around the edge of the cake. Do this in two stages, leaving a fair amount of fondant attached to the cake for the first cut, so you don't accidentally cut away too much fondant.

7. Cut around the cake a second time, this time more precisely, to remove excess fondant.

1. Roll out a bit of colored fondant and cut out polka dots with the large end of a pastry bag tip.

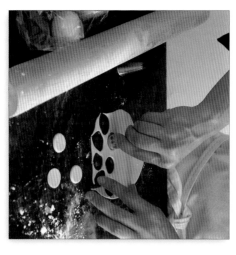

2. Arrange the dots on top of the fondant-covered cake.

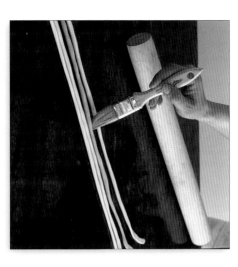

3. Roll the colored fondant into long, thin ropes.

4. Line the ropes up next to each other on the work surface.

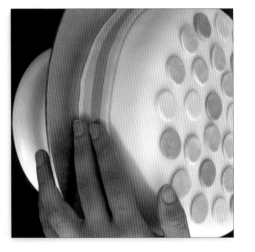

5. Roll the ropes into a thin strip.

6. Gently peel the strip from the work surface.

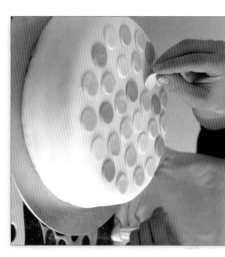

7. Wrap the strip around the base of the cake.

8. Cut the ends so they butt smoothly against each other and press gently to help the fondant strip adhere to the cake.

1. Spread warm melted chocolate on the acetate strip.

2. When the chocolate has cooled, gently lift the strip from the work surface, bringing the chocolate with it.

3. Wrap the acetate around the cake, with the layer of chocolate on the inside.

4. Let cool, and gently peel away the acetate strip.

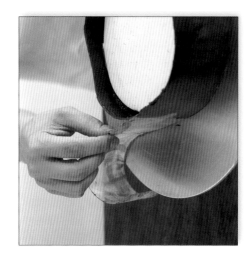

5. Cover the top of the cake with raspberries.

WRAPPING A CAKE WITH A WIDE CHOCOLATE STRIP

A wide chocolate strip wrapped around a cake is dramatic to look at and provides a contrasting crunch. To make it, you'll need to buy clear sheets of plastic called "acetate" at an art supply store or baking supply store. Melting the chocolate and then beating it as it cools tempers it, making it flexible enough to wrap around the cake in its solid state.

To wrap a 9 by 1½-inch cake, you'll need one 30-inch-long strip of 3-inch-wide acetate and 4 ounces of bittersweet chocolate.

Fill, frost, and refrigerate the cake. Spread the acetate strip on your work surface, weighting it down at the edges to keep it flat. The acetate must be perfectly clean and dry.

Melt the chocolate in a bowl over simmering water, and remove the bowl to an ice bath (a larger bowl of ice water). As it cools, stir it vigorously with a rubber spatula. Don't let even a drop of water get into the chocolate or it will seize. When the chocolate has cooled to about body temperature (touch it with the back of your finger—it should feel neither hot nor cold), spread it in a thin layer over the acetate sheet.

Allow the chocolate to cool on the work surface until it loses its sheen, about 5 minutes. Remove the cake from the refrigerator and place it on the work surface. Gently lift the chocolate-covered acetate strip off the work surface and wrap the acetate around the cake, with the layer of chocolate on the inside. Let cool for 15 minutes, then gently peel away the sheet of acetate. Decorate the top of the cake by covering it with raspberries.

DECORATING A CAKE WITH MERINGUE LOGS

You'll need one recipe's worth of meringue logs (page 41) to decorate the cake illustrated here. To decorate a crumb coated and frosted or iced

layer cake 3 by 9 inches, cut the meringue logs into irregular lengths that are taller than the cake by 1 or 2 inches. Press these pieces into the icing around the sides of the cake. Cut any remaining meringue logs into

irregular lengths of about 1 inch and arrange them on top of the cake. For a decorative touch, tie a ribbon around the cake.

DECORATING A CAKE WITH A PAPER CONE

While it takes some practice to master, using a paper cone to pipe thin ribbons of royal icing is an easy way to decorate cakes and pastries. See page 89.

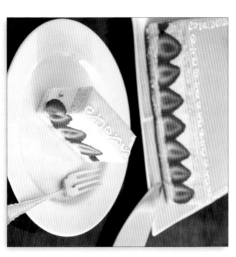

DECORATING THE SIDES OF A CAKE WITH LADYFINGERS

Ladyfingers are made by piping the separated-egg sponge cake (biscuit) into strips. If you're making strips of ladyfingers to wrap around the outside of cakes, pipe the ladyfingers close together so they form a strip (see page 15).

DECORATING A CAKE WITH CHOPPED OR SHAVED NUTS OR CAKE CRUMBS

Shaved almonds or coarse-ground nuts such as hazelnuts are easy to apply to the outside of a filled and frosted cake (see page 92). Toast the nuts first for more flavor. Save pieces of stale cake, process them in a food processor, and save in the freezer to use for decorating the sides of cakes.

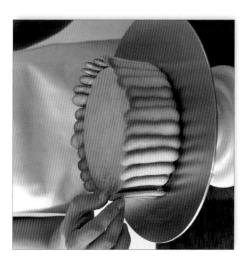

DECORATING A CAKE WITH FRESH FLOWERS

While fresh flowers are the easiest and perhaps the most elegant cake decoration, try to buy edible flowers from a food store, not the florist. Above: orange buttercream layer cake (page 77).

DECORATING A CAKE WITH CAT'S TONGUE COOKIES

These crisp little cookies are easily pressed against the sides of a cake as a decoration. Just make sure that the sides of your cake are well coated with something sticky such as mousse or buttercream so the cookies stick. For complete instructions, see page 81.

DECORATING A CAKE WITH A GELATIN MIRROR

A gelatin mirror is easy to make and creates an elegant effect. For complete instructions, see page 81.

DECORATING A CAKE WITH FRESH FRUIT

No cake decoration is simpler or more pleasing than fresh fruit.

DECORATING A CAKE WITH LAYERED CAKE SQUARES

This is a rather elaborate assembly involving making a layer cake with a sheet cake, slicing it into squares, and using those squares to decorate the sides of a mousse cake. These squares are easiest to use when you're constructing a cake in a cake ring or springform pan. Just press the squares against the inside of the springform pan or cake ring and trim the cake layers so they push against the squares and hold them in place. See page 98.

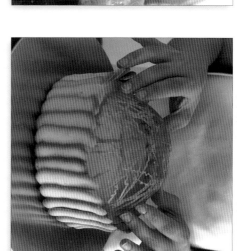

DECORATING A CAKE WITH A CARAMEL CAGE

This is one of those little tricks that looks very impressive and professional, but takes hardly any work. See page 85 for complete instructions.

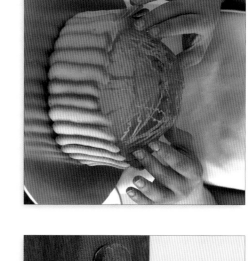

DECORATING A CAKE WITH COCOA POWDER

Cocoa powder comes alkalized (Dutch processed) or not. This is an important difference when baking it in cakes because the two kinds react differently to baking powder and baking soda. When using cocoa as a simple decoration as shown here, the type of cocoa isn't important.

DECORATING A CAKE WITH BUTTERCREAM

When it is at the right temperature, neither hot nor cold, buttercream has the perfect consistency for piping with a pastry bag (see page 64). If it gets hot and runny, cool it in the refrigerator for 10 to 15 minutes. It is fine to chill it right in the pastry bag.

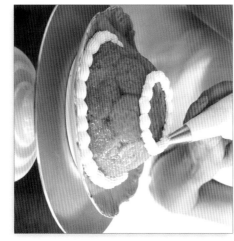

DECORATING A CAKE WITH SLICES OF ROLLED CAKE

Rolled cakes can be sliced and used to decorate the sides of a dome cake for a dramatic effect. See page 96.

DECORATING A CAKE WITH
CHOCOLATE CURLS

Even though this is a simple technique, much depends on the chocolate and the right temperature. The best chocolate for this is called "couverture"; it has a high cocoa butter content that makes it supple and malleable. If you're unsure of your chocolate, pay attention to how it behaves and adjust its temperature accordingly. If the chocolate breaks off into brittle pieces, try warming it in the microwave for 10 to 40 seconds to soften it ever so slightly. See page 71.

DECORATING A CAKE WITH
CONFECTIONERS' SUGAR

Here is an easy trick: lay metal skewers across the top of a cake and sprinkle with confectioners' sugar. Pictured above: peach crème mousseline cake (page 99).

DECORATING A CAKE
USING A SERRATED KNIFE

This method works especially well on cakes that have been coated with buttercream. Make sure the buttercream on top is perfectly level before sliding over it with a serrated knife. See page 76.

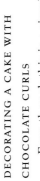

PIES, TARTS, AND PASTRIES

Basic Doughs

Basic Pie and Tart Pastry Dough (*Pâte Brisée*) · 130
Sweetened Basic Pie and Tart Pastry Dough · 131
Extra Buttery Sweet Pastry Dough (*Pâte Sablée*) · 134
Cream Cheese Tart and Pie Pastry Dough · 135
Flaky Pie and Tart Pastry Dough · 136
Sweet Crisp Pastry Dough (*Pâte Sucrée*) · 138
Linzer Pastry Dough · 140
Classic Puff Pastry Dough · 148
Quick Puff Pastry Dough · 151
Puff Pastry Cases · 152
Puff Pastry Rectangles · 153
Cream Puff Pastry Dough (*Pâte à Choux*) · 155
Croissant Dough · 157

Fillings and Glazes

Almond Cream · 159
Frangipane · 159
Pastry Cream · 160
Hazelnut Frangipane · 161
Praline Paste · 161
Cream Cheese Tart Filling · 161
Cheese Danish Filling · 162
Goat Cheese Filling · 162
Mushroom Filling (*Duxelles*) · 162
Liquid Fondant · 163
Chocolate Fondant · 163
Coffee Fondant · 163

Pies, Tarts, and Pastries

Blueberry Pie · 164
Cherry Pie · 167
Apple Pie · 169
Classic French Apple Tart · 170
Tarte Tatin · 173
Plum Tart · 174
Apricot Frangipane Tart · 175
Blueberry Frangipane Tart · 176
Hazelnut or Almond Tartlets · 176
Apricot Tartlets · 177
Cherry Tartlets · 178
Berry Frangipane Tartlets · 178
Plum, Kiwi, or Peach Frangipane Tartlets · 178
Raw Fruit Tarts · 179
Ganache Tart · 179
Raspberry-Ganache Tart · 179
Kiwi-Whipped White Chocolate Ganache Tart · 180
Raspberry-Classic Crème Mousseline Tart · 180
Blackberry-Peach Mousseline Tart · 180
Mixed Berry-Passion Fruit Mousse Tart · 181
Miniature White Chocolate Ganache Tartlets · 181
Miniature Dark Chocolate Ganache Tartlets · 181
Assorted Berry Tartlets · 182
Red Currant Barquettes · 182
Miniature Raw Fruit Tartlets · 182
Blackberry-Lemon Cream Tart · 183
Passion Fruit Meringue Tart · 184
Lemon Meringue Pie · 184
Alsatian Apple Tart · 186
Roast Pear Clafoutis · 188
Roast Pears in Butterscotch Sauce · 188

Pumpkin Pie · 191
Persimmon Tart or Tartlets · 191
Passion Fruit Tartlets or Tart · 191
Pecan Pie · 192
Lime Tart · 194
Key Lime or Lemon Tart · 194
Orange Tart · 194
Candied Orange Slices · 195
Banana Cream Pie · 196
Coconut Cream Pie · 199
Crispy Apple Tart · 201
Puff Pastry Pear Frangipane Tart · 201
Fruit-Hazelnut Puff Pastry Tartlets · 202
Miniature Puff Pastry Fruit Tartlets · 203
Individual Deep-Dish Berry Pies · 204
Blueberry Turnovers · 205
Almond-Puff Pastry Galette (Pithiviers) · 206
Linzertorte · 209
Éclairs · 210
Cream Puffs · 210
Cream Puffs · 213
Cream Puff Pastry Swans · 214
Croissants · 216
Chocolate Croissants · 219
Fruit Danish Tartlets · 220
Fruit and Cheese Danish Purses · 222
Miniature Cheese Danish Twirls · 223
Fruit Danish Packets · 224
Rolled Danish Pastries · 225
Napoleons · 226
Apple Strudel · 228
Pistachio Baklava · 232
Mushroom *Jalousie* · 234
Cheese Puffs (*Gougères*) · 235
Cheese Straws · 236
Vol-au-Vents · 237
Miniature Vol-au-Vents · 237
Quiche Lorraine · 238
Miniature Vol-au-Vents · 237

Methods and Techniques

MAKING AND WORKING WITH PASTRY DOUGH

Tips for Success with Pastry Dough • 129

Making Basic Pie and Tart Pastry Dough by Hand on a Work Surface • 132

Basic Pie and Tart Pastry Dough in a Stand Mixer: The Stages • 133

Making Extra Buttery Sweet Pastry Dough in a Stand Mixer • 134

Making Cream Cheese Tart and Pie Pastry Dough • 135

Making Flaky Pie and Tart Pastry Dough • 136

Making Sweet Crisp Pastry Dough (*Pâte Sucrée*) • 139

Making Linzer Pastry Dough • 140

Getting Rolled-Out Pastry Dough into the Pan • 141

Lining a Pie Pan with Pastry Dough • 142

Lining a Square or Rectangular Tart Pan with Pastry Dough • 142

Lining a Round Tart Ring or Fluted Tart Pan with Pastry Dough • 143

Lining a Tart Pan with Fragile Pastry Dough • 144

Troubleshooting Tarts and Pies • 145

Baking "Blind" • 145

Keeping the Edges of Tarts and Pies from Burning • 145

Making Prebaked Single-Serving Tart Shells • 146

Making Egg Wash for Pie Pastry • 146

Making Prebaked Miniature Tart Shells • 147

Using Puff Pastry Trimmings • 148

Making Classic Puff Pastry Dough • 149

Making Quick Puff Pastry Dough • 150

Puff Pastry Dos and Don'ts • 151

Making Puff Pastry Cases • 152

Making Puff Pastry Rectangles • 153

Thirteen Tips for Working with Puff Pastry Dough • 154

Making Cream Puff Pastry Dough • 155

Making Croissant Dough • 156

FILLINGS FOR TARTS AND PASTRIES

Making Raw Fruit Tartlets with Custard Filling • 159

Making Almond Cream and Frangipane • 159

Making Pastry Cream • 160

Peeling Hazelnuts • **161**

Making Liquid Fondant • 163

Flavoring Fondant • **163**

MAKING FRUIT AND CUSTARD PIES AND TARTS

Should I Precook Fruit for a Fruit Pie or Tart? • **164**

Making a Single-Crust Fruit Pie (Blueberry Pie) • 165

Making a Double-Crust Fruit Pie (Cherry Pie) • 166

Making a Double-Crust Fruit Pie (Apple Pie) • 168

Making a Classic French Apple Tart • 171

Making a Tarte Tatin • 172

Making a Plum Tart • 174

Making an Apricot Frangipane Tart • 175

Making Apricot Tartlets • 177

Making Cherry Tartlets • 178

Making Raw Fruit Tarts • 179

Making a Blackberry–Lemon Cream Tart • 183

Making a Strawberry–Lemon Cream Tart • 183

Making a Passion Fruit Meringue Tart • 184

Making a Lemon Meringue Pie • 185

Making an Alsatian Apple Tart • 187

Making a Roast Pear Clafoutis • 189

Making a Pumpkin Pie • 190

Making a Persimmon Tart or Tartlets • 191

Making a Pecan Pie • 192

Candying Citrus Zest • 194

Using Grated Citrus Zest • **194**

Making and Decorating Citrus Tarts • 195

Making and Using Candied Orange Slices • 195

Making Brown Butter • 196

Making a Banana Cream Pie • 197

Making a Coconut Cream Pie • 199

Making a Crispy Apple Tart • 200

Making a Puff Pastry Pear Frangipane Tart • 202

Making Fruit-Hazelnut Puff Pastry Tartlets • 202

Making Miniature Puff Pastry Fruit Tartlets • 203

Making Individual Deep-Dish Berry Pies • 204

Making Blueberry Turnovers • 205

MAKING ASSORTED PASTRIES

Making an Almond–Puff Pastry Galette (Pithiviers) • 207

Making a Linzertorte • 208

Making Éclairs • 211

Making Cream Puffs • 213

Making Cream Puff Pastry Swans • 215

Making Croissants • 217

Making Chocolate Croissants • 218

Croissants: How Big? • **219**

Making Fruit Danish Tartlets • 221

Making Fruit and Cheese Danish Purses • 222

Making Miniature Cheese Danish Twirls • 223

Making Fruit Danish Packets • 224

Making Rolled Danish Pastries • 225

Making Napoleons • 227

Decorating Napoleons with Confectioners' Sugar • **228**

Making an Apple Strudel • 230

Making Pistachio Baklava • 233

Making a Mushroom *Jalousie* • 234

Making Cheese Puffs (Gougères) • 235

Making Cheese Straws • 236

Making Vol-au-Vents and Miniature Vol-au-Vents • 237

Making a Quiche Lorraine • 238

BASIC DOUGHS

Pastry chefs working in the French tradition divide pastry into three different types: *pâte brisée* (pronounced bree-zay), which I also call "basic pie and tart pastry dough;" *pâte sucrée* (pronounced sue-kray), which I call "sweet crisp pastry dough;" and *pâte sablée*, which I call "extra buttery sweet pastry dough."

Most pie pastry dough, such as basic pie and tart pastry dough and extra buttery sweet pastry dough, is made by combining butter and flour; adding liquid such as egg, water, or cream; and then mixing just enough for the pastry dough to come together into a somewhat ragged-looking mass. The pastry dough is then smeared with the heel of the hand or gently kneaded just long enough to incorporate the butter and make the pastry dough possible to roll. Extra buttery sweet pastry dough contains sugar. Basic pie and tart pastry dough contains sugar only some of the time; when it does, it is called *pâte brisée sucrée*. I call it "sweetened basic pie and tart pastry dough."

The method for making sweet crisp pastry dough is different from any other pastry dough. The butter is creamed with sugar, eggs are incorporated into the mixture, and the flour is added all at once. The mixture is then combined just long enough to come together into a clumpy mass. Sweet crisp pastry dough makes crisp, cookielike crusts.

In addition to these three traditional pastries, I have included recipes for laminated (layered) pastry doughs for puff pastry, croissants, and Danish pastries; a flaky cream cheese tart and pie pastry dough; linzer pastry dough, a marvelously flavorful crumbly pastry made with almond flour; cream puff pastry dough; and flaky pie and tart pastry dough.

Except for sweet crisp pastry dough and cream puff pastry dough, these basic pastry doughs produce crusts that are both crumbly (like shortbread) and more or less flaky. Crumbly-style dough has long been preferred by Europeans, who like a crust to fall apart in the mouth and create an impression of a mouthful of delicate sand (*sable* means sand). Americans tend to prefer flaky crusts, frequently made with shortening or lard instead of butter. Pastry dough made with shortening or lard is more consistently flaky, but if you want a flaky crust and don't like these flavors, make the cream cheese pastry dough on page 135. Cream cheese behaves like shortening but has a richer flavor. You can also make flaky pastry dough by folding it over itself to form layers (see page 136). All of these pastry doughs can be made by hand (directly on a work surface or in a bowl), in a stand mixer with a paddle attachment, or in a food processor, but don't use a food processor for flaky dough because it mixes the butter into the pastry completely, leaving no pieces to create the flakes. The food processor does, however, make wonderfully fragile crumbly crusts.

PIE AND TART DOUGH

While pie and tart dough can be made using one of three methods—by hand, in a stand mixer, and in a food processor—when you're first getting started, it's helpful to make dough by hand as often as possible to develop a feel for it. Then again, if you're in a restaurant or some such place, you may never be called upon to make dough by hand and may make it in the mixer.

Tips for Success with Pastry Dough

Very few foods are as intimidating to make as pie and tart pastry dough. Some recipes are too simple, with vague amounts and methods, while others—in an effort to leave nothing to chance—are dauntingly complicated. Despite all the anxiety, pastry dough is easy to make.

TEMPERATURE: You must be very careful about only one thing: the pastry dough must never get warm. Pastry dough will withstand any number of mistakes—even the dreaded overworking—as long as the butter it contains never melts. So, regardless of the recipe or procedure you follow, you may need to refrigerate or freeze the pastry two or three times while you are making it, especially if you're working in a warm kitchen.

If your pastry dough never gets warm while you're making it or rolling it out, you'll almost invariably end up with a more than acceptable crust. But if you want an exceptional crust, there are a few other things to consider.

LIQUID: First, pastry dough must contain the right amount of liquid. If the dough is too dry, it will be impossible to roll out—at best it will crack as you try to place it in the pie dish. If it's too wet, it will be too sticky to roll out. Because different brands of flour absorb different amounts of liquid, and butter contains varying amounts of water, it's hard to provide an exact recipe. The first time you make the pastry dough, you'll need to experiment a little to get the amount of liquid just right. The next time you make it, you'll know exactly how much liquid to use, provided you continue to use the same brands of butter and flour. To judge the amount of liquid, you'll have to watch the consistency of the pastry as you're adding the liquid by pinching a piece to see if it comes together or falls apart in your hand. If it crumbles, it needs more liquid. If the pastry dough is too wet, you can incorporate extra flour as you roll it out by constantly flouring the work surface. If the pastry dough ends up too dry, it's more problematic. You can chill it, cut it into chunks, and process it with a tablespoon or two of cold liquid, but at the risk of overheating the dough. It's better to err in the direction of too wet than too dry.

The kind of liquid you use affects the texture of your crust. Liquids containing fat, such as heavy cream or beaten eggs, coat the flour and help prevent the formation of gluten. Water makes lighter pastry, but if the dough is overworked the gluten may develop, making the crust tough. For most pastry dough, different liquids can be used interchangeably, with only slight differences in the consistency of the pastry dough and the texture of the crust. Eggs make a crust soft and rich, while heavy cream makes it more delicate and brittle.

FLOUR: The flour you use determines the texture of your crust. American all-purpose flour contains a relatively large amount of gluten or, more accurately, two proteins that combine to form gluten when the dough is moistened and worked. Gluten is elastic when wet and causes pastry crusts to shrink and harden when baked. The best way to avoid too much gluten is to use a low-gluten flour. Most of the recipes given here use a combination of cake flour, which contains too little gluten, and all-purpose flour, which contains too much. Don't try making pastry dough with cake flour alone—it needs some gluten to hold it together.

OVERWORKING: Be careful not to overwork the pastry dough. Many of the techniques for making and rolling out pastry dough are designed to avoid activating the gluten in the flour by working the dough as little as possible. Fortunately, gluten that has been activated will be deactivated when the pastry dough is kept cold and allowed to relax. So, if your dough shrinks as you try to roll it out, put it in the refrigerator for 30 minutes and try again. As long as the pastry dough is kept cold, it can tolerate some overworking. The freezer is excellent for chilling pastry dough quickly, but keep in mind that it doesn't relax when frozen—freezing suspends the deactivation of the gluten.

FAT: You must decide what kind of fat to use and whether you want flaky or crumbly pastry. The recipes given here are made with butter because it has the best flavor, but some experienced bakers swear by and adore the flavor of lard. Some bakers prefer shortening, despite its inferior flavor, because it's easier to use than butter or lard and makes flakier pastry. But to make flaky pastry with butter isn't hard. There are three methods, used alone or in combination, that guarantee flaky crusts: leaving the butter in relatively large pieces in the pastry dough (this precludes using the food processor); folding the pastry dough over itself to create layers (a simple version of the method used for puff pastry; see page 136); and using a combination of cream cheese and butter. The amount of butter you use also has an effect. The more butter you use, the more delicate the crust will be. But pastry dough containing a lot of butter is difficult to roll out—if slightly too cold, it is too hard to roll and may crack; if slightly too warm, it melts and gets sticky.

continued

129

SUGAR: The texture of the crust is affected by the sugar—making it delightfully brittle—and because pastry dough containing sugar absorbs slightly less liquid, it may affect the amount of liquid you need to include. While sugar may make the dough sticky, it makes pastry that's more delicate and more resilient because it interferes with gluten development. Because of this, you can get by working sweetened pastry dough much more than unsweetened pastry.

FIXING: Pastry dough can be modified after it has been made. If it is too dry, cut it into 2-inch cubes and make sure they are very cold. Put them in a food processor with 2 tablespoons liquid per recipe and process them until they come together into a clumpy mass. Squeeze the pastry dough to make sure it holds together and, if not, process with 1 more tablespoon liquid. If the pastry dough is too wet and sticky, roll it out on a work surface while dusting liberally with flour. If the pastry dough breaks apart as you're rolling it, you can patch it as shown on page 144, or chill it thoroughly, squeeze it together into a ball, and roll it out again.

BREAKING: Last, regardless of how perfect your pastry dough is, it can break apart when you roll it and you might have to bunch it up and roll it out again. Pastry dough can tolerate this, even two or three times, as long as it never gets warm. Therefore, you can save trimmings to use for other dishes.

A NOTE ON AMOUNTS: The recipes included here make about 1 1/2 pounds, which is more than is absolutely necessary for a standard-size pie or tart. The reason for the extra is to provide you with plenty of dough to cover the sides of the pie or tart pan and form the border, even if your dough cracks around the edges when you roll it out. If you're an experienced baker, feel free to cut the dough recipes by one-third. If you're dividing eggs, remember that a large egg is 4 tablespoons.

A NOTE ON CAKE FLOUR: The pastry dough recipes given here include a percentage of cake flour to decrease the overall gluten in the flour. Some brands of flour, such as Heckers and White Lily, are already low in gluten and can be used alone, without combining with cake flour. If you experiment with the brands available in your area, you'll get to know which have more gluten by the amount of liquid your dough absorbs and by the texture of the dough after baking. Once you find the flour with the lowest gluten content, you may be able to dispense with the cake flour.

Basic Pie and Tart Pastry Dough (Pâte Brisée)

Many recipes for savory tarts, such as quiches, or for dessert tarts or pies with very sweet fillings call for unsweetened pastry. And if the filling is rich you may want to use a minimum amount of butter in your crust. Traditional recipes for this basic pastry, called pâte brisée in French, call for half as much butter by weight as flour. The pastry dough is moistened with water and includes no sugar. In this recipe, you have a choice of liquids, because water activates gluten and using eggs or a bit of heavy cream instead helps to keep the pastry from becoming tough. Water makes dough crispy and light, while cream and eggs make it softer and richer. A sweetened version, what professionals call pâte brisée sucrée, is included as a variation.

Take care not to overwork the pastry dough; keep it cold and resist the temptation to make the finished pastry dough perfectly smooth and homogeneous—when you roll it out it should look a little ragged, with pieces of butter suspended throughout.

This recipe gives full instructions for a variety of mixing methods—by hand, in a stand mixer, and with a food processor. The photographs on pages 132 and 133 show the steps of making the dough by hand on a work surface, but the stages look similar whether you mix by hand in a bowl or on a surface, or use a stand mixer or food processor.

MAKES 1 POUND 8 OUNCES DOUGH,
ENOUGH TO LINE ONE 11-INCH PIE OR TART PAN

1 cup cake flour
1 cup all-purpose flour
1/2 teaspoon salt
3/4 cup cold butter, cut into 1/3-inch cubes
7 tablespoons water or heavy cream, or 2 eggs, lightly beaten
2 tablespoons additional liquid, or 1 egg white, if dough is too dry

By hand in a bowl: Stir both flours with the salt in a bowl. Add the butter, toss lightly into the flour with your fingers, and cut in the flour with a pastry cutter or a bench scraper for about 2 minutes, or until the pieces of butter are no larger than hazelnuts and no smaller than baby peas. Don't worry if the pieces of butter aren't all the same size. Scrape off the dough that clings to the pastry cutter or bench scraper.

Add the liquid and cut it in for 2 to 3 minutes, or until there is no loose flour in the bottom of the bowl and the dough looks like gravel. If the dough is still powdery, like grated Parmesan cheese, pinch a piece. If it doesn't come together, sprinkle in 2 more tablespoons of liquid and continue to cut in until the dough looks like gravel.

Dump the dough onto a work surface. Use your fingertips to pinch it together until it starts to come together into a ragged mass; or smear the pastry dough with the heel of your hand, or, for flakier pastry, knead the dough just long enough to get it to hold together. Scrape up the pastry dough with a bench scraper.

Flatten the dough into a disk if you're using it for a pie or tart; roll it into a cylinder if you're making cookies or tartlets. If you are not using the pastry dough right away, wrap it in plastic wrap and refrigerate.

By hand on a work surface: Stir both flours with the salt in a pile on a work surface. Add the butter, toss lightly into the flour with your fingers, and cut into the flour with a pastry cutter or a bench scraper for about 2 minutes, or until the pieces are no larger than hazelnuts and no smaller than baby peas. Don't worry if the pieces are different sizes. Scrape off the dough that clings to the pastry cutter or bench scraper.

Make a well in the center of the pile with your fingers. Pour the liquid into the well. Combine the liquid and flour by gradually pulling the flour into the well with your fingertips. Cut the liquid into the pastry dough for about 3 minutes, or until it looks like gravel with no loose flour on the work surface. If the pastry remains powdery, like grated Parmesan cheese, pinch a piece. If it doesn't come together, sprinkle in 2 more tablespoons of liquid and continue cutting in until the pastry looks like gravel.

Use your fingertips to pinch the dough together until it starts to come together into a ragged mass; or smear the pastry dough with the heel of your hand, or, for flakier pastry, knead the dough just long enough to get it to hold together. Scrape up the pastry dough with a bench scraper.

Flatten the dough into a disk if you're using it for a pie or tart; roll it into a cylinder if you're making cookies or tartlets. If you're not using it right away, wrap it in plastic wrap and refrigerate.

In a stand mixer: A stand mixer has the advantage of not overheating the pastry dough, and unlike a food processor it leaves the butter in pieces so the pastry is flakier. But don't start off at too high a speed or flour will fly around your kitchen!

With the paddle attachment, mix both flours and the salt on slow speed for about 30 seconds. Add the butter and combine it with the flour on low to medium speed, for about 1 minute. Add the liquid and mix the dough on low to medium speed for 40 seconds to 2 minutes, or until it looks like gravel, depending on the temperature of the ingredients. If it is still powdery, like grated Parmesan cheese after 2 minutes, pinch a piece to see if it comes together. If it falls apart, add 2 more tablespoons of liquid; if it holds together in a clump, continue mixing. If at any point the dough no longer feels cold, put the mixer bowl in the refrigerator or freezer for 15 minutes. Mix the dough on low to medium speed for 1 to 4 minutes, until it clumps together into a cohesive mass—you'll hear the motor straining.

Flatten the dough into a disk if you're using it for a pie or tart; roll it into a cylinder if you're making cookies or tartlets. If you're not using the pastry dough right away, wrap it in plastic wrap and refrigerate.

In a food processor: Making pastry dough in a food processor is by far the easiest method. The only disadvantage is that it mixes in the butter so completely that the dough is less flaky and more crumbly. Much is made about overworking dough in the food processor, but overheating it is more of a problem, because the food processor warms it very quickly. The secret is to chill all of the ingredients thoroughly before starting and, if need be, to chill the dough in the food processor bowl if it gets too warm while you're making it.

Combine both flours and the salt in a food processor and process for 15 seconds. With the processor off, add the butter and liquid, and process for 30 seconds. If the dough still looks powdery, like grated Parmesan cheese, pinch a piece. If it falls apart in your fingers, add 2 more tablespoons of liquid. Process for 15 seconds more. Feel the dough with the back of a finger. If it's no longer cold, put the entire work bowl in the freezer or refrigerator for 15 minutes. Dislodge any pastry dough sticking to the sides or bottom of the work bowl with a rubber spatula. Process for 10 to 30 seconds more, until the dough clumps together or clings to the sides of the food processor.

Flatten the dough into a disk if you're using it for a pie or tart; roll it into a cylinder if you're making cookies or tartlets. If you're not using it right away, wrap it in plastic wrap and refrigerate.

VARIATION

SWEETENED BASIC PIE AND TART PASTRY DOUGH: To make a sweetened version of basic pie and tart pastry dough—what professionals call *pâte brisée sucrée*—mix 1/2 cup granulated sugar with both flours in the first step.

1. Cut cold butter into 1/3-inch cubes.

2. Scatter the butter over the dry ingredients on a work surface and use a bench scraper to cut in the butter until the pieces are no larger than hazelnuts and no smaller than baby peas.

3. Slide the bench scraper under the dough and lift. Tilt the scraper so any loose flour you scraped up is now on top of the mixture.

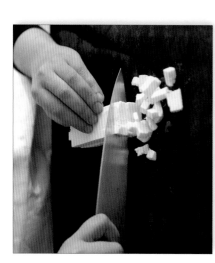

4. Bring the flour/butter mixture together in a pile and make a well in the center with the tips of your fingers.

5. Pour the liquid into the center of the well and move the tips of your fingers around in the well to incorporate the flour into the liquid.

6. As the dough gets sticky, use the bench scraper to clean off your fingers.

7. Cut in the liquid with the bench scraper.

8. Slide the bench scraper under the dough, lift, and fold, so loose flour, which sinks to the bottom, is folded over the top.

9. If the pastry dough remains powdery after 3 minutes of cutting, pinch a piece. If it falls apart in your hand, sprinkle in 2 tablespoons more liquid, while tossing until the dough looks like gravel.

BASIC PIE AND TART PASTRY DOUGH IN A STAND MIXER: THE STAGES

First, the dough looks like grated Parmesan cheese,

. . . then fine gravel,

. . . then coarse gravel,

. . . then lumps together, after 1 to 4 minutes of mixing.

10. When the ingredients are well combined, the dough should look like gravel with no loose flour.

11. Use the heels of your hands to smear the dough, one-eighth at a time, over the work surface until it comes together in a single mass.

12. You can also knead it with your fingertips.

13. Use a bench scraper to bring the dough together into a mound.

14. If you're not using the dough right away, flatten it, wrap it in plastic wrap, and keep it cold.

1. In a stand mixer, work the mixture on medium speed for 1 to 2 minutes, or until it looks like gravel.

2. Squeeze the dough and if it is still powdery, pinch a piece. If it crumbles, add another egg yolk. Continue to mix the dough on low to medium speed, until it clumps together and you hear the motor straining—from 1 to 4 minutes.

3. Flatten the dough so it cools more quickly.

hand, or, for flakier pastry, knead the dough just long enough to get it to hold together. Scrape up the pastry dough with a bench scraper.

Flatten the dough into a disk if you're using it for a pie or tart; roll it into a cylinder if you're making cookies or tartlets. If you're not using the pastry dough right away, wrap it in plastic wrap and refrigerate.

In a stand mixer: A stand mixer has the advantage of not overheating the pastry dough, and unlike a food processor it leaves the butter in pieces so the pastry is flakier. But don't start off at too high a speed or flour will fly around your kitchen!

With the paddle attachment, mix both flours, the salt, and sugar on low speed for 30 seconds. Add the butter and continue mixing on low to medium speed for about 2 minutes, or until the butter is well combined. Add the egg and egg yolk and mix on low to medium speed for 1 to 2 minutes, or until the dough looks like gravel. If after 2 minutes the pastry dough is still powdery, like Parmesan cheese, pinch a piece to see if it holds together. If it doesn't, add another egg yolk and mix again for 1 to 4 minutes, until the pastry dough looks like fine gravel, then coarse gravel, and finally until it comes together in a clumpy mass and you hear the mixer motor straining.

Flatten the dough into a disk if you're using it to make a pie or tart crust; roll it into a cylinder if you're making tartlets or cookies. If you're not using the pastry dough right away, wrap it in plastic wrap and refrigerate.

Extra Buttery Sweet Pastry Dough
(Pâte Sablée)

Extra buttery French-style sweet dough, pâte sablée, makes a rich and delicate pie crust—and great cookies—because it contains a high proportion of butter, and eggs are the only liquid. Because of all this butter, the pastry dough can be hard to roll out. If too cold, the butter congeals and the pastry is rock hard. If too warm, the butter melts and the pastry falls apart. Keep in mind, though, that the very things that make it hard to work with—the sugar and butter—make it less likely to toughen as it bakes. So if it keeps melting and you need to let it cool off in the refrigerator several times, don't panic—it will probably be fine. Because it is so buttery, sweet, and crumbly, extra buttery sweet pastry dough makes a great base for raw fruit tarts or any tarts and pies with fillings that aren't too sweet.

The photos at right show extra buttery sweet pastry dough being made in a stand mixer; the stages look very similar whether you are mixing by hand, in a stand mixer, or in a food processor (full directions for all of which are given in the recipe).

MAKES 1 POUND 10 OUNCES DOUGH,
ENOUGH TO LINE ONE 11-INCH PIE OR TART PAN

⅔ cup cake flour

1⅓ cups all-purpose flour

½ teaspoon salt

1 cup confectioners' sugar

1 cup cold butter, cut into ⅓-inch cubes

1 whole egg

1 egg yolk plus additional if needed

By hand in a bowl: Stir both flours with the salt and sugar in a bowl. Add the butter, toss lightly into the flour with your fingers, and cut into the flour with a pastry cutter or a bench scraper for about 2 minutes, or until the pieces of butter are no larger than hazelnuts and no smaller than baby peas. Scrape off the dough that clings to the pastry cutter or bench scraper. Don't worry if the pieces aren't the same size.

Add the egg and egg yolk and cut them in for 3 minutes, or until the pastry dough looks like gravel. If the pastry dough still looks powdery, like grated Parmesan cheese, pinch a piece. If it doesn't come together, cut in another egg yolk and continue cutting in until the pastry dough looks like gravel.

Dump the dough onto a work surface. Use your fingertips to pinch it together until it starts to come together into a ragged mass; or smear the pastry dough with the heel of your

BAKING

In a food processor: Making pastry dough in a food processor is by far the easiest method. The only disadvantage is that it mixes in the butter so completely that the pastry is less flaky and more crumbly. Much is made about overworking pastry dough in the food processor, but overheating it is more of a problem, because the food processor warms it very quickly. The secret is to chill all of the ingredients thoroughly before starting and, if need be, to chill the pastry dough in the food processor bowl if it gets too warm while you're making it.

Combine both flours, the salt, and sugar in a food processor and process for 15 seconds. With the processor off, add the butter and liquid. Process for about 10 seconds, or until the mixture looks like grated Parmesan cheese. Feel the pastry dough with the back of your finger. If it no longer feels cold, put the entire processor work bowl in the freezer for 15 minutes.

Dislodge any pastry dough sticking to the sides or bottom of the work bowl with a rubber spatula. Process for 10 seconds more. At this point, the pastry dough should hold together when you squeeze a piece. If it doesn't, add 2 more table- spoons of liquid or an egg yolk and process for 10 seconds more, or until it clumps together or clings to the sides of the food processor work bowl. Dump the pastry dough out onto a work surface.

Flatten into a disk if you're using for a pie or tart; roll into a cylinder if you're making cookies or tartlets. If you're not using it right away, wrap the dough and refrigerate.

Cream Cheese Tart and Pie Pastry Dough

· ·

Cream cheese pastry dough creates a delicious counterpoint to cooked fruit. Use it to line tarts or pies made with cooked berries, or tarts filled with lemon or other fruit curds.

This dough is made in the same way as the basic pie and tart pastry dough shown on page 130, except that the butter is augmented with cream cheese. Even when made in a food processor, it is flaky because the cream cheese forms layers in the same way as shortening. The dough is easier to work with than most because cream cheese doesn't melt as easily as butter when warm or harden as much when cold.

Depending on the flour, butter, and cream cheese, you may need to add more liquid to get the dough to hold together, requiring extra time in the food processor, which can cause the dough to overheat. Feel the dough with the back of a finger at each stage to make sure it is still cold. If it isn't, stick the entire food processor work bowl in the freezer for 15 minutes.

MAKES 1 POUND 8 OUNCES DOUGH, ENOUGH TO LINE ONE 11-INCH PIE OR TART PAN

1 cup cake flour

1 cup all-purpose flour

1/2 teaspoon salt

3/4 cup plus 1 tablespoon cold butter, cut into 1/3-inch cubes

4 1/2 ounces cold cream cheese, cut into 1/3-inch cubes

1/4 cup plus 2 tablespoons heavy cream, 2 eggs, or 1/4 cup plus 2 tablespoons ice water

1 to 2 tablespoons cream, beaten egg, or ice water if needed

Combine both flours and the salt in a food processor and process for 15 seconds. Turn off the processor. Add the butter, cream cheese, and cream. Process for about 10 seconds, or until it has the texture of grated Parmesan cheese.

Pinch a piece of dough. If it falls apart in your hand, add 1 more tablespoon of liquid and process for 10 seconds, or until clumpy. If it still won't form clumps, add 1 more tablespoon liquid and process for 10 seconds, or until it clumps. Dump the pastry dough onto a work surface.

Flatten the dough into a disk if you're using it for a pie or tart; roll it into a cylinder if you're making cookies or tartlets. If you're not using the pastry dough right away, wrap it in plastic wrap and refrigerate.

MAKING CREAM CHEESE TART AND PIE PASTRY DOUGH

1. When the mixture has the texture of grated Parmesan cheese, press together a small amount of the dough. If it remains mealy when you pinch it, add 1 more tablespoon liquid and process for 10 seconds more.

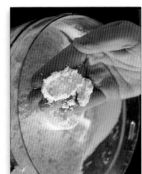

2. Pinch again to see if the dough holds together.

3. Process the dough for about 10 seconds more, or until it clumps together. Dump the dough onto a work surface and use it, or shape it and wrap it in plastic and refrigerate.

1. Scatter the butter cubes over the flour, then pour in the liquid. Fold the mixture so all the flour on the bottom of the bowl is moistened.

2. Dump the dough onto a sheet of plastic wrap and gather it in a mound along the center of the plastic wrap. Cover with a second strip of plastic wrap.

Flaky Pie and Tart Pastry Dough

Those of us who like the flavor of butter, which makes pastry crumbly, but also like our pastry flaky, as though made with lard or shortening, have to fold the pastry dough over itself a few times to create layers and hence flakes. You can make virtually any pastry flaky by rolling out the dough, folding it over itself like a letter, rolling it out again, and folding it again. You can repeat this folding up to 3 times; after that, continued folding makes no difference. This pastry dough is especially flaky because the butter is left suspended in relatively large pieces. When the dough is exposed to sudden heat, the moisture in the butter vaporizes and presses apart the layers of flour and water, creating a flaky effect. But whereas puff pastry dough, the ultimate folded pastry, is meant to puff up, this dough is meant simply to be flaky—and it is very flaky.

Because it contains a lot of butter, which can melt if the room is even slightly warm, you'll need to refrigerate the dough periodically to keep it from getting too sticky or too soft to work with. You should also refrigerate it if it starts to become elastic. Refrigerate the dough when it's rolled out in a rectangle instead of when it is folded so it chills faster.

More liquid is used in this dough than in others because the butter is not mixed thoroughly into the dough, contributing little to its moistness. This method won't work for dough that has been made in a food processor, because the butter is so thoroughly mixed into the flour it won't form flakes.

MAKES 1 POUND 8 OUNCES DOUGH,
ENOUGH TO LINE ONE 11-INCH PIE OR TART PAN

1 cup cake flour

1 cup all-purpose flour

1/2 teaspoon salt

1 cup cold butter, cut into 1/2-inch cubes

3 eggs, beaten, 1/2 cup plus 2 tablespoons heavy cream or ice water, or a combination of liquids totaling 1/2 cup plus 2 tablespoons

Stir together both flours and the salt in a bowl and sprinkle the butter over the mixture. Pour in the liquid and stir until there is no loose flour in the bottom of the bowl.

Place a 2-foot-long strip of plastic wrap on a work surface and put the dough on top of it. Form the dough into a mound about 15 inches long. Cover with a second sheet of plastic wrap. Pound the dough with a rolling pin and with the heel of your hand, and press it with your fingers, to coax it into a rectangle about 6 by 18 inches. Press the dough with your fingers or with the heel of your hand to combine loose pieces of butter and flour and to flatten the dough so it covers most of the plastic wrap and ends up being an inch or two larger in each direction. Refrigerate for 15 minutes.

Remove the top layer of plastic wrap and fold the dough as though it were a letter so it has 3 layers. Lift one end of the dough by holding onto the bottom layer of plastic wrap. Support the fragile dough with a bench scraper while you're folding it.

Pound the dough with a rolling pin to shape it into another rectangle the same size as the first. Wrap with plastic wrap and refrigerate for 30 minutes.

Fold the two ends of the dough so they meet in the center with just a little space separating them, then fold the two ends together again so you have a packet with four layers. The dough now has 12 layers.

Roll the dough out into another rectangle and fold it so the ends meet in the center as before, then fold the two ends together again. Cover with plastic wrap to prevent a crust from forming and refrigerate for 15 minutes. The dough now has 48 layers and is ready to use.

BAKING

3. Pound the dough to flatten it into a rectangle about 3 times longer than it is wide.

4. Press the dough with your fingers or with the heel of your hand to combine loose pieces of butter and flour and to flatten the dough so it covers most of the plastic wrap. Refrigerate for 15 minutes.

5. Remove the top sheet of plastic wrap. Fold the pastry dough like a letter: lift one end of the pastry dough by holding onto the bottom sheet of plastic wrap, supporting the fragile pastry dough with a bench scraper while you're folding.

6. Make the first fold.

7. Press the fold in place.

8. Lift the other end of the dough and fold it over so the dough is now a rectangle 3 layers thick.

9. Pound on the dough with a rolling pin to form it into another rectangle. Chill as needed.

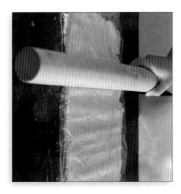

10. Continue pounding or gently rolling the dough until it is about 3 times longer than it is wide.

11. Fold the 2 ends of the dough so they meet in the center.

12. Fold the 2 ends together again so you have a packet with four layers. The dough now has 12 layers.

13. Pound and roll the dough into another rectangle and refrigerate for 15 minutes. Make another 4-layer-thick packet, for a total of 48 layers.

Sweet Crisp Pastry Dough
(Pâte Sucrée)

. . . .

The traditional French sweet pastry dough called pâte sucrée, used for fruit tarts with tart fillings (in both senses of the word) such as lemon curd, is made differently from most pie and tart pastry dough. The butter is not cut into small pieces with the flour; instead, it is creamed with sugar before beaten egg is added, a little at a time. The flour is then added all at once and mixed in just long enough for the whole thing to pull together.

MAKES 1 POUND 8 OUNCES DOUGH,
ENOUGH TO LINE ONE 11-INCH PIE OR TART PAN

1/2 **cup plus 2 tablespoons cold butter, cut into small cubes**

2/3 **cup confectioners' sugar, or** 1/2 **cup superfine sugar**

1 **cold egg plus 1 cold egg yolk, well beaten, plus additional egg yolk if needed**

1 **cup cake flour**

1 **cup all-purpose flour**

1/2 **teaspoon salt**

By hand in a bowl: Using a wooden spoon, cream the butter in a bowl and sift over the sugar. Beat until smooth and creamy. Beat the egg mixture into the butter-sugar mixture a little at a time.

Switch to a whisk as the mixture becomes more liquid. When the mixture has the consistency of sour cream or small curd cottage cheese, sift both flours over it and add the salt. Stir just long enough to incorporate the flour.

Flatten the dough into a disk if you're using it for a pie or tart; roll it into a cylinder if you're making cookies or tartlets. Wrap it in plastic wrap and refrigerate for at least 30 minutes before using.

In a stand mixer: A stand mixer has the advantage of not overheating the pastry dough, and unlike a food processor, it leaves the butter in pieces so the pastry is flakier.

Cream the butter and sugar with the paddle attachment on medium speed for about 2 minutes, or until smooth and creamy. Scrape down the sides of the bowl with a rubber spatula once during the creaming.

Beat in the whole egg until well combined. Scrape down the sides of the bowl with a rubber spatula, then beat in the egg yolk and scrape down the sides of the bowl again.

Turn off the mixer and add both flours and the salt all at once. Turn the mixer on low speed (so the flour won't fly around) for about 10 seconds, then turn it to medium. Continue mixing for about 30 seconds, or until the pastry clumps together, you hear the motor straining, and you see no more loose flour.

Flatten the dough into a disk if you're using it for a pie or tart; roll it into a cylinder if you're making cookies or tartlets. Wrap it in plastic wrap and refrigerate for at least 30 minutes before using.

In a food processor: Making pastry dough in a food processor is by far the easiest method. The only disadvantage is that it mixes in the butter so completely that the pastry is less flaky and more crumbly. Much is made about overworking pastry dough in the food processor, but overheating it is more of a problem, because the food processor warms it very quickly. The secret is to chill all of the ingredients thoroughly before starting and, if need be, to chill the pastry dough in the food processor bowl if it gets too warm while you're making it.

Process the butter and sugar for about 10 seconds, or until smooth. Scrape down the food processor bowl with a rubber spatula.

Add the egg mixture and process for 5 seconds. Scrape down the bowl again with a rubber spatula and process for 5 seconds more.

Add both flours and the salt and process for about 10 seconds, or until the mixture comes together in a single mass, but not so long that it forms a ball. If the dough doesn't come together, add 1 more egg yolk and try again.

Flatten the dough into a disk if you're using it for a pie or tart; roll it into a cylinder if you're making cookies or tartlets. Wrap it in plastic wrap and refrigerate for at least 30 minutes before using.

1. Sift the confectioners' sugar over the creamed butter, and cream the sugar and butter with a wooden spoon until smooth.

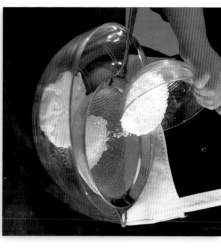

2. Work in the beaten egg–egg yolk mixture a table-spoon or so at a time. As the mixture becomes more liquid, switch to a whisk.

3. Sift over both flours and add the salt, and work the flour into the egg-sugar-butter mixture just long enough to moisten all the flour and eliminate lumps.

4. Press the dough with a spatula to flatten it (if you are using it for a pie or tart) or roll it into a cylinder (if you are using it for cookies or tartlets).

5. In a stand mixer, stop mixing when the pastry dough clumps together; then shape, wrap, and refrigerate.

6. In a food processor, process until the dough comes together in a cohesive mass, but stop before it forms a ball; then shape, wrap, and refrigerate.

Linzer Pastry Dough

. . . .

Besides its use for a linzertorte, linzer pastry dough can also be used to make cookies—one restaurant in Paris saves the tiny raspberry seeds left in the strainer used for making coulis, cooks the seeds with a little sugar, and spreads the mixture over a sheet of linzer dough. Another sheet is unrolled over and little cookies are cut out and baked.

Linzer pastry dough's delicate almond flavor goes well with virtually any fruit and gives a surprising dimension of complexity to fruit tarts and even apple pie. Because linzer pastry dough includes almond flour, which contains no gluten, the cooked pastry is even more crumbly and delicate than the richest tart doughs, extra buttery sweet tart and pie pastry, and cream cheese pastry.

**MAKES 1 POUND 8 OUNCES DOUGH,
ENOUGH FOR ONE 10-INCH TORTE**

²/₃ **cup almond flour, or 1 cup blanched almonds**

1²/₃ **cups cake flour**

¹/₂ **cup plus 2 tablespoons cold butter, cut into
small cubes**

³/₄ **cup confectioners' sugar**

¹/₂ **teaspoon salt**

1 egg, beaten

1 teaspoon vanilla extract

If using, toast the blanched almonds in a 350°F oven for 15 minutes, let cool, and grind for 2 minutes in a food processor. **By hand in a bowl:** Combine both flours (or the flour and ground almonds), the butter, sugar, and salt in a bowl. Toss them together and put the bowl in the freezer for 10 minutes.

Pinch the butter cubes to flatten them so they form thin flaky layers when incorporated into the dough. Stir in the egg and vanilla. Beat the mixture with a wooden spoon just long enough for it to come together into a ragged mass.

Flatten the dough into a disk if you're using it for a pie or tart; roll it into a cylinder if you're making cookies or tartlets. If you're not using the dough right away, wrap it in plastic wrap and refrigerate.

In a food processor: Making pastry dough in a food processor is by far the easiest method. The only disadvantage is that it mixes in the butter so completely that the dough is less flaky and more crumbly. Much is made about overworking dough in the food processor, but overheating it is more of a problem, because the food processor warms it very quickly. The secret is to chill all of the ingredients thoroughly before starting and, if need be, to chill the dough in the food processor bowl if it gets too warm while you're making it. Because linzer dough contains virtually no gluten, it's hard to overwork it, but you mustn't let it overheat in the food processor.

Put both flours (or the flour and ground almonds), the butter, sugar, and salt in the food processor and process for 10 seconds. Feel the dough with the back of a finger to make sure it isn't overheating. If it no longer feels cool, put the whole processor work bowl, with the dough in it, in the freezer for 15 minutes. Process for about 30 seconds, or until the dough comes together into a single mass.

Flatten the dough into a disk if you're using it for a pie or tart; roll it into a cylinder if you're making cookies or tartlets. If you're not using the dough right away, wrap it in plastic wrap and refrigerate.

MAKING LINZER PASTRY DOUGH

Don't worry if the finished dough looks a little shaggy. If you're not using it right away, shape it, wrap it in plastic wrap, and refrigerate.

Rolling out pastry dough may be the most exasperating of all baking techniques. Pastry dough, especially pastry dough that contains a lot of butter, can melt and tear if it gets too warm; if it's too cold, it's next to impossible to roll and may crack if you force it. Fortunately, if the dough tears or cracks, you can always patch it together when it's in the tart or pie dish. If the pastry dough starts to fall apart, quickly put it in the refrigerator to rest for 10 minutes. If the pastry dough is still difficult to roll, gather it up into a ball, flatten it into a disk, and roll it again.

Most pastry dough, especially dough that contains sugar or extra butter, can withstand some reworking as long as it never gets warm and the butter never melts. If you're working in a hot kitchen, try rolling the pastry dough out on a sheet of parchment paper (waxed paper will tear) so you can easily refrigerate it if it gets too warm. For a fragile pastry dough, hammer the dough with a rolling pin until you get it into

a disk shape, then roll it out. If the dough cracks as you're rolling it, place a piece of dough over the crack as soon as it forms so that when you continue rolling, the patch will be held in place.

One secret to rolling out dough successfully is to keep the dough from sticking to either the surface or the pin. Professional pastry chefs dust their work surface by artfully throwing a small handful of flour at the table such that the flour disperses evenly over just the right area. Short of that, sprinkle flour over the surface holding it high above so it spreads out. Dust the surface thoroughly, put the pastry in place and dust it. Rub flour on the rolling pin. Roll with the pin exactly crosswise in front of you; don't hold it diagonally. (This forces you to move the dough instead of the pin.) Keep the dough in constant motion by moving it in an arc over the work surface such that the flour on the surface attaches itself to the dough. Keep dusting and moving the dough, rolling as needed.

For a pie pan, roll the pastry dough 4 inches larger in diameter than the pan (pan bottom plus the sides).

For a round tart ring or tart pan or a fluted porcelain tart dish, roll the dough out so the diameter is 2 inches greater than the pan's diameter (4 inches for a fragile dough; see page 144). Because tart rings have no bottoms, plan ahead and bake these tarts on something you can serve them from—in the photos on page 144, we use a small round baking pan. If you don't have anything presentable to bake it on, you can gently transfer the finished tart to a cardboard disk before transferring the tart to a serving dish.

For a square or rectangular tart ring or pan, roll the dough 2 inches larger than the ring or pan on all sides (roll it 4 inches larger if you are using a fragile dough; see page 144).

Getting Rolled-Out Pastry Dough into the Pan

Of all baking frustrations, few are as annoying as the tendency for pastry dough to tear as you move it from a work surface to the pie or tart dish. The usual method, rolling it up on the pin and unrolling it over the dish, is fine in a cool kitchen, but pastry dough that's too warm may just fall apart as you roll it and dough that's too cold may crack. It's often easier just to fold the rolled-out pastry dough in half, quickly pull the dough up over the dish so the fold runs across the dish in the middle, and then unfold it. If the pastry dough is cold, hard, and brittle, quickly slide your splayed hands under it and move it over the pie dish or tart pan. You can also put the rolled-out pastry dough on a sheet pan—rolling the dough on parchment paper makes it easy to get the dough from surface to sheet pan—and freeze the dough until it's rock hard. You then only need to position the hardened round of pastry dough over the pan and let the dough thaw before pressing it into the dish.

If, when you finally get the pastry dough into the pie dish, there are cracks or holes, just press on the cracks with your fingers until they fuse together; patch any holes with small pieces of dough.

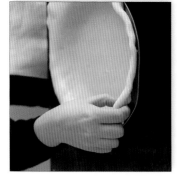

1. Unroll a sheet of pastry dough over a buttered or nonstick pie pan.

2. Cut around the dough with scissors so you have about an inch of extra dough hanging over the sides.

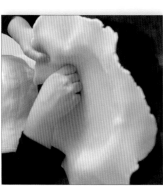

3. Tuck the extra dough under so the fold is even with the edge of the pie pan. Press the fold gently to form a thick border.

4. To flute the edge, press against both sides of the rim of the pie pan to get the pastry to rise up above it (but don't make it too thin). Press with 2 fingers on 1 side and 1 finger on the other to form a fluted edge.

1. Drape the pastry dough over the pan.

2. Press the pastry dough into the edges of the pan in the same way you would a round fluted tart pan (see opposite page).

1. If you are using a bottomless tart ring, brush it with softened butter.

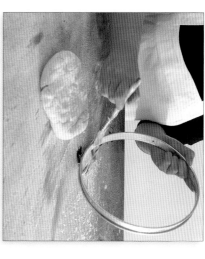

2. If you are using a fluted tart pan with a removable bottom or a porcelain tart dish, brush the sides and bottom with butter.

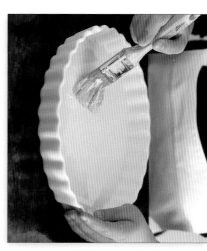

3. Roll the pastry dough up on the rolling pin or use another way to transfer it (see sidebar, page 141).

4. Unroll the pastry dough over the tart ring or dish. If you are using a bottomless tart ring, make sure it is on the surface you're using for baking the tart, because you can't move it once it's lined with dough.

5. Gently lift the pastry dough with one hand while gently pressing the dough into the corners.

6. Work around the ring, pushing a little extra pastry dough into the ring or dish and pressing on the rim of the ring or dish with your thumb to detach the extra dough around the sides.

7. Roll over the ring with a rolling pin to completely detach the extra pastry dough; pull away the excess dough.

8. Gently pinch the excess pastry dough that you left inside the ring so that the dough rises slightly above the edges of the ring and forms a border that comes about 1/4 inch above the ring.

9. Slide a paring knife between the dough and the edge of the ring so that no dough covers the edge of the ring. This makes it easier to lift up and take the ring off the finished tart.

Working with Fragile Pastry Dough

Some pastry dough, especially that which contains a lot of butter (such as puff pastry or *pâte sablée*) or contains very little liquid (such as shortbread dough, which contains none), can be almost impossible to roll without it cracking. You can always rework the pastry dough by kneading it slightly with the heel of your hand, but you risk warming it and making it tough.

A better if not terribly elegant solution is to just patch the pastry dough here and there where it cracks. If the pastry dough completely falls apart, just press the pieces together into the pie or tart dish. Because fragile pastry dough will fall apart if you try to roll it up on the rolling pin, it's better to fold it in half, move it over the tart dish, and unfold it. If the pastry dough is hard and brittle, don't even fold it—just slide your splayed hands under the dough and quickly move it over the dish; if it's soft, freeze it first.

Baking an Empty Pie or Tart Shell (Baking "Blind")

For some pies and tarts, the shell is baked empty, something bakers call baking "blind," before any filling is added. Blind baking the shell is necessary when the filling needs no baking, such as the filling in a banana cream pie or the filling and fruit in a raw fruit tart. When liquid or semiliquid fillings are cooked in a shell, the shell must be prebaked or the filling will keep the shell from getting hot enough to become crispy.

When baking blind, place a square of parchment paper or aluminum foil over the pastry dough. Make sure the parchment paper is large enough that it's easy to pick up by the ends when it's time to remove the weights. Don't use waxed paper, which smokes. Use dried beans or rice to keep the shell from puffing up in the oven. You can reuse them, but don't try cooking and eating them. Don't bother with those little aluminum beans made especially for bakers—they're too heavy and leave indentations in the dough.

When baking empty, most pie and tart shells should be baked at 400°F for 15 minutes for the edge of the tart to turn pale brown (when it's time to take out the beans or rice) and about 15 minutes more for the inside of the shell to turn golden brown and look matte instead of shiny. The exact baking time depends on the thickness of the pastry and the amount of sugar in the dough. Thinner shells and pastry with sugar brown more quickly.

During baking, if the inside of the shell isn't done but the outside edge is threatening to get too brown, cover the edge with a ring of aluminum foil (see opposite page).

1. Notice that the pastry dough is very crumbly. Hammer the pastry dough with a rolling pin until you get it into a disk shape.

2. Roll out the pastry dough. If it cracks as you're rolling it, place a piece of dough over the crack as soon as it forms so that when you continue rolling, the patch will be held in place.

3. Make sure the dough is at least 4 inches wider in diameter than the pan you're using.

4. Fold the dough in half and transfer it to the pan.

5. Press the pastry dough into the corners of the pan and press the dough against the rim of ring to cut off the excess.

6. If the dough cracks, patch it with another piece.

Troubleshooting Tarts and Pies

When prebaked shells are used to hold liquid mixtures, such as the custard mixture for a quiche, they need to be sealed so the liquid doesn't soak through and make them soggy. The usual method is to brush the prebaked shell with egg wash and put it back in the oven for 5 minutes or so to cook the seal. But if the shell has any cracks, liquid will seep through anyway. To seal cracks, don't bother with the egg wash, but instead whisk together 1 tablespoon flour and 2 tablespoons water into a smooth paste. Brush the inside of the shell with the paste—concentrate on any cracks—and bake for 5 minutes.

Another problem that sometimes arises is that the rim of the tart shell becomes brown before the rest of it. To prevent this, fold aluminum foil as though making a paper airplane and then cut off the top of the cone. When you unravel it, it will form a circle that you can use to cover the edge of the tart shell.

BAKING "BLIND"

1. Place a sheet of parchment paper over the dough-lined pan and pour in enough dried beans to come up the sides.

2. Bake until the edges are golden brown.

3. Remove the parchment paper and beans. Notice that the tart shell is shiny and gray.

4. Bake until the inside of the tart shell is golden brown.

KEEPING THE EDGES OF TARTS AND PIES FROM BURNING

1. Fold a square of aluminum foil, about 2 inches longer and wider than the tart, in half.

2. Fold in half again so you now have a square one-fourth the size of the first square.

3. Fold on a diagonal as though making a paper airplane.

4. Fold again so you have a narrow long triangle.

5. With the sharp point of the triangle at the center of the tart shell, cut the triangle about 1 inch from the edge of the tart, cutting off the point of the triangle.

6. Unfold the wider end of the triangle into a circular strip, and use it to cover the edge of the tart or pie shell when you put it back in the oven to finish baking.

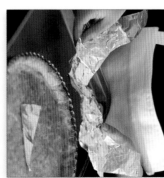

4. Press the dough into the corners of the ring.

3. Roll each 1/8 to 1/4 inch thick. Check the dough with a tartlet ring—there should be about 1 inch extra dough all around.

2. If they are hard, pound the rounds of dough to soften them.

1. Roll the dough into a cylinder and slice it 1 tartlet at a time (each is one-sixth of the dough).

8. Line the shells with parchment paper or aluminum foil and fill with dried beans. Bake until the edges are golden, remove the beans, and finish baking.

7. Slide the tip of a paring knife between the rim and the dough right along the edges to make the ring easier to remove once the tart is baked.

6. Roll over the tartlet with a rolling pin to detach the excess dough. Pinch the excess dough around the tartlet to reinforce the walls and form a border.

5. Press the extra dough that surrounds the tartlet about 1/3 inch toward the center and press down on the rim to cut through the dough and hold it in place.

9. If you're using the shells to hold liquid, brush them with egg wash or flour-and-water paste and bake for 5 minutes more to seal them.

Making Prebaked Single-Serving Tart Shells

To make six 3 1/2-inch tart shells, use 1 recipe basic pie and tart pastry dough (page 130) or one of the richer or sweet doughs such as extra buttery sweet pastry dough (page 134) or cream cheese tart and pie pastry dough (page 135).

Butter six 3 1/2-inch tart rings or fluted tartlet molds. Preheat the oven to 400°F. With your hands, roll the pastry dough into a cylinder. Cut off rounds of dough, one at a time, as you line the rings. If the dough rounds are hard, pound them, giving them a quarter turn after each couple of poundings.

When the pastry dough is about 1/2 inch thick or it has softened, roll out the circles until 2 inches greater in diameter than a tartlet ring and from 1/8 to 1/4 inch thick.

Place the round of pastry dough over a tartlet ring and press it down into the ring by lifting the edge of the dough and holding it upward while you press it into the corners—where the ring touches the pan—with the fingers of your other hand. When you've pressed the dough into the rings all around, push some of the excess dough that encircles the ring inward toward the center. Press down on the dough with your thumb to hold it in place, attached to the rim.

Making Egg Wash for Pie Pastry

Brushing pie pastry with an egg wash gives it an attractive golden sheen. A classic egg wash is made with an egg yolk, a whole egg, and salt, but you can play around with the ingredients, adding another yolk if you want a darker glaze, or another white if you want a lighter glaze. For convenience, a single whole egg beaten with 1/2 teaspoon salt will work well on most pastries.

Roll over the ring with a rolling pin to detach the excess dough (see opposite page), leaving a little extra dough within the tart ring to form a border. Form a border by pinching this extra pastry dough so some of it goes down and reinforces the tartlet wall and some of it pushes up over the edge. Slide the tip of a paring knife between the rim and the dough along the edges.

Cover the tartlet shells with parchment paper or aluminum foil and fill them with dried beans. Bake for about 15 minutes, or until golden brown on the edges. Remove the beans and bake for about 10 minutes more, or until the inside is pale brown. If the shells are being used to hold liquid mixtures, brush them with egg wash or flour-and-water paste and bake them for 5 minutes more.

Making Prebaked Miniature Tart Shells

To make these miniature tart shells, only a little larger than quarters, you'll need a stack of little molds. The more you buy, the more efficient the whole process will be since you need two molds per tartlet shell—one to hold the pastry dough and another to rest on top to hold it in place. Like tarts and pies, tartlets can be made starting with raw pastry or with pastry that's been cooked blind in the shells before anything is added. You may want to make a batch of prebaked tartlet shells—they freeze well—to use as holders for sweet fillings such as fruit curds or for savory fillings such as diced meats or curried seafood. They're great to have around for last minute hors d'oeuvres. The smallest molds take about 1/3 ounce dough each, while larger molds take close to 1 ounce.

To make 30 to 50 miniature tart shells, use 1 recipe sweetened basic pie and tart pastry dough (see page 131). To line the tiny molds, brush them with melted butter and roll the dough out into a thin sheet, no more than 1/8 inch thick. Nestle the molds as close to each other as possible, so as not to waste dough, and unroll the dough over. Press the dough in place with your fingers or with a ball of dough and press on the edges of the molds to detach the dough. Cut away the excess dough. If you keep the dough cold, you can roll out and use the trimmings. Brush the bottoms of another set of molds with butter and place these in the lined molds so the dough keeps its shape. If you're short on molds, stack the molds on top of each other—you can stack as many as six this way, but they won't cook evenly, so you'll need to take some out of the oven sooner than others.

Preheat the oven to 400°F. Bake for 15 minutes, take off the top molds, and bake for about 5 minutes more, or until the pastry is golden brown.

1. Brush half of the molds with melted butter.

5. Press around the inside edges of the pastry dough to adhere to the molds.

2. Roll a sheet of pastry dough up on the rolling pin. Brush off any excess flour.

6. Cut off any excess pastry dough with a paring knife.

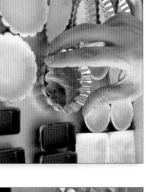

3. Unroll the dough over the molds that have been arranged close together.

7. Place a duplicate mold with the bottom buttered in each tartlet.

4. Press the dough into the molds with your fingers or with a little ball of dough.

8. Bake the shells for 15 minutes, remove the top molds, and bake 5 minutes more.

MAKING PUFF PASTRY AND OTHER LAYERED DOUGHS

Layered, or laminated, pastries are folded over themselves, usually along with a layer or chunks of butter, to create a series of thin sheets of pastry that produce vapor when heated. The vapor causes the layers to separate and the dough to rise. We've already seen this technique used to make so-called crumbly pastry more flaky, but it is also the method used for making classic puff pastry, quick puff pastry, and croissant dough.

Classic Puff Pastry Dough

Classic puff pastry dough scares people because it sounds complicated. Yes, to make it perfectly takes some practice, but if you follow a few dos and don'ts (see page 151), you should be able to make dramatic puff pastry the first time. Remember, you're basically enclosing a packet of butter in some pastry dough and then rolling it out and folding it over itself to create layers. This recipe is somewhat unorthodox because it calls for working the basic dough that you use to enclose the butter. This is heresy to anyone trained in the classic method in which the dough is worked as little as possible, but the results are dramatically better. The only downside is that the initial dough has to rest overnight before you can get to the next step.

**MAKES 1³/₄ POUNDS DOUGH,
OR A LITTLE OVER ³/₄ POUND FOR A HALF RECIPE**

2 cups all-purpose flour

1/2 cup water

3 tablespoons vegetable oil

1 teaspoon salt

3/4 cup plus 2 tablespoons butter

Combine the flour, water, oil, and salt by hand on a work surface or in a stand mixer or food processor. Mix until they come together in a smooth, homogeneous mass. Don't hesitate to knead the mixture to smooth it out. Form the dough into a squarish disk and score the top deeply with a knife, to help the gluten relax. Wrap tightly in plastic wrap and let rest overnight in the refrigerator.

Using Puff Pastry Trimmings

There are lots of preparations that call for puff pastry dough, but don't need the drama of perfectly even puffing. Tarts, tartlets, turnovers, cheese sticks, and napoleons can all be made with puff pastry trimmings. If you have tiny little trimmings, just bunch them together; but if you have sheets of pastry dough, keep them together so they're even when you roll them out. Keep trimmings tightly wrapped in plastic wrap in the refrigerator for up to a few days or in the freezer for up to a few weeks.

On a clean work surface, crush the butter with the heel of your hand or work it in a mixer with the paddle attachment until it is creamy, smooth, and spreadable, with the consistency of buttercream. Refrigerate for 15 minutes. Wrap the butter in plastic wrap and shape it into a square about 5 inches on each side and 1½ inches thick. Work the square of butter as needed with your hands to smooth it.

Flour the work surface and set the dough on it. Press firmly down on the dough disk at its four "edges." Roll out each edge so that you end up with a mound of dough in the center surrounded by four flaps. The flaps should be long enough to enclose the cube of butter.

Place the cube of butter on the central mound of dough and fold over the flaps, tucking excess dough into the folds so the butter is completely enclosed in a neat parcel of dough. Hammer gently on top of the packet of dough until it stretches out into a rectangle measuring 9 by 18 inches. Run your hand along the surface of the rectangle to make sure the butter is spreading out evenly inside the envelope of dough. Fold the rectangle into thirds as though it were a letter: starting with a narrow end, fold the bottom third up and fold the opposite end down. Turn the dough so that the large single fold, like the spine of a book, is on your left. Roll it out into another rectangle about the same size, and fold it in the same way. If the dough is difficult to roll, refrigerate for 30 minutes. Make two imprints with your fingers to indicate that it's had two "turns." Wrap in plastic wrap and refrigerate for at least 1 hour. Continue in this way until you have given the pastry seven turns total.

1. After mixing by hand or in a mixer or food processor, knead the mixture as necessary until smooth.

2. Form the dough into a squarish disk, score the surface of the dough with a knife, wrap in plastic wrap, and refrigerate overnight.

3. Wrap the butter in plastic wrap and pound it into a rectangle, working it with your hands as needed to smooth it out.

4. Press down and roll out each of the "edges" of the dough disk.

5. Roll the dough out so there are four flaps and a mound in the middle. Brush off any excess flour.

6. Close the butter up in the pastry.

7. Tuck excess dough in the folds to form a neat parcel of dough.

8. Roll the parcel of butter and dough out into a rectangle.

9. As you roll, check to make sure the butter reaches evenly across the length and width of the rectangle to its edges.

10. Fold one end of the rectangle halfway up the rectangle like a letter.

11. Fold the other end over and brush off any excess flour.

12. Roll out into another rectangle. Repeat the folds.

13. Fold again, and mark the dough with your fingers to indicate it has had two turns. Wrap and refrigerate for 1 hour.

14. Roll out into another rectangle. Fold, mark, wrap, and refrigerate, and continue until you've given the pastry a total of seven turns.

1. Combine the flour and salt and stir in the water. Don't overwork the dough—it should look ragged.

2. Gently toss the butter with the dough. If the butter starts to soften, refrigerate the mixture for 15 minutes. Pull the dough together into a mound.

3. Flour the work surface, place the dough on top, and press on the dough or hammer it with the rolling pin to flatten it.

4. Keep hammering, pressing, rolling, and shaping the dough into a rectangle. Refrigerate as needed if it starts to soften.

5. Fold the 2 ends of the rectangle toward the middle so they meet in the center.

6. Fold the 2 ends together to form a small packet. This is the first double turn.

7. With the large single fold, like the spine of a book, on your left, roll the dough into a rectangle.

8. Fold in a packet the same way as before. This is the second double turn.

9. Mark the dough with 2 fingers to show it has had 2 double turns. Repeat the rolling and folding one more time for flaky pastry and two more times for pastry for which height of rise is important.

Quick Puff Pastry Dough

....

Quick puff pastry is great for preparations in which you need the flaky effect of puff pastry but don't need it to rise as dramatically as classic puff pastry. The advantage, of course, is that quick puff pastry can be made in less time. One caveat: If your kitchen is terribly hot, don't try to make quick puff pastry; the butter will melt and make it very hard to work. Also, keep in mind that when you start folding over the dough it's going to look like you're trying to fold piles of gravel, but gradually, almost miraculously, it will come together and smooth out.

MAKES 1½ POUNDS DOUGH,
OR ¾ POUND FOR A HALF RECIPE

1½ cups butter

2 cups flour

½ teaspoon salt

⅔ cup cold water

Cut the sticks of butter lengthwise into quarters. Slice the quarters crosswise into cubes and refrigerate.

In a bowl or on a work surface, combine the flour and salt. Stir in the water with your fingers or a wooden spoon until the water disappears. Don't overwork the dough—it should look ragged.

Add the cold butter, form the mixture into a mound on a work surface, and pound it with a rolling pin until it is about 6 by 18 inches. Give the rolling pin a little twist at the instant it comes in contact with the dough while you're pounding to keep the pieces of butter from sticking. If the butter starts to soften, refrigerate for 15 minutes.

Fold in the 2 ends of the rectangle so they meet in the center and fold again to form a packet with 4 layers of dough. The dough now has 1 double turn. If the dough felt elastic as you were rolling, refrigerate for 30 minutes, covered with plastic wrap, before continuing.

With the large single fold, like the spine of a book, on your left, roll the dough into a 6 by 18-inch rectangle. If at any point the butter starts to soften, melt, or stick to the work surface, refrigerate the dough for 20 minutes. Fold the rectangle as before, into 4 layers. This is the second double turn; mark the dough with 2 fingers to show it has had 2 double turns. Refrigerate for at least 20 minutes.

Repeat the rolling and folding once more for the third turn. If you need the pastry to puff rather than just be flaky, give it 1 more double turn. Refrigerate the dough, wrapped in plastic wrap, for at least 1 hour before rolling out and baking.

A Note about Baking Temperatures

Pastries sometimes brown too much on the bottom before cooking through. This is because the oven is usually hotter on the bottom, near the heat source. To avoid this, preheat the oven 250°F hotter than the baking temperature called for and turn it down to the correct baking temperature once you start baking. Don't open the oven door any sooner than you need to. In this way, the oven doesn't ignite as soon so less heat comes up from the bottom. On the other hand, when baking a soufflé, it helps to have heat coming from the bottom so the body of the soufflé heats faster than the top. If the top cooks first, the crust can keep the soufflé from rising. For soufflés, preheat the oven 25°F lower than the eventual baking temperature and turn the heat up as soon as you put the soufflés in the oven.

Puff Pastry Dough Dos and Don'ts

If at any point your dough feels elastic and tries to shrink back into its original position as you're rolling it, wrap it up and put it in the refrigerator for an hour before rolling any more. If you force it, you'll break the layers.

Work the butter with the heel of your hand or with the paddle attachment in a mixer until smooth with no lumps. The butter should be cold but spreadable. If it contains lumps, these will harden as the dough rests and they will refuse to roll out and will cut through the dough.

Control the consistency of the butter with temperature. If the butter is too cold when you roll it, it will crack; if it's too warm, it will ooze out between the layers. It should have the same consistency as the dough itself. The best way to prepare the butter is to take it out of the refrigerator and knead it on a work surface with the heel of your hand.

When cutting pieces out of a sheet of puff pastry dough, make sure the dough is very cold—you can even stick it in the freezer for a moment—but not frozen so that when you cut it you don't crimp it. Use a sharp knife and cut quickly. Turn the pieces upside down on a sheet pan sprinkled with cold water: upside down so any crimping is on the bottom; cold water on the sheet pan to prevent the bottom of the pastry dough from burning.

When brushing dough with egg wash, don't let any get on the sides where it will harden and prevent rising. Start in a very hot oven, with convection if you have it, and then turn down the oven once the dough has puffed so it cooks through without browning more.

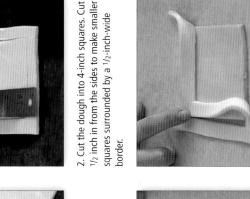
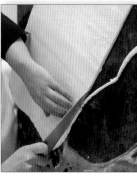

2. Cut the dough into 4-inch squares. Cut ½ inch in from the sides to make smaller squares surrounded by a ½-inch-wide border.

1. Roll out a sheet of puff pastry dough between ⅛ and ¼ inch thick. Trim off the edges.

3. Brush the inside square with water.

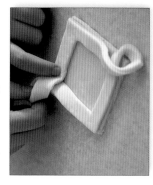

4. Lift one corner of the outer square and fold it diagonally so that its corner is directly over the opposite corner of the inner square. Press the corner gently in place.

5. Repeat with the opposite corner.

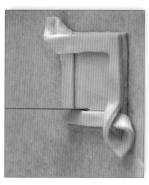

6. Press to hold the corner in place.

7. Press gently all around the square to keep the border in place. Brush the border and the curled corners with egg wash. Don't let any drip down the sides.

8. Cut halfway down into the inner square all around the inside border. Bake.

Puff Pastry Cases

These puff pastry square cases make elegant little holders for sweet or savory fillings—ice cream, fresh berries, creamed spinach, sautéed mushrooms, or seafood stews to name a few. The holder's gentle crunch offers a subtle contrast to the filling.

When cutting a sheet of puff pastry dough into smaller sections, be sure it is well chilled, almost frozen. This will prevent the edges from crimping as you cut and will also make it easier to move pieces of the pastry from one surface to the other without their changing shape. As you make these cases, you may have to move them to the freezer several times to keep the dough cold. You'll need about two-thirds of a recipe of dough to make the amounts given here. Before starting, review Thirteen Tips for Working with Puff Pastry Dough on page 154.

MAKES SIX 4-INCH SQUARE CASES

⅔ recipe classic puff pastry dough (page 148) or quick puff pastry dough (page 151)

Egg wash (see sidebar, page 146)

Line a sheet pan with parchment paper. Roll the dough into a 9 by 13-inch sheet, between ⅛ and ¼ inch thick. Transfer the dough to the prepared sheet pan (see page 141). Preheat the oven to 425°F. Chill the dough in the freezer for 5 minutes, or until firm but not hard. Using a knife or metal bench scraper, trim ½ inch off all 4 sides of the dough so you're left with an 8 by 12-inch sheet.

Cut the rectangle into six 4-inch squares. Work on parchment paper with space around each square so you can transfer the squares without the squares losing their shape. Cut a 3-inch square out of each of the larger squares and leave it in place. Wet the smaller squares. Lift the upper right corner of a larger square and bring it down on top of the lower left corner of the smaller square. Press the dough in place where it rests along the smaller square. Do the other side by lifting the lower left corner of the larger square and turning it over onto the upper right corner of the smaller square and again pressing the dough in place. Cut halfway down along the border of the inner square. Repeat for the other 5 squares.

Brush with the egg wash and bake for about 20 minutes, or until puffed and golden brown. Turn down the oven to 300°F and continue baking for about 20 minutes more to cook the dough through. Let cool on a cake rack.

When the pastry has cooled, notice how the center is a square. Cut around this center square and gently lift out the square of golden brown pastry and reserve this as the lid. Pull out and discard any raw dough.

Puff Pastry Rectangles

In classic and traditional French cooking, foods are sometimes served in cases such as those shown on the opposite page. Less formal, but in a way more elegant, are puff pastry rectangles. The baked rectangles are cut in half crosswise, and ingredients are placed over the bottom half of the rectangle, while the other half serves as a lid. You can make puff pastry rectangles any size you like. They're especially good with asparagus.

MAKES EIGHT 1½-INCH RECTANGLES

½ recipe classic puff pastry dough (page 148) or quick puff pastry dough (page 151)

Egg wash (see sidebar, page 146)

Line a sheet pan with parchment paper. Roll the dough into a 6½ by 8½-inch sheet, ⅛ to ¼ inch thick. Transfer the dough to the prepared sheet pan (see page 141). Preheat the oven to 425°F. Freeze the dough for 5 minutes, or until firm but not hard. Trim a ¼-inch strip off all 4 sides. Cut the dough into eight 1½ by 4-inch rectangles. Brush with the egg wash. Freeze for 15 minutes.

Bake for about 30 minutes. If the rectangles are golden brown before the time is up, turn down the oven to 300°F so the insides will finish cooking without the exterior becoming too brown.

Slice the rectangles in half horizontally and pull out any uncooked dough. When time to serve, place foods on the bottom half and cover with the top half.

9. Cut around the inside of the prebaked shells and gently pull away the little square on top to use as a lid.

10. Pull out and discard any uncooked dough.

11. Place the filling inside—raspberries with whipped cream is shown here—and place the lid on top.

MAKING PUFF PASTRY RECTANGLES

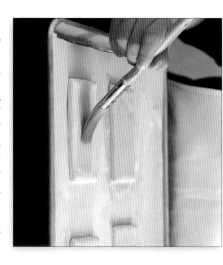

1. Roll out a sheet of dough and trim the edges. Cut the dough into rectangles and brush them with egg wash.

2. When the rectangles come out of the oven, cut them in half crosswise.

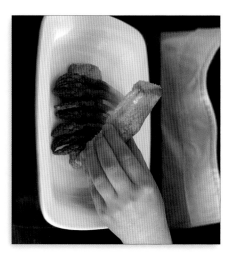

3. Steamed asparagus spears in puff pastry are shown here.

PIES, TARTS, AND PASTRIES

153

Thirteen Tips for Working with Puff Pastry Dough

Rolling out puff pastry dough and folding it over itself is a satisfying ritual, almost as satisfying as seeing the dough puff up in the oven. Classic puff pastry, made by sealing butter in a packet of dough and continually rolling it out and folding it on itself, is the most fun. While classic puff pastry dough takes more time to make than quick versions, it's actually easier to work with because the butter is sealed in and less likely to stick to a work surface. If you're making puff pastry for the first time, don't try it on a hot day or you won't be able to take your time with it without the butter melting.

1. Keep puff pastry dough cold or the butter it contains will melt and the integrity of the layers will be lost.

2. Don't ever force puff pastry dough while you're rolling it. If it shrinks as you press on it with the rolling pin, let it rest for at least 30 minutes in the refrigerator before trying again. If you try to force it, you'll tear the layers.

3. Never roll the dough thicker than 1/4 inch; when you bake the pastry, it won't rise efficiently.

4. Before baking, trim off the edges. The edges are likely to be crimped and can inhibit the pastry's rise.

5. Make sure the pastry dough is cold and hard—but not brittle—before you trim it, or you'll crimp it as you trim. Put it in the freezer for 10 minutes or so before trimming.

6. Sprinkle the sheet pan with a little water before putting on the dough. The water helps keep the bottom of the dough from burning.

7. Turn the sheets of puff pastry dough upside down onto the sheet pan so any crimped edges will be on the bottom.

8. Once you've rolled out the pastry dough and cut it to the size and shape you want, stick the whole sheet pan in the freezer for 15 minutes just before baking. The colder the dough and the greater the difference in temperature between the dough and the oven, the more dramatic the rise will be.

9. Don't cut or shape puff pastry dough into its final form before moving it to the sheet pan, or it may lose its shape. It's better to trim the dough right on the sheet pan or on a sheet of parchment paper that can be transferred to the sheet pan. This also makes it easier to move it in and out of the refrigerator or freezer.

10. When you brush puff pastry dough with egg wash to give it a golden sheen (see sidebar, page 146), don't let any of the egg wash drip down the sides or it may harden in the oven and keep the pastry from rising.

11. When sealing 2 pieces of dough together, such as for the vol-au-vents on page 237, seal them together with water, not egg wash. Egg wash would ooze down the sides and create a seal.

12. When baking puff pastry dough, always start with high heat, at least 425°F, to get the most rise. If the dough isn't cooked through even though it's puffed and golden brown, turn down the oven to 300°F so the pastry continues to cook on the inside without browning any more.

13. If you have a convection oven or a convection option on your oven, use it. Keep in mind that the movement of air in a convection oven creates the effect of higher heat. In general, bake at 50°F lower when using a convection oven (i.e., start the pastry dough at 375°F instead of 425°F).

Cream Puff Pastry Dough
(Pâte à Choux)

Cream puff pastry dough, commonly known as choux pastry, is made by beating eggs, one by one, into a cooked paste—called a panade—of flour, water, and butter. Cream puff pastry dough is used to make éclairs, cream puffs, profiteroles, and little cheese puffs called gougères. The techniques for making each of these are virtually the same; only the size and fillings differ. Éclairs are filled with pastry cream and coated with fondant; cream puffs are filled with sweetened whipped cream; and profiteroles are filled with ice cream (chocolate sauce is poured over them at the last minute). Cheese puffs have no filling—their flavoring, cheese, is combined with the uncooked pastry before baking.

It's hard to go wrong with cream puff pastry dough, but remember to slice the butter so it melts quickly when you heat it with water. If you add it in one big chunk, it will take too long to melt and too much of the water will evaporate, throwing off your proportions. As you cook the panade, continue stirring with a wooden spoon so the dough holds together in a single mass and leaves a film of cooked flour adhering to the bottom and sides of the saucepan. This process usually takes only about 3 minutes and ensures that you've forced as much water out of the mixture as possible, meaning that you can add more egg—and the more egg, the lighter the finished baked pastry will be. Keep in mind that the exact number of eggs you use depends on the flour. Don't just add all the eggs called for in the recipe without checking

(continued right column top) the consistency of the mixture. You've added enough eggs when a groove made in the top of the dough slowly folds in on itself and when the dough droops from a wooden spoon.

MAKES 1½ POUNDS DOUGH

1 cup water
½ teaspoon salt
½ cup butter, sliced
1 teaspoon sugar
1 cup flour, sifted
4 eggs
1 egg white plus more as needed

Combine the water, salt, butter, and sugar in a saucepan and bring to a simmer over high heat. There's no need to stir. Turn the heat down to medium and add the flour all at once. Stir with a wooden spoon for about 3 minutes, or until the mixture forms a cohesive mass and pulls away from the sides of the pan, leaving a film of flour on the sides of the pan.

Transfer the panade to a bowl or a stand mixer and beat it with a wooden spoon or the paddle attachment for about 1 minute, or until slightly cooled.

Beat in the eggs, 1 at a time, until you've added 4. Check the consistency of the batter by pulling a wooden spoon through it. When the groove it makes slowly closes in on itself, you've added enough eggs. Another way to check is to see if the batter droops from the spoon when it is held sideways. If so, it is ready. Add more egg whites as needed until the batter passes the groove test. While the dough is best used right away, it will keep for several hours in the refrigerator.

1. If you are mixing in a bowl, you'll know you've added enough eggs when a wooden spoon pulled quickly through the mixture leaves a groove in the dough that slowly closes in on itself.

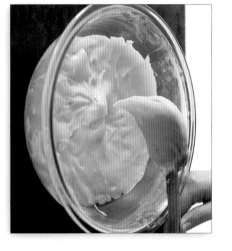

2. Pull the wooden spoon up out of the dough. The dough should droop off the spoon and not stick straight out.

3. If you are mixing in a stand mixer, you'll know you've added the right number of eggs when the dough pulls away from the paddle attachment in a thick rope.

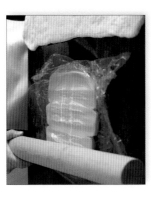

1. Pour the flour in a mound onto a work surface. Make a well in the middle. Pour in the milk and add the sugar, then the dry yeast. Use your fingers to gradually pull the flour away from the inside of the well.

2. Sprinkle over the salt, then use a bench scraper to pull the dough into the center with the liquid. Press on the dough until it comes together in a loose shaggy mass.

3. Pull the dough together with your hands. Knead for 7 minutes. Refrigerate the dough for 1 to 3 hours, covered with plastic wrap.

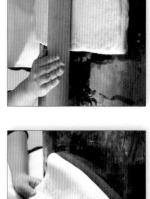

4. Pound the butter between 2 sheets of plastic wrap into an 8-inch square.

5. Uncover the dough and flatten it with the heel of your hand, then roll it into a rectangle.

6. Place the butter on one end of the rectangle. Align the sides of the butter and the dough with the sides of your hands.

7. Fold the other half of the dough over the butter so you end up with a square.

8. Press gently on one side of the square with one hand, while firming up the edge with the other to even out the square.

9. Gently pound the dough with the rolling pin to stretch the dough and the butter in it.

10. Roll the dough into another rectangle.

11. Fold the rectangle like a letter so you have three layers. This is the first "turn."

12. With the thick fold on your left, roll the packet into another rectangle.

13. Again, fold the rectangle like a letter. This is the second turn.

14. Pound the dough with the rolling pin to flatten it and roll it into another rectangle.

15. Fold in thirds, again, like a letter to make the third turn.

16. Pound and then roll with the rolling pin to form a rectangle. Fold as before to make the fourth turn. The dough can now be rolled out and used.

Croissant Dough

Croissant dough is similar to classic puff pastry dough—butter is folded in the dough to create layers—except that it is also leavened with yeast. You must take care not to let the yeast overferment while you're working with it, or it won't have any life left when you're ready to shape the croissants and let them rise. To avoid this, don't make the dough wait a long time between turns and keep the dough cold as you work with it—this means frequent chilling in the refrigerator. When the dough is finished, it will keep for up to 24 hours refrigerated before it must be shaped and proofed. In fact, 12 to 24 hours in the refrigerator before proofing improves its flavor. One last precaution: Never allow the salt to come in contact with the yeast all at once, or it will kill the yeast.

Note: A slightly different method of starting the dough is shown in the photographs. Either method works.

MAKES 2³/₄ POUNDS DOUGH, ENOUGH FOR 12 CROISSANTS

3¹/₂ cups flour

1 cup barely warm water

1 teaspoon active dry yeast

¹/₃ cup heavy cream

1 teaspoon salt

1³/₄ cups cold butter

Combine 1 cup of the flour with the water and yeast just long enough to break up the lumps of flour, and let rise for 1 hour.

Stir in the remaining flour, the cream, and salt and knead the mixture for 1 minute. Cover and let rest for 20 minutes.

Knead the mixture by hand for about 10 minutes or with a stand mixer fitted with the dough hook for about 20 minutes, or until smooth and elastic. Refrigerate for 30 minutes.

Work the butter with the heel of your hand or the paddle attachment until there are no lumps. Shape the butter into an 8-inch square. Roll the dough out into a 9 by 17-inch rectangle and place the square of butter on one end. Fold over the dough so the butter is encased in a square. Press together the edges of the square to seal in the butter. Press gently on the square with one hand while firming up the other sides to even out the square. Gently hammer on the square of dough with a rolling pin to stretch the dough and the butter in it.

Roll the dough into a 9 by 18-inch rectangle. Fold the rectangle into thirds as though it were a letter. Starting with a narrow end, fold the bottom third up and fold the opposite end down. If the dough is difficult to roll, refrigerate for 30 minutes. When the dough is easy to work, turn it so that the large single fold, like the spine of a book, is on your left, roll it out into another rectangle, about the same size, and fold it in the same way. Make two imprints with your fingers to indicate that it's had two "turns." Wrap in plastic wrap and refrigerate for at least 1 hour. Continue in this way until you have given the dough 4 turns total.

The dough is now ready to roll out for making croissants, pains au chocolat, or Danish pastry.

FILLINGS FOR TARTS AND PASTRIES

This section contains a number of fillings for tarts and pastries, both sweet and savory. More tart and pastry fillings can be found in the cakes chapter and in the custards chapter.

Almost all fruit tarts have a layer of filling spread over the tart shell before the fruit is added. The filling helps hold the fruit in place and balances its flavor by providing sweetness and, at times, a tangy acidity. If the filling and fruit are cooked together in the tart, the filling absorbs liquid released by the fruit and helps prevent the crust from getting soggy.

Fillings for raw fruit tarts are most often pastry cream or fruit curds—lemon curd is a favorite—but any kind of filling that might be used in a cake will also work in a tart. Mousses, mousselines, *crème chiboust* (pastry cream lightened with Italian meringue), white or dark chocolate ganache (whipped or not), mascarpone, stabilized whipped cream (flavored or not; perhaps folded with a fruit curd to make a light mousse), or buttercream can all be spread over a prebaked tart shell before the fruit is arranged on top. Fruit custards gently baked in prebaked tart shells and allowed to cool can also be used as a base for raw fruit.

Fruit curds, especially lemon curd, are among the most popular tart fillings because they're light and sweet without being too sweet and because they provide a tangy and refreshing accent to the fruit. Most fruit curds contain butter, or even brown butter (*beurre noisette*), which attenuates the curd's sourness and makes the tart richer and the curd stiffer when cold. Brown butter imparts a subtle butterscotch flavor. Most fruit curds are made by adding butter to the fruit mixture while it's still hot, but you can also beat room-temperature butter into the cold curd—as much as $1/2$ cup butter per 1 cup of curd—to make the curd fluffy and rich.

Mousses, such as white chocolate mousses or fruit mousses, make marvelous fillings. The most common fruit mousse is a Bavarian cream made by combining fruit puree, crème anglaise, whipped cream, and a little gelatin to hold the whole thing together.

Pastry cream, the filling used in éclairs, can be flavored and used as the base for a tart. It is best when flavored with brown butter or made richer with whole butter, which turns it into a mousseline. When pastry cream is combined with Italian meringue, it becomes crème chiboust, which is lighter. You can also make pastry cream with an appropriate fruit puree instead of milk and use this fruit-based pastry cream as the base for a fruit mousseline (by beating in cold butter), a fruit crème chiboust (by folding it with Italian meringue), or as the base for a fruit mousse by folding it with whipped cream or stabilized whipped cream.

White or dark chocolate ganache (essentially a mixture of cream and chocolate) is sometimes used to fill a prebaked tart shell before berries or other fruits are arranged on top. For a lighter effect, the ganache is sometimes whipped.

Fruit custards, made by combining fruit purees or juices with eggs and cream, can be baked in prebaked shells and the resulting tarts served as is (see pages 186 to 194), or the fruit custard tarts can be covered with raw fruit.

Mousseline, made by beating butter into cold pastry cream, makes a silky, luxurious filling because the richness of the mousseline balances the fruit, which by itself or with lemon curd, is sometimes too austere. There are two basic kinds of mousseline. One, classic mousseline, is made by beating room-temperature butter into pastry cream, usually $1/2$ cup butter to 1 cup pastry cream. The other mousseline, a fruit mousseline, starts out with a pastry cream made with strained fruit puree or fruit juice instead of milk. Butter is then beaten into this fruit pastry cream in the same way as for a classic mousseline.

Mascarpone, the rich creamlike Italian cheese, makes a lovely tart filling. Since mascarpone can be hard to find and is expensive, you can substitute cream cheese that's been worked with sour cream.

Stabilized whipped cream—cream held together with a little gelatin so it doesn't release liquid as it sits—can be used alone but is better flavored with a small amount of fruit curd or fruit puree (see pages 58 and 61).

Buttercream is usually reserved for cakes, but it can be used in a tart. Because it's very sweet, it should be spread rather thinly before the fruit is put on top. Buttercream can also be lightened by whipping it with fruit curd—one part fruit curd to two parts buttercream.

If the tart is to be cooked with a filling, almond or hazelnut cream (mixtures of ground nuts, eggs, and butter) or almond or hazelnut cream thickened with a little cornstarch are good candidates. For some fruit tarts, such as classic French apple tart, some of the fruit is cooked down into a thick "compote" and used to line the tart shell under the fruit.

Making Raw Fruit Tartlets with Custard Filling

Many tart recipes call for spreading cooked lemon curd, lightened with whipped cream or not, on the bottom of a prebaked tart shell before arranging fruit, usually berries, on top. You can also use fruit custard, cooked in the prebaked shell(s) and allowed to cool before arranging over the fruit. You can use any flavor of custard you like; if you want the flavor of the curd to match the fruit you put on top, prepare the persimmon curd on page 191, substituting the appropriate pureed fruit. When baking custard-filled tartlets that you're going to use to hold fruit, put in less filling—a little more than 2 tablespoons per tartlet instead of 3 to 4 tablespoons. Shown below are assorted fruits on top of tartlets filled with baked lemon custard curd.

Glazing assorted fruit tartlets.

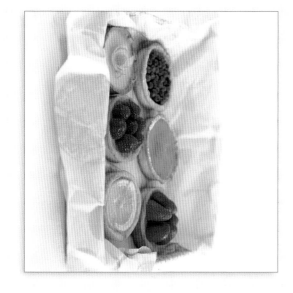

To make strawberry tartlets, cut a wedge out of the strawberries so you can nestle them closer to each other in the tartlet. Arrange the strawberries in the shell with the custard cream.

Almond Cream

. . . .

Almond cream is not almond paste. Almond cream is a mixture of eggs, butter, and almond flour or ground almonds—made from sweet, not bitter, almonds—while almond paste contains some bitter almonds to give it its distinctive flavor. Almond cream is often used to line tart shells for both cooked and raw fruit tarts. When almond cream is combined with pastry cream it becomes frangipane, which is lighter than almond cream and preferred by some bakers for lining tarts (see variation). You can also substitute other nuts to make other nut creams—toasted hazelnuts are especially good.

MAKES 2 CUPS

1½ cups almond flour, or 2 cups blanched almonds

½ cup butter

½ cup plus 2 tablespoons sugar

1 egg

1 egg yolk

2 tablespoons dark rum (optional)

If using, toast the blanched almonds in a 350°F oven for 15 minutes, let cool, and grind for 2 minutes in a food processor. Cream together the butter and sugar until smooth. Beat in the egg and egg yolk, one by one, adding the yolk only when the mixture is even and smooth.

Mix in the almond flour (or ground almonds) and the rum. Keep covered in the refrigerator or freezer for up to 3 days until needed.

VARIATION

. . . .

Frangipane is made by combining 1 part pastry cream (page 160) with 2 parts almond cream.

MAKING ALMOND CREAM AND FRANGIPANE

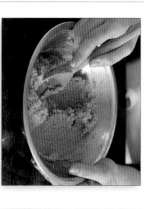

To make almond cream, cream sugar and butter until smooth, then work in the eggs. Work in the almond flour (or ground almonds) and rum.

To make frangipane, stir together almond cream and pastry cream.

1. Bring the milk to a simmer with the vanilla. Whisk together the sugar, egg, egg yolks, and cornstarch until smooth and pale.

2. When the milk comes to a simmer, stir half of the hot milk into the egg mixture.

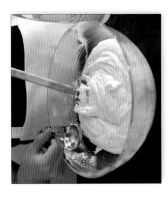

3. Return the mixture to the saucepan with the rest of the milk and stir over medium heat . . .

4. . . . until the mixture boils and thickens.

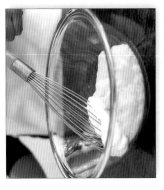

5. To loosen pastry cream that has gotten stiff in the refrigerator, beat with a whisk.

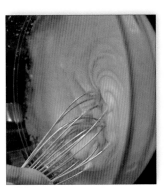

6. To lighten the pastry cream with whipped cream, whisk in about one-fourth of the whipped cream, then whip in the rest of the whipped cream.

7. To lighten the pastry cream with Italian meringue, whisk about one-third of the Italian meringue into the pastry cream, then whisk in the rest. Then stir in the flavoring (if any).

Pastry Cream

. . . .

Pastry cream is a custard somewhat like crème anglaise, but much thicker because it contains cornstarch or flour. Because the starch stabilizes it, pastry cream, unlike crème anglaise, can be allowed to boil. In fact it must boil for the starch to thicken it properly. Pastry cream is perhaps best known as the filling for éclairs, but it is at its best when combined with other mixtures such as whipped cream, Italian meringue, butter, brown butter, or lemon curd. It is used as a base for raw fruit tarts, as a filling for éclairs and napoleons, and occasionally as a cake filling. Pastry cream can be flavored with chocolate, vanilla, liqueurs, spirits, coffee, nut butters, praline, and spices.

MAKES ABOUT 2½ CUPS

2 cups milk

1 teaspoon vanilla extract

½ cup plus 1 tablespoon sugar

1 egg

3 egg yolks

¼ cup cornstarch

Bring the milk to a simmer in a heavy-bottomed saucepan over medium heat and add the vanilla.

In a bowl, whisk together the sugar, egg, egg yolks, and cornstarch until smooth. When the milk comes to a simmer, stir half of it into the egg mixture. Pour the egg mixture back into the saucepan containing the rest of the milk, place over medium heat, and stir the mixture with a whisk or wooden spoon. Reach into the corners of the saucepan so the pastry cream doesn't hide out there and scald.

When the pastry cream comes to a boil and thickens, transfer it to a bowl and cover with plastic wrap touching its surface so a crust doesn't form. Refrigerate for up to 4 days. To loosen pastry cream that has gotten stiff in the refrigerator, whisk it by hand or in a mixer.

VARIATIONS

METHODS FOR LIGHTENING PASTRY CREAM: To lighten pastry cream with whipped cream, combine one part whipped cream to three parts pastry cream. Whisk one-fourth of the whipped cream into the pastry cream and then fold the pastry cream with the remaining whipped cream. If you're using this mixture in something that's not going to be served immediately, use stabilized whipped cream (see page 62).

To lighten pastry cream with Italian meringue (*crème chiboust*), combine equal parts Italian meringue and pastry cream. Whisk one-third of the Italian meringue into the pastry cream and then fold the pastry cream with the remaining Italian meringue. You can also add 1 tablespoon brown butter (see page 196) to each cup of this mixture to give it a nutty flavor, or you can flavor with spirits such as kirsch.

Hazelnut Frangipane

Classic recipes for frangipane combine one part pastry cream to two parts almond cream. While this may make sense in a professional kitchen, most of us don't want to make a batch of pastry cream just to make frangipane. You can also substitute other nuts for the almonds. This hazelnut version of frangipane is made as a single recipe. If you want to make almond frangipane, substitute 2 cups blanched and toasted almonds for the hazelnuts.

MAKES 2½ CUPS

2 cups hazelnuts, peeled as much as possible (see sidebar at right)
1/3 cup sugar
2 tablespoons cornstarch
2 eggs
1/4 cup butter

Grind together the hazelnuts and sugar in a food processor (see above right). Add the cornstarch and eggs and process for about 1 minute, or until smooth. Add the butter and process for 30 seconds more.

Praline Paste

Praline paste is a sweetened nut butter made with hazelnuts or almonds. It's usually made from praline, which is a kind of candy made by cooking nuts in caramel. You can skip this step, however, by roasting the nuts and then grinding them with sugar in a food processor.

MAKES 2 CUPS

2 cups hazelnuts, roasted and peeled as much as possible (see sidebar, below)
1/2 cup sugar

Grind the hazelnuts and the sugar in a food processor for about 4 minutes, or until the hazelnuts are oily. Scrape the food processor work bowl with a rubber spatula to incorporate any of the mixture that is clinging to the sides and bottom.

Peeling Hazelnuts

Roast the nuts in a 350°F oven for 15 minutes. While still hot, rub them vigorously together between two towels. This procedure gets rid of most, but not always all, the peel. To get off more, boil for a minute, drain, and rub again in a towel.

Cream Cheese Tart Filling

This filling is very much, in fact almost exactly, like cheesecake.

MAKES 2¼ CUPS, ENOUGH FOR ONE 9½-INCH TART

8 ounces cream cheese, at room temperature
3/4 cup confectioners' sugar, or more as needed
1 teaspoon vanilla extract, or 1 tablespoon kirsch
2/3 cup sour cream, or more as needed

Beat the cream cheese using a wooden spoon or a stand mixer fitted with the paddle attachment until softened. Beat in the sugar and vanilla.

As the cream cheese gets easier to mix, switch to a whisk and add the sour cream, one-fourth at a time. Whisk until smooth. Add more sour cream as needed to obtain the desired consistency, which should be smooth and silky but still thick.

Cheese Danish Filling

Use this filling in cheese Danish (page 222) or in miniature cheese Danish twirls (page 223).

MAKES 1½ CUPS

½ cup confectioners' sugar

8 ounces cream cheese, at room temperature

1 teaspoon vanilla extract

1 tablespoon grated lemon zest
(½ lemon; see page 194)

1 egg

Use a heavy wooden spoon—or the paddle attachment of a stand mixer if you're making a lot—to combine all the ingredients except the egg. When the mixture is smooth, work in the egg. Refrigerate, covered, for up to 2 days before using.

Goat Cheese Filling

Use this filling for vol-au-vents (page 237) or for square or rectangular puff pastry cases (pages 152 and 153).

MAKES ABOUT 1½ CUPS

8 ounces soft or medium goat cheese

4 tablespoons heavy cream

2 to 3 tablespoons extra virgin olive oil (optional)

In a bowl with a wooden spoon, work the goat cheese to soften it. Add 2 tablespoons of heavy cream and work it into the cheese, then add another tablespoon at a time until the mixture has the consistency of sour cream. If you like the flavor of olive oil, work in 2 or 3 tablespoons.

Mushroom Filling (Duxelles)

Mushrooms are among the tastiest of all vegetables and are delicious when chopped and cooked down to concentrate their flavor. This chopped mushroom filling, called duxelles, can be used as the filling for turnovers, galettes like the Pithiviers (page 206; substituting duxelles for the almond cream), or a jalousie (page 234), or they can be spread over a prebaked tart shell (see page 146) with freshly sautéed wild mushrooms arranged on top. To make the easiest and least rich version of this filling, just cook the chopped mushrooms down until any water they release evaporates. Heavy cream is added to hold them together and give them a luxurious flavor and texture.

If you use cultivated white mushrooms, this recipe will yield 2 cups; if you use creminis, it will yield somewhat more (they have the same flavor as cultivated white mushrooms but contain less water).

MAKES ABOUT 2 CUPS

2 pounds mushrooms, preferably cremini

1 tablespoon butter

½ teaspoon chopped fresh thyme, 2 teaspoons chopped fresh tarragon, or 1 teaspoon chopped fresh marjoram (optional)

½ cup heavy cream (optional)

Salt

Pepper

Chop the mushrooms in a food processor. They should retain some of their texture; pulse them for a few seconds at a time to avoid turning them into a puree.

Melt the butter in a heavy-bottomed pan over high heat and add the mushrooms and thyme. Stir so the mixture heats evenly. Soon the mushrooms will be submerged in their own liquid. Continue to cook over high heat until all the liquid evaporates and the mixture is dry.

Add the cream. Continue cooking until there is no liquid in the pan. Season to taste with salt and pepper. Use as a filling for pastries, or as a stuffing for virtually anything.

Liquid Fondant

....

Most of us had our first encounter with fondant icing on the top of an éclair. Home bakers don't use fondant very often because it can be messy to work with and, until recently at least, no one knew they could make it at home.

To make fondant by hand, you have to pour soft ball sugar syrup (see page 47) onto a pastry marble and then knead it—starting out with a wooden spoon—until it takes on its characteristic opaque but shiny appearance. To replicate this technique with a food processor, just pour the soft ball sugar syrup into the food processor, let it cool to 147°F, and process it for about 5 minutes, or until the right consistency. Don't be tempted to process the syrup before it has cooled to 147°F. If you process it while it's too hot, the processing will cause water to evaporate and the fondant will be too dry and hard, making it impossible to work with.

Fondant can be stored in tightly sealed plastic containers for months at room temperature.

MAKES 2 CUPS

3 cups sugar

1½ cups water

¼ cup plus 2 tablespoons light corn syrup

Combine the sugar, water, and corn syrup in a heavy-bottomed saucepan and bring to a simmer over medium heat. Cook to the soft ball stage (when a candy thermometer reads 238°F).

Dip the bottom of the saucepan in cold water for about 5 seconds, to cool the syrup but not so long that it hardens.

Pour the syrup into a food processor work bowl. Let sit for about 15 minutes, or until the temperature of the syrup drops to 147°F on an instant-read thermometer. Process the fondant for about 10 minutes, or until milky and opaque. Let cool. Don't try to process until cool—the movement of the processor actually heats the fondant.

Note: If at any point the fondant gets too stiff—which invariably happens when you store it or it sits out—heat it slightly (so it's a little warmer than body temperature) over simmering water or in a microwave, and if necessary thin it with 1 to 2 teaspoons water per cup of fondant.

1. Prepare sugar syrup and cook it to the soft ball stage in a heavy-bottomed saucepan. Dip the bottom of the saucepan in cold water for about 5 seconds to cool the syrup but not so long that it hardens. Cool to 147°F, process for 10 minutes, then transfer to a plastic container.

2. As fondant sits, it gets harder. To thin it, heat it to slightly warmer than body temperature, and if necessary thin it with 1 teaspoon or more of water.

Flavoring Fondant

Fondant can be flavored and colored, but keep in mind that a very small amount of liquid will make it too thin. Because of this, fondant is hard to flavor with spirits. It's easily flavored, however, with melted bitter chocolate or concentrated instant coffee.

Chocolate Fondant: Melt 4 ounces grated or finely chopped bittersweet chocolate, or 2 ounces bitter chocolate in a double boiler and add the chocolate to 2½ cups warm fondant (or melt the chocolate directly in the fondant) and stir until smooth. If the fondant has hardened, heat the mixture over a saucepan of simmering water or in a microwave. If necessary to thin it, add 1 to 2 teaspoons water per cup of fondant.

Coffee Fondant: Dissolve 2 teaspoons instant coffee in 1 teaspoon hot water. Add this mixture to 1 cup fondant.

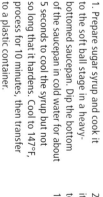

FRUIT PIES AND TARTS

Whereas pies and tortes are usually baked in a relatively deep pie pan with sloping sides (linzertorte is an exception; it's baked in a tart pan), tarts are thinner and have straight or nearly straight sides. Many pies have two crusts, whereas tarts do not. Tarts are removed from the pan or ring before they're served, while pies are usually served right out of the pie pan. Tarts are baked in pans, usually metal but sometimes porcelain, with fluted sides. Most metal tart pans have removable bottoms, which makes it easy to serve the tart.

The fruit in fruit pies is cooked as the pie cooks, whereas a fruit tart sometimes is made with raw fruit arranged in a prebaked shell, usually with some kind of filling such as lemon curd. When tarts are made with cooked fruit, the fruit is cooked along with the tart. Since most fruit releases liquid as it bakes, fruit tarts often contain a layer of frangipane (see page 159) or another filling (see page 179) below the fruit to absorb the liquid.

Should I Precook Fruit for a Fruit Pie or Tart?

It depends on the fruit. Some fruit, such as apples or pears, release so little liquid that the fruit can be baked right in the pastry without any worry that the liquid will make the pie soggy. Most berries release a lot of liquid and can be precooked and drained, and the liquid they release can be boiled down to a syrup. Cherries release less liquid and are sturdier, so they can be cooked directly in the liquid they release without going through the draining process. Tree fruits, such as apricots or peaches, can be cooked ahead—roasted with sugar and butter is great—or cooked directly in the tart since the amount of liquid they release will usually evaporate.

Blueberry Pie

Because berries release a lot of liquid as they cook, they'll turn into soup or at least make the bottom crust soggy when baked in a pie. To avoid this, cook the fruit long enough for it to release its liquid and for some of the liquid to evaporate, and then thicken the mixture with cornstarch. You can also cook the berries just long enough to get them to release their liquid, then drain them over a pan and boil down the liquid. The liquid and berries can then be reunited, sometimes with cornstarch, before baking. Berry pies should not be served as soon as they come out of the oven or the inside will be too runny. A little lime juice is included to wake up the flavor of the berries. If you are not a veteran piemaker, review pages 129 to 130 for advice about working with pastry dough.

MAKES ONE 9- TO 10-INCH PIE

1 recipe sweetened or unsweetened basic pie and tart pastry dough (page 130)

Egg wash (see sidebar, page 146)

4 pints blueberries

1 cup sugar or more as needed

1/4 cup lime juice (2 to 3 limes)

1 tablespoon cornstarch combined with 2 tablespoons cold water

Use a 9- to 10-inch pie pan. Roll the dough into a round about two inches larger than the pie pan (see page 142). Line the pie pan, fold under the edge to make it a double thickness, and make a fluted edge. Brush the inside of the pie shell with the egg wash to help prevent the bottom crust from becoming soggy. Refrigerate the pie shell. Preheat the oven to 400°F.

Cook the blueberries in a wide sauté pan with the sugar and lime juice, covered, over medium heat for about 10 minutes, or until they release their liquid. Drain the berries over a large saucepan and boil down the liquid until you have about 2 cups. Stir in the cornstarch mixture, bring back to a boil, and let cool. Combine with the blueberries.

Put the blueberry mixture in the lined pie shell and bake for 90 minutes, or until bubbling.

Let cool for 2 hours at room temperature, then refrigerate for 2 hours more before serving.

1. Roll the pastry dough in a circle large enough to come up the sides of a pie pan with enough left over to form the border.

2. Transfer the pastry dough to the pie pan (see page 142).

3. Push the pastry dough into the sides of the pie pan.

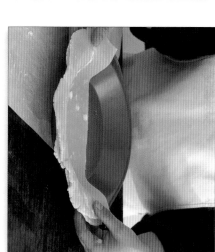

4. Pinch the pastry dough around the rim of the pie to form a border.

5. Pinch the dough to flute the edge (see page 142).

6. Brush the inside of the pie shell with egg wash to help prevent the bottom crust from becoming soggy.

7. Stir the berries in a wide pan with the sugar and lime juice over medium heat until they're swimming in their own liquid. Boil down the liquid, stir in the cornstarch, and return to a boil. Let cool and combine with the berries.

8. Pour the berry mixture into the pie shell and jiggle the pie back and forth to settle the mixture. Bake until bubbling.

3. Toss the cherries with the sugar, cornstarch, and lime juice.

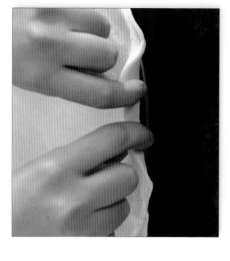

6. Lift up the edge of the pastry dough and fold under the excess. Pinch it all around the pie to form a thick border.

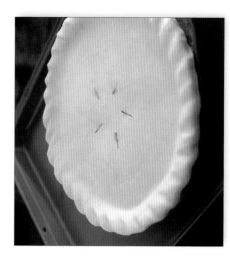

9. Make slits in the top crust to allow steam to escape.

2. Use the side of your forefinger to push the dough into the corners of the pie dish.

5. Trim the pastry dough around the pie so both the top and bottom crusts stick out about 1 inch from the rim.

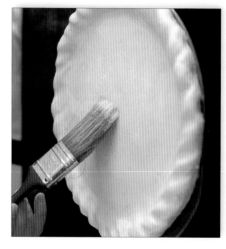

8. Brush the crust with egg wash and sprinkle it with granulated sugar.

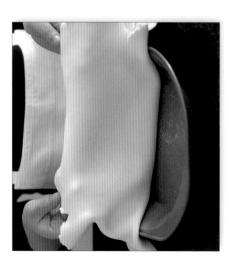

1. Butter a 9- to 10-inch pie dish and unroll or unfold a sheet of pastry dough over the pie dish.

4. Spread the cherries in the pan so they come level with the top of the pie pan. Place the frozen round of pastry dough over the pie and let it soften.

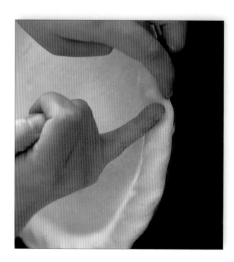

7. Use the side of a finger to gently press the pastry dough at an angle to form a fluted edge.

Cherry Pie

. . . .

Because cherries release less liquid when baked than, for instance, blueberries, they can be baked raw in a pie without too much liquid accumulating. However, toss the cherries with cornstarch, which thickens the liquid they release as they cook. It is important that the pie get very hot—cherry juice should bubble up through the slits in the top—to cook the cornstarch, otherwise it won't thicken properly. The pie should be allowed to sit for 3 hours after it comes out of the oven so the fruit filling can set. If you are at all apprehensive about working with pastry dough to make a pie crust, read pages 129 to 130.

MAKES ONE 9- TO 10-INCH PIE

2 recipes sweetened or unsweetened basic pie and tart pastry dough (page 130)

5 cups Bing or sour cherries, pitted, or three 12-ounce bags frozen pitted cherries, thawed, about 5 cups

1/2 cup sugar if using Bing cherries, 3/4 cup if using sour cherries, plus more for the pie top

3 tablespoons cornstarch

2 tablespoons lime juice (1 to 2 limes), optional

Egg wash (see sidebar, page 146)

Use a 9- to 10-inch buttered pie pan. Roll half the dough into a round about two inches larger than the pie pan and 1/8 to 1/4 inch thick and use the dough to line the pie pan. Refrigerate the pie shell. Roll the remaining dough to the same size and thickness as the first, and place it on a sheet pan and freeze. Preheat the oven to 400°F.

Toss the cherries with the sugar, cornstarch, and lime juice and place them in the lined pie pan. The cherries should be level with the top of the pie pan, or slightly mounded. Lift the frozen round of pastry dough and place it on top of the pie. Wait for about 5 minutes for it to soften, then trim the two rounds of pastry dough with scissors so they each protrude about 1 inch out from the rim. Pinch them together to form a fluted edge.

Brush the pie with the egg wash and drizzle sugar over it. Make several slits near the center of the pie with a paring knife to allow steam to escape. Bake for about 30 minutes, or until the top browns, then place a sheet of aluminum foil loosely over it to keep it from browning more. Turn down the oven to 350°F. Bake for about 30 minutes more, or until bubbles and juice are coming out of the slit. Continue baking for 10 minutes more to make sure the cornstarch thickens the liquid released by the cherries. Let cool for at least 3 hours on a cake rack. Serve at room temperature or slightly cool.

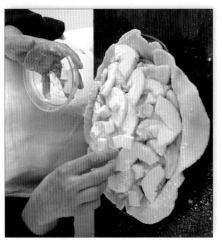

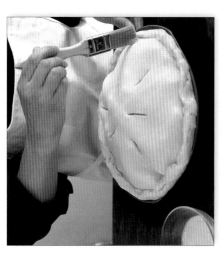

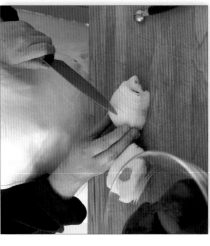

1. Line a pie pan with the pastry dough, leaving at least ³/₄ inch dough hanging over the rim, and refrigerate. Roll a second round of pastry dough the same size as the first, place it on a sheet pan, and freeze it.

2. Peel, halve, core, and slice the apples slightly less than ¹/₂ inch thick.

3. Toss the apples gently with the sugar and flour. Heap them in the pastry-lined pie pan and dot them with the butter.

4. Place the frozen round of pastry dough on top of the pie and let it thaw slightly.

5. Working around the pie, pinch together the top and bottom rounds of dough and roll them to form the edge.

6. Make at least 6 vents in the top of the pie to let out steam, then brush the top of the pie with the egg wash and sprinkle with sugar.

7. Bake until steam and juice come out of the vents and the top crust is golden brown.

Apple Pie

· ·

Apples make great pies because they don't release a lot of liquid, which can make the crust soggy. Buy tart apples, preferably heirloom varieties from a local farmers' market. The sliced apples are tossed with a small amount of flour to thicken what little liquid they do release. If you are unsure of your pastry-handling skills, you may want to review pages 129 to 130.

MAKES ONE 9- TO 10-INCH 2-CRUST PIE

2 recipes sweetened or unsweetened basic pie and tart pastry dough (page 130)

7 large tart apples (3 pounds), such as Cortland, Northern Spy, or Rome

2/3 cup sugar plus more for the pie top

3 tablespoons flour

1/4 cup butter, cut into 1/4-inch cubes

Egg wash (see sidebar, page 146)

Preheat the oven to 375°F. Use a 9- to 10-inch pie pan. Roll half the dough into a disk about two inches larger than the pie pan. Line the pie pan. Refrigerate the pie shell. Roll the remaining dough to the same size and thickness as the first disk. Place on a sheet pan and refrigerate or freeze.

Peel, halve, core, and slice the apples slightly thinner than 1/2 inch. Toss the sliced apples with the 2/3 cup sugar and the flour and put them in the lined pie pan. Be gentle so you don't break up the slices. Dot the apples with the butter. Place the second pastry round over the pie and let thaw slightly.

Trim the edges of the pastry rounds with scissors so each protrudes about 1/2 inch out from the rim. Pinch the edges together and roll up to seal the pie with a ropelike border.

Make 6 slits in the top of the pie with a paring knife. Brush the edges and top of the pie with the egg wash. Sprinkle the top of the pie with sugar. Bake for 90 minutes, or until golden brown with bubbling juices coming out of the vents. Let cool for at least 1 hour before serving.

Classic French Apple Tart

. . . .

For this tart, some of the apples are cooked down into a thick chunky apple sauce, which is spread over the raw tart shell. The remaining apples are then sliced thin (see note) and arranged over the applesauce. Slice the apples as thin as you can so they'll be flexible when you fan them in the tart shell; if they are too thick, they'll crack.

MAKES ONE 9- TO 10-INCH TART

8 large (about 4 pounds) Golden Delicious or other tart apples

1/2 lemon

1/2 cup sugar plus 1 tablespoon for the tart top

1 vanilla bean, split in half lengthwise (optional)

1/2 cup water

1 recipe sweetened or unsweetened basic pie and tart pastry dough (page 130)

3 tablespoons butter, melted

2 tablespoons hot apricot glaze (see page 61), optional

Peel, halve, and core the apples and rub the halves with the lemon. Squeeze the juice of the lemon into a wide pan or pot. Cut half of the apple halves into 1/3-inch cubes and put them in the pan with the lemon juice. Add the 1/2 cup sugar, the vanilla bean, and water. Cook over medium heat, stirring with a rubber spatula, for about 15 minutes, or until the apples soften and all the liquid they release evaporates. Let cool. Slice the remaining apples as thin as you can with a chef's knife or plastic mandoline (see Note).

Preheat the oven to 375°F. Use a 9- to 10-inch tart ring or fluted tart pan. Roll the dough into a round 2 inches larger than the pan and use it to line the pan (see page 143). Spread the cooked apple mixture in the pan and press the sliced apple halves together in your hands to get them to fan out slightly. Arrange them around the side of the tart, with the fanned

end up against the sides of the tart, fitting extra slices in here and there to make them even. Place some broken-up apple slices—use the small end pieces—in the middle of the tart to mound up the apples that are arranged in the middle. Make another ring of apple slices inside the first but facing in the opposite direction. Use a few apple slices for the tiny round in the middle. Brush generously with the melted butter and sprinkle the 1 tablespoon sugar over all. Bake for about 1 hour and 15 minutes, or until deep golden brown. Brush with the glaze while the tart is still hot.

Note: Here is a trick to make the slicing easier: Cut across the apples as thin as you can, but leave the slices attached along the side of the apple. Cut along the side of the apple to slice off the strip where the apples are attached. This leaves the slices nestled together and makes them much easier to fan.

1. Halve the apples, core them with the end of a vegetable peeler or with a melon baller, and rub the halves with lemon.

2. Use half of the apple halves to make the applesauce filling. Place the apple halves, flat side down, on a work surface and cut through them sideways so you end up with 3 slices per half. Slice into strips, then cubes.

3. Toss the cubes with the lemon juice and put them in a heavy-bottomed pot with the sugar, water, and the optional split vanilla bean. Cook until the liquid evaporates. Stir occasionally but not so much that the cubes lose their shape.

4. Allow the applesauce to cool and spread it over the lined tart ring. Mound it up slightly in the center to support the apples and to create a more dramatic effect.

5. Slice the remaining apple halves as thin as you can. Leave the slices barely attached on one side of the apple half so they stay in place as you slice. Cut off the strip where the slices are attached, and fan them out to make sure they're all detached.

6. Arrange the apple slices around the outside of the tart so that each slice covers the indentation where the core was removed of the slice beneath it. Use a knife to nudge the slices so they meet evenly. Put aside the small or uneven apple slices from the ends of the apples.

7. Mound the little apple slices you saved in the center of the tart.

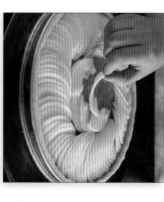

8. Make another ring of apple slices inside the first but facing in the opposite direction. Use your fingers to even out the inner slices.

9. Arrange half-slices over the center of the tart, brush with melted butter, and sprinkle with granulated sugar.

10. Bake until deep golden brown. Let cool and gently lift off the tart ring. If the tart ring sticks, slide a paring knife between the ring and the crust along the top edge. Gently transfer the tart to a serving dish or serve right from the baking dish.

11. Brush the tart with hot apricot glaze while the tart is still hot.

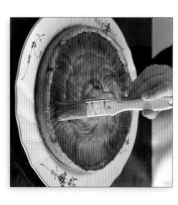

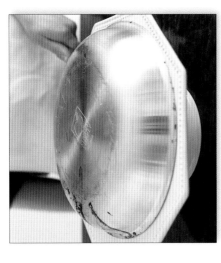

3. Cut out a disk of pie pastry dough about 2 inches wider than the pan, using a pan lid or plate as a template. Pull off any excess dough. Put the round of dough on a sheet pan and freeze for 10 minutes.

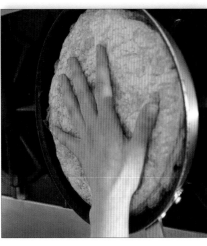

2. Place the pan over medium heat and as the apples shrink, force in more apples. Continue to cook the apples until they release their liquid and this liquid reduces to about 1/2 inch deep and is syrupy. Remove from the heat.

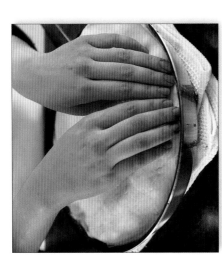

1. Arrange the apple quarters over the sugar-butter mixture, starting from the outside and working in. Continue adding apple wedges until they fit tightly in the pan and all stand on end.

4. Transfer the now hard pastry disk to the top of the apples. When the disk softens slightly, tuck it in and around the apples. Bake.

5. To unmold, heat the pan on the stovetop. Splay your hand over the tart and rotate it to loosen it completely from the pan.

6. Set a serving plate over the pan, hold them together, and invert them so that the tart unmolds onto the plate.

Tarte Tatin

A Tarte Tatin is a French upside-down apple tart. Because it needs to cool thoroughly and then warm to room temperature for serving, it's best started the day before. You'll be buying a ludicrous number of apples, but keep in mind that they shrink a lot as they cook. Golden Delicious apples are used because, despite what one would think, they hold their shape better than, say, Granny Smiths. If you're lucky enough to find Macintosh, Northern Spy, Cortlands, or a tart heirloom variety for baking, use those instead.

MAKES ONE 12-INCH TART

15 medium to large baking apples (about 7 pounds), Golden Delicious or another type (see above)

³/₄ cup butter

³/₄ cup sugar

1 recipe basic pie and tart pastry dough (page 130) or cream cheese tart and pie pastry dough (page 135)

Peel, halve, and core the apples, then cut into quarters. Combine the butter and sugar in a heavy-bottomed 12-inch nonstick oven-safe sauté pan with sloping sides. Cook the mixture over medium heat, while stirring with a wooden spoon, for about 5 minutes, or until the butter begins to brown and smell fragrant.

Arrange the apple quarters standing up, in a circle, around the perimeter of the pan. If the butter starts to brown too much, take the pan off the heat until the bottom of the pan is covered. Continue adding apples, working inward. As you add more apples, you'll be able to keep them standing upright, on end. Add as many apples as you can to keep them tightly together. Keep the pan over low to medium heat. Move the pan every 5 or 10 minutes to a different position over the heat so the apples brown evenly.

Because the apples shrink as they cook, you'll need to keep adding more apple quarters to force them to stay on end. If there aren't enough apples in the pan, they will fall over, instead of being tightly packed, on end. Continue adding apple quarters until you can't add any more, then wait as the apples cook, and add more. Fifteen minutes from when you started adding the apples, you'll see liquid coming about halfway up their sides. Continue cooking for about 20 minutes, or until the liquid evaporates to syrup and comes only about ¹/₂ inch up the sides of the apples. At this point, gently pull out one of the apple quarters and look at the end that was against the

bottom of the pan and check to make sure it's golden brown. Take a few samples from around the pan and, if necessary, continue to cook until golden brown. Carefully replace the apples in the exact position they were. When the apples are all golden brown, remove the pan from the heat.

Preheat the oven to 400°F. While the apples are cooking, roll out the dough and cut out a 14-inch round. Put the pastry dough on a sheet pan—it may reach a little over the sides— and freeze it.

Place the frozen round of pastry dough over the apples. Let it soften for a couple of seconds so you can tuck the extra dough down along the sides of the apples. Bake for about 40 minutes, or until the dough is golden brown. Take the tart out of the oven and let it cool for a couple of hours. Refrigerate it for 3 to 12 hours or more so the apples cling together for the unmolding.

To get the tart out of the pan without it falling apart, place the pan on the stove over high heat and move it around for about 40 seconds to heat the entire bottom of the tart. Turn off the heat and with your splayed palms, give the tart one full rotation to make sure that it doesn't stick to the pan when you unmold it. Put a serving plate upside down over the pan. While holding the pan and plate together, turn the tart over. Gently pull away the pan.

Plum Tart

You can make this tart with any round tree fruit such as peaches, plums, and nectarines. When fruits, such as plums, release a lot of liquid as they bake, it's best to cover the tart shell with a layer of frangipane (essentially a mixture of eggs, butter, and ground almonds) to absorb the fruits' liquid as it's released and keep the shell from getting soggy. Another approach is to cook the fruit first, with sugar and butter, and boil down the released liquid into a syrup that you can then use to glaze the tart.

MAKES ONE 9¹/₂-INCH TART

1 recipe sweet crisp pastry dough (page 138), extra buttery sweet pastry dough (page 134), or sweetened basic pie and tart pastry dough (page 131)

2 cups frangipane (page 159)

6 large plums (about 1¹/₂ pounds)

2 tablespoons butter, cubed

1 tablespoon granulated sugar

Strawberry, red currant, or apricot glaze (see page 61), or confectioners' sugar

Use a 9¹/₂-inch tart ring or fluted tart pan. Roll the dough 2 inches larger than the ring or pan and line the pan with it (see page 143). Spread the frangipane over the bottom of the tart shell and refrigerate. Preheat the oven to 300°F.

Cut the plums in half, scoop out the pits with a melon baller or small measuring spoon, and cut each half into 3 wedges. Arrange the plum wedges in a ring around the perimeter of the tart shell,

overlapping the wedges slightly. Make another ring of wedges facing in the opposite direction as the first or, as shown here, arrange just a few more wedges in the center to fill it. Dot with the butter and sprinkle with the granulated sugar. Bake the tart for about 30 minutes, or until it is golden brown and you see the frangipane puff up slightly between the plum wedges. Brush with glaze or dust with confectioners' sugar (see Note) just before serving. Serve warm or at room temperature.

Note: To avoid getting sugar on the rim, cover the edge of the tart with a foil ring (see page 145) or brush off the sugar with a dry brush.

MAKING A PLUM TART

1. Line a tart ring or fluted tart pan with pastry dough and spread the frangipane over it.

2. Cut the plums in half vertically. Scoop out the pits with a melon baller or small measuring spoon. Cut each half into 3 wedges.

3. Arrange the plum wedges, overlapping slightly, around the perimeter of the tart. Make another ring of wedges facing in the opposite direction as the first or, as shown here, arrange just a few more wedges in the center to fill it.

4. Dot the tart with butter and sprinkle with granulated sugar. Bake for about 30 minutes, or until the rim of the tart is golden brown and you see the frangipane puff up slightly between the plum wedges.

5. Brush the tart with glaze or dust it with confectioners' sugar. To avoid getting sugar on the rim, cover the edge of the tart with a foil ring or brush off the sugar with a dry brush.

Apricot Frangipane Tart

This is another example of using frangipane to line a tart shell and absorb liquid released by cooking fruit. Surprisingly, this tart is good made with canned apricots, so you can even make it out of season. This tart is only 7 inches in diameter, so you can make it with a half recipe of pastry dough. If you want to make a full-size tart—9 or 10 inches—use a full recipe of pastry dough and double the frangipane and fruit amounts called for.

MAKES ONE 7-INCH TART

1/2 recipe sweetened basic pie and tart pastry dough (page 131), or extra buttery sweet pastry dough (page 134), or sweet crispy pastry dough (page 138)

5 fresh apricots, or 10 canned apricot halves

1 cup frangipane (page 159), almond cream (page 159), or hazelnut frangipane (page 161)

1 tablespoon butter, melted

2 teaspoons sugar

Apricot glaze (see page 61), optional

Use a 7-inch tart ring or fluted tart pan. Roll the dough into an 8-inch round and line the tart ring or pan with it (see page 143). Refrigerate the tart shell for at least 30 minutes. Preheat the oven to 300°F.

If using fresh apricots, halve them. Cut the halves into 3 wedges each. Spread the frangipane in the tart shell and arrange the apricot wedges on top. Brush the tart with the melted butter and sprinkle with the sugar.

Bake for about 45 minutes, or until well browned on the edges. Brush with glaze as soon as the tart comes out of the oven. Serve warm or at room temperature.

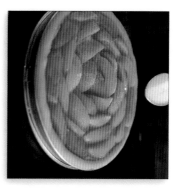

1. Arrange the apricot wedges on top of a tart shell spread with frangipane. Brush with the melted butter and sprinkle with the sugar.

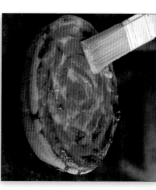

2. Bake until well browned on the edges, then brush with the apricot glaze.

Blueberry Frangipane Tart

You can use any berry you like to make this tart. Just spread the berries over a tart shell lined with frangipane.

MAKES ONE 9¹/₂-INCH TART

1 recipe sweetened basic pie and tart pastry dough (page 131)

2 cups frangipane (page 159), almond cream (page 159), or hazelnut frangipane (page 161)

¹/₂ pint blueberries

1 tablespoon butter, melted

Apricot glaze (see page 61) or confectioners' sugar (optional)

Use a 9¹/₂-inch tart ring or fluted tart pan. Roll the dough into a round about two inches larger than the tart ring or pan and line the pan with it (see page 143). Refrigerate the tart shell for at least 30 minutes. Preheat the oven to 400°F.

Spread the frangipane over the tart shell and arrange the blueberries over it. Pat them down gently with the flat of your hand to press them just slightly into the frangipane. Brush with the melted butter.

Bake for about 1 hour, or until deep brown on the edges. Brush with the glaze as soon as the tart comes out of the oven, or wait until just before serving and powder with confectioners' sugar.

Hazelnut or Almond Tartlets

These tartlets are a simple variation on cooked fruit tartlets—you just leave off the fruit from nut cream–filled tartlets. They are a snap to make if you have hazelnut frangipane or almond cream on hand.

MAKES SIX 3¹/₂-INCH TARTLETS

1 recipe basic pie and tart pastry dough (page 130)

1¹/₂ cups hazelnut frangipane (page 161) or almond cream (page 159)

Preheat the oven to 300°F. Use six 3¹/₂-inch tartlet rings or fluted tartlet pans. Roll the dough into a cylinder (see page 146) and line the tartlet rings or pans with it (see page 143). Spread about 3 tablespoons of the cream over the inside of each of the tartlets with an offset spatula.

Bake for about 45 minutes, or until golden brown. Let cool before serving.

Apricot Tartlets

....

Virtually any fruit can be baked in a tart or tartlet. Canned or frozen fruit can be used without precooking because it will have already released much of its liquid.

Alternatively, you can line the tartlet shells with a layer of frangipane, almond cream, or hazelnut cream and use raw fruit. But cooking the fruit shrinks it and concentrates its flavor. If you use cooked fruit, decrease the amount of fruit by about one-third.

MAKES SIX 3- TO 4-INCH TARTLETS

1 recipe sweetened basic pie and tart pastry dough (page 131), extra buttery sweet pastry dough (page 134), or sweet crisp pastry dough (page 138)

18 large uncooked apricot halves, or 12 cooked apricot halves

3 tablespoons granulated sugar

2 tablespoons butter plus 1 tablespoon melted

³/₄ cup frangipane (page 159), almond cream (page 159), or hazelnut frangipane (page 161)

Apricot glaze (see page 61) or confectioners' sugar (optional)

Use six 3- to 4-inch tartlet rings or fluted tartlet pans. Roll the dough into a 10-inch rectangle and line the tartlet rings or pans with it (see page 143). Refrigerate the tartlet shells. Preheat the oven to 300°F.

If you're using fresh apricot halves, sprinkle them with 2 tablespoons of the granulated sugar and sauté them in 2 tablespoons of the butter over medium heat for about 10 minutes, or until soft and lightly browned. Let cool.

Spread about 2 tablespoons of the frangipane in each of the lined tartlet rings and arrange the apricot halves, overlapping, on top (see Note). Brush the apricots with the melted butter and sprinkle with 1 tablespoon of the granulated sugar. Bake for about 45 minutes, or until the tartlets are golden brown on the edges.

Brush with glaze as soon as they come out of the oven, or just before serving, dust with confectioners' sugar.

Note: If the apricots are ripe and sweet, use less sugar when sautéing. You can also cut the apricot halves into wedges and arrange them as shown on page 175.

MAKING APRICOT TARTLETS

1. Sauté the apricot halves in the butter and granulated sugar until golden brown.

2. Line tartlet rings or fluted molds with dough. Spread a layer of frangipane over the bottoms of the raw tartlet shells and arrange the apricot halves over the filling.

3. Brush the apricots with the melted butter and spoon over a thin layer of granulated sugar.

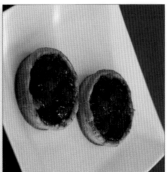

4. Bake until the edges of the tartlets are golden brown and brush with the apricot glaze.

Cherry Tartlets

These are a variation on the apricot tartlets with frangipane (page 177); another—for berry tartlets—follows this recipe.

MAKES SIX 3- TO 4-INCH TARTLETS

12 ounces fresh cherries, or one 12-ounce package frozen cherries

½ cup water

1 tablespoon sugar or more, plus additional for sprinkling

1 recipe sweetened basic pie and tart pastry dough (page 131) or cream cheese tart and pie pastry dough (page 135)

¾ cup frangipane (page 159), almond cream (page 159), or hazelnut frangipane (page 161)

2 tablespoons butter, melted

Pit the cherries by twisting a fluted pastry bag tip in one end of the cherry and pushing out the pit. Cut them in half or leave them whole. Put the cherries, water, and 1 tablespoon of the sugar into a saucepan over medium heat. Bring to a simmer, cover the saucepan, and cook for about 15 minutes, or until the cherries release their juices. Taste a cherry, judge the sweetness, and add more sugar if needed. Remove the cherries from the saucepan with a slotted spoon and reserve. Boil down the juice released by the cherries until it is thick and syrupy, and reserve.

Preheat the oven to 400°F. Use six 3- to 4-inch tartlet rings or fluted tartlet pans. Roll the dough into a cylinder (see page 146) and line the tartlet rings or pans with it (see page 143).

Spread about 2 tablespoons frangipane over the bottom of each tartlet and arrange the cherries on top. Brush with the melted butter and sprinkle with sugar.

Bake for about 45 minutes, or until the shells are golden brown on the edges. Brush with the reserved cherry glaze and let cool before serving.

VARIATIONS

BERRY FRANGIPANE TARTLETS: To make frangipane tartlets with berries, substitute 12 ounces berries for the cherries. Don't cook the berries, just press them into the frangipane in each tartlet. Brush with melted butter, sprinkle with sugar, and bake in a 400°F oven for about 45 minutes, or until golden brown.

PLUM, KIWI, OR PEACH FRANGIPANE TARTLETS: Tree fruits such as plums, kiwis, or peaches can be cut into tiny wedges or slices, layered over the frangipane, and baked in the same way.

MAKING CHERRY TARTLETS

1. Simmer the cherries in a covered saucepan with water and sugar until they release their juices.

2. Take the cherries out of the liquid with a slotted spoon. Cook the cherry liquid down until syrupy.

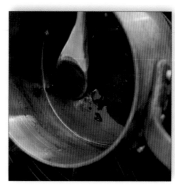

3. Line tartlet rings with the dough, then spread frangipane over them. Arrange the cherries over the frangipane.

4. Brush the cherries with melted butter and sprinkle with granulated sugar. Bake until golden brown, then brush with the reserved cherry liquid.

Making Raw Fruit Tarts

A raw fruit tart is made by prebaking a pastry shell in a tart pan or ring, covering the shell with some kind of filling, and then arranging the fruit on top. You can use just about anything for the filling, and if you're in a situation where you have more than one filling left over from something else, you can even combine them. Here are some basic filling possibilities (2 cups of filling is about right for a 9-inch tart):

Fruit curds (plain, lightened with whipped cream, or with butter or brown butter added)

Mascarpone

Whipped cream cheese, alone or combined with sour cream or crème fraîche

Crème fraîche

Devon cream

Ganache (white or dark chocolate; whipped or not)

Pastry cream (with butter added, to make mousseline; with brown butter added; or lightened with whipped cream)

Fruit mousses

Custards (baked sweet custard filling, such as for crème brulée)

This section contains a multitude of ideas for other raw fruit tarts and tartlets. All use prebaked tart or tartlet shells (see pages 146 and 147), and all can be glazed with apricot glaze (see page 61), but it's optional (1/2 cup of glaze is about right for a 9-inch tart).

Ganache Tart: A rectangular tart with a simple ganache filling is a dramatic break from the usual round tart. You can use a classic ganache of equal parts chocolate and heavy cream (see page 51), but if you want a denser texture use less cream or whisk 1/4 cup butter per 8 ounces chocolate into the ganache. To fill a standard 91/2-inch tart pan, you'll need 3 cups ganache; for the 8 by 11-inch rectangle shown here, you'll need 4 cups. You can also use whipped ganache (see page 51) for a lighter alternative.

Ladle hot ganache into a prebaked tart shell. Allow it to settle and set slightly.

To give the surface a luxurious sheen, wave a blow torch over the tart—hold it about a foot away from the top of the tart—just long enough to barely melt the surface of the ganache.

Raspberry-Ganache Tart: Spread whipped ganache (page 51) or pour melted ganache into a prebaked tart shell and let set. Arrange the raspberries on top. Use 3 cups (about 1 pound) raspberries for an 8-inch round or square ganache tart. For a 91/2-inch tart, use 2 pints raspberries.

Arrange raspberries in diagonal rows, starting in a corner.

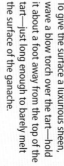

Within 1 hour of serving, take out of the refrigerator. Sprinkle with confectioners' sugar just before serving.

Kiwi–Whipped White Chocolate Ganache Tart: This 8-inch tart is made with 1 1/2 cups whipped white chocolate ganache (page 51) and 6 kiwis. For a 9 1/2-inch tart, increase the whipped ganache to 3 cups and increase the number of kiwis to 10.

1. Cover the bottom of the tart shell with the whipped white chocolate ganache.

2. Use a spoon to peel the kiwis and slice them into 6 or more slices each.

3. Arrange the slices, overlapping, around the tart, starting from the outside and working in.

4. Once you get to the center of the tart, use a knife to position the last slices.

5. Brush the tart with apricot glaze (see page 61) if you like.

Raspberry–Classic Crème Mousseline Tart: This 8-inch tart is lined with 1 cup of classic crème mousseline (pastry cream with butter beaten in, page 57) and covered with 2 cups raspberries. For a 9 1/2-inch tart, use 2 to 3 cups mousseline and 4 cups raspberries.

Dust the tart with confectioners' sugar before serving. Hold the shaker a foot or so over the tart so the sugar coating is even.

Spread the mousseline on a prebaked tart shell and arrange over the raspberries, starting from the outside and working in.

Blackberry–Peach Mousseline Tart: For an 8-inch tart, use 1 cup peach mousseline (page 58) to line the tart and 2 cups blackberries to cover it. For a 9 1/2-inch tart, use 2 to 3 cups peach mousseline and 4 cups berries.

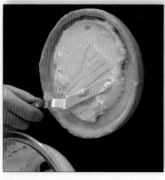

Arrange the berries over the mousseline, starting from the outside and working in. Brush with apricot glaze (see page 61) if you like and serve cool.

Spread the mousseline over the prebaked tart shell.

Mixed Berry–Passion Fruit Mousse Tart: In this tart, whipped cream is stabilized with gelatin and combined with passion fruit curd (page 364); 4 cups of mixed berries are used to cover a 9½-inch tart. Soak 1 teaspoon gelatin in 1 tablespoon cold water for 5 minutes. Add 2 tablespoons cream and heat the mixture in the microwave until the gelatin dissolves, about 5 seconds. Beat ¾ cup cream to medium peaks and beat in the gelatin mixture and ½ cup passion fruit curd.

Spread the passion fruit mousse over the bottom of a prebaked tart shell.

Arrange the berries on top in concentric circles and brush with glaze (see page 61).

Miniature White Chocolate Ganache Tartlets: Make a white chocolate ganache with 2 ounces white chocolate, finely chopped, and ¼ cup heavy cream, by stirring the two together in a double boiler. Flavor with a teaspoon of kirsch if you like. Spoon or pipe into prebaked miniature tartlet shells. Decorate with melted dark chocolate.

Pour hot white chocolate ganache into prebaked tartlet shells. Allow to set.

If you like, decorate the tartlets with melted bittersweet chocolate squeezed from a paper cone (see page 87).

Miniature Dark Chocolate Ganache Tartlets: Make a ganache with 1 ounce finely chopped bittersweet chocolate and 2 tablespoons heavy cream, by stirring the two together in a double boiler. Spoon the ganache into prebaked shells. Decorate with gold or silver leaf.

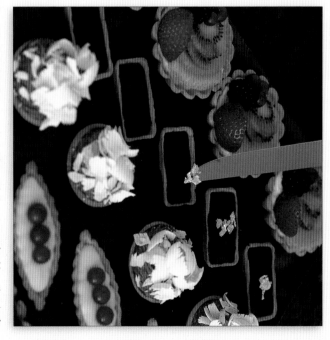

Decorate dark chocolate ganache tartlets with tiny pieces of gold or silver leaf.

continued

Assorted Berry Tartlets: To cover and fill twelve 3- to 4-inch lined tartlet shells, beat 1/4 cup cream to stiff peaks and fold it with 1/2 cup pastry cream (page 160). Flavor with vanilla or kirsch and spread it in the shells. Cover with assorted berries.

2. Arrange the raw fruit over the lined shells.

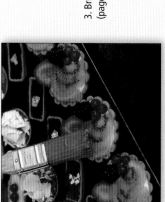

1. Pipe a layer of lightened, flavored pastry cream into the cooked shells.

3. Brush the tartlets with apricot glaze (page 61, optional).

Red Currant Barquettes: A *barquette* is a little boat. Lemon curd (page 364) or passion fruit curd (page 364) is piped into the miniature shells with a paper cone and red currants are placed on top.

Decorate with red currants or other fruit.

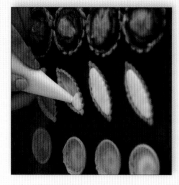

Fill a paper cone (see page 87) with fruit curd and cut the tip of the cone so there's an opening about 1/4 inch wide. Pipe the curd into the prebaked shells.

Miniature Raw Fruit Tartlets: These tiny shells are prebaked (see page 147) and filled with lemon curd (page 364) before fruit is arranged on top.

2. Top the lemon curd with berries.

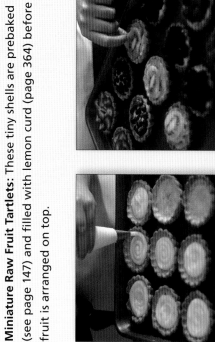

1. Use a pastry bag or spoon to fill the tartlet shells with lemon curd.

3. Brush with apricot or strawberry glaze (optional).

Blackberry–Lemon Cream Tart

This tart is a variation on countless others made with lemon curd and various fruits. What makes this tart a little different is that the lemon curd is lightened with whipped cream. If you just want to line the perimeter with blackberries, then you only need a couple of dozen. You can also make it with strawberries, raspberries, or kiwifruits.

MAKES ONE 9½-INCH TART

1 recipe sweetened basic pie and tart pastry dough (page 131), sweet crisp pastry dough (page 138), or extra buttery sweet pastry dough (page 134)

²/₃ cup heavy cream

4 teaspoons sugar

1 cup lemon curd (page 364)

2 pints blackberries

Apricot glaze (see page 61), optional

Use a 9½-inch tart ring or fluted tart pan. Roll the dough into a round about two inches larger than the ring or pan and line the ring or pan with it (see page 143). Prebake the tart shell (see page 146).

Beat the cream to stiff peaks with the sugar. Fold the lemon curd and whipped cream together and spread the mixture in the prebaked tart shell. Arrange the berries on top and brush the fruit with the glaze.

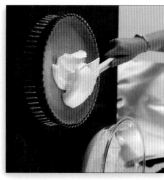

1. Fold together the lemon curd and the whipped cream. Use a rubber spatula to transfer the lemon cream to a prebaked tart shell.

2. Use an offset spatula to spread the cream over the surface of the tart, then arrange berries around or over the tart.

MAKING A STRAWBERRY–LEMON CREAM TART

1. To make a strawberry–lemon cream tart, cut a little wedge out of each strawberry to get them to nestle more tightly.

2. Arrange the strawberries, starting on the outside and working in. Brush with glaze.

MERINGUE PIES AND TARTS

Meringue, or beaten and sweetened egg whites, can be used as a soft topping for fruit curd–filled pies and tarts, like this passion fruit tart covered with piped stars of meringue. Baked, it can also serve as a crispy, crunchy, airy pie shell itself, as it does in the lemon meringue pie recipe.

Passion Fruit Meringue Tart

This tart is filled with passion fruit curd and topped with meringue stars. The curd base can also be used for berries and other fruits—just skip the meringue and arrange the fruit over the curd.

MAKES ONE 9½-INCH TART

1 recipe sweetened basic pie and tart pastry dough (page 131)

3 cups passion fruit curd (page 364)

¾ cup brown butter (page 196)

4 egg whites

Tiny pinch of cream of tartar, if not using a copper bowl

⅔ cup sugar

Use a 9½-inch tart ring or fluted tart pan. Roll the dough 2 inches larger than the ring or pan and line the pan with it (see page 143). Prebake the tart shell (see page 145). Beat the mixture slightly to loosen it and then beat in the brown butter. Spread the mixture in the tart shell.

In a bowl or a stand mixer, combine the egg whites with the cream of tartar (if using) and beat until medium peaks form. Add the sugar and continue beating until stiff peaks form.

Fit a pastry bag with a ½-inch fluted tip and fill it with the meringue. Starting at the edge of the tart, pipe little rosettes over the fruit curd.

Preheat the broiler. Set the tart on a rack so the top is about 5 inches from the broiler and rotate it constantly—be careful, it browns very quickly—for about 30 seconds, or until the tips of the meringue stars are browned.

Lemon Meringue Pie

A traditional lemon meringue pie is made by filling a prebaked pie crust with lemon curd, topping with soft meringue, and baking. In this version, a hard meringue shell replaces the traditional pie crust and an especially tangy lemon curd is used as a counterpoint to the sweet crust and soft meringue topping. Whipped cream is added last. The delicate interplay of flavors and textures—the crunch of the meringue shell, the tang of the lemon curd, the softness of the meringue topping, and the whipped cream—makes an irresistible combination.

For this pie, you need to make two kinds of meringue: The first meringue is used for the crunchy shell. Made with relatively little sugar, it works fine on dry cool days; but if you are making it on a humid day, the meringue will need additional confectioners' sugar folded in at the end to keep it crunchy. The second meringue, for the soft topping, is made with less than the usual amount of sugar beaten into the whites so that it will remain soft after baking. Most recipes for lemon curd contain at least some whole eggs, but this recipe uses all egg yolks because they are at hand from making the meringue. This lemon curd contains no cornstarch.

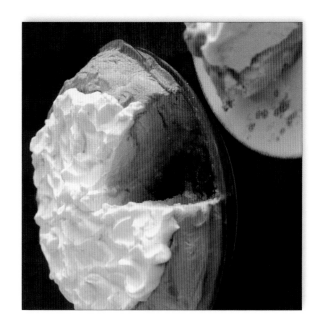

MAKING A PASSION FRUIT MERINGUE TART

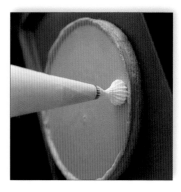

Fill a prebaked tart shell with the fruit curd and pipe meringue stars onto the curd using a pastry bag.

Quickly brown the tips of the meringue under the broiler.

Meringue shell

Room-temperature butter and confectioners' sugar for the pie pan

6 egg whites

Pinch of cream of tartar, if not using a copper bowl

3/4 cup plus 2 tablespoons granulated sugar

11/3 cups confectioners' sugar, if it is a humid day (see head note)

Lemon curd

8 egg yolks

2/3 cup sugar

Grated zest of 1 lemon (see page 194)

2/3 cup lemon juice (about 5 lemons)

1/4 cup plus 2 tablespoons butter, sliced (optional)

Whipped cream

1 cup heavy cream

2 tablespoons sugar

1 teaspoon vanilla extract

Meringue topping

4 egg whites

Pinch of cream of tartar, if not using a copper bowl

1/4 cup plus 2 tablespoons sugar

Butter a 10- to 11-inch pie plate and coat it with confectioners' sugar. Preheat the oven to 250°F.

To prepare the meringue shell, beat the egg whites with the cream of tartar (if using) in a stand mixer for 1 minute on medium speed, then for about 4 minutes on high speed, or until stiff peaks form. Then add the granulated sugar in a steady stream and beat for 2 minutes more on high speed. If it's a humid day, fold in the confectioners' sugar. Spread the meringue over the pie pan. Leave an indentation in the middle to hold the lemon curd. Bake the shell for at least 3 hours, or until hard and dry to the touch. If it starts to brown, turn down the oven to 200°F.

To prepare the lemon curd, whisk together the egg yolks and sugar in a medium heatproof bowl or in a saucepan with sloping sides for about 2 minutes, or until pale. Add the zest and lemon juice. If you're using a bowl, put it over a saucepan of simmering water and gently stir the mixture until it stiffens. If you're using a pan, put it directly over medium heat and whisk constantly until the mixture stiffens. Stir in the butter.

Stir with the whisk for a couple of minutes to cool it slightly and then transfer to a bowl if necessary and cover with plastic wrap. Let cool at room temperature for 1 hour and then refrigerate for at least 1 hour more.

Preheat the oven to 350°F. To prepare the meringue topping, in a stand mixer on high speed, beat the egg whites with the cream of tartar (if using) to stiff peaks. Add the sugar and beat for 2 minutes more.

Spread the lemon curd over the indented part of the meringue shell and spread the soft meringue over the whole shell. Bake for about 15 minutes, or until medium brown. Let cool for 1 hour on a cake rack.

To make the whipped cream, just before serving, combine the cream, sugar, and vanilla in a bowl and whip until stiff peaks form. Spread the whipped cream over the pie.

MAKING A LEMON MERINGUE PIE

1. Cover the prepared pie plate with a thick layer of stiff meringue. Leave an indentation in the middle to hold the lemon curd. Bake until hard and dry to the touch.

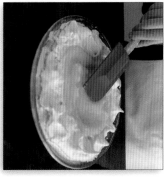

2. Spoon the lemon curd into the middle of the baked shell.

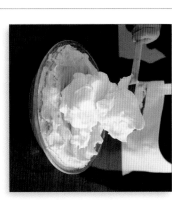

3. Spread the soft meringue over the whole shell. Bake at 350°F for about 15 minutes, or until medium brown. Let cool for at least 1 hour.

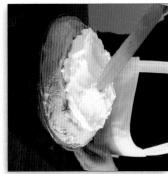

4. Just before serving, spread the whipped cream over the browned meringue.

FRUIT CUSTARD PIES AND TARTS

Custard is a liquid mixture that contains eggs and sets when it is cooked. The best-known custards, such as crème brulée or crème caramel, are made with milk or cream, but custards can also be made with purees of fruit or vegetables—a pumpkin pie, for example, is filled with pumpkin custard. Any fruit can be used to make a fruit custard; the sugar should be adjusted according to how sweet the fruit is. The custard fillings for fruit custard tarts and pies are very similar to fruit curds except that fruit curds are cooked on the stove and usually contain butter, while fruit custard fillings are baked in the oven and contain cream. Though fruit custard tarts or tartlets make fine stand-alone desserts, they can also be used as the base for raw fruit tarts—just arrange berries or other fruit on top.

Alsatian Apple Tart

This is a traditional Alsatian apple tart. You can adapt the recipe to use virtually any fruit. Just cook the fruit on the stove or in the oven before you bake it in a tart surrounded with this simple vanilla custard. The vanilla bean is optional, but it elevates this tart's flavor into higher realms.

MAKES ONE 9¹/₂-INCH TART

1 recipe sweetened basic pie and tart pastry dough (page 131)

3 large apples (1 pound 8 ounces), such as Golden Delicious or Rome

1/2 lemon

1/4 cup butter

1 vanilla bean, split in half lengthwise, or 2 teaspoons vanilla extract

1/4 cup plus 1/3 cup granulated sugar

2 eggs

1 cup milk

Confectioners' sugar for dusting

Use a 9¹/₂-inch tart ring or fluted tart pan. Roll the dough 2 inches larger than the ring or pan and line the tart ring or pan with it (see page 143). Prebake the tart shell (see page 145). Preheat the oven to 325°F.

Peel the apples and rub them with the lemon. Halve and core them, and cut each half into 3 or 4 wedges, depending on their size. Put the apples in a nonstick sauté pan with the butter over medium heat. Add the vanilla bean, if using, and gently toss or stir the apples for about 12 minutes, or until they're a golden brown. Sprinkle the 1/4 cup granulated sugar over the apples. Continue to toss or stir for about 5 minutes longer, or until the apple wedges are deep brown on both sides. Be careful not to break them. Remove from the heat.

To make the custard, whisk together the eggs and the 1/3 cup granulated sugar for about 2 minutes, or until the mixture gets a little pale. Stir in the milk. If you used the vanilla bean, scrape out the seeds in each of the halves and add these to the egg mixture; otherwise, add the vanilla extract.

Arrange the apples in the prebaked tart shell and pour the custard mixture over them. Bake for about 30 minutes, or until the custard sets—when it no longer moves in the middle when you jiggle the sheet pan slightly (don't move the tart). Dust with confectioners' sugar just before serving.

1. Sauté the apples in butter with a split vanilla bean (optional). When the apples start to brown, sprinkle over ¼ cup of the granulated sugar.

2. Continue sautéing until the apples are deep, dark brown on both sides.

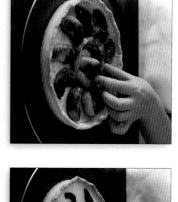

3. Arrange the apples in a prebaked tart shell placed on a sheet pan.

4. Whisk together the eggs and ⅓ cup granulated sugar until smooth and add the milk. Pour the mixture into the tart shell.

5. Bake until the custard no longer jiggles when you move the sheet pan gently back and forth.

6. Allow to cool, and sprinkle with confectioners' sugar just before serving.

Roast Pear Clafoutis

A clafoutis (klah-fou-tee) is a kind of pie or tart made by baking fruit arranged in a round pan and partially submerged in sweetened crepe batter. The only difference between a clafoutis and custard tarts, such as the Alsatian tart on page 186, is that a clafoutis contains some flour and salt. While not traditional, adding melted butter to the batter makes it lighter and less starchy because it helps prevent the flour from forming gluten. Here the batter is flavored with the caramelized butter that is left in the pan after roasting the pears with butter and sugar. This recipe calls for 10 pear halves, but if the pears are especially large, you may only need 7 or 8 (as shown in the photographs opposite). If your pears are large and you don't want extra pear halves, roast only 4 pears, but leave the butter and sugar amounts the same.

If you're making a clafoutis with a fruit other than pears—say cherries—add ²/3 cup sugar, at the same time as the eggs, to the batter amounts given here. If you want your clafoutis richer and to have a lighter consistency, stir in ¹/2 cup butter, either melted or made into brown butter (page 196).

MAKES ONE 10-INCH CLAFOUTIS

5 underripe pears

¹/2 cup granulated sugar

¹/2 cup butter, sliced

3 large eggs

¹/4 teaspoon salt

³/4 cup flour

1 cup milk

2 teaspoons vanilla extract

Confectioners' sugar for sprinkling on top

Preheat the oven to 400°F. Peel the pears with a vegetable peeler, removing the stem from both ends, and cut the pears in half lengthwise. Remove the cores, including the small strip at the narrow end of the pear, with a melon baller or paring knife. Place the pear halves, flat side up, in a heavy-bottomed pan just large enough to hold them in a single layer. Sprinkle the granulated sugar and butter over them.

Depending on the ripeness and size of the pears, roast for 25 minutes to 1 hour, until the butter and sugar mixture is golden brown and the pears are soft when you poke one with a knife. Remove the pear halves with a slotted spoon and reserve, leaving the juices in the pan. Place the pan over medium heat. If the sugar hasn't yet browned and clung to the bottom of the pan, stir the mixture until the sugar browns.

If the sugar is stuck to the bottom of the pan, put ¹/2 cup of water in the pan and boil it down by half, while scraping the bottom of the pan with a wooden spoon. Set the oven to 350°F.

In a bowl, stir the eggs and salt into the flour to create a thick paste. If the mixture is too dry, add some of the milk, but only enough to make a thick paste. (If you add the liquid to the flour all at once, the flour won't combine well and the mixture will be lumpy.) Stir the paste with a whisk until there are no lumps, then stir in the remaining milk and the vanilla. Pour or ladle the pear butter and sugar mixture from the pan into the clafoutis batter. Arrange the pears in a buttered tart or pie dish with the narrow ends of the pears toward the center and, if there is room, put one or two pear halves in the center. Strain the batter, then pour it over so that it comes almost all the way to the tops of the pears.

Bake for about 45 minutes, or until puffed and golden brown on top. Just before serving, sprinkle with confectioners' sugar and serve in wedges, each containing an entire pear half.

VARIATION

ROAST PEARS IN BUTTERSCOTCH SAUCE: Whisk ¹/2 cup heavy cream into the hot caramelized pan juices. Stir over medium heat until the cream, butter, and sugar emulsify together into a rich and delicious pear-butterscotch sauce. If it gets too thick, thin it with 1 to 2 tablespoons water. Serve the pears with the sauce poured over.

1. Stem, peel, halve, and core the pears. Use a paring knife to cut along both sides of the small strip of core at the narrow end of the pear and snap out this strip.

2. Arrange the pear halves, flat side up, in a single layer in a pan just large enough to hold them. Sprinkle the sugar and butter over them.

3. Bake until the pears are easily penetrated with a knife and the butter and juices are golden brown. Remove to the stovetop.

4. When the milk has been added, the batter should have the consistency of heavy cream.

5. Spoon the butter/sugar mixture from the bottom of the pan used for roasting the pears into the batter. Stir with a whisk until smooth.

6. Strain the batter.

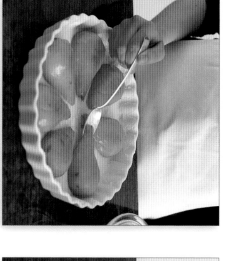

7. Arrange the pear halves in a buttered tart dish (don't use one with a false bottom or the batter will leak out) with the thin stem ends facing toward the center.

8. Ladle over the batter so that it comes almost all the way to the tops of the pears.

9. Bake until puffed and golden brown. Sprinkle with confectioners' sugar just before serving.

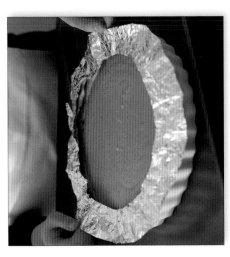

1. Combine the pumpkin puree with the sugar, eggs, and spices, and stir until smooth. Add the heavy cream and salt and stir until smooth and evenly colored.

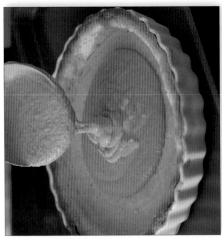

2. Fill a prebaked pie shell—a porcelain quiche dish is shown here—with the pumpkin mixture.

3. Set on a sheet pan and bake until the center doesn't jiggle when you move the sheet pan back and forth. If the edges start to get too brown, cover with an aluminum foil ring.

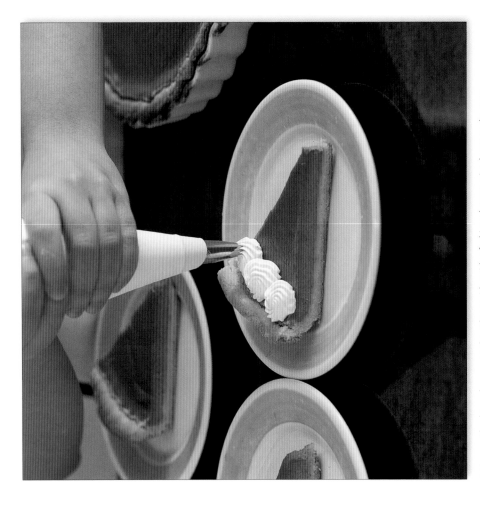

4. Serve with whipped cream on the side or with swirls of whipped cream piped next to the crust.

Pumpkin Pie

Pumpkin pie filling is a custard made with eggs and pumpkin puree. Here the puree is flavored with spices and given a luxurious texture with cream before it is baked in a prebaked pie or tart shell. If you keep in mind that one egg sets at least 2/3 cup puree when baked, it's easy to use this recipe as a model for other custard pies made with other purees, such as on pureed spinach or sweet potato puree. Savory versions, based on pureed spinach or mushrooms, are also made in the same way, without, of course, the sugar and spices.

MAKES ONE 9½-INCH PIE OR 10-INCH TART

1 recipe sweetened basic pie and tart pastry dough (page 131), extra buttery sweet pastry dough (page 134), or sweet crisp pastry dough (page 138)

One 15-ounce can pure pumpkin puree (no spices added)

1 cup light brown sugar

3 eggs

1/2 teaspoon ground cinnamon

1/2 teaspoon ground ginger

1/4 teaspoon ground cloves

Scant 1/4 teaspoon nutmeg

1½ cups heavy cream

1/2 teaspoon salt

Whipped cream for serving

Use a 9½-inch pie pan or 10-inch tart ring or fluted tart pan. Roll the dough into a round about two inches larger than the pie pan or tart ring or pan and line the pan or ring with it; if using a pie pan, flute the edge (see page 143). Prebake the pie or tart shell (see page 145). Preheat the oven to 325°F.

In a bowl, whisk the pumpkin puree and brown sugar together. Add the eggs, one by one, whisking well after each addition. Stir in the spices, cream, and salt. Pour the mixture into the prebaked pie or tart shell and set it on a sheet pan. Bake for about 45 minutes, or until the center doesn't move when you move the sheet pan back and forth. If at any point the rim of the pie or tart starts to get too brown, cover it with a foil ring (see page 145).

Serve with whipped cream on the side. If you like, you can pipe swirls of whipped cream around the perimeter before serving.

VARIATIONS

PERSIMMON TART OR TARTLETS: To make one 8-inch tart or eight 3½-inch tartlets, puree the pulp from two very ripe persimmons and whisk it with 2 eggs, 1/2 cup sugar, 1/4 cup lemon juice, and 1/2 cup heavy cream. Pour the mixture into the prebaked shells and bake in a 300°F oven for 30 to 40 minutes, until set. You can decorate the tarts or tartlets with a few strips of candied lemon zest (see page 194) or with additional thinly sliced ripe persimmon. Because more pastry is required to make 8 tartlets than one 8-inch tart, use extra buttery sweet pastry dough (page 134) for the tartlets because the recipe makes more dough. To make one 9½-inch tart, increase the ingredients by 50 percent.

PASSION FRUIT TARTLETS OR TART: To make one 9½-inch tart or twelve 3½-inch tartlets, whisk together 4 eggs and 3/4 cup sugar until smooth. Whisk in 3/4 cup passion fruit puree and 1 cup heavy cream. Preheat the oven to 300°F. Pour the filling into prebaked shells made with sweetened pie and tart dough. Bake at 300°F for 30 to 40 minutes until set.

MAKING A PERSIMMON TART OR TARTLETS

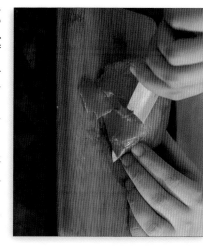

1. Carefully peel a ripe persimmon with a sharp paring knife.

2. Slice the persimmon as thinly as you can.

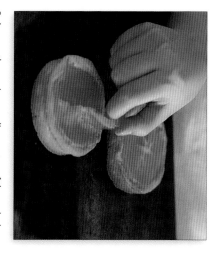

3. Arrange the persimmon slices on top of the cooked and cool tart or tartlets.

Pecan Pie

This pecan pie is made in the style of a tart, using a fluted tart pan with a removable bottom. It can also be made in a classic pie pan. A pecan pie is little more than a very sweet custard poured over pecans and baked. Pecan pie is made with both chopped pecans and whole pecan halves, which are used to decorate the top. While you could buy all pecan halves and chop some of them, it is less expensive to buy both pecan pieces and halves and use the halves only for the decorative finish. Because the filling is very sweet, you may want to use unsweetened pastry to make the crust.

MAKES ONE 9¹/₂- TO 11-INCH TART

1 recipe basic pie and tart pastry dough (page 130) or cream cheese tart and pie pastry dough (page 135)

3 eggs

¹/₂ cup sugar

¹/₂ cup dark corn syrup

¹/₃ cup butter, melted, plus 2 tablespoons melted butter for brushing the pie (optional)

¹/₂ teaspoon salt

1 teaspoon vanilla extract

1 cup pecan pieces

³/₄ cup whole pecan halves

Use a 9¹/₂- to 11-inch tart ring or fluted tart pan. Roll the dough into a round about two inches larger than the tart ring or pan and line the ring or pan with it (see page 145). Prebake the tart shell and seal it (see page 143). Preheat the oven to 350°F.

In a bowl, beat the eggs with the sugar and corn syrup. When the sugar dissolves, beat in the ¹/₃ cup melted butter, the salt, and vanilla. Stir in the pecan pieces.

Pour the mixture into the prebaked tart shell. Arrange the pecan halves on top. Brush with the 2 tablespoons melted butter. Bake for about 40 minutes, or until the surface of the pie no longer moves when you gently move it back and forth. If the edges start to get too brown, place a foil ring over the edges to stop further browning (see page 145).

MAKING A PECAN PIE

Pour the pecan custard mixture into the prebaked tart shell and smooth it.

Arrange the pecan halves on top of the tart and brush them with melted butter (optional). Bake for about 40 minutes, or until the surface no longer moves when you jiggle the sheet pan.

Lime Tart

Much is made about Key lime pie, but you can make a perfectly delightful pie, based on a lime custard, with everyday supermarket limes. Aficionados of Key lime pie insist that it be made with condensed milk, but cream is used in this recipe. Substitute condensed milk if you like, but if you use sweetened condensed milk such as Eagle brand, reduce the sugar in the recipe by half.

MAKES ONE 9½-INCH TART

1 recipe sweetened basic pie and tart pastry dough (page 131), extra buttery sweet pastry dough (page 134), or sweet crisp pastry dough (page 138)

3 eggs

2 egg yolks

¾ cup granulated sugar

1½ cups heavy cream

Grated zest from 1 lime (see sidebar, below right)

6 tablespoons lime juice (3 limes)

Confectioners' sugar (optional)

Pinch of candied lime zest (see sidebar below; optional)

Use a 9½-inch tart ring or fluted tart pan. Roll the dough 2 inches larger than the ring or pan and line the ring or pan with it (see page 143). Prebake the tart shell (see page 145). Set the oven to 300°F.

In a bowl, beat the eggs, egg yolks, and granulated sugar for about 2 minutes, or until the mixture turns pale. Beat in the cream, lime zest, and lime juice.

Pour the mixture into the prebaked tart shell. Bake for about 45 minutes, or until the custard sets—it no longer moves when you move the tart gently back and forth. Let cool at room temperature. Refrigerate for 1 hour before serving.

Dust with confectioners' sugar and decorate with candied lime zest just before serving.

VARIATIONS

KEY LIME OR LEMON TART: If you're making a Key lime tart, substitute Key lime juice and zest for the Persian limes shown here. If you want to make a lemon tart, substitute lemon juice and zest for the lime juice and zest. To make a 9½-inch pie instead of a tart, use 4 eggs, 2 egg yolks, 1 cup sugar, 2 cups heavy cream, and ½ cup lime juice.

ORANGE TART: For one 9½-inch orange tart, use 1 prebaked 9½-inch tart shell made with sweetened basic pie and tart pastry dough (page 131). For twelve 3½-inch orange tartlets, use 12 prebaked 3½-inch tartlet shells. Follow the same method as for the lime tart, with the following amounts of ingredients: 3 eggs, ⅔ cup sugar, ¾ cup heavy cream, ¼ cup lime juice, 1 teaspoon grated orange zest, 1 cup orange juice, 2 tablespoons Grand Marnier (optional), ½ teaspoon orange oil (optional), confectioners' sugar, candied orange zest, and 24 candied orange slices (page 195; optional).

Candying Citrus Zest

To candy up to 3 tablespoons citrus zest, peel the zest off in strips, leaving as little pulp attached to the zest as possible. If you see pulp still attached to the zest, shave the pulp off with a sharp knife while pressing firmly against a work surface with the side of the knife. Continue to shave off the zest. When you have the amount you need, slice it into very thin strips. Place it in a saucepan with 3 tablespoons sugar and 5 tablespoons water. Bring the water to a boil and turn the heat down to very low. Cover the pot for 15 minutes. Uncover the pot, turn the heat to high, and boil until the water turns into a thick syrup. Strain the zest. Put it on a plate with 2 tablespoons sugar and pinch them to get the sugar to adhere, separating and sugar coating them as you go. To lightly candy sliced citrus fruits, see opposite page.

Using Grated Citrus Zest

Recipes often call for citrus zest because it contains the essential oils that give these fruits their flavor. Usually, recipes recommend grating off the zest with the fine teeth of a box grater or a long thin grater called a rasp. But in some dishes, such as the citrus tarts shown here, little bits of zest interfere with the smooth silky consistency of the filling. To avoid this, grate the zest with the kind of grater that has tiny punch outs rather than teeth so the zest ends up in a paste instead of in tiny strips. To get the paste off the side of the grater, whack the grater over a sheet of waxed paper on a work surface.

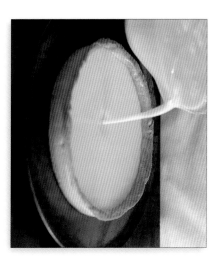

1. Pour the citrus mixture into a prebaked shell.

2. Bake until the custard no longer moves in the center of the tart when you move it very gently. Dust with confectioners' sugar just before serving and decorate with candied lime zest.

3. Lime tart decorated with confectioners' sugar and candied lime zest.

Cut the ends off the orange, set the orange on end, and cut it in half vertically. Lay the orange halves their cut sides and slice both halves crosswise into $1/8$-inch-thick slices. You should end up with about 50 slices.

Place the orange slices in a roasting pan with sides at least 2 inches high; there's no need to arrange them as I show here, arranged in neat rows. Pour the hot syrup over the slices and cover with a sheet of parchment paper or aluminum foil. Set the oven to 250°F (no need to preheat), and bake the oranges for about 12 hours, or until the white part of the rind looks waxy and translucent. If at any point the syrup begins to simmer, turn down the oven. If most of the syrup evaporates and it gets very thick, pour in 1 cup hot water. Check every 4 hours or so.

Transfer the orange slices to a cake rack set over a sheet pan and let drain for 30 minutes. Store on sheets of waxed paper—don't stack the slices or they'll adhere to each other—for up to 2 months in the refrigerator or indefinitely in the freezer.

Candied Orange Slices

Thinly sliced citrus fruits, lightly candied in sugar syrup, make an elegant topping for tarts and tartlets. They provide a concentrated flavor with a delightful hint of bitterness.

MAKES ABOUT 50 ORANGE SLICES, ENOUGH FOR TWO 9½-INCH TARTS, OR TWELVE 3½-INCH TARTLETS

2 cups sugar

2 tablespoons light corn syrup

2 cups water

1 large navel orange

Combine the sugar, corn syrup, and water in a heavy-bottomed saucepan and bring to a gentle simmer. Continue simmering, stirring constantly, until all the sugar dissolves.

MAKING AND USING CANDIED ORANGE SLICES

1. Simmer the sugar and water until the sugar dissolves. With the orange slices in a roasting pan, ladle over the hot syrup.

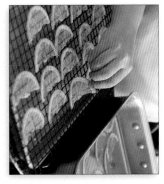

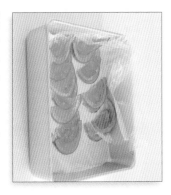

2. Cover loosely with parchment paper or aluminum foil and let cook in a slow oven for 12 hours. Drain on a cake rack and let dry slightly before using.

3. To store the slices, arrange them, without stacking, on sheets of waxed paper.

4. Orange tartlet decorated with candied orange slices.

CREAM PIES

Actually custard pies, cream pies are based on American-style pudding, which is almost identical to pastry cream in that it is a custard stabilized with cornstarch. It differs from pastry cream, however, in that it contains less starch.

Banana Cream Pie

This recipe differs from the classic in that it contains brown butter to give it a nutty butterscotch flavor.

MAKES ONE 9- TO 10-INCH PIE

1 recipe basic pie and tart pastry dough (page 130)

3 cups milk

1 vanilla bean split lengthwise, or 1 teaspoon vanilla extract

2 eggs

2 egg yolks

3/4 cup sugar

1/3 cup cornstarch

1/4 cup plus 2 tablespoons brown butter (left)

3 ripe bananas

Use a 9- to 10-inch pie pan. Roll the dough into a round about two inches larger than the pie pan. Line the pie pan with the dough, fold under the edge to make it a double thickness, and make a fluted edge (see page 143). Prebake the pie shell (see page 145). Set the oven to 400°F.

In a saucepan, bring the milk to a simmer with the vanilla bean or extract. In a bowl, whisk together the eggs, egg yolks, sugar, and cornstarch until smooth. Pour half of the milk into the egg mixture, stir to combine thoroughly, and pour the mixture back into the saucepan with the rest of the milk. Stir the mixture over medium heat with a whisk for about 5 minutes, or until it bubbles and thickens. Remove the vanilla bean, if using. Transfer the custard mixture to a bowl, whisk in the brown butter, cover with plastic wrap, and allow to cool to room temperature.

Cover the bottom of the pie shell with one-third of the pudding. Slice 2 of the bananas between 1/8 and 1/4 inch thick and place one half of them over the pudding in a single layer. Spread half of the remaining pudding over the banana slices. Place the remaining sliced bananas on top of the pudding, then cover the bananas with the remaining pudding.

Refrigerate for at least 1 hour before serving, but serve at room temperature. Shortly before serving, slice the remaining banana and arrange on top of the pie.

Making Brown Butter

This cooked butter is also called *beurre noisette*. Unlike whole butter, brown butter contains no water, so it has an intense buttery flavor. It also helps stiffen whatever mixture it is added to once the mixture is cold—for example, pastry cream and lemon curd—while giving it a delicious nuttiness.

To make brown butter, cook whole butter in a heavy-bottomed saucepan over medium heat. As it melts, you'll notice a lot of foam. After about 3 minutes, the foam will subside and the milk solids will coagulate into small but visible particles. After about 2 minutes more, the particles of milk solids will brown. Brown particles will also cling to the sides and bottom of the saucepan.

Immediately plunge the saucepan into a bowl of cold water to keep the butter from burning. Using a fine-mesh strainer lined with a paper towel or coffee filter, strain the brown butter into a storage container. Refrigerate if not using immediately. Brown butter keeps for months in the refrigerator.

One cup of whole butter yields 3/4 cup brown butter.

1. Melt butter in a heavy-bottomed saucepan over medium heat. You'll notice a lot of foam.

2. As the butter cooks, after about 3 minutes, the foam will subside and the milk solids will coagulate into small but visible particles.

3. After about 2 minutes more, the particles of milk solids will brown. Brown particles will also cling to the sides and bottom of the saucepan.

4. Here, the milk solids have caramelized to just the right degree. Immediately plunge the saucepan into a bowl of cold water to keep the butter from burning. Strain through a fine-mesh strainer lined with a paper towel.

1. Bring the milk and vanilla bean to a simmer. Whisk together the eggs, egg yolks, sugar and cornstarch. Ladle or pour half the hot milk into the egg mixture and stir.

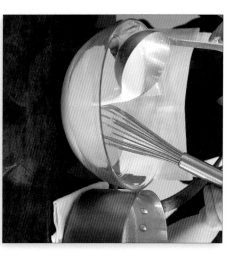

2. Pour the egg mixture into the saucepan with the rest of the milk.

3. Stir the pudding over high heat until it bubbles and thickens.

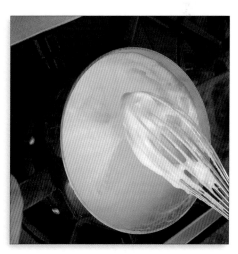

4. Transfer the pudding to a bowl. Whisk the brown butter into the pudding. Cover with plastic wrap and let cool.

5. Spread one-third of the pudding over the bottom of the prebaked pie shell. Arrange a layer of banana slices over the pudding.

6. Layer more pudding, then more banana slices, and the rest of the pudding. Refrigerate for at least 1 hour.

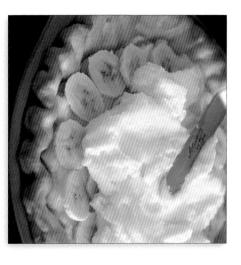

7. Spread over the last layer of banana slices just before serving.

8. Serve the pie in wedges.

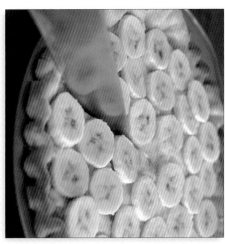

Coconut Cream Pie

To make this American classic, simply fold shredded sweetened coconut into American-style pudding and spread the pudding in a prebaked pie shell. To give it an intense coconut flavor, use coconut milk to make the pudding—not the sweetened coconut cream used to make piña coladas, but the unsweetened kind, usually from Thailand.

MAKES ONE 9- TO 10-INCH PIE

1 recipe basic pie and tart pastry dough (page 131)

3 cups milk or canned unsweetened coconut milk

1 teaspoon vanilla extract

2 eggs

2 egg yolks

1/2 cup plus 2 tablespoons sugar

1/4 cup plus 2 tablespoons cornstarch

One 14-ounce package (4 cups) sweetened shredded coconut

1 cup heavy cream

Use a 9- to 10-inch pie pan. Roll the dough into a round about two inches larger than the pie pan. Line the pie pan with the dough, fold under the edges to make it a double thickness, and make a fluted edge (see page 143). Prebake the pie shell (see page 145). Set the oven to 350°F.

In a medium saucepan, bring the milk to a simmer with the vanilla. In a bowl, whisk together the eggs, egg yolks, the 1/2 cup sugar, and the cornstarch until smooth. Pour half of the milk into the egg mixture, stir to combine, and pour the mixture back into the saucepan with the rest of the milk. Stir the mixture with a whisk over the heat until it bubbles and thickens. Transfer to a bowl, cover with plastic wrap, and allow to cool to room temperature.

Fold three-fourths of the coconut into the pudding and spread this mixture in the pie shell. Chill for at least 1 hour.

Combine the heavy cream with the 2 tablespoons sugar and beat it to stiff peaks. Spread the whipped cream over the pudding mixture, doming the cream in the center, and sprinkle the remaining coconut over it.

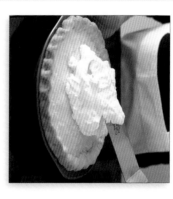

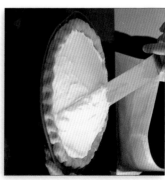

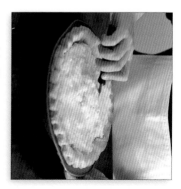

1. Fold three-fourths of the coconut into the custard filling.

2. Spread the filling in the prebaked pie shell.

3. Cover the top of the pie with a layer of sweetened whipped cream.

4. Rotate the pie, with the spatula held at an angle, as you apply the whipped cream so the pie is domed in the middle.

5. Sprinkle the top of the pie with the remaining coconut.

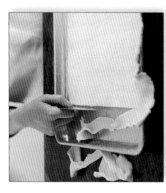

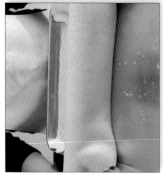

1. Pound the puff pastry to soften it slightly.

2. Roll out the dough. It should be slightly more than 1/8 inch thick.

3. Sprinkle a sheet pan with cold water to keep the bottom of the tart from burning, and unroll the dough over the sheet pan.

4. Trim off the rough edges of the dough.

5. Dock the pastry with a fork to keep it from puffing.

6. Arrange the apples in rows, over-lapping slightly and changing direction with each row.

7. Sprinkle the apples with the sugar and cover with thin slices of butter.

8. Bake the tart. After about 20 minutes, check to make sure the pastry isn't puffing. If it is, poke the pastry with a paring knife to deflate it. If necessary, use the tip of the knife to reposition any apples.

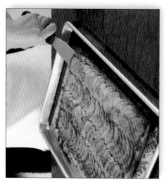

9. Bake for another 20 to 30 minutes, until deep golden brown. Scrape under the tart with a metal spatula to loosen it.

10. Trim off the edges. It's normal that these are slightly burned.

Puff pastry can be rolled out and used in the same way as pastry that is not layered (nonlaminated pastry)), but it should be rolled out very thin so that it doesn't remain raw in areas where it's covered with some kind of filling. Because it puffs, you can roll out puff pastry into a rectangle or square and spread filling over, leaving a 1/2-inch border or so. In this way, the border puffs and forms a natural enclosure for the filling.

Crispy Apple Tart

This tart manages to taste intensely of butter and apples at the same time. You will also feel a delightful delicate crunch when you bite into a piece.

If you are making puff pastry just for this tart, you need to give it only four turns instead of the traditional six (this is a good opportunity to use puff pastry trimmings or quick puff pastry; flaky pie and tart pastry dough, however, doesn't quite do the trick). Slice the apples as thin as you can—if you slice very very thin, you'll need only 3 apples, but it's better to have 4 just in case. Avoid Granny Smiths—they turn mushy.

MAKES ONE 11 BY 14-INCH TART

1 recipe puff pastry dough, 4 turns (page 148) or quick puff pastry dough (page 151)

4 large apples (2 pounds), such as Golden Delicious, Macintosh, or local tart varieties for baking, but not Granny Smiths

2/3 cup sugar

1/2 cup butter, sliced very thin

Preheat the oven to 425°F. Sprinkle cold water on a 13 by 17-inch sheet pan to keep the bottom of the tart from burning. Roll the dough into a 12 by 15-inch rectangle and transfer it to the prepared sheet pan (see page 141). Trim the edges of the rectangle so it measures 11 by 14 inches and dock it (poke it with holes) to keep it from puffing up in the oven.

Peel, halve, and core the apples. Cut the apple halves into thin slices, leaving them barely attached on the side away from where you are cutting (see page 170). Cut off the strip where the apples are attached and fan out the slices. Arrange the apple slices in 4 rows along the length of the pastry, overlapping the slices so that each one covers about half of the one before it and changing direction with each row. Sprinkle the tart with the sugar and cover evenly with the butter. Bake for about 50 minutes, or until the edges are a deep golden brown. Start checking the tart after 20 minutes to make sure it isn't puffing up and forcing off the apples. If it is puffing, poke the puffed part with the tip of a paring knife to deflate it and use the tip of the knife to gently rearrange any slices that have moved.

Let it cool on the sheet pan for a minute and then, with a long metal spatula, scrape under the tart to loosen it before you remove the tart from the sheet pan—it always sticks and usually burns a little on the bottom. If you notice any burned parts, just scrape them off with a spatula. Cut into rectangles and serve.

Puff Pastry Pear Frangipane Tart

If nothing is weighting it down, puff pastry expands upward as it bakes. You can use puff pastry to make a tart without using a tart ring or mold because the pastry edge rises to form a rim. The method is simple: Spread a sweet filling—frangipane is used here—on a sheet or round of puff pastry and arrange fruit on top. Leave a border of about 1 inch uncovered so the edges of the pastry will puff up. Unlike fillings for regular tarts, which are held in place by the tart shell, fillings for puff pastry tarts must be stiff and not runny, even when hot, because the tart has no rim to keep the filling from running out before the pastry puffs up. Frangipane, made from almonds or hazelnuts, makes a perfect sweet and nutty filling that will stay in place during baking. Frangipane also helps absorb any liquid released by the fruit.

Because most fruit releases liquid as it cooks, which can make the crust soggy, it's helpful to precook the fruit. This tart is very rich, so I usually make an 8-inch version instead of a 9 1/2-inch version. To convert this recipe to a 9 1/2-inch tart, increase the ingredients by 50 percent.

MAKES ONE 8-INCH TART

1/2 recipe classic puff pastry dough (page 148) or quick puff pastry dough (page 151)

Egg wash (see sidebar, page 146)

1/2 cup almond frangipane (page 159) or hazelnut frangipane (page 161)

5 or 6 roasted pear halves, allowed to cool (see page 188)

2 tablespoons butter, melted, or the butter-sugar mixture from the roasted pears

2 teaspoons sugar

Apricot glaze (see page 61), optional

continued

Fruit-Hazelnut Puff Pastry Tartlets

The process for making these tartlets is almost identical to that for making the puff pastry cases on page 152. Here, the pastry is covered with hazelnut cream and raw fruit. As the pastry bakes, the sides puff up to form a border, while the liquid released by the baking fruit is absorbed by the hazelnut cream. You can use more than one kind of fruit, using one kind per tartlet or a mixture for each tartlet.

MAKES SIX 4-INCH SQUARE TARTLETS

1/2 recipe classic puff pastry dough (page 148) or quick puff pastry dough (page 151)

Egg wash (see sidebar, page 146)

1/4 cup plus 2 tablespoons hazelnut frangipane (page 161), almond cream (page 159), or frangipane (page 159)

2 cups fruits, such as raspberries, blackberries, strawberries, cherries, and/or apricot halves

2 tablespoons butter, melted

2 tablespoons sugar

Apricot glaze (see page 61), optional

MAKING FRUIT-HAZELNUT PUFF PASTRY TARTLETS

1. Brush the borders and corners of the unbaked pastry cases with egg wash. Don't let any drip down the sides.

2. Spread a thin layer of hazelnut cream on the center of each tartlet.

3. Arrange assorted fruits—berries and cooked apricot halves are shown here—on top of the hazelnut cream. Brush the tops with melted butter and sprinkle with sugar.

4. Bake until well risen and golden brown. Brush the fruit with apricot glaze.

MAKING A PUFF PASTRY PEAR FRANGIPANE TART

1. Cut a round of puff pastry dough out of an almost-frozen sheet. Pull away the excess dough (save the trimmings for other projects).

2. Brush the round with egg wash and dock with a fork, leaving a 1-inch-wide border undocked.

3. Spread the round with frangipane (don't get any on the border). Arrange pear halves in a circle on the frangipane. Brush the pears with melted butter or the butter-sugar mixture from the pears. Sprinkle with sugar, freeze, and bake.

4. Brush the finished tart with apricot glaze while it's still warm.

Puff Pastry Pear Frangipane Tart, continued

Sprinkle the bottom of a sheet pan with water to keep the bottom of the tart from burning. Roll the dough from 1/8 to 1/4 inch thick and transfer it to the prepared sheet pan (see page 141). Place the sheet pan in the freezer for about 5 minutes, or until the dough is nearly frozen.

Cut out an 8-inch round of the dough. Pull away the excess dough and save the trimmings for other projects. Brush the round with the egg wash. Dock the round to keep it from rising, leaving a 1-inch border all around it undocked. Spread over the frangipane (don't get any on the border). Arrange the pears over the frangipane with the narrow stem ends facing the center of the tart. Brush with the melted butter and sprinkle with the sugar.

Preheat the oven to 425°F. Freeze the tart for 15 minutes, then bake for about 40 minutes, or until golden brown on the edges. Brush with the glaze while still warm. Serve at room temperature or warm.

Using the puff pastry dough, prepare 6 puff pastry cases (see page 152), but don't bake them. Brush the borders with the egg wash.

Preheat the oven to 425°F. Spread 1 tablespoon hazelnut cream on the center of each of the pastry squares. Top each pastry square with one-sixth of the fruit. Brush the fruit with the melted butter and sprinkle with the sugar.

Bake for about 25 minutes, or until golden brown. Brush with the glaze while still warm.

Miniature Puff Pastry Fruit Tartlets

These tartlets are 2½ inches across and make a delightful bite or two for breakfast or tea. You can serve three or four as a dessert or use them as petits fours. For fruits that release a lot of liquid, such as peaches and apricots, sauté them as shown on page 177 or bake them as shown on page 188, then allow them to cool before using them to make these tartlets. Make sure the fruit is completely cool before putting it on the pastry round.

MAKES THIRTY 2½-INCH TARTLETS

1 recipe classic puff pastry dough (page 148) or quick puff pastry dough (page 151)

Egg wash (see sidebar, page 146)

2 cups almond cream (page 159) or frangipane (page 159)

2 cups assorted fruits such as berries, bananas, kiwis, apricots (halves sautéed, page 177), or roasted pears (page 188)

Melted butter for brushing on the tartlets

2 tablespoons sugar

Apricot glaze (see page 61), optional

Sprinkle a sheet pan with water to keep the bottoms of the tarts from burning. Roll the dough into a 13 by 16 by ⅛-inch sheet, and transfer to the prepared sheet pan (see page 141).

Use a 2½-inch cookie cutter to cut thirty 2½-inch rounds, 5 rows of 6 rounds each. Pull away the excess pastry. Brush the rounds with egg wash and dock them by poking holes in them with a fork. Leave a ½-inch border on all sides undocked. Spread 1 tablespoon almond cream on the center of each round, leaving the ½-inch border uncovered. Arrange the fruit on top, leaving the border uncovered. Brush the fruit with the melted butter and sprinkle with the sugar.

Preheat the oven to 400°F. Freeze the tartlets for 15 minutes. Bake for 15 to 20 minutes, until the sides puff up and turn golden brown. Brush with glaze while still hot.

When the tartlets are cool, warm the glaze and glaze the tartlets again.

MAKING MINIATURE PUFF PASTRY FRUIT TARTLETS—

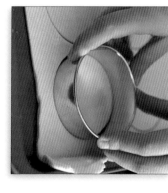

1. Roll out a ⅛-inch-thick sheet of puff pastry dough. Cut out 2½-inch rounds. Pull away the excess dough.

2. Brush the rounds with egg wash. Dock with a fork; don't dock the outer ½ inch, which will form the rim.

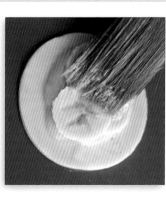

3. Spread almond cream over the center of each of the tartlets; leave a ½-inch border. Place raw or cooked fruit on top of the almond cream. Brush the fruit with melted butter.

4. Sprinkle the fruit with granulated sugar. Bake until the rims puff up and turn golden brown. Brush with glaze while still hot.

5. Glaze the tartlets again when cool.

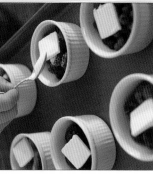

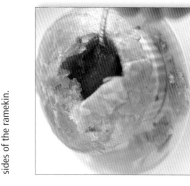

1. Arrange ramekins on a sheet pan—leave a little space between them—and spoon in the jam and fruit. Don't overfill.

2. Put a pat of butter in each ramekin. Sprinkle over sugar.

3. Roll out the dough into a sheet and cut into rounds 2 inches wider than the ramekins. Brush one side of each of the rounds with egg wash.

4. Place a round of pastry, egg-wash side down, over each ramekin, and gently fold down the sides until they conform to the sides of the ramekin.

5. Brush the tops of the pies with egg wash and bake until puffed and golden brown.

Individual Deep-Dish Berry Pies

These little fruit potpies can be made with any sort of berries. Jam provides steam and flavor, but you can also use fruit puree—ideally, the same fruit you're using in the pies. Berries, butter, sugar, and a puff pastry lid complete this simple dessert. You can use any size ramekins you want; just adjust the amounts and cooking time.

MAKES 6 INDIVIDUAL PIES

1/4 cup plus 2 tablespoons blueberry jam or fruit preserves, or 3/4 cup fruit puree

3 1/2 cups blueberries or other berries

3 tablespoons butter, cut into 6 pieces (optional)

2 tablespoons sugar or more as needed

1 recipe classic puff pastry dough, 4 turns (page 148) or quick puff pastry dough (page 151)

Egg wash (see sidebar, page 146)

Crème fraîche (optional)

Whipped cream (see page 62), optional

Arrange six 6-ounce ramekins on a sheet pan, leaving a little space between them. Put 1 tablespoon jam or preserves or 2 tablespoons fruit puree in each ramekin, then divide the berries equally among the ramekins. Put in enough berries to come about three-fourths up the sides of the ramekin. Don't overfill. Don't let any of the fruit touch the rim of the ramekin; it will touch the pastry, cause the pastry to melt where it touches, and a crack will form. Put 1 piece of butter in each of the ramekins. Spoon 1 teaspoon of the sugar (more if you're using a tart fruit puree instead of preserves) over each.

Roll the dough into a 13 by 16 by 1/8-inch sheet. Unroll it onto a sheet pan (see page 141). Use a cookie cutter or cardboard round to cut out six 1/8 to 1/4-inch-thick rounds, 2 inches in diameter larger than the ramekins. The ramekins shown here are 3 1/2 inches in diameter, so the pastry rounds are 5 1/2 inches.

Working one at a time, brush the rounds on one side with egg wash. Turn the round over onto a ramekin, egg-washed side down, and gently press the dough against the sides of the ramekins. Start by pressing with your fingers and then with the sides of your hands so that the pastry is tightly sealed. Don't press against the ramekin's rim or you'll cut through the pastry. Brush the tops with egg wash.

Preheat the oven to 425°F. Refrigerate or freeze the pies for 30 minutes.

Bake for about 25 minutes, or until the pastry is golden brown and mounded. Serve with crème fraîche or whipped cream.

Turnovers are one of the most versatile pastries that you can make in any size, using virtually any fruit. These miniature turnovers are made from 4¹/₂-inch rounds of puff pastry. (Traditional turnovers are made from 6-inch rounds.) For the filling, the blueberries are cooked with sugar until the mixture is thick enough to hold its shape. If you want to use other berries for the filling, cook them in the same way.

MAKES 8 SMALL TURNOVERS

1 recipe classic puff pastry dough (page 148) or quick puff pastry dough (page 151)

2 cups blueberries

¹/₄ cup water

2 teaspoons granulated sugar or more as needed

Egg wash (see sidebar, page 146)

Confectioners' sugar for dusting

Crème fraîche or whipped cream (see page 62) for serving (optional)

Line a sheet pan with parchment paper. Cut the dough in half and roll each half into a 10-inch square slightly thicker than ¹/₈ inch. Put each square on the prepared sheet pan and freeze until firm but not hard. Use a cookie cutter or bowl to cut out four 4¹/₂-inch circles from each square and pull away the trimmings.

Combine the blueberries, water, and granulated sugar in a saucepan; bring to a boil, cover, and simmer for about 4 minutes, or until the blueberries release their liquid. Remove the lid and cook over medium heat for about 15 minutes, or until the mixture thickens. Stir every minute or so to prevent sticking and burning. You should end up with about ¹/₂ cup blueberry filling. Let cool, sweeten to taste if necessary, and refrigerate until cold.

Preheat the oven to 425°F. Place 1 tablespoon of the cold blueberry mixture slightly off center on each of the puff pastry circles. Brush the opposite half of the circle with the egg wash, so when you fold it over it will form a seal. Fold the pastry over and gently press on the edges to hold them in place. Press along the edges of the turnovers with a fork to make a decorative seal. Brush the turnovers with egg wash.

Bake for about 25 minutes, or until golden brown. For a shiny glaze, sift a little confectioners' sugar over the turnovers about 5 minutes before they come out of the oven. Serve warm or at room temperature with crème fraîche or whipped cream, if you like.

1. Roll the pastry into two 10-inch squares. Cut four 4¹/₂-inch rounds from each square.

2. Stack the trimmings and save them for another use.

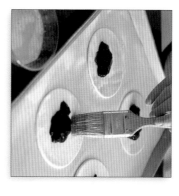

3. Place 1 tablespoon of blueberry filling slightly off center on each round. Brush the round, around the filling, with the egg wash.

4. Fold the half of the round with egg wash over the other half. Gently press around the edges of the fold.

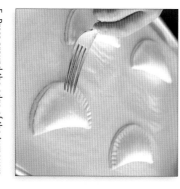

5. Press around the edge of the turnovers with a fork to make a decorative seal. Brush any excess flour off the turnovers and brush them with egg wash. Bake until golden brown.

6. Five minutes before the turnovers have finished baking, dust them with confectioners' sugar.

ASSORTED PASTRIES

Most pastries are made by combining butter and flour, sometimes sugar, and sometimes a liquid such as water or egg. Much of what gives each pastry its distinctive flavor and texture comes about from manipulating the ingredients slightly (or sometimes not so slightly) differently. Pastries can be sweet or savory, but most of the pastries here are sweet—in part because so many of them contain fruit.

Almond–Puff Pastry Galette (Pithiviers)

A galette is made by sealing ingredients between 2 layers of puff pastry. A pithiviers, named after the village that specializes in them, is made by sealing a layer of almond cream in puff pastry. It's probably the best-known galette. You can bake any number of ingredients between 2 layers of puff pastry; for example, the almond cream can be replaced by cooked fruit or mushrooms (see page 163), pâté mixtures, seafood mousses, or slices of partially cooked fish or meat layered with chopped mushrooms.

This pithiviers is decorated with a series of arcs, cut about 1/16 inch deep. The decorative arcs allow the dough to expand and "crack" along the cuts. Without the arcs, the dough can expand and crack randomly.

Chill the pastry thoroughly before cutting out the circles, and work on a sheet pan or over a sheet of parchment paper so you can move the pastry after it's been shaped without having it droop and lose its shape.

MAKES ONE 9-INCH GALETTE

1 recipe classic puff pastry dough (page 148) or quick puff pastry dough (page 151)

1 cup cold almond cream (page 159)

Egg wash (see sidebar, page 146)

Preheat the oven to 300°F. Line 2 sheet pans with parchment paper. Cut the dough in half and roll one piece into a 10½-inch square from 1/8 to 1/4 inch thick. Transfer the square to a prepared sheet pan (see page 141), and refrigerate. Roll the other piece into a 9½-inch square from 1/8 to 1/4 inch thick and transfer to the other sheet pan.

Using a bowl or cake ring, cut out a 9-inch circle from the second square and pull away the trimmings. Place the almond cream in the center and shape it into a flattened mound, leaving a 2-inch border all around. Brush the border with water. Place the larger cold square over the almond cream, wait a minute or two for it to soften a little, then press gently around the sides of the mound to force any air toward the outside. Smooth the pastry, working outward from the mound to eliminate air pockets. Gently press the border to seal the top and bottom. Center over the galette the same bowl or cake ring you used to cut out the first round of pastry and cut around it so the edges of both layers are even. Pull away the extra pastry.

Use the back of a knife to make a series of indentations, about 1/4 inch apart, all around the edge of the galette. Make a series of arcs, like the spokes of a wheel but curved, from the center to the edge. Don't cut all the way through to the almond cream, but cut, ideally, about halfway into the pastry. Brush very lightly with egg wash—if you use too much egg wash it will accumulate around the base of the mound—and freeze for 15 minutes.

Bake for about 40 minutes, or until golden brown and puffed. If the galette browns before 40 minutes, turn down the oven to 300°F for the rest of the baking. Let the galette cool before serving. Serve in wedges.

1. Roll out two squares of puff pastry dough. Use a bowl to cut out a circle. Pull away the excess dough (stack and save for another use).

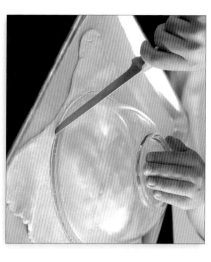

2. Press cold almond cream in the center of the pastry circle to form a flattened mound surrounded by a 2-inch border. Brush the border with water.

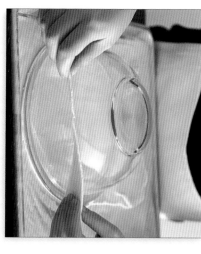

3. Roll the second sheet of puff pastry over the first.

4. Center the bowl you used to cut out the first circle over the galette—make sure it is even with the bottom edges of pastry. Cut around the bowl; pull away the extra dough.

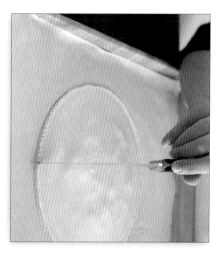

5. Decorate the edges of the galette by making indentations with the back of a knife.

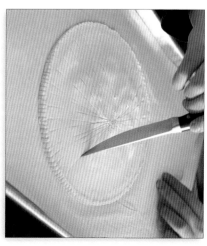

6. Cut a series of arcs from the edge to the center. Brush the top of the galette with egg wash.

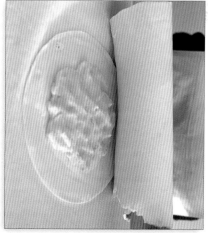

7. Put the galette in the freezer for 15 minutes, then bake until golden brown.

1. Roll the pastry dough into a 1/8-inch-thick round large enough to fill the tart ring or pan. Transfer the round to a buttered tart ring or tart pan.

2. Line the ring with the dough, pressing it against the outer rim of the ring to remove excess dough. Push the edge of the dough up slightly all around the edge to make a slight lip.

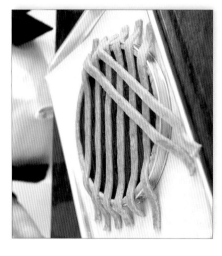

3. Spread the almond cream over the pastry-lined tart ring or mold.

4. Spread the raspberry jam over the cream.

5. Roll out the excess pastry dough into a rectangle and trim the edges off the rectangle so the ends are perfectly straight.

6. Cut the rectangle into 1/2-inch strips. Cut a small square from the first strip to use as a guide to keep the strips the same width.

7. Arrange the strips over the torte, leaving about 3/4 inch between each strip.

8. Arranged a second row of dough strips diagonally over the first strips, to make lozenge shapes.

9. Slice the ends of the strips with the knife at an angle to form a slanted beveled edge.

Linzertorte

A torte is a tart with some sort of covering. In the case of a linzertorte, it's a lattice covering made with strips of dough. This recipe contains somewhat less jam than the classic and is hence a little bit nuttier.

MAKES ONE 9- TO 11-INCH TORTE

1 recipe linzer pastry dough (page 140)
2 cups almond cream (page 159)
1 cup raspberry jam
Egg wash (see sidebar, page 146)
Apricot glaze (see page 61), optional
Confectioners' sugar for sprinkling

Butter a 9- to 11-inch tart ring or fluted tart pan. Roll the dough 2 inches larger than the ring or pan and line the ring or pan with it (see page 143). Refrigerate the tart shell. Reserve the remaining dough to make the lattice top. Preheat the oven to 350°F.

Spread the almond cream in the torte shell and then spread the raspberry jam over the cream. Roll the reserved pastry dough into a rectangle 9 by 11 by ⅛ inch. If the kitchen is hot, roll the rectangle on parchment paper so it can be placed easily in the refrigerator to cool.

Cut the rectangle into six ½ by 9-inch strips. Arrange the strips on the torte leaving about ¾ inch between the strips. Cut a second row of strips and place them diagonally over the bottom strips to form a lattice top. Slice the ends of the strips

with the knife at an angle to form a slanted beveled edge. Brush the lattice with egg wash, taking care not to let any drip down the sides of the lattice into the preserves. Bake for about 1 hour, or until golden brown.

Let the torte cool on a cake rack and remove the tart ring or pan. Brush the torte with the glaze. Place a round of cardboard over the torte, slightly off center, leaving a half inch or so of the rim exposed. Sprinkle confectioners' sugar over the exposed rim. Reposition the cardboard round and continue to sprinkle confectioners' sugar until the entire rim is covered.

10. Brush the lattice with egg wash. Don't let any drip down into the raspberry jam.

11. Bake. When the tart has cooled, remove the ring. Brush with apricot glaze (optional).

12. Place a round of cardboard over the tart, slightly off center, leaving part of the rim exposed. Sprinkle over confectioners' sugar. Reposition the cardboard round and continue to sprinkle until the entire rim is covered.

Éclairs

Éclairs are made with cream puff pastry dough (pâte à choux) and are essentially the same thing as cream puffs, except that éclairs are long, filled with pastry cream, and glazed with fondant; cream puffs are round, filled with whipped cream, and not glazed. You can fill éclairs in one of two ways—by cutting them in half lengthwise, piping in the filling, and replacing the top; or, more elegantly, by piping the mixture through holes cut in the bottom. Instructions for the second method are included here.

You can flavor the pastry cream for éclairs however you like: by simmering a vanilla bean, split down the middle, with the milk used to make the pastry cream (or you can add vanilla extract to the milk); by adding instant coffee to the hot milk (or you can infuse fresh ground coffee into the milk as shown on page 353); by combining cocoa powder with the egg-cornstarch mixture at the beginning of making the pastry cream; or by adding a liqueur or fruit brandy to the finished pastry cream after it has cooled.

Two cups fondant are called for—you'll only use ½ cup, but it's hard to work with that small an amount. The excess drips off and can be scraped up with a spatula and reused. The fondant can be flavored with chocolate, coffee, or vanilla, depending on the flavor of the pastry cream, but they don't have to match.

MAKES 12 ÉCLAIRS

1 recipe cream puff pastry dough (page 155)

Egg wash (see sidebar, page 146)

2½ cups pastry cream, flavored with vanilla, coffee, chocolate, or fruit brandy (page 160)

2 cups liquid fondant, flavored with chocolate or coffee (page 163)

Preheat the oven to 425°F. On a 13 by 17-inch sheet of parchment paper, use a pencil to make twelve 4½-inch vertical lines starting 1½ inches in from the end of the sheet pan and then every 2 inches to the other end so that you have 2 rows of 6 each. Fit a pastry bag with a ½-inch plain tip and fill it with the dough batter. Pipe tiny dollops of batter into the corners of the sheet pan, turn over the parchment paper, and press it onto them to hold it in place. Pipe 12 strips of batter, 1 by 4½ inches, along each of the lines. Brush each strip with egg wash.

Turn down the oven temperature to 400°F. Bake the éclairs for about 20 minutes, or until golden brown and puffed, then turn down the oven to 300°F and bake for about 25 minutes more, or until the éclairs feel light. If the éclairs start to look too brown, turn down the oven to 250°F. Let cool for at least 20 minutes on a cake rack.

Use a ⅓-inch fluted pastry bag tip to make two holes, one near each end, in the bottom of each éclair. Fit a pastry bag with a ⅓-inch plain tip, fill with pastry cream, and squeeze pastry cream into each hole until the éclairs are filled. Warm the fondant to slightly warmer than body temperature—it should barely feel warm when you touch the bottom of the bowl—or until it has the consistency of cold maple syrup. Dip the éclairs, top side down, into the fondant. Lift them out of the fondant without turning them upright right away so any excess fondant drips off. Place on a rack and allow the fondant to set for at least 30 minutes before serving.

1. Draw twelve 4½-inch lines on a sheet of parchment paper. Turn the parchment paper over and place on a sheet pan.

2. Pipe a small dollop of batter under each corner of the parchment paper to hold it in place.

3. Pipe the batter along the lines, pulling the pastry bag back along the line and squeezing as you go. When you reach the end of the éclair, move the bag quickly in the opposite direction (toward the end where you started) without squeezing, to detach the batter from the tip.

4. Brush the strips with egg wash and smooth out any irregularities with the brush.

5. Bake the éclairs and let them cool. Using a small fluted tip, make two holes, one on each end, in the bottom of each éclair.

6. Use a pastry bag to fill the éclairs, using the holes at each end. Use the side of a knife to wipe away any excess filling.

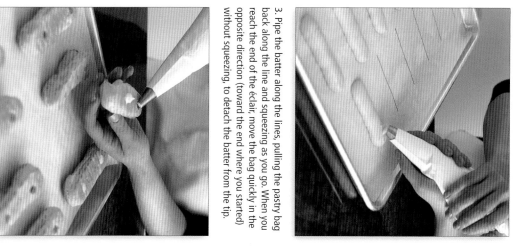

7. Dunk the tops of the éclairs in the liquid fondant.

8. Carefully wipe away excess fondant with your finger.

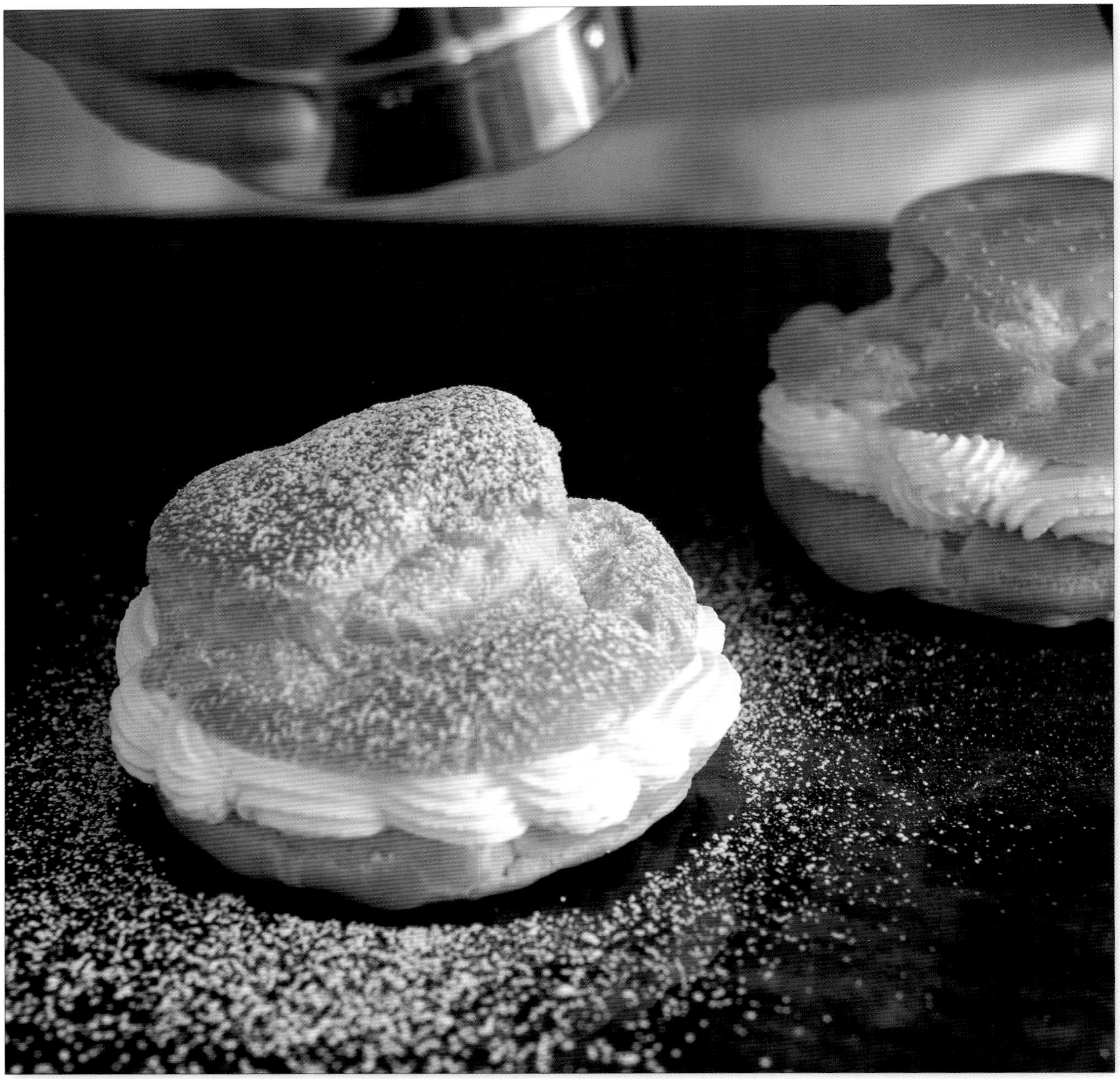

Cream Puffs

Cream puffs may be the most delightful of all cream puff pastry desserts because they're filled with whipped cream instead of something heavier like pastry cream. Cream puffs are at their best when baked shortly before serving and filled at the last minute so they don't have time to get soggy. If your pastry bag isn't big enough, you may have to pipe out the cream puffs in two stages.

MAKES 6 LARGE CREAM PUFFS

1 recipe cream puff pastry dough (page 155)

Egg wash (see sidebar, page 146)

1 cup heavy cream

2 tablespoons granulated sugar or more as needed

2 teaspoons vanilla extract

Confectioners' sugar for sprinkling on top

Preheat the oven to 400°F. Fit a pastry bag with a 1/2-inch plain tip and fill it with the dough. Pipe tiny dollops of dough into the corners of a sheet pan, and press a sheet of parchment paper onto them to hold it in place.

Make 2 rows of 3 cream puffs each. Start by holding the pastry bag about 3/4 inch above the sheet pan and squeezing. If the pastry bag tip is too close, the cream puffs won't be thick enough; if it's too far away, they won't be wide enough. As the round of pastry takes shape, lift the pastry bag until it is about 1 1/2 inches above the sheet pan. The mounds of dough should be about 3 1/2 inches in diameter and about 1 1/2 inches high in the center. Brush with egg wash, lightly smoothing the surface with the brush at the same time. Bake the cream puffs for about 20 minutes, or until puffed and golden. Turn down the oven to 300°F and continue baking for 20 minutes more. Let cool for at least 20 minutes on a cake rack.

In a bowl, combine the cream with the granulated sugar and vanilla and beat to stiff peaks. Use a serrated knife to cut the cream puffs in half horizontally. Pull away any undercooked dough from both halves. Pipe with a fluted tip or spoon the whipped cream generously onto the bottom halves, put on the tops, and sprinkle with confectioners' sugar.

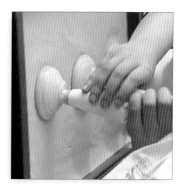

1. On a parchment paper–lined baking sheet, pipe out large mounds—about 1 1/2 inches high and 3 1/2 inches wide—of cream puff pastry dough.

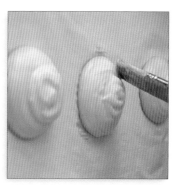

2. Coat the mounds with egg wash and bake until they are puffed and golden. Reduce the heat to finish the baking.

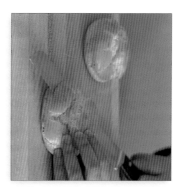

3. Let the cream puffs cool for at least 20 minutes before slicing them in half through the middle.

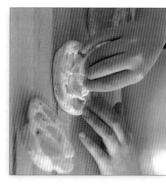

4. Pull out any moist, undercooked dough from each half.

5. Fill with the whipped cream (scallop shapes are shown here).

6. Put on the tops and sprinkle with confectioners' sugar.

Cream Puff Pastry Swans

Even though puff pastry swans are one of those old-fashioned decorations that look great on dessert plates or platters, most of us don't bother with them any more, in part because they look a lot harder to make than they are. The only tricky steps are piping out the teardrop shapes that form the swan bodies and the S-shaped necks. If you have trouble, pipe them out as best you can and if you're not satisfied, just scrape up the dough and use it to try again. You can serve these swans as dessert or you can put one on a dessert plate to decorate another dessert.

MAKES 10 TO 12 SWANS

1 recipe cream puff pastry dough (page 155)

Egg wash (see sidebar, page 146)

1 cup heavy cream

2 tablespoons granulated sugar or more as needed

1 teaspoon vanilla extract

Confectioners' sugar for decoration

Preheat the oven to 400°F. Fill a pastry bag fitted with a 1/2-inch tip with dough. Pipe tiny dollops of dough into the corners of 2 sheet pans, and press a sheet of parchment paper onto each one to hold it in place. Working on the side of a sheet pan farthest away from you and holding the pastry bag tip about 1/2 inch above the surface of the sheet pan, squeeze as though you were making a small round. When the round is slightly larger than 1 inch across, pull the pastry bag toward you while squeezing gently so that the amount of pastry released by the bag gradually decreases and you form a teardrop shape, about 3 inches long. Continue until you have between 10 and 12 teardrops. Brush with egg wash.

Bake for about 20 minutes, or until golden brown. Turn down the oven to 300°F and bake for 20 minutes more. When you take the teardrops out of the oven, turn it back up to 400°F. Let the teardrops cool for a minute and peel them off the parchment paper.

Make a paper cone (see page 87) and cut the tip to form a 1/8-inch opening. Fill the cone with dough and pipe 12 S-shapes onto the second sheet pan, to form the necks. Give a little extra squeeze at the beginning of each S to form the heads. Bake for about 15 minutes, or until golden brown. Let the S-shapes cool for a minute and peel them off the parchment paper.

Cut the teardrops in half crosswise—the top half will be shorter than the bottom half, which will be the body. Cut the top halves in half down the middle to form the wings.

In a bowl, beat the cream to stiff peaks with the sugar and vanilla. Load the whipped cream into a pastry bag fitted with a 1/2-inch fluted tip. Pipe the whipped cream into the bottom halves of the teardrops, using a slight up and down movement as you pull the pastry bag toward the back of the swan to create a ripple effect. The amount of cream should taper down as the point of the teardrop narrows.

For each pastry, anchor the bottom end of an S-shape in the whipped cream, where the neck would be. Place the two halves of the top of the teardrop on the whipped cream to form the wings. Sprinkle with confectioners' sugar just before serving.

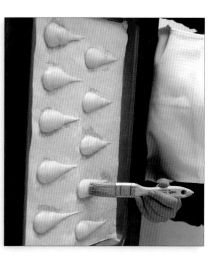

1. Pipe the swan bodies by starting as though you were making a round dollop, but pull back while decreasing the squeezing pressure on the pastry bag, so the bodies taper. Brush with egg wash. Bake until golden brown.

2. Use a paper cone to pipe the S-shaped necks. Leave a little extra dough on one end to make the head. Bake until golden brown.

3. Cut each of the swan bodies in half crosswise, leaving the bottom half deeper than the top.

4. Cut the top half in half to make 2 wings.

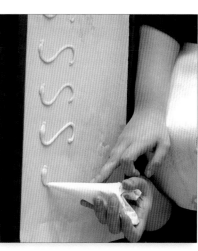

5. Use a pastry bag or spoon to fill the bottoms of the bodies with the sweetened whipped cream.

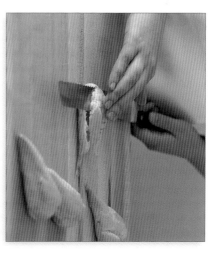

6. Attach the necks by sticking the end without the extra dough into the whipped cream in the front of the swan.

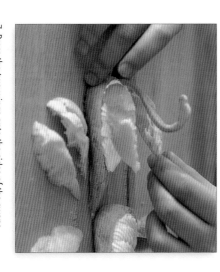

7. Press the two wings onto the sides of the swans.

8. Sprinkle the swans with confectioners' sugar.

Croissants

Few pastries are as satisfying as a buttery croissant. When well made, with authentic croissant dough, a croissant is rich and buttery like good brioche and flaky and light like the best puff pastry. Real croissants—not the breadlike kind found at the corner deli, which are more often than not made with margarine—are made from a kind of layered dough made by folding butter between sheets of yeast-leavened bread dough. When you pull apart a croissant, it should unravel in spirals of flaky, buttery bread.

Once you've made the croissant dough, you've done most of the work and finished most of the tricky parts, but there are still a few things to watch out for.

Once you shape the croissants, they must proof, either for a couple of hours at room temperature or less in a warm place, or, ideally, in the refrigerator for about 12 hours where they'll develop a better flavor because of the slow rising time. If you're letting the croissants proof in a warm place, it should still never be warmer than 85°F or the butter will melt—you'll see it oozing out onto the sheet pan—and the separation of the layers will be lost.

If you want to fill the croissants with chocolate or savory ingredients such as ham or cheese, just roll pieces of the ingredients in regular croissants or into rectangular-shaped croissants (see page 218).

The trick to making croissants is to time them so they're ready in the morning, not at some hour of the night before they happened to rise to just the right degree. The best solution is to make and shape the croissants the night before and then let them rise in the refrigerator. The slow rising will actually improve their flavor. If your refrigerator is on the cold side, you may find that the croissants haven't risen. Take them out and let them rise in a relatively warm place, but no warmer than 85°F.

MAKES 12 CROISSANTS

1 recipe croissant dough (page 157)

Egg wash (see sidebar, page 146)

Line 2 sheet pans with parchment paper. Roll the dough into two 6½ by 20-inch rectangles from ⅛ to ¼ inch thick. Transfer one of the rectangles to one of the prepared sheet pans (see page 141). Repeat for the other rectangle. Trim any uneven edges. Refrigerate for 20 minutes, or until firm but not brittle.

For each rectangle, measure 5 inches from the end and make a tiny notch to mark the base of the first triangle. Continue in this way until you've made 3 notches, each 5 inches apart, along the length of the rectangle. One side of the rectangle will now be marked off into four 5-inch sections.

On the other long side of the rectangle, make a notch 2½ inches from the end. Make another notch 5 more inches in, then 2 more notches 5 inches apart. The second side will now be marked into 5 sections, with the 2 sections at the ends each 2½ inches long and the ones in the middle 5 inches long. The notches on the first side are for the bases of the croissant triangles and the notches on the second side form the tips of the triangles.

Use a large knife to cut out the triangles by connecting the notches on the first side with those on the second side. You'll end up with 6 full triangles, each 5 by 6½ inches, and two half triangles, which are trimmings, on the ends.

Make a small cut at the center of the base of each of the triangles. As you begin to roll up the croissants, curl the two sides of the triangle on each side of the cut away from each other. Continue rolling with both hands, each one on half of the triangle. Point your hands away from each other as you roll. Roll the triangle so the tip is underneath and bend the 2 ends toward each other like a little crab. You should see 3 distinct layers as the dough curls around to form the croissant.

Arrange the croissants on a sheet pan and cover them with plastic wrap to proof. They should be well covered, but don't tuck the plastic wrap under them. Set them aside until they've doubled in size, overnight in the refrigerator, 3 hours in a cool place, or 1 hour in a warm place.

Preheat the oven to 375°F. Brush the proofed croissants with egg wash and bake for about 35 minutes, or until puffed and golden brown. Let cool, on a cake rack, to room temperature before serving.

1. Roll the dough into a rectangle and cut it into triangles.

2. Make a slit in the base of each triangle in the center.

3. Begin forming the croissant by rolling each side of the triangle at each side of the slit. Roll tightly.

4. Roll on both sides of the slit, pressing and pinching as you go.

5. Continue rolling while turning your hands out away from the center of the croissant. This helps make the classic croissant shape.

6. Continue rolling until the dough is rolled into a log. Roll with the little tail held in place under the log.

7. Shape the croissant by bending the two ends in so they're facing each other.

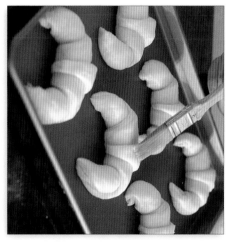

8. Arrange the croissants on a sheet pan, cover, and proof until doubled in size. Brush the croissants with egg wash.

9. Bake until golden brown.

4. Place a stick of chocolate 1½ inches from one end of the dough rectangle.

8. Cut the dough where the croissant ends.

3. Cut the chocolate sticks with a hot knife.

7. Fold the dough over again so the chocolate sticks are each in one of the folds.

2. Trim off the edges.

6. Place another stick of chocolate on top of the folded dough.

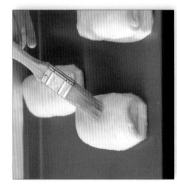

10. Cover the croissants and proof. When each layer is nearly twice its original thickness, brush with egg wash. Bake until golden brown and let cool.

1. Cut the croissant dough into 4 pieces. Keep the others cold as you roll out a piece into a long rectangle. Brush off excess flour.

5. Fold the dough over the chocolate.

9. Turn over the croissant, lift up the top flap of dough, and brush it with egg wash. Place on a sheet pan. Fill the other half of the dough rectangle with chocolate. Repeat for the remaining rectangles.

Chocolate Croissants

·····················

Here the word croissant is a misnomer, because these chocolate-filled pastries aren't crescent shaped at all. In France, they are called pains au chocolat. But they are made from croissant dough and have the same lovely flakiness as regular croissants. These rectangles of croissant dough are filled with little strips of chocolate, but you could just as well use strips of ham, cheese, or both. To cut a chocolate bar crosswise into strips, hold an old knife over the stove flame for a few seconds before cutting.

MAKES 8 CHOCOLATE CROISSANTS

1 recipe croissant dough (page 157)
One 4-ounce bittersweet chocolate bar, cut crosswise
   into 16 sticks
Egg wash (see sidebar, page 146)

Line 2 sheet pans with parchment paper. Divide the croissant dough into 4 parts. Roll each part into a 4 by 18½-inch rectangle about ¼ inch thick. Roll each rectangle up on the rolling pin and unroll it over the prepared sheet pan (see page 141). Trim the edges of the rectangles so each now measures 3½ by 18 inches. Keep the dough rectangles and completed pastries refrigerated while you're forming the croissants.

Place a chocolate stick crosswise 1½ inches in from one end of the rectangle. Fold over the end of the dough so you cover the chocolate and the end of the flap is 2 inches from the end of the fold. Place another chocolate stick on top of the flap and roll the whole thing over. You now have a flattened roll of dough with three layers and a piece of chocolate in each of the 2 folds.

Croissants: How Big?

The size you make croissants is flexible: Don't worry too much if your croissants don't fit these exact dimensions. Sometimes the rectangle just won't roll out to the width you want, so if it's wider than 6½ inches, make the base of the croissants not quite as long, maybe 4½ inches, to make up for the extra bulk they'll gain by 8 inches of rolled up dough rather than 6½ inches. The point is, use your own judgment and shape the croissants according to what works best and what suits your taste. You can even make mini croissants.

Cut the chocolate croissant away from the rest of the rectangle. Turn the roll over and brush under what is now the top flap with egg wash and gently press the flap to hold it in place. Turn the croissant back over, and place it on a sheet pan for proofing. Repeat with the second half of the rectangle. Repeat with the remaining 3 rectangles so you have 2 chocolate croissants per rectangle. When all of the croissants are on a sheet pan, cover with plastic wrap, and let rise until almost, but not quite, doubled in volume, overnight in the refrigerator, 1 hour in a warm place, or 3 hours in a cool place.

Preheat the oven to 375°F. Brush the croissants with egg wash. Bake for about 45 minutes, or until golden brown. If the croissants start to get too dark, turn down the oven to 300°F to finish baking. Let cool before serving on a cake rack.

DANISH PASTRIES

If you've eaten only the typical Danish pastries sold in grocery stores and corner doughnut places, you have never tasted the real thing. Authentic Danish pastries are not like bread or cake but are instead flaky and buttery and very rich; they're made with croissant dough.

Strictly speaking, Danish pastry dough is only slightly different from croissant dough, but calling it a different name is more the result of tradition than because of any discernable difference in the result; it is so hard to distinguish that it's hardly worth learning very similar steps. The real distinction between Danish pastries and croissants is, of course, the numerous shapes Danish pastry takes.

The best known style of Danish pastry is made by spreading a sheet of dough with some kind of filling—cream cheese, almond cream, dried fruits, preserves, and nuts are all used—rolling the whole thing up, and slicing it into the characteristic round pastries, which are then proofed and baked.

Fruit Danish Tartlets

There are several styles you can use for enclosing fruit in Danish pastry. Ideally, the fruit should be cooked ahead of time so it doesn't release a lot of liquid as it bakes, making the pastry soggy. If you want to use berries, it is best to use them in the form of preserves or cook them down with sugar as on page 205, and put them in the Danish twirls shown on page 223. Round fruits such as apricots, pears, plums, and peaches can be halved and sautéed with sugar and butter or baked until any liquid they release caramelizes.

These pastry cases are made to hold fruit, much like the puff pastry holders shown on page 153. The cases are lined with almond cream, but you can also use cream cheese and a sprinkling of sugar. Use a small marble slab that can be placed in the refrigerator as needed to chill the dough and keep it cold.

MAKES 6 FRUIT DANISH TARTLETS

1 recipe croissant dough (page 157)

¹/₄ cup plus 2 tablespoons almond cream (page 159)

6 large or 12 small pieces fresh fruit, sautéed (see page 177), or canned fruit, such as apricot halves, pear halves or slices, peach halves or wedges

1 tablespoon butter, melted

³/₄ cup slivered almonds (optional)

1 tablespoon sugar

Egg wash (see sidebar, page 146)

Line a sheet pan with parchment paper. Roll the croissant dough into a 9¹/₂ by 14-inch rectangle about ¹/₄ inch thick and transfer to the prepared sheet pan (see page 141). Trim the edges of the rectangle so it measures 9 by 13¹/₂ inches. Refrigerate for about 20 minutes, or until firm but not brittle.

Cut the rectangle into six 4¹/₂-inch squares. Make sure the dough is very cold. Cut a 4-inch square out of the inside of each of the squares, leaving a ¹/₂-inch border. Leave the smaller squares in position, but make sure the inner squares are detached from the outer squares.

Brush the edge of the inner square with water. Lift up the upper right corner of the outer square and gently press it against the lower left corner of the inner square. Press the pastry so it stays in place. Lift the lower left corner of the outer square and press it against the upper right corner of the inner square. Press against the pastry to hold it in place. Refrigerate the pastries.

Danish pastry shapes (from front): purse, tartlet, twirl (left), packet (right).

MAKING FRUIT DANISH TARTLETS

Spread the inside of each tartlet with 1 tablespoon almond cream. Place a piece or two of cooked fruit on the almond cream. Brush the fruit with the melted butter. Arrange slivered almonds around the fruit. Sprinkle 1/2 teaspoon sugar over the fruit in each tartlet. Cover with plastic wrap and let proof until the sides have almost, but not quite, doubled in height, about 1 hour at room temperature. Brush the pastry with egg wash.

Preheat the oven to 400°F. Bake for about 20 minutes, then check whether the pastries are browning too quickly. If so, turn down the oven to 325°F. Continue baking for about 15 minutes, or until golden brown.

1. Roll the croissant dough into a rectangle and cut it into squares. Cut smaller squares within each larger square.

2. Brush the edges of the inner square with water.

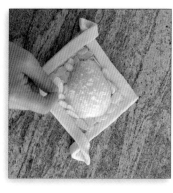

3. Lift up one corner of the outer square and gently press it against the opposite corner of the inner square.

4. Pick up the corner of the outer square opposite the first and gently press it against the opposite corner of the inner square.

5. Spread almond cream over the inside squares. Place a piece or two of cooked fruit on the layer of almond cream (a pear half is shown here). Brush the fruit with melted butter.

6. Arrange slivered almonds around the pear. Sprinkle over sugar.

7. Cover with plastic wrap and let proof until the sides are almost twice as high. Brush with egg wash and bake until golden brown.

8. Finished fruit Danish tartlet.

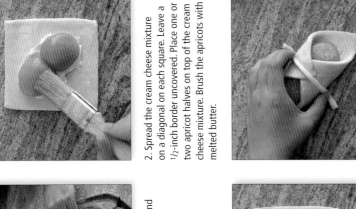

2. Spread the cream cheese mixture on a diagonal on each square. Leave a 1/2-inch border uncovered. Place one or two apricot halves on top of the cream cheese mixture. Brush the apricots with melted butter.

4. Fold the other corner over the flap that you egg washed and press it gently into place. Wrap the purse with a thin strip of dough brushed on one side with egg wash.

1. Roll the dough into a rectangle and trim the edges. Cut it into squares.

3. Sprinkle the apricot halves with granulated sugar. Fold one corner of the dough over the apricots. Brush the tip of the flap you just made with egg wash.

5. Cover the purses with plastic wrap and let proof until the dough has almost doubled in thickness.

6. Brush the purses with egg wash and bake until golden brown.

7. Finished purse.

Fruit and Cheese Danish Purses

These little purses are some of the easiest Danish to make. You just line a square of croissant dough with sweetened cream cheese, place fruit on top, and fold up two opposite corners of dough. Virtually any fruit will work, but it must be at least partially cooked or it will release liquid in the pastry and make it soggy.

MAKES 6 DANISH PURSES

1 recipe croissant dough (page 157)

1/4 cup plus 2 tablespoons cream cheese tart filling (page 161)

6 large or 12 small apricot halves, lightly sautéed in butter (page 177), or other cooked fruit such as roasted pears (page 188), or cooked cherries (page 178)

2 tablespoons butter, melted

2 tablespoons sugar

Egg wash (see sidebar, page 146)

Line a sheet pan with parchment paper. Roll the croissant dough into an 8 1/2 by 12 1/2-inch rectangle about 1/4 inch thick and transfer it to the prepared sheet pan (see page 141). Trim the rectangle so it measures 8 by 12 inches. Refrigerate for about 20 minutes, or until firm but not brittle. Save the trimmings.

Cut out six 4-inch squares from the chilled rectangle. Spread 1 tablespoon cream cheese filling on a diagonal on each square, leaving a 1/2-inch border untouched. Place one or two cooked apricot halves on top of the cream cheese mixture. Brush the apricots with the melted butter and sprinkle each of them with 1 teaspoon sugar. Fold one corner of the dough over the opposite edge of the apricots and brush the tip with egg wash. Fold the other corner over the flap that you egg washed and press it gently into place. Roll the trimmings into 6 thin strips. Brush one side of the strips with egg wash and wrap one around each purse. Cover with plastic wrap and let proof for about an hour, until the edges of the dough are almost doubled in thickness.

Preheat the oven to 400°F. Brush the purses with egg wash. Bake for 20 minutes and check whether the purses are browning too quickly; if so, turn down the oven to 325°F. Bake for about 15 minutes longer, or until golden brown. Let cool on cake racks.

222

BAKING

Miniature Cheese Danish Twirls

. . . .

You can make these any size you like. These miniature ones are perfect in a breakfast basket, but you can also make large ones, like those sold in American bakeries and cafes. These versatile Danish pastries have a hollow spot in the middle into which you can put just about anything from the cream cheese, preserves, and walnuts used here, to various cooked fruits, almond cream, or Nutella.

MAKES 12 MINIATURE DANISH TWIRLS

1/2 **recipe croissant dough (page 157)**
1/4 **cup cream cheese tart filling (page 161)**
1/4 **cup fruit preserves**
1/4 **cup chopped walnuts**
Egg wash (see sidebar, page 146)

Line a sheet pan with parchment paper. Roll the dough into a 12 1/2-inch square slightly less than 1/4 inch thick and transfer it to the prepared sheet pan (see page 141). Trim the square to 12 inches. Refrigerate for about 15 minutes, or until firm but not brittle.

Cut the square into 12 strips, each 1 by 12 inches. Twist the two ends of the strips in opposite directions until you can no longer see the insides of the strips. Wrap the strips around in a loose spiral. Tuck one end under the spiral, bring it up into the hole, and press on it with your forefinger to hold it in place and make an indentation for the filling. Place 1 teaspoon cream cheese filling in the center of each twist and then spoon in 1 teaspoon preserves. Divide the walnuts evenly among the 12 twists. Cover with plastic wrap and let proof until the edges of the pastry look swollen and puffed, about an hour.

Preheat the oven to 400°F. Brush the twists with egg wash. Bake for about 20 minutes, then check whether the pastries are browning too quickly; if so, turn down the oven to 325°F. Bake for about 10 minutes longer, or until golden brown.

MAKING MINIATURE CHEESE DANISH TWIRLS

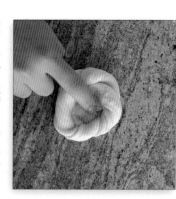

1. Twist both ends of the dough strips in opposite directions.

2. Twist until you no longer see the inside of the strip.

3. Wrap the strip around into a loose spiral.

4. Bring the end of the strip on the outside in through the opening in the middle of the coil.

5. Press in the middle to make a hollow and keep the strip in place.

6. Spoon filling in the middle of the circle and press the filling into the Danish with your finger.

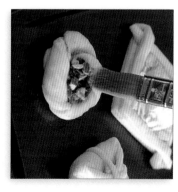

7. Add fruit preserves. Sprinkle in chopped walnuts. Cover with plastic wrap and let proof.

8. Brush with egg wash and bake until golden brown.

Fruit Danish Packets

. . . .

You can fill these little packets with cooked-down fruit, or preserves and almond cream, or cream cheese filling. This recipe uses the same blueberry mixture used as a filling for the blueberry turnovers on page 205.

MAKES 8 FRUIT DANISH PACKETS

1 cup blueberries

1/2 cup water

2 teaspoons sugar or more as needed

1/2 recipe croissant dough (page 157)

1/3 cup almond cream (page 159) or cream cheese tart filling (page 161)

Egg wash (see sidebar, page 146)

Combine the blueberries, water, and sugar in a covered saucepan and simmer for about 4 minutes, so the blueberries release any liquid they contain. Remove the lid and continue cooking over medium heat for about 15 minutes, or until the mixture thickens. Stir every minute or so to prevent sticking and burning. You should end up with about 1/4 cup plus 2 tablespoons cooked blueberries. Let cool and add more sugar if necessary, then refrigerate until cold.

Line a sheet pan with parchment paper. Roll the dough out into an 8 1/2 by 16 1/2-inch rectangle about 1/4 inch thick and transfer it to the prepared sheet pan (see page 141). Trim the rectangle so it measures 8 by 16 inches. Refrigerate the rectangle for about 20 minutes, or until firm but not brittle. Reserve the trimmings in the refrigerator.

Cut the rectangle into eight 4-inch squares. Put 2 slightly rounded teaspoons almond cream in the center of each square, followed by the same amount of the cooked blueberries. Fold one corner over the filling and brush the tip with egg wash. Fold the opposite corner over the first and press gently to seal them. Brush the top with egg wash, fold up another corner, brush with egg wash again, and fold up the last corner. Gently push down on the center to hold the flaps together. Pinch the corners and edges to seal them.

Roll the reserved trimmings into 8 thin strips about 6 inches long. Halve each strip. Place 2 strands over each packet and tuck them underneath. Place the packets on a sheet pan and cover with plastic wrap. Let proof until the dough's almost twice as thick, about 1 hour.

Preheat the oven to 400°F. Brush the packets with egg wash. Bake for about 20 minutes, then check whether the pastries are browning too quickly; if so, turn down the oven to 325°F. Bake for about 10 minutes longer, or until golden brown. Serve warm or at room temperature.

MAKING FRUIT DANISH PACKETS

1. Roll out and cut the croissant dough into eight 4-inch squares. Add the almond cream and cooked blueberries. Fold the first corner into the center.

2. As you fold the corners into the center, brush them with egg wash.

3. Brushing as you go, press one flap on top of the next . . .

4. . . . until you've formed a tight little packet.

5. Wrap the packet with two thin strips of dough.

6. Tuck the strips underneath the packet. Cover with plastic wrap and let proof. Brush with egg wash and bake until golden brown.

Rolled Danish Pastries

These are an authentic version of the Danish pastries most of us are used to seeing. They are filled with almond cream, raisins, and walnuts, but fillings are easy to improvise. Cream cheese filling, hazelnut cream, diced dried fruit, and cooked fresh fruit are all possibilities. Because these Danish expand sideways as they proof, they must be proofed on an oiled sheet pan, which will allow them to expand.

MAKES 12 ROLLED DANISH PASTRIES

2 pounds croissant dough (page 157)

2 cups almond cream (page 159), cream cheese tart filling (page 161), or hazelnut frangipane (page 161)

2 tablespoons sugar

1 cup golden raisins, soaked in just enough water to cover for 30 minutes and drained

1 cup coarsely chopped walnuts

Egg wash (see sidebar, page 146)

Apricot glaze (see page 61), optional

Royal icing (page 67), optional

Line a sheet pan with parchment paper. Roll the dough into a 12 by 15-inch rectangle, a little less than ¼ inch thick and transfer it to the prepared sheet pan (see page 141). Refrigerate for about 20 minutes, or until firm but not brittle.

Spread the almond cream over the rectangle in an even layer and sprinkle with the sugar. Sprinkle the raisins and the chopped walnuts over the almond cream. Begin rolling up the rectangle by pinching it along one short end. Continue rolling, as tight as you can, alternating between tucking under the dough with your fingers and rolling it with the flats of your hands, until you've rolled it up into a log.

Brush a sheet pan with oil. Slice the roll into 12 rounds. Tuck the little flap of dough from the end of the roll under the center to hold it in place and arrange the rounds on the sheet pan, leaving at least 2 inches between each one to allow for expansion. Cover with plastic wrap and let proof until each layer of dough has expanded by 50 percent, about 1 hour.

Preheat the oven to 400°F. Brush the pastries with egg wash. Bake for about 20 minutes, then check whether they're starting to get too brown. If so, turn down the oven to 325°F. Bake for about 15 minutes longer, or until golden brown.

Remove the pastries from the oven and brush with the glaze while still hot. Drizzle with royal icing, using a paper cone (see page 87), or a fork dipped in the icing and waved over the Danish.

MAKING ROLLED DANISH PASTRIES

1. Roll out a rectangle of croissant dough about ¼ inch thick. Spread over almond cream in a thin layer and sprinkle with the sugar.

2. Sprinkle with raisins and chopped walnuts. Start rolling the pastry dough by pinching it at one end and so you start out with a very tight roll.

3. Continue rolling, as tight as you can, alternating between tucking under the dough with your fingers . . . .

4. . . . and rolling it with the flats of your hands.

5. Slice the dough into rounds and place them on the oiled sheet pan. Leave room to allow for expansion. Tuck under the little flap of dough on the side of each round so it is held in place during baking.

6. Cover and allow to expand, then brush with egg wash. Bake until golden brown.

7. While they're still hot, brush the pastries with apricot glaze. Drizzle royal icing over them in a decorative pattern.

PIES, TARTS, AND PASTRIES 225

Napoleons

Classic napoleons are rectangular pastries made by stacking three thin, crisp sheets of baked puff pastry with filling in between. The classic filling is pastry cream, but passion fruit mousseline or crème chiboust (see page 158) can also be used.

For napoleons, puff pastry dough is rolled very thin and baked between two sheet pans to keep it from puffing. It's baked to a very deep brown for maximum flavor and crispiness. Napoleons are by definition rectangular, but the principle—sandwiching filling between sheets of brittle puff pastry—can be used to make round or square pastries with virtually any filling, provided that it's stiff enough so it doesn't ooze out when you're cutting through the layers.

Traditional napoleons are covered with fondant decorated with chocolate chevrons, but simpler and easily as elegant are napoleons that are dusted with confectioners' sugar with a grid pattern burned in with a hot skewer. See the sidebar on page 228.

One cup fondant is enough to coat the 5 by 12-inch rectangle, which is to say 60 square inches, a convenient formula when figuring out how much you need. For a 5 by 9-inch rectangle, enough for 6 napoleons, you'll need enough fondant for 45 square inches, about ¾ cup, but use a cup to be sure.

MAKES 6 NAPOLEONS

1 recipe classic puff pastry dough (page 148) or quick puff pastry dough (page 151)

2 cups filling such as pastry cream (page 160), passion fruit mousseline (page 58), or crème chiboust (page 161)

1 cup liquid fondant (page 163)

1 tablespoon finely grated bittersweet chocolate

Preheat the oven to 400°F. Line a 13 by 17-inch, or larger, sheet pan with parchment paper. Roll the dough into a 13 by 17-inch rectangle and transfer it to the prepared sheet pan (see page 141). Trim the sides if necessary. Refrigerate for about 20 minutes, or until firm but not brittle.

Dock the rectangle to keep it from puffing by poking it with a fork. Cover it with a sheet of parchment paper, put another sheet pan on top, and bake for 20 minutes. Remove the top sheet pan and the parchment paper on top of the pastry and bake for 20 minutes more, or until a deep golden brown.

Trim the edges so the rectangle is perfectly even. Measure the rectangle and cut it across into 3 rectangles the same size. If the pastry shrinks in the oven (to be expected), you will have a 12 by 15-inch rectangle, which will yield 3 cut rectangles approximately 12 by 5 inches. Cut a piece of cardboard the same size as the rectangles to serve as a base that will make it easier to finish the sides of the napoleons. Set aside about ⅓ cup of the filling. Place the first rectangle on the cardboard and spread it with half of the remaining filling. Press on the second rectangle and spread all but the reserved filling. Place the last rectangle on top, with the flat bottom side on top. Use a small metal spatula to smooth the reserved filling along the sides of the rectangle. Chill the pastry for at least 1 hour to make it easier to cut.

Warm the fondant and, if necessary, adjust its consistency with a tiny bit of water so it runs in a thick steady stream from a fork. Combine 1 tablespoon fondant with the chocolate and stir until smooth. You may need to heat it and thin it with 2 or 3 drops water so it will form threads when piped with a paper cone (see page 87).

Fill a paper cone with the chocolate fondant. Spread the plain fondant over the pastry and immediately pipe 5 lines of chocolate fondant an equal distance apart, along the length of the pastry. With a straight edge (a bench scraper, thin ruler, or straight knife), press very slightly into the surface of the chocolate fondant. Move the edge about ½ inch in one direction. Wipe the edge and repeat in the opposite direction, ¾ inch further down the rectangle (for 1½-inch-wide napoleons). Continue, alternating directions, until the plain fondant is decorated with chevrons. After the napoleon is sliced, the tops of the individual napoleons should have a row of chevrons with the chevron points in the center. Slice the napoleon crosswise into 6 equal portions and serve.

Note: Fondant can be tricky to work with because it hardens very quickly once it's allowed to sit or cool. It's best to cover the pastry rectangle with the fondant before the rectangle is sliced into individual napoleons. Keep in mind that the width of the chevrons should match the width of the individual napoleons so they all look the same. For example, if the rectangle is 9 inches long, you can make 6 napoleons, each 1½ inches wide. The chevrons should be made every ¾ inch.

1. Roll out a thin sheet of puff pastry dough onto a parchment paper–lined sheet pan. Trim the edges. Dock the dough by poking it with a fork.

2. Cover the dough with parchment paper and put a sheet pan on top of that. Bake until golden brown.

3. Trim the edges of the pastry rectangle to make it even. Mark the edges of the pastry into thirds and cut the pastry into 3 rectangles all the same size.

4. Cut a piece of cardboard the same size as the pastry rectangles. Place one of the rectangles on the cardboard and spread about half of the filling over it. (Reserve a little filling for the sides.)

5. Press the second rectangle over the filling. Spread the remaining filling (except that reserved for the sides) over the second rectangle.

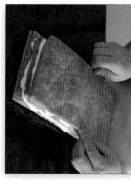

6. Press the last rectangle—the smoothest side up—over the filling.

7. Smooth off the sides of the rectangle with the reserved filling. It is helpful to hold the pastry at shoulder level while doing this.

8. Pour the plain fondant, all at once, over the pastry rectangle.

9. Immediately spread the fondant to cover with an offset spatula.

10. Pipe 5 straight lines of chocolate fondant along the length of the rectangle.

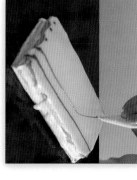

11. Press a straight edge very lightly into the surface of the fondant and pull to create the chevron effect.

12. Trim the edges of the rectangle.

13. Slice the napoleon crosswise into 6 smaller rectangles. Slice so the tips of the chevrons are in the middle of the rectangles.

Decorating Napoleons with Confectioners' Sugar

To decorate napoleons with confectioners' sugar, sprinkle or sift the sugar liberally over the top of the pastry rectangle. Heat a metal skewer until almost red hot over the flame of a gas stove or with a butane torch. Press it on the surface of the rectangle on a diagonal and repeat on the opposite diagonal to burn a diamond pattern into the sugar. (As you get used to this, you can use more than one skewer at a time.)

Apple Strudel

Strudel is made by wrapping paper-thin layers of dough around a filling. The dough is brushed with melted butter to keep the layers from sticking together and to add flavor. To make strudel dough, knead dough made with bread flour until it's smooth and very elastic. You need to make it at least two hours before you plan to use it; it's even better made the day before. After resting the dough, pull on it and stretch it until it's almost paper thin. It is easier if you have two people working. This recipe uses a classic filling of raisins and apples, but strudel can be made with virtually any filling, sweet or savory, such as sautéed chicken livers, diced dried fruits, foie gras, or cheese such as brie or Camembert.

MAKES ONE 20 BY 6-INCH STRUDEL

Dough

2 cups bread flour

1/2 cup plus 2 tablespoons water

3 tablespoons vegetable oil

1/2 teaspoon salt

Filling

1 cup raisins, soaked in enough water to cover or in 3 tablespoons flavorful spirits, such as Cognac, rum, or grappa

5 tart apples (2 1/2 pounds), preferably crisp heirloom local apples

1 1/2 cups coarsely chopped walnuts

1/4 cup granulated sugar or more as needed

Strudel

1/2 cup butter, melted

1/2 cup breadcrumbs combined with 2 tablespoons melted butter (optional)

1/2 cup sour cream

Confectioners' sugar for dusting

To make the dough, combine the flour, water, oil, and salt in a bowl and stir with a wooden spoon until the mixture pulls together into a single, shaggy mass.

On a floured work surface, knead the dough with the heel of your hand for about 15 minutes, or until it's very smooth and you can form a thin translucent sheet when you pinch it in 2 places and pull up a little. The dough can also be made in a food processor by processing for 2 minutes and then kneading by hand for 2 minutes. Cover with plastic wrap and let rest for at least 2 hours or, better, overnight.

To make the filling, drain the raisins if soaked in water. Peel, core, and dice the apples. Toss together the raisins, apples, walnuts, and the 1/4 cup granulated sugar, including any spirits used for soaking the raisins. Taste the mixture. If the apples are especially tart, you may want to add more sugar. Cover until needed.

To assemble and bake the strudel, preheat the oven to 350°F and line a sheet pan with parchment paper. Cover a table with a lint-free cloth (polyester is good) at least 3 feet square. Leave at least 6 inches of cloth hanging over one end and one of the corners of the table. Flatten the dough into a disk and start by stretching it all around with your hands. As the dough gets thinner, slide your hands, with the palms down, under the dough and lift while separating your hands. Alternate stretching and lifting until the dough is about 2 by 2½ feet. Fold one end of the dough over the corner of the work surface where the cloth is hanging over. Anchor the dough by pinching it over the edges of the table and placing a roll of aluminum foil or other object on the edges where you're not pulling. Continue stretching until the dough is about 2 by 3 feet and you can see your hands through it; brush it with melted butter to keep it from drying out.

Arrange the filling in a 14-inch-long, 6-inch-high mound about 8 inches in from one of the shorter ends of the dough—the end you left the extra cloth hanging from. Leave at least a couple of inches at each end of the mound. Place the bread-crumbs in a line along the top of the filling. Pipe or spoon over the sour cream.

Lift the extra cloth hanging over the end and pull it over the mound of filling so that it brings the 6 inches of dough with it. Peel the cloth away and leave the dough over the filling. Use the flats of your hands to push the dough against the sides of the filling. Roll the cylinder until you've used up all the dough. Press all over the log to make sure the dough adheres. Cut off any excess dough from the ends of the log, but leave a couple of inches on each end to seal it. Fold the extra dough under the ends of the log. Transfer to the prepared sheet pan and brush with melted butter.

Bake for about 60 minutes, or until golden brown. Let cool. Just before slicing, dust with confectioners' sugar, then cut into 1-inch-thick slices.

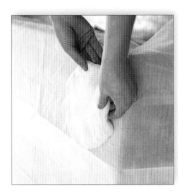

1. Stir together all the dough ingredients until the dough comes together in a shaggy mass.

2. Knead the dough by hand for about 15 minutes, or until it is perfectly smooth on the surface. It's ready when you stretch a section and can see through it. Wrap the dough and let it rest.

3. Combine the diced apples, soaked raisins—with their soaking liquid, if you used spirits—chopped walnuts, and sugar. Use your hands to combine the mixture.

4. Cover a work surface with lint-free cloth. Pull on the dough to shape it into a disk.

5. Continue pulling on the sides of the dough with your fingers to stretch it. Slide your hands, back sides up, under the dough and gently lift while separating your hands.

6. Fold one end of the dough over the corner of the work surface and continue to use the back of your hands to stretch it.

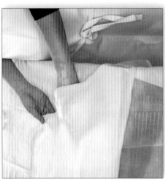

7. Continue stretching and pulling . . .

8. . . . until you can see your hands through the dough.

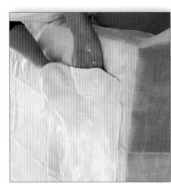

9. Anchor the dough with a roll of aluminum foil. It's also helpful to have two people working.

10. Immediately brush the stretched dough with melted butter to keep it from drying out.

11. Arrange the filling in an elongated mound running along the width of the dough. Leave 2 or 3 inches at each end with no filling and about 6 inches extra dough on the end you'll be rolling.

12. Place the buttered breadcrumbs in a line over the mound of filling. Use a pastry bag to pipe a line of sour cream over the filling.

13. Lift the cloth and fold it over the filling bringing the dough with it.

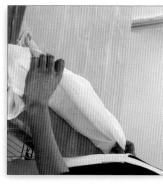

14. Use your hands to compress the log. Alternate lifting the cloth and pressing the log until all the dough is completely rolled up.

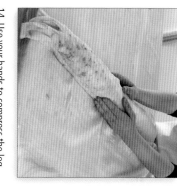

15. Trim the dough where it ends so the seam is straight.

17. Fold under the excess dough at each end of the log.

18. Transfer the log to a sheet pan by rolling it up in a sheet of parchment paper and sliding a long metal spatula under the length of it. Make sure the seam is hidden at the bottom. Brush with melted butter.

16. Trim off excess dough from each end of the log. Leave two inches of extra dough at each end of the log to fold over and seal in the filling.

19. Bake until golden brown. Allow to cool and dust with confectioners' sugar.

20. Serve the finished strudel in slices.

Pistachio Baklava

This is a refined version of baklava—made with pistachios instead of the usual almonds or walnuts—that is not quite as sweet and has fewer layers than those encountered in most Middle Eastern restaurants. But you can add as many layers as you want and use whatever nuts you like. This baklava is also made with brown butter instead of just melted butter, which gives it an intense nutty flavor.

Filo dough comes frozen in rolls and is so thin that a 1-pound package contains dozens of sheets. Fortunately, it can be frozen and refrozen so you only need to unroll what you need and put the rest back in the freezer. Filo is easy to work with, but dries out very fast when exposed to air. Keep it covered with a damp towel as you work with it.

The baklava shown here are made in a 10 by 15-inch sheet pan with relatively low sides. If you want to make baklava with more than the 2 layers, use a smaller baking dish with higher sides. Don't hesitate to adjust the amounts and sizes given here to match whatever pan you have and just keep building the baklava until you run out of nuts.

When shopping for pistachios, buy shelled nuts and, if possible, nuts with the thin reddish membrane-like peel removed. Pistachios with the peel removed will be bright green. If you can't find shelled and peeled pistachios, follow the peeling directions in the note below.

MAKES ABOUT 35 TWO-INCH BAKLAVA

4½ cups pistachios, shelled and, if possible,
    with thin peel removed (see Note)

1¼ cups sugar

1 cup honey

1½ cups water

1 cup brown butter (page 196)

12 ounces filo dough

Preheat the oven to 350°F. Toast the pistachios for about 10 minutes, or until you can smell them. Don't let them brown. Let the nuts cool, but leave the oven on. Chop the toasted nuts coarsely with a knife or with very short pulses in a food processor until they're the size of raisins. In a bowl, toss the nuts with ½ cup of the sugar.

Make the syrup by combining the remaining sugar, the honey, and water in a saucepan. Bring to a simmer and stir until the sugar dissolves. Let cool.

Brush a 10 by 15-inch sheet pan or baking dish, preferably nonstick, with sides at least ½ inch high, with the brown butter. Unroll the filo and cut 9 sheets to the size of the sheet pan. Immediately roll up and refreeze the filo you aren't using. Keep the 9 sheets covered with a moist towel while you're working.

Place 1 sheet filo in the sheet pan and brush with a thin layer of brown butter; keep in mind that you're going to butter 9 layers, so ration the brown butter accordingly. Add a second layer of filo, brush it with butter, then add a third layer of filo and brush with butter. Spread 1¾ cups chopped pistachios over the buttered filo. Cover with 3 more layers of filo, brushing each layer with brown butter. Sprinkle another 1¾ cups chopped pistachios over the buttered filo, then stack on another 3 sheets of filo, with butter brushed on each sheet. Bake for about 30 minutes, or until golden brown on top.

Ladle the syrup over the baklava—there should be enough syrup so that when you press down on the top of the sheets of filo with your fingertip, the syrup surrounds it. Cover with plastic wrap and let sit for 1 hour before cutting it into squares.

Cut into 2-inch squares and sprinkle the rest of the pistachios over them. Baklava will keep for up to 1 week in the refrigerator. They can be kept, covered with plastic wrap, in the pan they were baked in, or they can be transferred to a platter and refrigerated.

Note: If the pistachios still have their inner peel—if they're not green—peel them by plunging them into boiling water for 2 minutes, draining them, and rubbing them vigorously in a kitchen towel before sorting out the peels.

1. Plunge the unpeeled pistachios into boiling water for 2 minutes, drain, and immediately rub between two towels. Pick out the nuts. Roast them lightly and chop them in a food processor.

2. Combine the chopped nuts with 1/2 cup of the sugar. Brush a nonstick pan with the brown butter.

3. Unwrap the filo and cut 9 sheets, at one time, to the size of the sheet pan.

4. Keep the filo covered with a moist—not wet—towel while you're working.

5. Stack 3 sheets of filo on the sheet pan with brown butter brushed on each sheet.

6. Sprinkle over pistachio nuts.

7. Stack another 3 sheets of filo over the nuts, brushing each sheet with brown butter. Spread over a layer of pistachios and another 3 sheets of filo, each brushed with butter. Bake until golden brown.

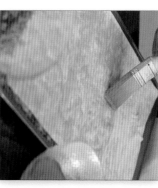

8. Pour over the syrup.

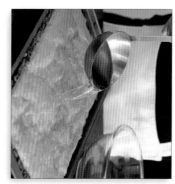

9. Cover the baklava with foil or plastic wrap and let cool. Cut into squares or diamonds.

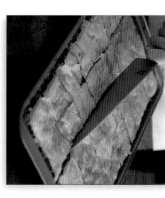

10. Sprinkle with more pistachios and serve.

SAVORY PASTRIES

Savory pastries are made just like sweet pastries except that the sugar is left out. Basic pie and tart pastry, puff pastry, and croissant dough can all be used to make savory pastry.

Mushroom Jalousie

. . . .

A jalousie—a window with slatted blinds—presumably gets its name for its ability to protect those inside from the inquiring eyes of jealous lovers. In any case, it's easy to see the resemblance to this pastry, which has slats on top that allow a peek at what is inside. A classic jalousie has a fill- ing of almond paste covered with jam, but it is one of those versatile pastries that you can fill with just about anything sweet (such as cooked fruit) or savory (such as foie gras, pâté, seafood, cooked chopped vegetables). Whatever filling you decide on should not release liquid as it bakes, which would make the jalousie's bottom crust soggy.

MAKES ONE 7 BY 10-INCH JALOUSIE

1 recipe classic puff pastry dough (page 148) or quick puff pastry dough (page 151)

2 cups mushroom filling, chilled (page 163)

Egg wash (see sidebar, page 146)

Line 2 sheet pans with parchment paper. Roll the dough into a 10½ by 14½-inch rectangle between ⅛ and ¼ inch thick and transfer it to a prepared sheet pan (see page 141). Freeze the dough for 10 minutes. Cut the dough in half crosswise and trim the pieces to make two 10 by 7-inch rectangles. Transfer one of the rectangles to the other prepared sheet pan. Preheat the oven to 425°F.

Spread the filling over one of the rectangles, leaving about a 1-inch border all around. Refrigerate.

Put the second rectangle of dough in the freezer for about 5 minutes, or just long enough to firm it slightly, but not so long that it cracks when you fold it. Fold it in half lengthwise to create a 5 by 7-inch strip of folded dough. With a long, sharp knife, cut slits about ¾ inch apart, cutting through the top

1. Roll out a piece of dough into a rectangle on a sheet of parchment paper.

2. Trim the edges of the dough with a sharp knife, then cut the rectangle in half. Put each rectangle on a piece of parchment paper.

3. Transfer one of the rectangles to a sheet pan. Use an offset spatula to spread the mushroom mixture over the rectangle in the sheet pan. Leave a 1-inch border all around the mushroom mixture. Refrigerate.

5. Cut into the folded rectangle to make the slats for the *jalousie*. Leave about ¾ inch on each side uncut.

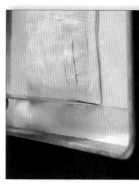

4. Freeze the second rectangle for about 5 minutes. Fold it in half.

6. Brush the border of the first rectangle with egg wash.

7. Transfer the slatted top onto the mushrooms, making sure the borders line up.

8. Unfold the top and press it gently over the egg-washed border to seal it. Trim the edges of the dough so they're exactly even. Brush the top of the *jalousie* with egg wash. Bake until golden brown.

and bottom layers of the dough but not cutting all the way to the fold. Leave about 3/4 inch of the fold and of the open side uncut to create the eventual center strip of dough and the border. Chill the dough so it's firm when you transfer it.

Brush egg wash over the edges of the bottom dough with the filling. Place the folded dough over the bottom dough with a minute or two if it's too stiff to work with. Unfold it so there's a strip of dough running up the center with the slats on both sides. Gently press the edges to seal the top to the bottom and cut away a tiny strip along all 4 edges, so the top and bottom edges are flush. Brush the top with egg wash. Freeze for 15 minutes.

Bake for about 30 minutes, or until puffed and golden brown. Turn down the oven to 300°F and bake for 20 minutes more. Cut into rectangles to serve.

1. Pipe the batter in little mounds in staggered rows on a parchment paper–lined sheet pan.

2. Brush the mounds lightly with egg wash and sprinkle a little grated cheese on each.

3. Bake until golden brown.

Cheese Puffs (Gougères)

These little cheese puffs are a traditional French hors d'oeuvre, perfect with a glass of wine or a cocktail. You can make them any size you like, but these are bite size. Most recipes for gougères call for Gruyère cheese, but Gruyère is a moist cheese that can make the puffs heavy. You'll have more success with well-aged Parmigiano-Reggiano or aged Gouda because they are dry and flavorful and don't weigh down the pastry.

MAKES ABOUT 40 BITE-SIZE HORS D'OEUVRES

3 ounces dry aged cheese
1 recipe cream puff pastry dough (page 155)
1 tablespoon paprika (optional)
Egg wash (see sidebar, page 146)

Preheat the oven to 425°F. Grate the cheese finely; you should have about 1 cup. Reserve 1/4 cup and mix the rest into the dough with a wooden spoon. Mix in the paprika.

Fill a pastry bag fitted with a 1/3-inch plain tip with dough. Pipe tiny dollops of dough into the corners of a sheet pan, and press a sheet of parchment paper onto them to hold it in place. Pipe the pastry in dollops about 1 inch apart, in staggered rows. When you've piped out the right amount—the pastry bag forms a mound about 1 inch wide at the base and about 2/3 inches high—give the tip a quick circular motion to detach it from the mound without leaving a little thread of pastry in the middle.

Brush the gougères with egg wash and smooth off the tops with the brush. Sprinkle with the reserved cheese. Bake for about 20 minutes, or until golden brown. Serve as soon as possible. They can also be frozen and gently reheated.

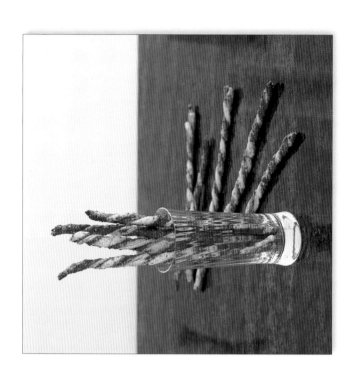

1. Spread over the cheese mixture so it completely covers the rectangle. Roll over the rectangle to get the cheese to stick to the dough.

2. Fold the rectangle in half and press down on it to hold it together.

3. Roll the rectangle out to its original dimensions—12 by 16 inches—and trim the sides. Cut the rectangle into 1/2 by 12-inch strips.

4. With your hands at each end, twist in opposite directions to make spirals. Bake until pale brown.

Cheese Straws

Once you've made puff pastry dough, you can throw together these straws in just a few minutes. If you have puff pastry trimmings, this is a perfect use for them. If you're working in a hot kitchen, make the cheese straws before you preheat the oven and keep them in the freezer until you are ready to bake them.

MAKES 24 STRAWS

1½ ounces firm, hard cheese such as Parmigiano-Reggiano or aged Gouda

1 tablespoon paprika or Spanish pimentón

1 recipe classic puff pastry dough (page 148) or quick puff pastry dough (page 151) or trimmings

Egg wash (see sidebar, page 146)

Grate the cheese—you should end up with 1/2 cup when gently pressed—and combine it with the paprika.

Roll the dough into a 12 by 16-inch rectangle. Brush the rectangle with egg wash and sprinkle the cheese mixture evenly over the entire surface. Roll over the surface with a rolling pin to ensure that the cheese will stick.

Fold the rectangle in half so it measures 8 by 12 inches and roll it out to its original size, 12 by 16 inches. Freeze until very firm, but not hard and brittle. Trim the edges of the rectangle and use a bench scraper or knife to cut the rectangle into 1/2 by 12-inch strips. Roll the ends of each strip in opposite directions with the flats of your hands until you see a distinct spiral pattern. While it would seem that a 16-inch rectangle cut into 1/2-inch strips would make 32 strips, it only makes 24 strips because of shrinkage and waste that falls off while you're slicing. Place the strips on a sheet pan and freeze until firm, but not brittle.

Preheat the oven to 425°F. Bake for about 12 minutes, or until pale brown. Let cool on a cake rack and serve.

Vol-au-Vents

One of the many uses of puff pastry is serving as a holder for both sweet and savory foods. A vol-au-vent is a round case with a lid. You can make vol-au-vents any size you want, from miniature bite-size cases for hors d'oeuvres to larger versions for main-course servings of stews and other mixtures. These vol-au-vents are filled with goat cheese, lightly creamed and flavored with herbs and olive oil (see page 162), but virtually anything, hot or cold, can be served in these holders. To make square puff pastry holders, see page 152, and to make less formal puff pastry rectangles, see page 153.

MAKES 6 VOL-AU-VENTS

1 recipe classic puff pastry dough (page 148) or quick puff pastry dough (page 151)

Egg wash (see sidebar, page 146)

Line a sheet pan with parchment paper. Roll the dough into a 13 by 16-inch sheet and transfer it to the prepared sheet pan (see page 141). Freeze for 10 to 15 minutes, or until the dough is very firm but not too hard to cut through.

With a 3½-inch round fluted cookie cutter, make 6 cutouts in the dough. Cut all the way through the dough, but leave the cutouts in place. Make 6 more cutouts with the 3½-inch cutter, but this time, center a 2½-inch fluted cutter inside the 3½-inch cutter and press down. Now you have six 3½-inch plain rounds and six 3½-inch rings with a 2½-inch round in the middle. If the dough is getting soft, freeze it again for 10 minutes or so to keep it firm.

Take the 2½-inch fluted rounds out of the center of the larger circles and reserve. These are the lids. Pull away the pastry that surrounds the cutouts and reserve. Dock 6 of the larger circles—those with no cutout in the middle—with a fork, brush them with egg wash, and place a ring (one of the rings that surrounds the lids) on top. Press on it gently to hold it in place. Brush the rings and the tops with egg wash—don't let any get on the sides—and freeze. You should now have 6 larger rounds with rings on top and six smaller rounds for the lids.

Preheat the oven to 400°F. Bake for about 25 minutes, or until puffed and golden brown. Let cool. Fill with the mixture of your choice.

VARIATION

MINIATURE VOL-AU-VENTS: To make miniature vol-au-vents, perfect for bite-size hors d'oeuvres, use a 1½-inch and a 1-inch round fluted cookie cutter to make 80 cutouts—8 rows of 10 each.

Preheat the oven to 400°F. Bake for about 20 minutes, or until puffed and golden brown. Let cool and fill. Put on the lids.

MAKING VOL-AU-VENTS AND MINIATURE VOL-AU-VENTS

1. Cut 3½-inch fluted rounds into the dough, and cut 2½-inch rounds in the centers of half of these.

2. To make miniature vol-au-vents, cut fluted 1½-inch rounds into a sheet of puff pastry dough and press a 1-inch fluted cookie cutter into the centers of half of the 1½-inch rounds.

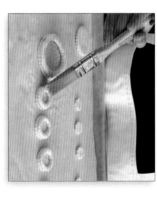

3. Take out the 2½-inch rounds from the larger circles and the 1-inch rounds from the smaller ones; these are the lids. Dock the remaining circles by poking with a fork. Pull away the excess dough.

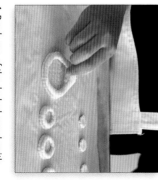

4. Brush one of the docked rounds with egg wash and put one of the rings from those that surround the smaller rounds—over it.

5. Brush the ring and the lids with egg wash. Bake until golden brown.

6. Fill the vol-au-vents with a mixture of your choice and put on the lids.

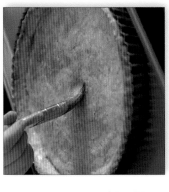

1. Cook the bacon over medium heat until it browns a bit and releases fat.

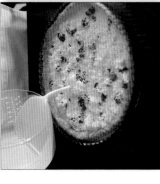

2. Prepare the custard mixture. Brush the prebaked tart shell with egg wash and bake for about 5 minutes more to create a seal before adding the filling.

3. If there are serious cracks in the tart shell, brush it with flour paste to create a seal and bake for 5 minutes.

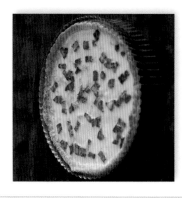

4. Sprinkle the tart shell with the bacon strips. Sprinkle the cheese over the bacon. Pour the custard mixture over the bacon and cheese.

5. Bake the quiche until you see no movement on the surface of the quiche when you gently move it back and forth.

Quiche Lorraine

A quiche is a savory custard baked in a prebaked tart shell. The most traditional quiche of all is a quiche Lorraine, made by pouring a custard mixture over pieces of bacon, and sometimes cheese, arranged in the tart shell. Because quiche is so versatile, you can arrange almost anything you like in the shell before pouring the custard mixture into it—the custard mixture stays the same. The quiche is then slowly baked until the custard sets. When making a quiche, or any tart filled with liquid, make sure that any holes or cracks in the tart shell have been sealed. For minor cracks or slits, the traditional brushing with beaten egg, followed by a 5-minute baking to set it, usually does the trick. For bigger cracks, or just to be sure, brush the baked shell with flour paste and bake it for 5 minutes (see page 145).

MAKES ONE 9- TO 10-INCH QUICHE

1 recipe basic pie and tart pastry dough (page 130) or cream cheese tart and pie pastry dough (page 135)

Egg wash (see sidebar, page 146) or flour paste (page 145), to seal tart shell

4 ounces flavorful cheese, such as Gruyère or Cheddar

6 ounces bacon, preferably slab or thick-sliced

2 eggs

1¼ cups milk

Freshly ground black pepper

Use a 9- or 10-inch tart ring or fluted tart pan. Roll the dough 2 inches larger than the ring or pan and line the tart pan or ring with it (see page 143). Prebake the tart shell (see page 145). Brush with egg wash and bake for 5 minutes more to seal. If the tart shell has serious cracks, brush with flour paste (see page 145) and bake for 5 minutes more.

Heat the oven to 300°F.

Finely grate the cheese—you should have about 1½ cups. If you're using slab bacon, cut it into ⅓-inch-thick slices. Cut the bacon slices crosswise into little strips—these are called *lardons*. Cook the strips over medium heat for about 6 minutes, until they render their fat and barely begin to brown. Remove with a slotted spoon, drain on a paper towel, and reserve.

Beat the eggs until the whites and yolks are thoroughly combined, then beat in the milk. Grind in a little pepper. Sprinkle the bacon over the tart shell and then spread the grated cheese over it. Pour over the egg mixture.

Place the quiche on a sheet pan and bake for about 40 minutes, or until set—there's no motion on the surface when you move it back and forth.

COOKIES

Basic Butter Cookie Dough • 246

Jelly Cookies • 247

Holiday Butter Cookies • 248

Sablée Cookies • 250

Chocolate Sablée Cookies • 250

Checkerboard Sablée Cookies • 250

Marbled Sablée Cookies • 252

Spiral-Patterned Sablée Cookies • 252

Shortbread Cookies • 256

Pecan Fingers • 257

Chocolate Chip Cookies • 259

Madeleines • 260

Cakey Madeleines • 261

Financiers • 262

Cat's Tongue Cookies
(*Langues de Chat*) • 263

Almond Tuiles • 264

Lacy Blood Orange Tuiles • 265

Macarons • 266

Coconut Macarons • 267

Florentine Almond Cookies • 268

Biscotti • 269

Palmiers • 271

Brownies • 272

Lemon Bars • 274

Methods and Techniques

Making Basic Butter Cookie Dough • 246

Making Jelly Cookies • 247

Making Holiday Butter Cookies • 248

Decorating Cookies with Royal Icing • 249

**Decorating Cookies with
Colored Sugar • 249**

Making Sablée Cookies • 250

Making Checkerboard Sablée Cookies • 251

Making Marbled Sablée Cookies • 252

Making Spiral-Patterned
Sablée Cookies • 253

**Making Sablée Cookies with
a Cookie Press • 254**

Making Shortbread Cookies • 256

Making Pecan Fingers • 257

Making Chocolate Chip Cookies • 258

Making Madeleines • 260

Making Cakey Madeleines • 261

Making *Financiers* • 262

Making Cat's Tongue Cookies • 263

Making Almond Tuiles • 264

Making Lacy Blood Orange Tuiles • 265

Making Macarons • 266

Making Coconut Macarons • 267

Making Florentine Almond Cookies • 268

Making Biscotti • 269

Making *Palmiers* • 270

Making Brownies • 272

Making Lemon Bars • 275

Basic Butter Cookie Dough

Many of the techniques used for making pies, tarts, cakes, and other pastries are also used to make cookies. Virtually any cookie is one of several kinds: pie dough–like cookies, such as sablées, jelly cookies, shortbread, pecan cookies, and tollhouse cookies; cakelike cookies, such as madeleines; meringue-based cookies, such as *macarons*; thin egg-white based cookies, such as *tuiles* and cat's tongue cookies (*langues de chat*); melted-butter cookies, such as *financiers*; puff pastry cookies, such as *palmiers*; and rusks, such as biscotti. In America, cookies are named by how they are shaped; hence, we have bars, icebox cookies, rolled cookies, and drop cookies. You will find examples of each in this chapter.

The basic dough for butter cookies, sugar cookies, and holiday cookies is made like a sweetened pie dough with extra butter and a little baking powder to make it richer and lighter. This dough can be shaped with your hands—as shown for the jelly cookies on the facing page—or rolled out with a pin as shown for the holiday cookies on page 248. Remember to always keep this dough cold.

shown for the jelly cookies on the facing page—or rolled out with a pin as shown for the holiday cookies on page 248.

MAKES ENOUGH FOR 30 COOKIES

2¹/₄ cups flour

³/₄ teaspoon baking powder

¹/₂ teaspoon salt

1 cup plus 3 tablespoons butter, at cool room temperature

1 cup superfine or granulated sugar

1 teaspoon vanilla extract

1 egg

1 egg yolk

In a bowl, whisk together the flour, baking powder, and salt. Using a whisk, a handheld beater, or a stand mixer with the paddle attachment, beat the butter with the sugar and vanilla until fluffy. Beat in the egg and egg yolk.

Sift the flour mixture over the butter mixture. Combine with a wooden spoon—don't beat it with a handheld mixer at this point, it's too stiff—or the stand mixer with the paddle attachment just until it's well combined and there's no loose flour. If you're using a stand mixer, start on slow speed so flour doesn't fly around, then increase to medium speed and beat for 30 seconds to 1 minute, until the dough pulls away from the sides of the bowl, it forms a cohesive mass, and you hear the motor straining. If there's any loose flour on the bottom of the bowl, fold it into the rest of the dough with a silicone spatula and combine for about 15 seconds more. The dough can be stored, tightly wrapped, in the refrigerator.

MAKING BASIC BUTTER COOKIE DOUGH

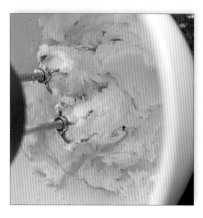

Beat together the butter, sugar, and vanilla until fluffy.

Beat in the egg and then the egg yolk. Sift the combined flour, baking powder, and salt over the batter. Mix just until the dough coheres and there's no loose flour on the bottom of the bowl.

Jelly Cookies

These cookies, which use basic butter cookie dough, are fun to make with kids. Play around with different flavors and colors of jams and jellies.

MAKES 30 COOKIES

1 recipe basic butter cookie dough (page 246)
¼ cup plus 1 tablespoon jelly or jam

Preheat the oven to 350°F. Unless you are using nonstick pans, line 2 sheet pans with parchment paper.

To keep the balls the right size, weigh 1 ounce of dough or spoon out 2 tablespoons, and roll it into a ball. Use it as a model to make the others the same size. Arrange them on the prepared sheet pans. Press them down with the heel of your hand to flatten them into 2-inch rounds. Press in the center to make an indentation—don't poke all the way through the cookie—and fill the indentation with ½ teaspoon jelly or enough to come up to the top of the indentation. Don't add too much or it will run down the sides of the cookies in the oven.

Bake for about 20 minutes, or until very pale brown around the edges. Let cool until set and then transfer to cooling racks, or cool in the pans set on racks. Store tightly sealed in an airtight container for up to 1 week.

1. Roll the dough into balls.

2. Arrange the balls on a sheet pan and use your hand to flatten them into 2-inch rounds.

3. Press a finger into the center of each of the rounds to make an indentation for the jelly.

4. Spoon just enough jelly into the holes so that it's level with the top.

5. Bake the cookies until they are just slightly pale brown on the edges.

Holiday Butter Cookies

These cookies use the basic butter cookie dough, but with a little more flour. Without the extra flour, the dough would be too soft to roll.

MAKES ABOUT 20 COOKIES, DEPENDING ON SIZE AND SHAPE

1 recipe basic butter cookie dough made with ½ cup more flour (page 246)

Pound the dough to flatten it and roll it into a 13 by 17-inch rectangle (the size of a standard sheet pan), ⅛ to ¼ inch thick. Roll it between parchment paper or waxed paper to avoid dusting it with flour and to make it easier to move. Refrigerate until cold.

When the dough is cold, cut it into shapes with cookie cutters and pull away the excess dough. Roll this dough out and cut out more cookies. If you like, decorate the cookies with colored sugar as shown opposite. Put the cookies, still on the parchment paper, on a sheet pan and refrigerate.

Preheat the oven to 325°F. Bake for 15 to 20 minutes, until very pale brown. Let cool until set and then transfer to cooling racks, or let cool in the pans set on racks. Store tightly sealed in an airtight container for up to 1 week.

Decorate with royal icing (see facing page), if you like.

MAKING HOLIDAY BUTTER COOKIES

1. Pound the dough to flatten it.

2. Roll the dough between sheets of waxed paper or parchment paper.

3. Trim the excess dough around the paper.

4. Slide the sheet of dough, still on the parchment paper, onto a sheet pan.

5. Cut the dough into cookie shapes with cookie cutters. Press very hard to completely detach the cutouts.

6. Pull the cookies away from the surrounding dough—which you can save and roll out again. Chill the cookies and bake until very pale brown.

Decorating Cookies with Royal Icing

There are several ways to use royal icing (see variation, page 67) to decorate cookies. You can spread it out in a baking dish and dip the cookies face down into the icing; you can pipe it with a paper cone (see page 87); you can color it; and you can paint it onto the cookies with a brush.

1. Dip a cookie face down into the royal icing. Hold it suspended for a few seconds over the icing to allow excess icing to drip off.

2. Turn the cookie over. If it isn't evenly coated, rotate it around to distribute the icing.

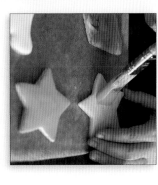

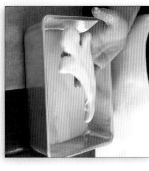

3. To create a marbled effect, spread one drop of food coloring in the royal icing with a fork. Dip the cookie face down in the colored icing.

4. Paint royal icing on cookies with a brush.

5. Some people prefer painting cookies holding them in one hand, while others like to paint the cookies set on the work surface as shown above.

6. Here the rim of a star cookie is decorated with yellow royal icing flavored with lemon oil, piped out of a paper cone.

Decorating Cookies with Colored Sugar

Colored sugar, called "sanding sugar," is easy to sprinkle over cookies cut into a variety of shapes. You can create different designs by covering parts of the cookies with waxed paper while sprinkling different colors over them. If you want all the cookies to be the same color, just decorate them right on the sheet pan. But if you're decorating them with different colors or in different ways (such as coating them with royal icing as shown at left), take them one at a time off the sheet pan and decorate them on the work surface so you don't accidentally scatter a little of the wrong color sugar over them. Make sure the dough is very cold—stick the cookies in the freezer as needed—so the cookies don't lose their shape while you're moving them to and from the work surface.

1. Brush the raw cookies with egg white beaten just enough to loosen it.

2. Sprinkle the sugar over the cookies.

3. To make stripes or to use more than one color, cover parts of the dough with strips or pieces of waxed paper while sprinkling the sugar.

Sablée Cookies

These cookies are made with the same dough used to make sweet crusts for pies and tarts. It is very similar to the shortbread dough on page 256—it has the same marvelous tendency to turn instantly into crumbs in the mouth—except it contains an egg and an egg yolk. You can also use this dough to make checkerboard cookies (below, right), marbled cookies (page 252), spiral-patterned cookies (page 252), and cookies made with a cookie press (page 254).

MAKES ABOUT 50 COOKIES

1 recipe extra buttery sweet pastry dough (page 134)

Cut the dough in half. On a floured work surface, roll half of the dough into a 1½ by 8-inch log, using the palms of your hands. Repeat with the remaining dough. Wrap the logs separately in plastic wrap and refrigerate for 30 minutes. If you're not using the dough right away, keep it tightly wrapped in the refrigerator or freezer. It will keep in the refrigerator for about 3 days and in the freezer for about 3 months.

Preheat the oven to 350°F. Unless you are using nonstick pans, line 2 sheet pans with parchment paper or silicone baking mats.

Slice the cylinders into ⅓-inch-thick rounds and arrange them on the prepared baking sheets, spacing them about ½ inch apart. Bake for about 12 minutes, or until a barely perceptible browning is visible on the edges of the cookies. Transfer to a cooling rack or let cool in the pans set on racks. Store tightly sealed in an airtight container for up to 1 week.

Chocolate Sablée Cookies

Chocolate cookie dough can be used to make simple chocolate butter cookies or it can be combined with plain cookie dough to make checkerboard cookies (below), marbled cookies (page 252), spiral-patterned cookies (page 252), and cookies made with a cookie press (page 254).

MAKES 10 OUNCES DOUGH, ENOUGH FOR 25 COOKIES

¾ cup flour
⅓ cup confectioners' sugar
¼ cup unsweetened cocoa powder
¼ teaspoon salt
¼ cup plus 2 tablespoons cold butter, cut into ⅓-inch slices
1 egg white

Unless you are using nonstick pans, line a sheet pan with parchment paper or silicone baking mats. In a food processor, combine the flour, sugar, cocoa powder, and salt and process for 15 seconds, or until well mixed. Add the butter and egg white and process for about 20 seconds, or until the dough comes together in a lumpy mass. Remove the dough from the processor and shape into a 1½ by 15-inch log. Refrigerate the dough for 45 minutes.

Preheat the oven to 375°F. Slice the dough ⅓ to ½ inch thick. Arrange the cookies in rows on the prepared sheet pan. Bake for 20 minutes, or until firm but not hard. Let cool until set and then transfer to cooling racks, or let cool in the pan set on racks. Store tightly sealed in an airtight container for up to 1 week.

Checkerboard Sablée Cookies

To make these cookies, you'll need chocolate sablée dough and extra buttery sweet pastry dough. These are rolled into ropes that are then pressed together to make the cookies.

MAKES ABOUT 50 COOKIES

½ recipe extra buttery sweet pastry dough (page 134)
Confectioners' sugar for dusting
1 recipe chocolate sablée dough (above)
Cocoa powder for dusting
1 egg white, lightly beaten

MAKING SABLÉE COOKIES

1. Roll the dough into logs, wrap in plastic wrap, and refrigerate for 30 minutes.

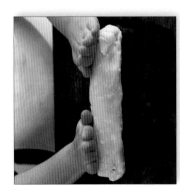

2. Slice the log into ⅓-inch-thick disks and bake until barely brown.

1. Roll the plain sablée dough, using confectioners' sugar to prevent sticking, into 2 ropes, each about 1/3 inch thick.

2. Roll the chocolate sablée dough, using cocoa powder to prevent sticking, into 2 ropes, each about 1/3 inch thick. Brush off extra cocoa and sugar.

5. Cut the strip in half. Brush one half with egg white. Place the other half, turned over, so plain alternates with chocolate, on the egg white–brushed half. Roll gently with the rolling pin to press together.

6. Cut the strip in half again, brush one half with egg white, and arrange the other strip on top. Gently press the strips together, both from the top and from the sides, to hold the ropes together.

Unless you are using nonstick pans, line 2 sheet pans with parchment paper or silicone baking mats. On a work surface dusted with confectioners' sugar, divide the extra buttery sweet pastry dough in two and roll each piece into a 1/3-inch-thick rope about 17 inches long. Dust the work surface with cocoa powder and repeat with the chocolate sablée dough.

Brush excess confectioners' sugar and cocoa off the ropes. Arrange the 4 ropes next to each other, alternating chocolate and plain dough. Roll over them gently with a rolling pin, pressing them together into a strip about 1/3 inch thick and 1 inch wide and squaring them off. Alternate gentle rolling with pressing on the sides of the strip with a flat edge—a ruler and spatula are shown above—to square off the strip. Refrigerate as needed if the dough starts to soften and gets sticky.

3. Align the ropes so there are 4 lengths, alternating chocolate and plain. Roll them gently with a rolling pin to make the round ropes into a squared-off strip.

4. Press on the sides of the ropes with straightedges to square off the sides.

7. Slice the strips into 1/3-inch-thick cookies. Bake until barely brown.

Cut the strip in half crosswise into 2 equal lengths. Brush one half with egg white and place the other half on top, flipping it over so the colors are alternating. Roll gently with the rolling pin to press the strands together. Cut the now-double strip in half. Brush one half with egg white, and place the other half—again alternating colors—on top. Roll lightly with the rolling pin to make sure the 4 layers hold together. Cut the dough into 1/3-inch-thick slices and arrange on the prepared sheet pans. Refrigerate for at least 30 minutes.

Preheat the oven to 350°F. Bake for about 12 minutes, or until only the slightest hint of browning is visible on the edges of the cookies. Let cool until set and then transfer to cooling racks, or let cool in the pans set on racks. Store tightly sealed in an airtight container for up to 1 week.

Marbled Sablée Cookies

These little cookies are great if you have trimmings of plain sablée and chocolate sablée left over. They indeed have a marbled appearance and combine the flavors of butter and chocolate in a nutty, crumbly cookie.

MAKES 50 COOKIES

¹/₂ recipe extra buttery sweet pastry dough (page 134)

1 recipe chocolate sablée dough (page 250)

Unless you are using nonstick pans, line 2 sheet pans with parchment paper or silicone baking mats. Squeeze each dough into rough strips and bunch the strips together. Use your hands to roll the mixed doughs into a cylinder, slightly less than 1¹/₂ inches in diameter. Slice the cylinder into ¹/₃-inch-thick rounds and arrange the rounds on the prepared sheet pans. Chill for 30 minutes.

Preheat the oven to 350°F. Bake for about 12 minutes, or until only the slightest hint of browning is visible on the edges of the cookies. Let cool until set and then transfer to cooling racks, or let cool in the pans set on racks. Store tightly sealed in an airtight container for up to 1 week.

MAKING MARBLED SABLÉE COOKIES

1. Bring the 2 doughs together in strips.

3. Slice the cylinder into ¹/₃-inch-thick rounds. Bake until barely brown

Spiral-Patterned Sablée Cookies

To make these elegant cookies, roll out a sheet of chocolate sablée dough and press it onto a sheet of plain extra buttery sweet dough. Then roll the whole thing up and slice it. The spiral cookies combine the flavors of chocolate and butter.

MAKES ABOUT 50 COOKIES

¹/₂ recipe extra buttery sweet pastry dough (page 134)

1 recipe chocolate sablée dough (page 250)

Confectioners' sugar for rolling

Cocoa powder for rolling

1 egg white, lightly beaten

Unless you are using nonstick pans, line 2 sheet pans with parchment paper or silicone baking mats. Using confectioners' sugar for the plain dough and cocoa powder for the chocolate dough, roll each dough into a 7 by 16-inch sheet, ¹/₈ to ¹/₄ inch thick.

Brush the plain dough sheet with egg white and place the chocolate dough sheet on top. Trim the edges so the sheets are flush. Brush the chocolate sheet with egg white. Starting on one of the longer sides, roll up the sheets together as tightly as you can. Pinch the seam so the cookies don't unravel. Refrigerate for 30 minutes.

Preheat the oven to 350°F. Slice the cylinder into ¹/₃-inch-thick cookies and arrange them on the prepared sheet pans. Bake for about 12 minutes, or until only the slightest hint of browning is visible on the edges of the cookies. Let cool until set and then transfer to cooling racks, or let cool in the pans set on racks. Store tightly sealed in an airtight container for up to 1 week.

2. Squeeze the dough together and then roll into a cylinder.

1. Roll out a rectangle of extra buttery sweet pastry dough and brush it with egg white. Roll out a rectangle of chocolate sablée and set it on top of the sheet of plain sablée.

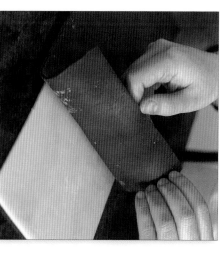

2. Trim the edges of the two-layered rectangle.

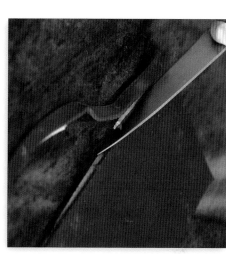

3. Brush the chocolate rectangle with egg white.

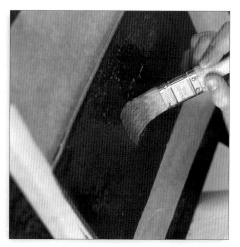

4. Pinch along one long side of the rectangle . . .

5. . . . roll it up.

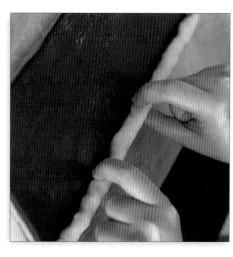

6. Pinch the edge of the cylinder against the rest of the roll so it doesn't unroll when baking.

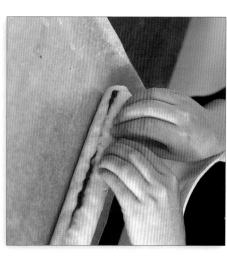

7. Slice the roll into 1/3-inch-thick cookies. Bake until barely brown.

Making Sablée Cookies with a Cookie Press

If you've never seen one before, a cookie press can be a bit perplexing. When you open the box, you'll find a metal cylinder, a handle connecting to a notched rod, and a myriad little metal disks. Each disk produces a cookie with a different shape, so it's easy to make a variety of different cookies with very little extra effort. This method works for virtually any cookie dough. To set the thing up, roll the dough—extra buttery sweet pastry dough is shown here—into logs that fit in the metal cylinder. Screw one of the disks onto one end of the cylinder and attach the handle/plunger mechanism. Here is the trick: Hold the end of the cylinder very firmly over a sheet pan and press down the

handle as far as it will go. Lift the whole gadget up with a very quick jerk. If you're too slow, the dough will stick to the cylinder instead of forming a cookie on the sheet pan. Use nonstick or buttered sheet pans—parchment paper can't be used because it will come up as you jerk up the press.

When you've pressed all the dough, refrigerate for 30 minutes. Fifteen minutes before baking, preheat the oven to 350°F. Bake for about 12 minutes, or until only the slightest hint of browning is visible on the edges of the cookies. Let cool until set and then transfer to cooling racks, or let cool in the pans set on racks. Store tightly sealed in an airtight container for up to 1 week.

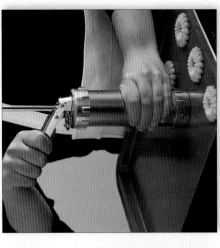

3. Hold the metal-disk end of the cylinder firmly over a nonstick or buttered sheet pan and press down firmly with the handle. Lift the press up very quickly. Bake until barely browned.

2. Roll the cookie dough into logs and slide one into the press.

1. The press with its various attachments.

4. Finished pressed cookies.

Shortbread Cookies

If you want to make the dough by hand instead of with a stand mixer, work the ingredients with a wooden spoon in the order—and to the same consistency—shown here. Shortbread dough is similar to extra buttery sweet pastry dough but contains no liquid. These cookies are quite salty—a delicious juxtaposition with their sweetness—but if you don't want the salt, cut it in half.

MAKES 35 COOKIES

1³/₄ cups flour
1 teaspoon salt
1 cup butter, cut into ¹/₂-inch slices
³/₄ cup granulated sugar
¹/₄ cup turbinado or granulated sugar (optional)

In a bowl, whisk together the flour and salt. Combine the butter and granulated sugar in the bowl of a stand mixer and cream the butter using the paddle attachment blade on medium to high speed for about 1 minute, or until fluffy. Scrape down the sides of the bowl with a silicone spatula, and beat for 1 minute more. Turn off the mixer, add the flour mixture, and turn the mixer on at low speed. Gradually increase the speed to medium and beat for about 1 minute, or until the dough clumps together and you hear the motor straining. The dough will first look like grated Parmesan cheese, then fine gravel, then coarse gravel, and finally a cohesive mass.

Transfer the dough to a sheet of parchment paper that will just fit into a sheet pan. Use a rolling pin and your fingers to press the dough into a 9 by 12-inch rectangle about ¹/₃ inch thick. Trim the sides to even up the rectangle and roll the trimmings into the center of the rectangle. Sprinkle evenly with the turbinado sugar, if using. Transfer the dough to a sheet pan by lifting each end of the parchment paper. Refrigerate for at least 30 minutes.

Preheat the oven to 375°F. Bake for about 15 minutes, or until golden brown on top. Slice the rectangle, while still hot, into 1-inch-wide strips. Cut across the strips by making four slices, 2¹/₄ inches apart, at about a 30-degree angle with the 1-inch strips, to form diamonds. Let cool completely on the parchment paper before serving. Store tightly sealed in an airtight container for up to 1 week.

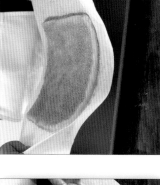

1. Mix the dough in a stand mixer until it comes together in a ragged mass.

2. Scoop the dough out onto a sheet of parchment paper, then flatten it by pounding it with a rolling pin.

3. Roll the dough into a 9 by 12-inch rectangle about ¹/₃ inch thick. Use a bench scraper to trim the sides.

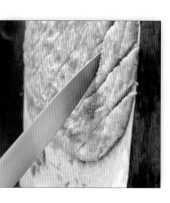

4. Press the trimmings back into the center of the dough.

5. Continue rolling, trimming, and pressing until the rectangle is even and smooth. Sprinkle the dough with turbinado sugar.

6. Lift the parchment paper up at each end and transfer the dough to a sheet pan.

7. Bake until golden brown on top. Cut into cookies while it's still hot.

Pecan Fingers

When you bite into one of these cookies, you'll get the impression of butter suspended in air, as the bite of cookie immediately falls apart into dust. Sometimes these fragile buttery cookies are called Russian tea cookies or Mexican wedding cookies. They can be made with pecans, hazelnuts, or walnuts. You can make the cookie dough by hand, with a stand mixer or a handheld mixer, or in a food processor.

MAKES 30 COOKIES

2 cups flour

1/4 teaspoon salt

1 cup butter, cut into 1/2-inch cubes

2/3 cup granulated sugar

2 teaspoons vanilla extract

2 cups pecans, roasted (see Note)

Confectioners' sugar for dusting

To make the dough by hand or with a mixer, sift together the flour and salt in a bowl and reserve. In a large bowl, with a heavy wooden spoon or a mixer, cream the butter and granulated sugar until fluffy. Mix in the vanilla. Process the pecans in a food processor for about 30 seconds, or until finely ground but not oily. Mix the nuts into the butter mixture until evenly distributed. Add the flour mixture and beat just long enough to eliminate lumps. Refrigerate for at least 20 minutes.

To make the dough in a food processor, whisk together the flour and salt in a bowl and reserve. Grind the pecans and granulated sugar together for about 1 minute, or until finely ground but not oily. Add the butter and vanilla and process for about 30 seconds, or until a paste forms with no lumps. Scrape down the sides of the processor work bowl with a silicone spatula halfway through the processing. Add the flour mixture all at once and process for 10 seconds. Scrape down the sides of the processor with a silicone spatula and process for about 10 seconds more, or until the mixture clumps together. Refrigerate for at least 20 minutes.

Unless you are using a nonstick pan, line a sheet pan with parchment paper or a silicone baking mat. Form about 2 tablespoons of dough into a finger shape about 3 inches long and place it on the prepared sheet pan. When you've formed all the cookies, refrigerate them on the sheet pan for 1 hour to harden the butter.

Preheat the oven to 275°F. Bake for about 25 minutes, or until pale brown on the bottoms. Let cool until set and then transfer to cooling racks, or let cool in the pans set on racks. Roll the cookies in confectioners' sugar. Store tightly sealed in an airtight container for up to 1 week.

Note: To roast the pecans, preheat the oven to 350°F. Place the nuts on a baking sheet and roast them for about 15 minutes, or until you can smell their aroma.

MAKING PECAN FINGERS

1. Shape the dough into finger shapes and arrange them on a sheet pan covered with parchment paper or a silicone mat. Bake until pale brown on the bottoms.

2. Allow to cool and sprinkle with or roll in confectioners' sugar and serve.

1. Combine all the ingredients except the chocolate and nuts in the food processor. Process the mixture for about 20 seconds, or until it clumps together into a solid mass.

2. Transfer the dough to a bowl and use a wooden spoon to mix in the chopped chocolate and chopped walnuts.

3. Spoon the dough onto nonstick or buttered baking sheets.

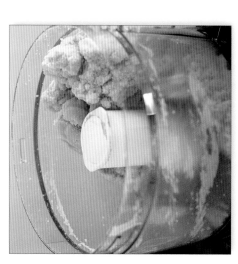

4. Dip a glass in a bowl of cold water and use it to press down on the cookies to flatten them. Bake until barely browned.

Chocolate Chip Cookies

Most bakers make chocolate chip cookies with the chocolate chips sold at the supermarket. To take your cookies up a notch, chop a piece of high-quality bittersweet chocolate. This recipe contains more butter and walnuts than the classic; it has gotten rave reviews.

MAKES ABOUT 16 COOKIES

6 ounces bittersweet chocolate or chocolate chips

1 cup flour

1/2 teaspoon baking soda

1/2 teaspoon salt

3/4 cup butter, sliced

1/4 cup brown sugar

1/4 cup granulated sugar

1 egg yolk

1/2 teaspoon vanilla extract

3/4 cup coarsely chopped walnuts

Unless you are using silicone baking liners or nonstick sheet pans, brush 2 sheet pans with room-temperature butter.

If you're using a chunk of chocolate, chop it into 1/2-inch pieces by hand or with a food processor using the pulse mechanism to avoid overchopping. In a bowl, sift together the flour, baking soda, and salt.

If you're making the dough by hand or with a stand mixer with the paddle attachment, mix together the butter and sugars until fluffy. Mix in the egg yolk and vanilla and add the flour mixture all at once. Stir or mix on low to medium speed until there's no loose flour visible. Stir in the nuts and chocolate.

If you're using a food processor, process all the ingredients except the chocolate and nuts for about 20 seconds, or until they clump together and you see no loose flour. If there's loose flour clinging to the bottom of the processor work bowl, scrape it up with a silicone spatula and process for 5 seconds more. Transfer the dough to a bowl and mix in the nuts and chocolate with a wooden spoon.

Refrigerate the dough for 30 minutes. Preheat the oven to 375°F.

For the first cookie, measure out 2 tablespoons of dough—you can use a 2-tablespoon ice cream scoop—and roll it into a ball. Set the ball on the sheet pan and press it into a 2³/4-inch disk with a glass (if it sticks, dip the glass in cold water) or the heel of your hand. Continue shaping the rest of the cookies.

Bake for about 15 minutes, or until the edges of the cookies brown slightly. Let cool until set and then transfer to cooling racks, or let cool in the pans set on racks. Store tightly sealed in an airtight container for up to 1 week.

Madeleines

. . . .

Madeleines are buttery little cakes baked in the shape of a scallop shell. They come in various sizes—large like the ones shown here and a miniature petits four size. They are made in one of two basic ways. One method, shown on the facing page, is almost identical to a classic sponge cake, a genoise (page 8), but with more butter. The other, shown here, has a melted butter batter, similar to the melted butter cake shown on page 16. These madeleines are denser and chewier than those on page 261, which are more cakelike. Most recipes for madeleines call for lemon zest; orange zest is substituted in this recipe. If you're using silicone madeleine molds, as shown here, there's no need to flour the molds; they should, however, be brushed with softened butter, which gives the outside of the madeleines a buttery crispiness.

MAKES 18 COOKIES

³/₄ cup sugar

³/₄ cup flour

¹/₂ teaspoon baking powder

1 tablespoon grated orange zest (see page 194)

4 egg whites

¹/₂ cup butter, melted

Confectioners' sugar for sprinkling

Preheat the oven to 400°F. Even if you are using nonstick molds, butter the molds with room-temperature butter. Unless you are using nonstick molds, also dust the molds with flour.

In a bowl, sift together the sugar, flour, baking powder, and zest and stir in the egg whites until smooth. Stir in the butter until smooth. Fill the molds not quite to the top with a spoon or a pastry bag fitted with a ²/₃-inch tip.

Bake for about 20 minutes, or until the madeleines swell above the molds, spring back to the touch, and are slightly browned around the edges. Sprinkle the madeleines with confectioners' sugar, then pop them out of the molds and onto cooling racks. Store tightly sealed in an airtight container for up to 1 week.

MAKING MADELEINES ——————

1. Butter the madeleine molds. If you're not using nonstick molds, flour the molds after buttering.

2. Fill a pastry bag with the batter and pipe the mixture into the molds (you can also use a spoon). Fill the molds not quite to the top to allow room for expansion.

3. Bake until the madeleines expand out of the molds, spring back to the touch, and are slightly browned around the edges. Sprinkle with confectioners' sugar and pop the madeleines out of the molds and onto cooling racks.

BAKING

These madeleines are made much like a whole-egg sponge cake, a genoise, but they're denser and much more buttery. They not only contain more butter, they're made with brown butter, which gives them a deep, nutty flavor. It's highly recommended to use a silicone mold for madeleines as they otherwise love to stick. If you don't have silicone, butter the molds twice—chill after the first brushing—before flouring.

MAKES 18 COOKIES

3 eggs, warmed to room temperature (see page 10)

1/2 cup granulated sugar

1/2 cup plus 1 tablespoon cake flour

1/2 cup butter, made into brown butter (see page 196)

Confectioners' sugar for sprinkling

Preheat the oven to 400°F. Even if you are using nonstick or silicone molds, brush the madeleine molds with butter. Unless you are using nonstick or silicone molds, dust the molds with flour.

In a bowl, combine the eggs and granulated sugar and beat on high speed with a stand mixer fitted with the whisk attachment for about 6 minutes or with a handheld mixer for about 15 minutes, or until the ribbon stage: When the beater is lifted, the mixture falls in a wide band onto the surface, forming a figure eight that stays for 5 seconds before dissolving. Sift the flour over the egg mixture while folding with a silicone spatula until there's no more loose flour. Scrape along the bottom of the bowl where the flour likes to hide. Whisk together one-fourth of the egg mixture with the brown butter and fold this mixture with the remaining egg mixture. Spoon the batter into the molds or use a pastry bag fitted with a 2/3-inch plain tip (see page 64).

Bake for 20 minutes, or until the madeleines swell above the molds, spring back to the touch, and are slightly browned around the edges. Sprinkle the madeleines in their molds with confectioners' sugar. Pop the madeleines out of the molds and onto cooling racks. Store tightly sealed in an airtight container for up to 1 week.

1. Combine the eggs and sugar and beat on high speed until the ribbon stage.

2. Sift the flour over the egg mixture while folding.

3. In a small bowl, combine the brown butter with about one-fourth of the beaten madeleine mixture. Fold this mixture with the rest of the batter.

4. Fill the molds slightly less than full. Bake until slightly browned, sprinkle with confectioners' sugar, pop the madeleines out of the molds, and let cool.

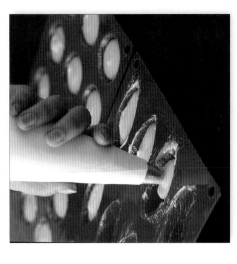

Butter the molds liberally, even if they're nonstick or silicone. Use a pastry bag or spoon to fill the molds almost, but not quite, full.

Finished *financiers*.

Financiers

. . . .

These rich, slightly chewy little butter cookies are made with melted butter—or, even better, brown butter—almond flour, and cake flour. Bake the financiers in a silicone mold. Even though silicone molds are completely nonstick, brush them with butter for more flavor and to give a slight crispness to the outside of the financiers. If you don't have silicone, butter the molds twice—chill after the first brushing—before flouring.

Traditionally, financiers are an elongated boat shape, but you can bake them in any mold you like, or you can spread the batter in a thin layer in a parchment paper–lined round cake pan and use it as a crisp, slender cake layer. The classic boat molds (shown here) hold 1 tablespoon plus 1 teaspoon of batter; the round molds hold 1 tablespoon plus 2 teaspoons of batter.

MAKES 20 TO 25 COOKIES

1 cup confectioners' sugar

1/2 cup almond flour

3 tablespoons cake flour

1/4 teaspoon salt

3 egg whites

1/2 cup butter, made into brown butter (see page 196), or melted

Preheat the oven to 400°F. Butter the molds; if you are not using silicone molds, butter them once, chill for 5 minutes, then butter them again. Flour the molds.

In a bowl, combine the confectioners' sugar, almond flour, cake flour, and salt. Add the egg whites and stir until smooth. Then add the butter and stir until smooth.

Spoon the batter into the molds or use a pastry bag fitted with a 1/2-inch plain tip (see page 64) so they are almost, but not quite, full.

Bake for about 25 minutes, or until pale brown. Pop the financiers out of the mold and onto cooling racks. Store tightly sealed in an airtight container for up to 1 week.

Cat's Tongue Cookies
(Langues de Chat)

. . . .

These delicate, crisp little cookies are lovely served with tea, coffee, or soft desserts such as ice cream to provide a contrasting texture. They are also used to decorate the mango cake on page 81.

MAKES 40 COOKIES

Room-temperature butter for the sheet pan unless using silicone baking liners or parchment paper

¹/₂ cup butter

1 cup confectioners' sugar

²/₃ cup plus 1 tablespoon flour

3 egg whites, lightly beaten

2 teaspoons grated lemon or orange zest (see page 194; optional)

1 teaspoon vanilla extract

Preheat the oven to 400°F. Cover 2 sheet pans with silicone baking liners or parchment paper or brush them with butter.

Cream the butter by hand with a wooden spoon or with a stand mixer fitted with the paddle attachment on medium speed for about 5 minutes, or until fluffy. Add the sugar and cream until smooth. Work in one-half of the flour and one-half of the egg whites. When absorbed, add the remaining flour and egg whites and work in. Stir in the zest and vanilla. Refrigerate for 30 minutes.

Fit a pastry bag with a ¹/₃-inch plain tip, fill it with the batter, and pipe the batter into ²/₃ by 3-inch strips ¹/₃ inch thick, leaving at least 2 inches between the sides and ends of the strips.

Bake for about 12 minutes, or until golden brown just around the edges. Rotate the pans if the cookies brown unevenly. Let cool just until hard enough that you can lift them off the sheet pans or peel them off the parchment paper. Don't wait too long or they'll stick. Transfer to cooling racks. Store tightly sealed in an airtight container for up to 1 week.

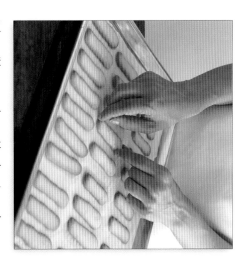

Use a pastry bag with a ¹/₃-inch tip to pipe out strips of batter.

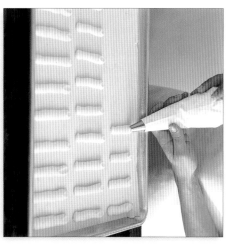

Bake until brown on the outside edges. Let cool slightly, then take the cookies off the sheet pan or parchment paper.

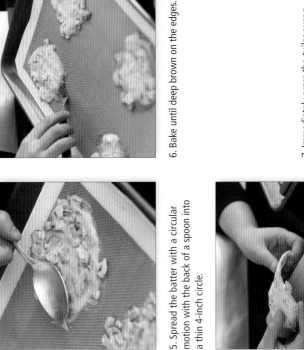

1. Combine the flour, sugar, orange zest, and egg whites.

2. Stir until smooth. Whisk in the vanilla and butter until smooth.

3. Stir in the sliced almonds. Be gentle or they'll break apart.

4. Place the batter, 1 tablespoon at a time, on the prepared sheet pans.

5. Spread the batter with a circular motion with the back of a spoon into a thin 4-inch circle.

6. Bake until deep brown on the edges.

7. Immediately press the *tuiles* over a rolling pin or place them in a *tuile* mold.

Almond Tuiles

Tuile is French for "tile," specifically a curved tile you might see on a roof in Italy or Los Angeles. There are many ways to make the pastry versions, but most contain egg white and just enough flour to get them to hold together when the batter is spread thinly on the surface of a buttered sheet pan or, better, on a silicone baking liner as shown here. These tuiles contain sliced almonds, which add flavor and crunch. Because they stiffen within seconds of coming out of the oven, they must be bent into shape immediately. This is easiest to do by draping the hot tuiles on top of a rolling pin and letting them harden for a minute or two. If you make tuiles a lot, you may want to invest in a mold, which makes it easier if you are making several batches. But don't try baking too many at one time or they'll harden before you shape them.

MAKES 18 TO 20 TUILES

³/₄ cup flour

1 cup confectioners' sugar

1 tablespoon grated orange zest (see page 194)

3 egg whites

1 teaspoon vanilla extract

¹/₄ cup plus 2 tablespoons butter, melted

1 cup sliced almonds

Preheat the oven to 350°F. Line as many as 3 sheet pans with silicone baking liners or brush nonstick pans with room-temperature butter.

In a bowl, combine the flour, sugar, and orange zest. Add the egg whites and stir with a whisk until smooth. Add the vanilla and butter and stir again until smooth. Gently stir in the almonds.

Measure out a mounded tablespoon of batter onto a prepared baking sheet. With the back of a spoon or a small offset spatula, spread the batter—if you're using a spoon, use a circular motion—until it forms a thin 4-inch-diameter circle. Repeat until you have at least 6 circles—2 rows of 3 each—on each of the sheet pans.

Stagger the baking so that no more than 1 sheet pan comes out of the oven at a time. Bake for 13 to 15 minutes, until the edges of the *tuiles* are deep brown and the insides are pale brown.

Working very quickly, lift the still-flexible *tuiles* off the sheet pan with a metal spatula and immediately place each one over a rolling pin, top side up, or place them in a *tuile* mold. If they don't droop on their own, press them gently against the pin. Store tightly sealed for up to 1 week.

Lacy Blood Orange Tuiles

....

These tuiles—inspired by the grapefruit tuiles in Claudia Fleming's elegant book The Last Course—have a delicious tang and are amazingly light and fragile. They're unusual because they contain no egg white. If you can't find blood oranges, use regular oranges or, better, tangerines. You'll need to use silicone baking liners or nonstick sheet pans—these tuiles will stick to regular sheet pans.

MAKES ABOUT 40 TUILES

Room-temperature butter unless using silicone baking liners

1¼ cups sugar

¾ cup flour

2 to 3 tablespoons lemon juice (1 lemon)

½ cup plus 2 tablespoons blood orange juice

½ cup plus 3 tablespoons blood orange juice

½ teaspoon grated blood orange zest (see page 194)

Preheat the oven to 350°F. Line two sheet pans with silicone baking liners or brush two nonstick sheet pans with room-temperature butter.

In a bowl, stir together the sugar and flour and whisk in the lemon juice a bit at a time. Whisk in the blood orange juice and stir vigorously until the mixture has the consistency of a smooth paste. Stir in the melted butter and the orange zest. Refrigerate for at least 2 hours.

Measure out 1 mounded teaspoon of batter on a baking sheet. With the back of a spoon or a small offset spatula, spread the batter—if you're using a spoon, use a circular motion—until it forms a 4-inch-diameter circle. Make 2 rows of 3 each per sheet pan.

Slide 1 pan into the oven. After 5 minutes, slide in the second one. Staggering the baking gives you time to shape the tuiles before they harden. Bake each sheet pan for 10 to 15 minutes (the exact time varies a lot), until the tuiles are evenly golden brown. Rotate the sheet pans as needed for the tuiles to brown evenly.

Take the first sheet pan out of the oven and let cool for 30 seconds to 2 minutes, until a tuile holds its shape when you slide an offset spatula under it. (If you lift up a tuile while it is still too hot, it will fall apart.) Transfer the tuiles to a rolling pin or mold and let harden for 1 to 2 minutes. Work quickly until you've draped all the tuiles. Repeat with the second sheet pan and continue until you've used all the batter. Store tightly sealed in an airtight container for up to 1 week.

MAKING LACY BLOOD ORANGE TUILES

1. Stir together the sugar and flour and whisk in the lemon juice a bit at a time and then the blood orange juice, until the mixture has the consistency of a smooth paste.

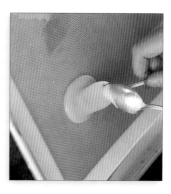

3. Measure out 1 teaspoon of batter on a prepared baking sheet.

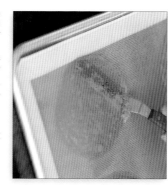

5. Bake until the circles are golden brown. Let cool until firm enough to lift off the pan with an offset spatula. Work fast as you lift off the tuiles or they'll harden before you shape them.

2. Stir in the melted butter, then stir in the orange zest. Cover and refrigerate for 2 hours.

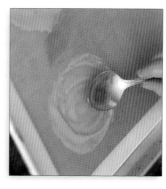

4. Spread the batter into circles about 4 inches in diameter.

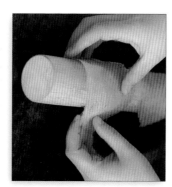

6. Immediately drape the tuiles over a rolling pin or tuile mold and let harden for about a minute.

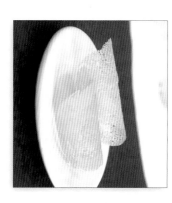

Macarons

Macarons are delicate little cookies that dissolve almost the instant they touch your tongue. The cookies, made by folding almond flour into beaten egg whites, are pasted together with some kind of filling. Jam is the most popular filling, but macarons are also good filled with with ganache, hazelnut praline, or fruit curds. (Coconut macaroons are something different: Coconut is substituted for the almond flour.) Plain macarons are white, but most macarons sold in French pastry shops have been colored with a tiny bit of food coloring.

MAKES ABOUT 60 COOKIES

³/4 cup plus 2 tablespoons almond flour
1¹/4 cups confectioners' sugar
4 egg whites
Pinch of cream of tartar, unless using a copper bowl
1 to 10 drops food coloring
¹/4 cup plus 1 tablespoon fruit jam
1 tablespoon kirsch (optional)

Preheat the oven to 375°F. Unless you are using nonstick pans, line 4 sheet pans with parchment paper. If you don't have enough sheet pans, work in stages.

In a large bowl, combine the almond flour and 1 cup of the confectioners' sugar with 2 egg whites and beat until smooth. In a bowl, beat the remaining 2 egg whites with the cream of tartar (if using) to medium peaks. Whisk in the remaining ¹/4 cup confectioners' sugar and beat to stiff peaks. It's all right if the egg whites are a little runny. Stir food coloring into the beaten egg whites until they are the color you like. (Mix the coloring into a small amount of the batter and then stir that in, in increments, until the color is right. This prevents overdoing it and making the cookies garish.) Fold the colored egg whites with the almond flour mixture.

Fit a pastry bag with a ¹/2-inch tip and fill with the batter (see page 64). Pipe little dollops into the corners of each sheet pan to hold the parchment paper in place. Pipe out 1¹/4-inch rounds about ¹/8 inch thick on a prepared sheet pan. Hold the tip of the pastry bag no more than ¹/4 inch above the surface of the parchment paper so the rounds stay flat. Move the tip

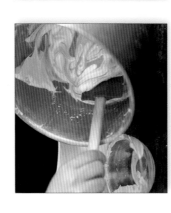

1. Beat the egg whites with the sugar and color a small quantity of the egg whites. Fold the colored egg whites, one-third at a time, into the rest of the whites.

2. Fold the beaten egg whites with the almond flour mixture.

3. Fit a pastry bag with a ¹/2-inch tip and fill it with the *macaron* mixture. Pipe tiny dollops into the corners of the sheet pan to hold the parchment paper in place.

4. Pipe the batter out into 1¹/4-inch rounds about ¹/8 inch thick.

5. Let the unbaked *macarons* sit out for exactly 15 minutes before baking so that a very fine skin forms on them. Bake for about 10 minutes, or until they don't stick to your finger when you touch them.

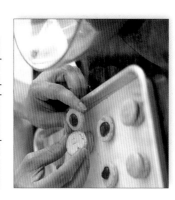

6. Flavor the jam with kirsch and put it in a paper cone with a ¹/4-inch opening. Pipe a ¹/4-teaspoon dollop of filling on the center of one cookie.

7. Press together two cookies, one with filling, one without.

8. Arrange the *macarons* on a tray. If you like, prepare them in a variety of colors.

quickly in a spiral motion as you pull away so you don't leave a little peak—like a Hershey's kiss—in the center. Don't make the rounds too thick or they'll crack in the oven. Let the rounds sit out at room temperature for exactly 15 minutes so a thin skin forms on their surface.

Bake for about 10 minutes, or until they don't stick to your finger when you touch them. Let cool on the sheet pan for 5 minutes and peel the rounds off the parchment paper. Flavor the jam with the kirsch. Spread the bottom of a cookie with 1/4 teaspoon jam, using a paper cone (see page 87) with a 1/4-inch opening or a small spoon. Top with another cookie, bottom down. Repeat for the remaining cookies. Store tightly sealed in an airtight container for up to 1 week.

Coconut Macaroons

··

Don't confuse these with macarons (facing page), which are little sandwiches of almond meringue. Coconut macaroons are sometimes made with almond paste or, shown here, as simple mounds of baked meringue with shredded coconut folded in.

MAKES 24 COOKIES

4 egg whites

3/4 cup sugar

One 12-ounce package sweetened shredded coconut

Preheat the oven to 200°F. Unless you are using a nonstick pan, line a sheet pan with parchment paper.

Beat the egg whites to medium peaks, add the sugar, and beat to stiff peaks. Reserve 1/2 cup coconut and fold the rest into the egg whites.

Make 2-inch rounds of the egg white mixture with 2 spoons or a pastry bag fitted with a 2/3-inch fluted tip on the prepared pan. Sprinkle the reserved coconut over the macaroons.

Bake for about 3 hours, or until the cookies are dry and feel hard to the touch. If the cookies start to brown, even slightly, turn down the oven between warm and the lowest temperature setting. Let cool until set and then transfer to cooling racks, or let cool in the pan set on a rack. Store tightly sealed in an airtight container for up to 1 week.

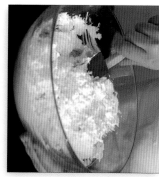

1. Beat egg whites to medium peaks, add the sugar, and beat to stiff peaks. Fold in all but 1/2 cup of the coconut.

2. Use a pastry bag with a fluted tip to pipe the macaroons onto the prepared sheet pan.

3. Sprinkle each macaroon with shredded coconut.

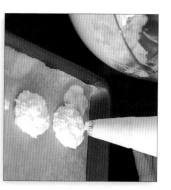

4. Bake for about 3 hours, or until the cookies are dry and hard.

Florentine Almond Cookies

To make these cookies, you will first make caramel and then cook the caramel with butter to make butterscotch. Stir sliced almonds into the butterscotch and spread the mixture over a prebaked sheet of pastry. When the butterscotch mixture hardens, cut the sheet of pastry into squares.

MAKES FIFTY 1¹/₂-INCH SQUARE COOKIES

1 recipe sweetened basic pie and tart pastry dough (page 131)

1¹/₂ cups sugar

9 tablespoons butter

2 cups sliced almonds

³/₄ cup heavy cream

Preheat the oven to 375°F. Line a sheet pan with parchment paper.

Roll out the dough into a sheet just large enough to fit in the sheet pan. Place the dough on the sheet pan and dock it (poke the dough with a fork). Cover the dough with another sheet of parchment paper and nest another sheet pan on top to keep the dough flat.

Bake for 20 minutes, then remove the top sheet pan and top layer of parchment paper. Bake for about 10 minutes more, or until pale brown. Rotate the pan if the pastry is browning unevenly. Let cool while you're making the topping. Leave the oven on.

Melt the sugar in a heavy-bottomed saucepan while stirring with a wooden spoon. Continue stirring until there are no lumps and the sugar has turned into deep brown caramel. Add the butter—stand back, it can spatter—and stir until the butter melts and boils up. Continue stirring for 30 seconds to 1 minute after the butter melts, until the mixture smells like butterscotch. Don't wait too long or you'll burn the butter. Stir in the almonds and continue stirring for 30 seconds to toast them. Add the cream, stir until smooth, and let the cream simmer for about 1 minute.

With the sheet of pastry still in the sheet pan, spread the hot caramel mixture evenly over it and bake for about 10 minutes, or until the mixture sets. Let cool, transfer to a cutting board, and cut into 1¹/₂-inch squares. Store tightly sealed in an airtight container for up to 1 week.

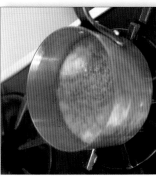

1. "Dock" a sheet of dough, cover it with parchment paper and another sheet pan, and bake. Remove the top sheet pan and the top parchment paper and continue baking until the pastry is pale brown.

2. Cook the sugar into caramel.

3. When the caramel is a deep brown, add the butter. Cook over low heat until the mixture smells like butterscotch.

4. Add the almonds and stir gently for 30 seconds. Stir in the cream. Simmer for about 1 minute.

5. Spread the almond mixture evenly over the sheet of prebaked dough. Bake until the nut mixture sets.

6. Let the sheet cool and transfer it to a cutting board. Cut it into squares.

Biscotti means "twice cooked"; the closest equivalent in English is "rusk." This basic dough is made in a food processor and stirred with chopped hazelnuts, dried berries, candied orange rind, and spices. These biscotti are flavored very much like the medieval panforte—hard, round disks, half cake, half bread—sold in Italy at Christmastime.

MAKES 35 COOKIES

2 cups flour

1 teaspoon baking powder

1/2 teaspoon salt

1/2 teaspoon ground cinnamon

1/4 teaspoon ground cloves

1/8 teaspoon ground nutmeg

3/4 cup sugar

2 eggs

3/4 cup butter, melted

1/2 cup dried currants, cherries, or cranberries, soaked in just enough warm water to cover for 30 minutes, drained

1 1/2 cups hazelnuts, coarsely chopped

1/4 cup diced candied orange zest (page 194), optional

Preheat the oven to 350°F. Unless you are using nonstick pans, line 2 sheet pans with parchment paper.

Combine the flour, baking powder, salt, spices, and sugar by hand, with a stand mixer fitted with the paddle attachment for 1 minute, or in a food processor for 15 seconds. Add the eggs and butter and stir, mix, or process until thoroughly combined and the mixture clumps together. Mix in the currants, hazelnuts, and orange zest by hand or with the mixer—not in the food processor.

On one of the prepared sheet pans, shape the dough into two 11-inch logs. Flatten the logs so they're each about 3 inches wide.

Bake for about 35 minutes, or until the tops of the logs turn pale brown. Turn down the oven to 300°F and remove the sheet pan. Let the logs cool for 15 minutes, then slice them with a serrated knife on a diagonal into 1/2-inch-thick cookies. Use a sawing motion with very little pressure. If the dough is soft and tears, let the logs cool for 5 minutes more. Arrange the biscotti cut side up on both sheet pans and bake for about 30 minutes, or until golden brown. Let cool until set and then transfer to cooling racks, or let cool in the pans set on racks. Store tightly sealed in an airtight container for up to 1 week.

1. Combine the flour, baking powder, salt, spices, and sugar in the food processor. Add the egg and butter and process. Put the dough in a bowl and fold in the currants, hazelnuts, and orange zest.

2. Divide the dough in half and shape it into two logs on a parchment paper–lined or nonstick sheet pan.

3. Flatten the logs.

4. Keep flattening and pressing the sides of the logs until they hold together and are even. Bake until pale brown.

5. Allow the logs to cool for 15 minutes, then slice them on a diagonal with a serrated knife.

6. Arrange the biscotti on the sheet pans and bake until golden brown.

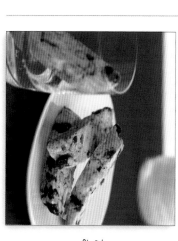

7. Finished biscotti (one dipped in a glass of kirsch).

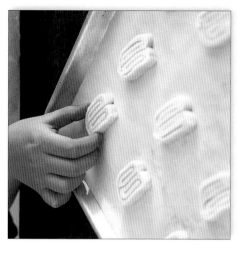

3. Fold up one side of the rectangle to form a 1-inch-wide flap.

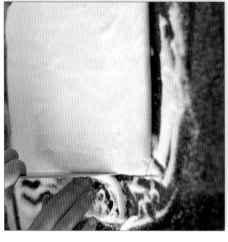

6. Roll gently over the rectangle to press the folds and keep them in place. Don't push too hard.

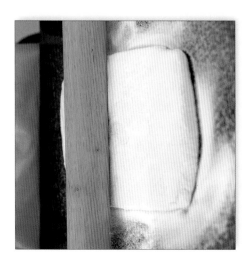

9. Chill the strip for at least 30 minutes and slice it into 1/4-inch-thick cookies. Arrange the cookies on a sheet pan covered with a sheet of parchment paper.

1. Roll puff pastry dough into a 9 by 14-inch rectangle about 1/4 inch thick. Use granulated sugar on the work surface.

2. Trim the edges of the puff pastry rectangle.

4. Repeat on the other side. Sprinkle the folded sides of the rectangle generously with sugar.

5. Fold the two sides so they meet in the center. Sprinkle with sugar.

7. Fold one more time.

8. Press gently along the sides of the strip with your hand and a bench scraper to even the strip, then press gently along the strip with a rolling pin.

BAKING

Palmiers

Palmiers are crisp buttery cookies made out of puff pastry dough that's rolled into a rectangle using granulated sugar on the work surface instead of flour. They'll keep for days but like most pastries are best eaten right away. It is best to bake these in two batches, one sheet pan at a time.

MAKES 30 TO 35 COOKIES

1 recipe classic puff pastry dough (page 148) or quick puff pastry dough (page 151)

Granulated sugar for rolling

Roll the pastry, using granulated sugar instead of flour when rolling out, into a 9 by 14-inch rectangle about ¼ inch thick. Trim the edges so the rectangle measures about 8 by 13 inches. Sprinkle the rectangle with sugar and fold in the sides so they make 1-inch-wide folds that run the length of the

rectangle on both sides. Sprinkle the folds with sugar and fold them again so they meet in the center of the rectangle. Roll over the surface of the rectangle with a rolling pin, pressing gently on the pin, to help the rectangle hold its shape; this will also lengthen it about 1 inch. Fold the two sides of the rectangle together. Press gently along the sides to even them out and roll over the now thin and long rectangle with the rolling pin. Chill for 30 minutes.

Preheat the oven to 400°F. Line a sheet pan with parchment paper. Slice the rectangle into ¼-inch-thick slices and arrange half of the slices on the prepared sheet pan. Leave at least 2 inches between the *palmiers* to allow them space to expand.

Bake for about 25 minutes, or until golden brown, then flip each *palmier* over. Bake for 5 minutes more. Transfer to cooling racks, or let cool in the pan set on a rack. Repeat with the remaining slices of pastry dough. Store tightly sealed in an airtight container for up to 1 week.

10. Bake until pale brown, then flip over the cookies with a spatula, and bake for 5 minutes more.

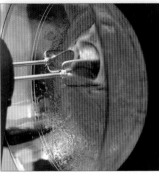

2. Beat the eggs, sugar, salt, and vanilla for about 2 minutes, or until frothy.

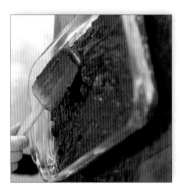

1. Combine bittersweet chocolate with butter in a bowl set over a saucepan of simmering water. Stir until smooth.

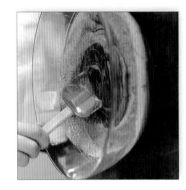

3. Stir the chocolate mixture into the beaten egg mixture.

4. Sift over the flour and fold until there are no lumps. Stir in the walnuts.

5. Spread the mixture into a buttered baking dish.

6. Bake for about 25 minutes, or until a knife stuck into the center comes out clean. Allow the brownies to cool and cut into rectangles.

Brownies

Brownie aficionados are divided into two camps: those who like them cakey and those who like them fudgy. At the risk of pleasing no one while trying to please all, these brownies fall in between. Regardless, these brownies are rich, very chocolaty, and not too sweet. Use the best chocolate you can find; it makes all the difference.

MAKES 9 BROWNIES

Room-temperature butter for the baking pan

³/4 cup butter, sliced

8 ounces bittersweet chocolate, chopped

3 eggs

¹/2 cup sugar

¹/2 teaspoon salt

1 teaspoon vanilla extract

¹/2 cup flour

1 cup toasted coarsely chopped walnuts (see Note; optional)

Preheat the oven to 325°F. Butter a 7 by 11-inch baking dish.

Place the butter and chocolate in a bowl set over a saucepan of simmering water and stir until both are melted and completely combined. Whisk or beat together the eggs, sugar, salt, and vanilla for about 2 minutes, or until frothy. Stir in the chocolate mixture. Sift over the flour and fold just until there are no lumps. Fold in the nuts. Spread the mixture evenly in the baking pan.

Bake for about 25 minutes, or until a knife stuck into the center comes out clean. Let cool on a cooling rack, then cut into rectangles with a metal spatula. Store tightly sealed in an airtight container for up to 1 week.

Note: To toast the walnuts, preheat the oven to 350°F. Place the nuts on a baking sheet and toast them for about 15 minutes, or until you can smell their aroma.

Lemon Bars

. . . .

Classic lemon bars are made by pressing extra buttery sweet dough into a baking dish, baking it, and, after cooling, spreading lemon curd over it. Most lemon curd is made with whole butter—regular butter that's just added as is. This recipe uses brown butter for a more pronounced butter flavor and a stiffer curd, but whole butter works fine, too.

MAKES 8 TO 10 BARS

Dough

²/₃ **cup all-purpose flour**

²/₃ **cup cake flour**

¹/₂ **cup confectioners' sugar**

¹/₄ **teaspoon salt**

¹/₂ **cup plus 3 tablespoons cold butter, cut into** ¹/₃-**inch cubes**

1 egg

Lemon curd

3 eggs

³/₄ **cup granulated sugar**

1 tablespoon grated lemon zest (see page 194)

³/₄ **cup lemon juice (about 7 lemons)**

¹/₂ **cup butter, made into brown butter (see page 196), optional, or sliced**

To make the dough, combine the flours, confectioners' sugar, and salt in a food processor and process for 15 seconds. Add the butter and egg and process for about 20 seconds more, or until the mixture clumps together. Flatten the dough, wrap in plastic wrap, and refrigerate for 15 minutes. Preheat the oven to 400°F.

To make the lemon curd, set a saucepan of water over medium heat and bring to a simmer. In a heatproof bowl that will fit over the saucepan, whisk together the eggs and

granulated sugar for about 2 minutes, or until pale, then whisk in the lemon zest, juice, and brown butter (if using). Set the bowl over the saucepan of simmering water. Stir constantly with a whisk for about 6 minutes, or until the mixture starts to thicken. If you're using a saucepan that doesn't have sloping sides, switch to a silicone spatula so you can reach into the corners. If you're not using brown butter, stir in the sliced butter. Cook for about 2 minutes longer, or until the butter is absorbed and remove from the heat. Cover with plastic wrap.

Roll out the dough into a square or rectangle about 1 inch wider and longer than your baking dish. (If using a 7 by 11-inch baking dish, roll out to 8 by 12 inches.) Press the dough into the pan and, with the side of your finger, press the edges of the dough against the sides of the baking pan to form a 1-inch-high border. Trim the edges so the border is even. Press the trimmings over any thin sections.

Bake for about 30 minutes, or until pale brown. Let cool for 15 minutes.

Spread the lemon curd over the still-warm pastry and let cool for 30 minutes at room temperature. Cover with plastic wrap—don't touch the surface of the curd with the wrap or it may leave marks—and refrigerate for at least 2 hours before serving.

Cut into rectangles and remove from the pan with an offset spatula. Store tightly sealed in an airtight container in the refrigerator for up to 1 week.

Note: You can cook the lemon curd over direct medium to high heat in a heavy-bottomed saucepan, ideally, one with sloping sides. Stir constantly with a whisk for about 4 minutes, or until the mixture starts to thicken. If you're using a saucepan that doesn't have sloping sides, switch to a silicone spatula so you can reach into the corners. If you're not using brown butter, stir in the sliced butter. Cook for about 2 minutes longer, or until the butter is absorbed; let cool.

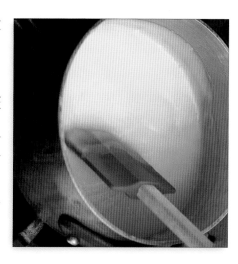

1. In a saucepan, whisk together the eggs and sugar, then the lemon zest, lemon juice, and brown butter, if using. When the lemon curd starts to thicken, switch to a silicone spatula so you can reach into the corners of the saucepan. Stir until thickened.

2. Pound the dough into a rectangle 1 inch longer and wider than the baking dish.

3. Press the dough into the baking dish. Use the side of your finger to press on the dough near the sides of the dish to force the dough up along the sides.

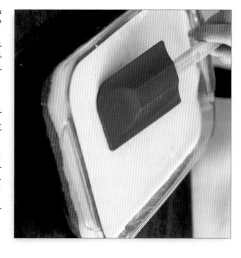

4. Trim the edge of the dough with a small knife so the edges are even.

5. Press the trimmings over any thin sections.

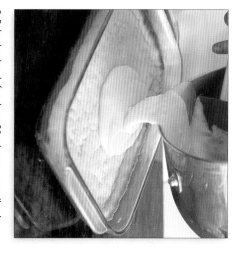

6. Bake the dough for about 30 minutes, or until pale brown. Let the dough cool for 15 minutes, then pour in the hot lemon curd.

7. Smooth the lemon curd with a spatula. Let cool for 30 minutes before cutting.

8. Cut the lemon bars into rectangles and remove from the pan with an offset spatula.

COOKIES

BREADS, QUICK BREADS, AND BREAD-BASED DESSERTS

Yeasted Breads

White Bread (Straight Dough) • 304
White Bread (Sponge Starter) • 306
White Bread (Mature Starter) • 307
Ciabatta • 309
Sourdough Bread • 313
Rye Bread • 314
Sourdough Whole Wheat Bread • 316
Sourdough Whole Wheat
  Raisin Bread • 316
Pumpernickel Bread • 318
Pizza Dough • 319

Pizza Margherita • 320
Roquefort and Walnut Pizza • 320
Pita Bread • 322
Bread Sticks (Grissini) • 323
Focaccia • 324
Brioche • 327
Panettone • 328
Challah • 330
Coffee Cakes • 333
Cinnamon Rolls • 334
Sticky Buns • 336

Quick Breads and Bread-Based Desserts

Banana Nut Bread Muffins • 338
Apricot Bread • 339
Popovers • 340
Blueberry Muffins • 341
Baking Powder Biscuits • 342
Scones • 343
Cherry Cobblers • 344
Strawberry Shortcakes • 345
Apple Charlottes • 346

Methods and Techniques

MAKING YEASTED BREADS

Proofing Yeast • 287

Making Starters • 287

Mixing the Dough Ingredients • 288

Kneading Dry Dough by Hand • 289

Kneading Wet Dough by Hand • 290

Using the Dough Hook to Knead
Dry Dough • 291

Using the Dough Hook to Knead
Moist Dough • 291

Using the Dough Hook to Knead
Wet Dough • 291

Kneading Dough with the Paddle
Attachment • 291

Kneading Dry Dough in a
Food Processor • 292

Kneading Moist Dough in a
Food Processor • 292

Kneading Wet Dough in a
Food Processor • 292

Punching Down Dough • 293

Dividing and Rounding Dough • 294

How Much Dough for Each Shape? • 295

Shaping a Sandwich Loaf • 295

Shaping a Baguette and a
Wheat Sheaf • 296

Shaping a *Boule* • 297

Shaping a *Bâtard* • 297

Shaping Rolls • 298

Shaping a Braided Loaf • 299

Shaping a *Fougasse* • 300

Shaping Split Loaves (*Pain Fendu*) • 300

Improvising Your Own Proofing Box • 302

Scoring Dough • 303

Judging When Bread Is Done • 303

**Judging Yeast Amounts and
Rising Times • 304**

Making White Bread (Straight Dough) • 305

Making a Sponge Starter • 306

Using Leftover Dough • 307

Kneading in a Food Processor • 308

Making a Mature Starter (*Pâte
Fermentée*) • 308

**Calculating the Amount of Liquid
in a Bread Recipe • 309**

Making Ciabatta • 310

How Sour Is Sour? • 311

Making and Maintaining a
Natural Starter • 312

Making Sourdough Bread • 313

Making Rye Bread • 315

Making Sourdough Whole
Wheat Bread • 317

Making Sourdough Whole Wheat
Raisin Bread • 317

Making Pumpernickel Bread • 318

Making Pizza Dough • 319

Making a Pizza • 321

Making Pita Bread • 322

Making Bread Sticks (*Grissini*) • 323

Making Focaccia • 325

Making Brioche Dough • 326

Making Individual Brioches • 326

Making a Brioche Loaf • 327

Candying Orange Peel • 328

Making Panettone • 329

Making Challah • 331

Making Coffee Cakes • 332

Making Cinnamon Rolls • 335

Making Sticky Buns • 337

MAKING QUICK BREADS

Making Banana Nut Bread Muffins • 338

Making Apricot Bread • 339

Making Popovers • 340

Making Blueberry Muffins • 341

Making Baking Powder Biscuits • 342

Making Scones • 343

Making Cherry Cobblers • 344

Making Strawberry Shortcakes • 345

Making Apple Charlottes • 347

YEASTED BREADS

Some of the most complex foods—wine, cheese, and bread—are made by manipulating one ingredient in a myriad ways to create finished products of great subtlety and variety. Bread, cheese, and wine all rely on microorganisms—bacteria, mold, and yeast—in often symbiotic combinations to shape the food's eventual flavor, aroma, and texture.

The bread we buy at the supermarket is made from a single strain of yeast, while artisan-style breads are manipulated to encourage the growth of bacteria and wild yeasts. Because virtually all environments have their own miniature ecosystems, artisan-style bread made in one place is often different from bread made in the exact same way somewhere else. By making slight changes in technique, kneading time, rising time, and baking temperature, we can make an enormous variety of breads without changing the basic ingredients. There are so many variables that even the slightest changes result in a different loaf; in a home environment, it is almost impossible to predict exactly how the bread will turn out. There will always be a little of the unanticipated, which is part of what makes bread baking fun.

The complete chemistry of bread making is very complex, but the central process—what makes the loaf rise—is not. When yeast comes into contact with starch, it releases enzymes that break the starch down into sugar; the yeast then secretes different enzymes that convert the sugar into alcohol and carbon dioxide. Bread rises because, when properly kneaded so that certain proteins bind together into a web of gluten, the carbon dioxide is trapped within the bread, forcing it to rise. If allowed to reproduce indefinitely, the yeast will die when all the fermentable starch is used up. All the subtle tricks used by bakers to make a successful loaf have to do with trapping carbon dioxide gas within the bread. Because only wheat flour contains gluten, virtually all breads—including breads made from other grains—must contain some wheat flour.

When baking some artisan-style breads, bakers also rely on secondary processes to get the most flavor out of the flour. While commercial yeast can be used to make a reliable and consistent loaf, it extracts relatively little flavor from the flour; because each commercial yeast cell is a clone—all the yeasts cells are genetically identical—they have very little character of their own. Artisan bakers take advantage of natural wild yeasts that live in flour—and which will eventually inhabit your kitchen—to produce bread with a deeper, more complex flavor. The deeper flavor comes about because

there are many strains of yeast in the same loaf. Because these strains are less aggressive than commercial yeast, they ferment more slowly and allow more time for the flavor to be extracted from the flour. Wild yeasts allow for a much slower fermentation, allowing beneficial bacteria in the air or in the flour to develop in the dough. Wild yeasts can live in an acidic environment, while commercial yeast cannot, which is why we can't make sourdough bread with commercial yeast alone. Bacteria act on flour and the alcohol produced by the yeasts and turn it into lactic acid and acetic acid, which give the bread its characteristic tang and also make the crumb tougher and more resilient. It is this dual process that produces sourdough bread and other naturally leavened loaves. The character of the finished loaf depends on the interplay of yeast and bacteria. By controlling these two basic processes, bakers can produce bread with a variety of flavors, colors, and textures.

Yeast and bacteria are very sensitive to temperature. Yeast is active between just above freezing and 130°F. Yeast is so sensitive to changes in temperature that a 17-degree increase in temperature will cause a loaf to rise twice as fast. Different bacteria are favored at different temperatures. Warmer temperatures encourage the growth of acetic acid–producing bacteria and lower temperatures encourage bacteria that produce lactic acid, which is less acidic. Bread that is allowed to rise slowly, in a relatively cool environment—even the refrigerator—will develop better flavor; if the temperature is too high—above 80°F—the dough will ferment very quickly and may develop "off" flavors and odors.

There are two basic methods used to make yeasted breads. The simplest is a direct method called the "straight dough" method, in which you just add yeast to the dough and let it rise. Because this method extracts less flavor from the flour than slower methods, most bakers ferment a portion of the dough separately—often in a cool environment so it has plenty of time to ferment and develop flavor—and at a later stage work this mixture (called a starter) with the rest of the dough. The use of a starter is called the indirect method. The simplest and wettest of these starters is a "sponge," sometimes called a *levain levure*, made by combining some or all of the commercial yeast called for in the recipe with some of the flour and water and allowing the sponge to rise before combining it with the rest of the dough. The less yeast added to the sponge and the cooler the temperature at which the sponge is allowed to rise, the slower the fermentation will be and the deeper the flavor. You can control the rising time of the sponge by altering the amount of yeast it contains and the temperature at which it is allowed to rise. There are many versions of a classic sponge, but equal parts flour and water by volume is typical.

Somewhat stiffer from a classic sponge but still relatively liquid is a starter called a *poolish*. A poolish is usually made with equal parts flour and water by weight. The amount of yeast added to the poolish depends on how long it is going to rise. Traditionally, poolish is allowed to rise at room temperature, but it can also be left to rise overnight in the refrigerator to develop more flavor. If too much yeast is added to the poolish or the poolish gets too warm, the yeast may die, rendering the starter lifeless and ineffective.

Some bakers prefer a stiffer starter, sometimes called a *biga*. A biga is easy to use because it has the same consistency as most bread dough and is easy to mix and knead, unlike a poolish, which is very sticky. A typical biga contains more than twice as much flour by volume as water. A biga is convenient because it can last up to 3 days in the refrigerator—there's more flour to feed on—before the yeast exhausts itself.

The "leftover dough" method, one of the easiest ways to make flavorful bread, is to save a piece of dough from a previous batch and include it in the next batch of dough. The dough should be used within 3 days if you refrigerate it, or if you are a regular bread maker, just save a little dough each time you make bread and you'll always have a starter. You can freeze the dough for up to 1 month. Because fermented dough lacks rising power—the yeast is old and tired—a small amount of

commercial yeast is sometimes added to the dough to help the process along.

The most intriguing starter is a sourdough starter, sometimes called a *levain*, which can be finicky. It takes at least several days to make a sourdough starter, because you have to cultivate the wild yeasts contained in the flour until you develop a strain that can survive in an acidic environment and is aggressive and fast acting enough to get your bread to rise. A sourdough starter requires only 2 ingredients, flour and water. A small amount of organic flour that contains large amounts of natural yeasts—whole wheat, rye, or pumpernickel—is combined with a small amount of water and covered with plastic wrap. Usually after 36 hours, the mixture bubbles up and becomes elastic and full of holes. You then add more flour and water and let it ferment for 24 hours. As you repeat this process, your starter will get continually more vigorous. Many bakers use sourdough starter when it takes no more than 8 hours to rise (usually after 5 or 6 days), while others insist that it takes at least 2 weeks to develop a starter with the correct mellow flavor. During this fermentation, natural bacteria are reproducing in the seed culture to give the finished starter and finished bread its characteristic tartness and tangy aroma. To some degree, the tartness of the seed culture and the finished starter can be controlled because yeast reproduces more quickly than bacteria. When the seed culture is ready to

STEPS FOR MAKING YEASTED BREADS

The following pages contain an illustrated overview of the basic steps of making yeasted breads: preparing and proofing the yeast and/or the starter; mixing the ingredients; kneading; fermentation (rising); punching down the dough; dividing the dough; rounding the dough; shaping the loaves; proofing the loaves; scoring the loaves; glazing the loaves; baking, and cooling.

Preparing and Proofing the Yeast and Starter

The recipes in this book are all made using active dry yeast because it is easy to find and more consistent than fresh yeast. Some bakers prefer instant yeast because there's no preliminary moistening, but because it's not always available, I don't call for it here. When yeast is added to bread dough, it must be first added to liquid, either the liquid contained in the dough or a separate tablespoon of liquid, a few minutes before it is kneaded into the dough. The liquid should be slightly warm, about 93°F (at this temperature liquid feels neither warm nor cold). One caveat: Don't let the yeast get too hot or cold when you first moisten it or you will slow it down or even kill it.

If you're uncertain about the viability of your yeast, proof it by combining it with a small amount of water, sugar, and flour and waiting 10 minutes to see whether the mixture bubbles and takes on the characteristic barroom-the-morning-after aroma. If you know your yeast is good, you still need to activate it by combining it with a small amount of water and letting it steep for a few minutes before combining it with other ingredients. If you're using instant yeast—not active dry yeast—you don't need to steep it this way.

To extract more flavor from the flour, most bakers make a starter with some of the yeast and water called for in the recipe and let this ferment before combining it with the rest of the ingredients. A good all-around formula is to make a starter with all of the yeast, one-fourth of the flour, and one-half of the water. When this has doubled in volume, simply combine it with the rest of the ingredients and then let the whole batch double in volume. To a degree, the longer your starter takes to double in volume, the more flavorful the bread will be. So to increase the rising time, either decrease the yeast amount or lower the temperature—1/4 teaspoon yeast will cause 1 cup flour to double in about 2 hours at room temperature or overnight in the refrigerator.

use, it usually needs to be expanded into a finished starter by combining it with additional flour and water. Sourdough starters are made in varying consistencies by adding more or less water and flour than called for in the recipe you're using. Some bakers prefer a stiff starter because it ferments more slowly and is easier to work with, while others prefer a liquid starter that is usually more acidic. Whatever the consistency of your starter, remember the amounts of flour and water that you used so you can deduct these amounts from the flour and water called for in the recipe. Some excellent sourdough starters are also sold commercially.

Starters are often the only leavening in an artisan-style loaf, but some bakers prefer the reliability of a "mixed" starter that contains the starter plus a small amount of commercial yeast. A mixed starter makes it possible to use a weak or finicky starter to contribute flavor, while the commercial yeast gets the bread to rise.

One mistake often made by beginning bakers is to use too much flour, which will make the dough heavy and too dry. It is hard to resist adding more flour when kneading by hand so the dough doesn't stick so tenaciously to your fingers, but if you want a loose, coarse crumb with plenty of holes, it is better to dip your hands in water to keep them from sticking while leaving the dough as wet as possible.

BAKING

1. Combine 1 yeast packet with 1 tablespoon barely warm water, 1/2 teaspoon sugar, and 1 tablespoon flour.

2. Stir to combine.

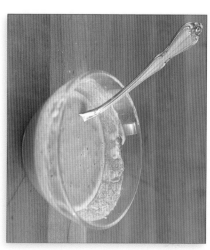

3. The yeast is ready to use after about 10 minutes.

1. Sponge starter, just mixed.

2. Sponge starter, ready to use.

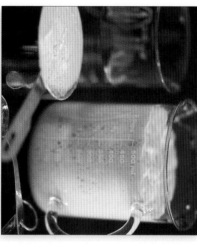

3. Poolish, just mixed.

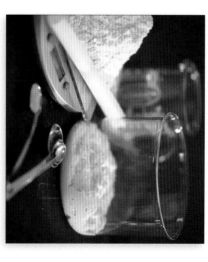

4. Poolish, ready to use.

5. Biga, just mixed.

6. Biga, ready to use.

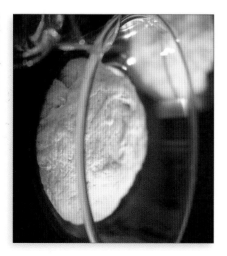

1. To mix by hand in a bowl, combine all the ingredients with a wooden spoon. When the mixture gets too stiff to stir, scrape the wooden spoon with a bench scraper.

2. Finish working the dough together with your fingers.

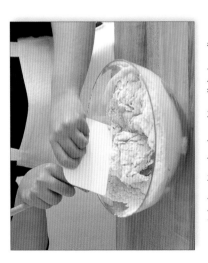

3. Let the dough rest before turning out onto a work surface.

4. To mix by hand on a work surface, put the flour in a pile on a work surface and make a well in the center with your fingers. Pour warm water into the well and sprinkle the yeast over it or add the starter. Let sit for 3 minutes, then combine the mixture by pulling the flour into the water with your fingers.

5. When the dough becomes stiff enough, knead it with your fingers.

6. To mix in a stand mixer, put the flour in the bowl of a stand mixer and pour the water (barely warmed) over it. Sprinkle in the yeast over the water and let sit for 3 minutes, or add the starter.

7. Turn the mixer on low for 3 minutes to moisten all the flour.

8. Cover the bowl with a moist towel or plastic wrap and let the dough rest for 20 minutes.

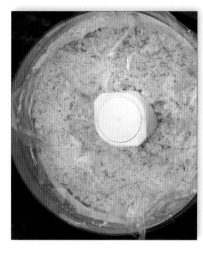

9. To mix in a food processor, put the flour in the work bowl of the food processor and pour the warm water over it. Sprinkle the yeast over the water, let sit for 30 minutes to moisten the yeast, and process for 10 seconds. If you are using a starter, add it to the mixture and process for 10 seconds. Cover the work bowl with plastic wrap and let the dough rest for 20 minutes.

BAKING

Mixing

While many bakers don't distinguish between mixing and kneading, here the initial combining of ingredients, before the actual kneading, is referred to as "mixing." The first stage of mixing is a simple stirring together of all the ingredients—including the starter if you're using one. After an initial mixing of usually about 3 minutes, the dough is covered and allowed to rest for 20 minutes. This resting—known to professionals by its French name *autolyse* (pronounced oh-toe-leeze)—allows the water to penetrate the flour and develop the gluten. The overall effect of resting is that the dough needs less actual mixing and kneading, which can cause the dough to oxidize or, if you're using a machine, to overheat.

When using active dry yeast, sprinkle it over the liquid in the flour before the liquid is worked in or moisten it with 1 tablespoon barely warm (95°F) water. It is important that active dry yeast be activated in water from 70°F to 90°F before it is mixed with the other ingredients; instant yeast can be combined, without proofing, with the other ingredients provided they're in this temperature range. Outside this temperature range, dry yeast—active and instant—will die if not moistened first, but once worked into the dough will live in a much wider temperature range.

Dough can be mixed by hand—in a bowl or on a work surface by making a well in the flour—or with a machine such as a stand mixer or food processor. It makes sense to mix with the same implement—hands, mixer, food processor—that you're going to use for kneading since this saves a dish or two.

Kneading the Dough

Kneading activates the gluten in the dough, then smooths out the strands of gluten so the dough is cohesive. Salt and butter are usually added to the dough during the kneading. This keeps the salt away from the unmixed yeast and prevents the butter from melting.

If you're kneading by hand, it is hard to overknead; but if you're using a machine, it is easy to overwork the dough, which breaks apart the gluten strands, or overheat the dough, especially when using a food processor. Properly kneaded bread dough is smooth—as a baby's bottom is an accurate cliché—and elastic. If you pinch a piece with two fingers and pull it away from the rest of the dough, the dough should stretch into a thin translucent "window" without tearing; this is known as the windowpane test. If the dough is firm, it will spring back to the touch; if you make an indentation with your finger, the indentation will fill up.

Kneading wet dough by hand is a messy job that is probably best avoided by using an electric mixer, but you should try it at least once because there is no other way to experience the intimate feel of the dough as it goes through its various stages.

KNEADING DRY DOUGH BY HAND

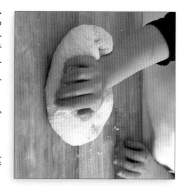

1. Push the dough away from you while smearing it over the work surface. You can switch hands, alternating left to right.

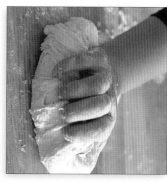

2. Pull the dough back toward yourself.

3. Fold the end of the dough farthest from you back over to the center of the dough.

4. Press the other end of the dough into the center.

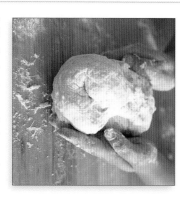

5. Give the dough a quarter turn and continue in the same way.

6. The dough is properly kneaded when a thin ridge, pinched along one side of the dough, stays in place or when you can stretch it to make a translucent window (see page 290).

Most dough can be kneaded in a stand mixer with either the dough hook or the paddle attachment. For making small amounts of dough—with 1 cup flour or less—the dough hook might not reach far enough down into the bowl, so it's better to use the paddle attachment. The paddle attachment also works better for especially wet dough. A stand mixer is excellent for very loose dough that would be cumbersome to knead by hand. When kneading dough with the dough hook, the dough sometimes clings around the hook without touching the sides of the bowl so the dough just turns around without being kneaded. To avoid this, you can pull the dough off the hook with your hands every 30 seconds or so, or you can turn the mixer to medium or even to high speed so that the centrifugal force pulls the dough off the hook. You can tell the dough is being kneaded by the sound of it slapping against the mixer bowl. If you have a large-capacity heavy-duty mixer, you can leave it on medium or high speed for most of the kneading. (Be careful: when on medium or high speed, mixers tend to creep along surfaces and can fall over.) If the dough is stubborn or dry, pull it off the hook and cut it into pieces with scissors before continuing to knead.

Step 1: Put the flour in the mixer bowl and pour the warm water over it. Add the yeast to moisten it. Turn the mixer on low speed and mix for about 3 minutes, or until the flour is moist. Cover the bowl with a moist towel or plastic wrap and let rest for 20 minutes; this is the autolyse (see page 289).

Step 2: Sprinkle the salt over the dough and mix for 3 minutes on low speed. At this point, the dough may cling to the dough hook and no longer adhere to the sides of the bowl. If the dough is clinging to the hook so that it's just moving around in the bowl and not being kneaded, turn the mixer up to medium or even high speed until the centrifugal force pulls the dough away from the hook. Knead on medium to high speed for 5 to 10 minutes, until the dough is smooth and pulls together into a single mass.

KNEADING WET DOUGH BY HAND

1. Pull the dough up with both hands . . .

2. . . . and slap it down on the table.

3. The dough should also be smooth and shiny. Notice how here it still has a rough uneven texture.

4. Here the dough no longer adheres to the work surface.

5. The dough is ready when it's smooth and shiny and you can pull it up into a translucent sheet or "window." Kneading wet dough until it pulls away from both hands and the table takes about 25 minutes.

1. After, yeast, and flour have been mixed and the dough has rested, add the salt and mix on low speed for 3 minutes. If the dough is clinging to the hook, turn up the mixer to medium or high until the dough is spun off the hook and slaps against the sides of the bowl.

2. Mix the dough on medium speed for 5 to 10 minutes, until smooth. You can cut the dough in pieces to get the kneading started.

1. After water, yeast, and flour have been mixed and the dough has rested, add the salt and mix on low speed for 3 minutes.

2. Turn the mixer to medium to high speed and mix the dough for 5 to 10 minutes, until it pulls away from the hook and slaps against the bowl.

1. After water, yeast, and flour have been mixed and the dough has rested, add the salt and mix the dough on slow speed for 3 minutes, or until the dough clings to the hook.

2. Turn the mixer to medium or high speed to get the dough to pull away from the hook and slap the sides of the bowl.

3. If the dough clings to the sides of the bowl, scrape the sides with a rubber spatula. Knead on medium speed for 5 to 10 minutes.

1. After water, yeast, and flour have been mixed and the dough has rested, add the salt and mix on low speed for 3 minutes.

2. Continue mixing for about 5 minutes, or until the dough pulls away from the mixer bowl, then add the salt.

3. The salt sucks moisture out of the dough so that it adheres, again, to the bowl.

4. Continue mixing for about 7 minutes longer, or until the dough pulls away from the bowl again.

1. Combine all the ingredients except the salt and mix until all the flour has been moistened. Cover with a moist towel or plastic wrap and let the dough rest for 20 minutes.

KNEADING DOUGH IN A FOOD PROCESSOR

Using a food processor is the fastest way to knead bread dough—rarely does it take longer than 1½ minutes, but it doesn't work well if you're working with very wet dough because it's too hard on the motor. If you hear the motor straining at any time while you're kneading the dough, turn the food processor off for 5 minutes before trying again. It may be necessary to finish kneading the dough by hand.

The food processor works at such high speeds that the friction it generates heats up the dough considerably. You can keep the temperature down by using ice water, but if you use ice water or even cold water it will kill dry yeast if you put the yeast in at the same time as the water. If you're adding starter, however, any water you add should be very cold. If you notice the dough getting very warm, stick the whole food processor work bowl with the dough in it in the freezer for 15 minutes. You can also proof the yeast separately and add it after about 1 minute of processing, after the dough has warmed in the food processor.

Step 1: Put the flour in the food processor bowl and pour warm water over it. Sprinkle the yeast over the water and set aside for 3 minutes. Process for 10 seconds to moisten the flour. Drier doughs will look a little like couscous at this stage, while wet doughs come together into a wet mass. Cover the dough with a moist towel or plastic wrap and let rest for 20 minutes.

KNEADING MOIST DOUGH IN A FOOD PROCESSOR

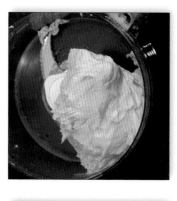

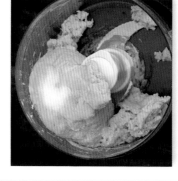

1. After the water, yeast, and flour have been mixed and the dough has rested, add the salt and process for 30 seconds. Let rest for 5 minutes. If the dough is warm, put the work bowl in the freezer with the dough in it during the rest period.

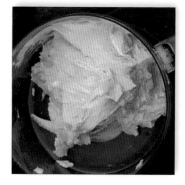

2. Process for 30 seconds more, then let rest for 5 minutes. Again, if the dough is warm, put it in the freezer, then process for 30 seconds more.

KNEADING WET DOUGH IN A FOOD PROCESSOR

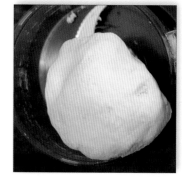

1. After the water, yeast, and flour have been mixed and the dough has rested, add the salt. Process for 30 seconds and let rest for 5 minutes. If you hear the motor straining, stop the machine for 5 minutes, then try again.

2. Process for 30 seconds more, putting the work bowl in the freezer if the dough gets warm. Let rest for 5 minutes, then process for 30 seconds more.

KNEADING DRY DOUGH IN A FOOD PROCESSOR

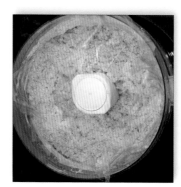

1. Put the flour in the food processor's work bowl and pour the water or the starter and water over it. Sprinkle the yeast over the water and let moisten for 3 minutes. Process for 10 seconds to moisten the flour, then cover with a moist towel or plastic wrap; let rest for 20 minutes.

2. Add the salt and process for 30 seconds. Let rest for 5 minutes. If the dough is distinctly warm, put the work bowl in the freezer with the dough in it. The dough may have formed little pellets; this is fine.

3. Process for 30 seconds more, and let rest for 5 minutes. Again, if the dough feels warm, put the work bowl in the freezer.

4. Process for 30 seconds more. Gather the dough together into a smooth mass.

Step 2: Add the salt and process for 30 seconds. Let rest for 5 minutes. If the dough is warm, put the work bowl in the freezer for this resting time. Process for 30 seconds more. Let rest for 5 minutes and process for 30 seconds more. At this point, the dough may have formed little pellets. These are fine. You'll notice that the dough will come together into a smooth single mass when you pick it up and knead it for a few seconds in your hands. The dough is now ready for fermentation.

KNEADING DOUGH IN A BREAD MACHINE

Most bread machines let you knead dough without going through the whole baking cycle. Bread machines knead dough very gently and are especially good for wet doughs. Combine the ingredients and transfer them to the bread machine. Knead until smooth, then cover and let rise. Twenty minutes of kneading is usually enough.

FERMENTATION AND PUNCHING DOWN

Once dough is kneaded, it is usually allowed to rise until doubled or tripled in volume. The rising is caused by the fermentation of the yeast, which creates carbon dioxide. The gas is caught by the strands of gluten in the dough, which causes the dough to expand and gives the bread its pattern of air holes in the crumb. Most breads have only one rising before the dough is shaped, but some have as many as three. More risings result in a finer crumb. Most of the flavor of the eventual bread is formed during this first fermentation, not the fermentation that occurs after shaping, which is usually called "proofing" (see page 302). Because most of the bread's flavor develops during the first fermentation, it's best to allow as much time as is practical. To keep the dough from rising too quickly, you can use very little yeast or increase the time. Of course if you're using a starter, a long rising is less important because the starter provides flavor. If you're making dough with sourdough starter, the dough can be allowed to rise at room temperature and it will still have plenty of time to develop flavor. Dough that is properly fermented will hold an indentation made with a fingertip.

When dough is fermenting, cover it with plastic wrap touching its surface to prevent a crust from forming, but don't tuck the plastic under the dough in any way or it will prevent it from rising completely. For a longer rise, leave the dough at room temperature for 1 hour to get it started, then refrigerate it overnight; for a longer room-temperature rise, decrease the amount of yeast or starter. If you don't have a warm place in your kitchen, consider letting the dough rise in a proofing box in the same way as shaped dough (see page 302).

One of the most useful tools in bread making is the refrigerator. Dough can be refrigerated at virtually any stage to slow down the process of fermentation. It may take some practice to get the refrigerator to do exactly what you want. Every refrigerator is different and much depends on the amount of dough you're preparing, the temperature of the water and flour that you use to make it, the kind of bowl you use, and how much time you have. For example, if you make dough on a warm day, even if you put the dough in the refrigerator, it will take so long to chill that the dough may rise more than you want. To compensate for this, use less yeast. If, on the other hand, your refrigerator is especially cold and/or you're making a small amount of dough, you may need to leave the dough at room temperature long enough to get the fermentation started before refrigerating it. By manipulating the temperature and the amount of yeast, you can make bread according to your own schedule.

Punching down—which is not literal punching, but a gentle pressing or stirring—is designed to force out carbon dioxide and expose the yeast to fresh oxygen while redistributing the ingredients within the dough. To deflate the dough, press it with your closed fist or stir it around in the bowl with your fingers until it loses about half its volume. You can also place the dough on a work surface and flatten it with a bench scraper or with your hands. Dough for fine-crumbed breads should be thoroughly punched down, but dough for rustic breads with large holes should be handled very gently—with no real pressing at all—to keep from deflating the holes.

PUNCHING DOWN DOUGH

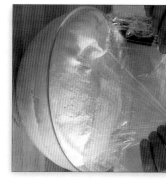

Risen dough will be about twice as voluminous as it was when you finished kneading it.

To "punch down," gently deflate the dough with your fist or fingers until it loses half its volume.

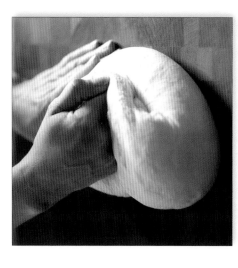

3. To round the dough, fold it from the outside into the center all around.

2. Notice the gluten structure of the divided bread.

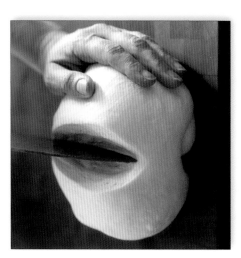

1. Don't pull dough apart; cut it using a bench scraper, a knife, or scissors.

4. Pull the dough together at the bottom.

5. Press in the sides to make the top of the dough more firm.

Dividing and Rounding Dough

If you are making rolls or more than one loaf with your batch of dough, you'll have to divide it. Don't pull it apart—you'll tear the gluten strands—but instead cut it with a bench scraper, a knife, or scissors. A scale is invaluable for even division; if you don't have one, you'll have to eyeball it.

Regardless of the final shape of the bread, each section of dough should be rounded. By rounding the dough, you stretch the gluten on the surface and increase its surface tension. This tension helps the dough hold its shape during proofing and in the oven and helps prevent the dough from expanding out instead of up. To round a piece of dough, place it on a work surface and pull each of the 4 corners toward the center on top. Use all the fingers of one hand to pinch the

ends of the dough together. Turn the dough over and use the sides of your hands to press the dough inward around the bottom to tighten and round it. If you're making a long loaf, use the same method but leave the dough closer to an oval in shape. Some bakers recommend letting the dough rest at this point. This rest is called "benching" and is designed to relax the gluten and make it easier to give the dough its final shape. If the dough is elastic and relentlessly pulls back into its original shape as you work with it, it may require 2 or even 3 benchings of 10 to 20 minutes each before it reaches its final shape. Cover the dough with plastic wrap during any rest periods to prevent a crust from forming, taking care not to tuck the plastic under the dough.

BAKING

294

Shaping Loaves and Rolls

Beginning bakers are often intimidated by the prospect of shaping their bread. Some shapes do take a little practice to perfect, but in any case, bread that doesn't look perfect has its own homespun charm. This section contains illustrated instructions for shaping a variety of loaves—often called by their French names. For example, a *baguette* is essentially a stick, a *boule* is a sphere, and a *bâtard* is a thick tapering loaf sometimes called a country loaf.

How Much Dough for Each Shape?

One recipe of any of the basic doughs will make your choice of the following:

2 seventeen-inch-long baguettes
1 *boule*
1 fourteen-inch-long *bâtard*
10 rolls
1 eight-cup pan loaf
4 two-cup pan loaves

SANDWICH LOAVES

To shape bread dough into a basic sandwich loaf, press the dough into a rectangle on a floured work surface. Fold both sides of the rectangle into the center and fold both ends of the rectangle into the center. Roll the dough toward you to form a cylinder. Press down along the front of the cylinder. Press down along the surface of the loaf. Roll on the ends a bit to elongate the cylinder, then fold under the ends of the cylinder to make the loaf fit snugly in an oiled loaf pan. Cover the loaf with plastic wrap and let rise.

SHAPING A SANDWICH LOAF

1. Press the dough into a rectangle.

2. Fold both ends of the rectangle into the center.

3. Roll the dough toward you to form a cylinder.

4. Press down along the front of the cylinder.

5. Roll the cylinder to elongate.

6. Fold under the ends of the cylinder.

7. Place the loaf in an oiled loaf pan and cover with plastic wrap.

8. Let rise. Remove plastic wrap before baking.

1. Press along the dough with your fist to stretch it.

2. Fold the dough along one side into the center and press it into the loaf with your fingers. Repeat along the other side of the dough.

3. Continue folding and pressing until the baguette is the length you want.

4. Roll the baguette to even it.

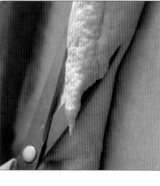

5. Fold down the ends and pinch together. The plain baguette is now ready to proof.

6. To shape a wheat sheaf loaf, cut along the top of the baguette with scissors so the bread becomes sectioned with the sections coming apart.

7. Move the flap to one side.

8. Repeat the cutting, about 2 inches down the loaf.

9. Move the flap to the opposite side as the first flap.

10. Continue cutting and moving the flaps the entire length of the baguette.

BAGUETTES

To coax bread dough into a baguette shape, press along one side of the dough to elongate it. As it spreads into an oval, fold the sides into the center and press the dough into the center position. As you continue in this way, the dough will lengthen. You can also pull on the dough to stretch it.

A variation on the baguette is wheat sheaf bread, or *pain epis*; it is shaped by snipping flaps in the shaped baguette to make the finished loaf look like a stalk of ripe wheat (see opposite).

BOULES

To shape a *boule* (ball), start with a rounded ball of dough and press along the bottom of the dough with the sides of your hands to stretch the top of the loaf tight and smooth. This will create creases in the bottom of the loaf; turn it over and pinch these together to seal. Turn it right side up to proof; you can let it proof in a cloth-lined basket called a *bânneton*, which helps the loaf hold its shape as it rises.

SHAPING A BOULE

1. Press along the bottom of the ball of dough with the sides of your hands.

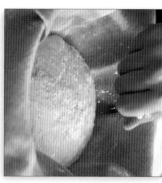

2. Turn the dough over and pinch the creases together in the center.

3. Turn the boule over, right side up, to proof. Place it in a cloth-lined basket.

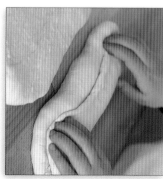

4. Sprinkle with flour to prevent sticking and fold the cloth over the dough.

BÂTARDS

The classic *bâtard* is a torpedo-shaped loaf—sort of halfway between a *boule* and a baguette. To make shaping the dough into a *bâtard* easier, first stretch the dough into an oval and let it rest, covered with a moist towel or plastic wrap, for 20 minutes before shaping it further. Then fold the sides into the center and press along the center as illustrated here.

SHAPING A BÂTARD

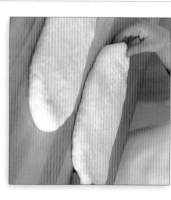

1. Form the dough into an oval, cover, and let it rest.

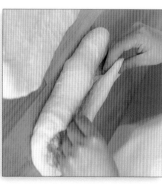

2. Fold one side of the dough into the center and press the edge in place.

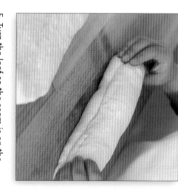

3. Repeat along the other side of the dough.

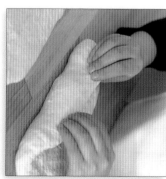

4. Press along the center and fold as needed until the loaf is the size you want—here, 14 inches.

5. Turn the loaf so the seam is on the bottom. Roll the dough on the counter to help round it.

6. Roll over the ends to give the loaf a tapered effect. Place the loaf on a floured sheet pan for proofing.

ROLLS

To shape rolls, round the dough slightly to tighten its surface. Weigh it so you know how much you have and how to divide it. You'll need about 2½ ounces per roll. Using a bench scraper or knife, cut the dough into equal pieces, then round each to make them easier to section into rolls. Now cut each dough piece into equal sections about 2½ ounces each. Roll each piece over a tiny bit of flour to keep it from sticking to the surface or to your hands. Roll each piece against the work surface between your palm, your forefinger, and the inside of your thumb. Sprinkle more flour over as needed as you shape the rolls. Place them on a nonstick pan to proof.

SHAPING ROLLS

4. Sprinkle each roll with a tiny bit of flour and roll the dough against your forefinger and the inside of your thumb.

8. Sift flour over the rolls before baking.

3. Cut each piece of dough into 2½-ounce pieces.

7. You can use scissors to make 4 cuts to create a star on each roll.

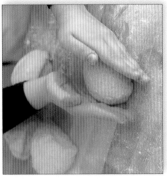

2. Round the pieces of dough to make them easier to section.

6. Leave the balls as they are or make decorative cuts into the dough before baking. Here are two methods: The first, shown here, is to make a single cut on the top of each of the rolls to create a little flap.

1. Cut the dough into equal pieces for the rolls (here the dough is cut into 4 pieces, each of which will be divided into 3 rolls for a total of 12 rolls).

5. Continue rolling. Curl your fingers down to create a small cage for the ball as you're rolling. Move your hand over the dough and let it roll around in the "cage." Place the finished balls on a nonstick sheet pan.

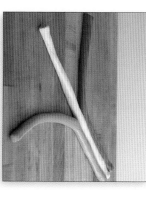

1. Arrange the three strands next to each other and spread the two outer strands away from the center. Stand behind the strands.

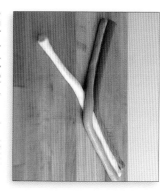

2. Take the left (blue) strand and fold it over the center (white) and next to the right (red) strand.

3. Take the right (red) strand and lift it over the blue strand and next to the center (white) strand.

4. Take the center (white) strand and place it over the left (red) strand and next to the right (blue) strand.

5. Take the right (blue) strand and place it over the center (white) strand and next to the left (red) strand.

6. Take the left (red) strand and place it over the blue (center) strand.

7. Take the right (white) strand and place it over the center (red) strand.

8. Proceed until you have reached the end of the strands, then pinch the strands together at the end.

9. Returning to the center of the loaf, braid the strands together in this way in the opposite direction.

BRAIDED LOAVES

Challah (page 330) is the classic braided loaf, and shaping it can feel intimidating to the uninitiated. The photographs above use colored dough to clarify the sequence of shaping a three-strand braided loaf.

Start by dividing the dough into three equal sections. Round the sections by pressing along the sides near the bottom with the sides of your hands. Roll and stretch each ball of dough into a rope about 24 inches long. Since the dough is very elastic, you'll need to stretch it in several stages, allowing it to rest for 10 minutes between each stretching and

rolling: Arrange the three strands next to each other on a work surface and, midway along the line formed by the three strands, spread the two outer strands away from the center strand. Working on alternate sides, bring the outer strand of dough over the center strand, so that it becomes the new center strand. When you reach the end of the loaf, pinch the ends of the strands together and tuck the pinch under the loaf. Working from the center again, braid the other half of the loaf in the same way, until the whole loaf is neatly braided.

FOUGASSE

A *fougasse* is a flat loaf that looks vaguely like a snow shoe or a leaf. It can be made with any of the basic doughs, such as basic white bread (page 304) or sourdough bread (page 313). To make it, prepare a basic dough and let it ferment until it has doubled in volume. Punch it down and shape it by pulling on the ends and by rolling over it with a rolling pin until you have an oval 12 inches long and 9 inches wide in the center. With a sharp paring knife, make six 2-inch slits in the dough, radiating diagonally from the center of the loaf. Let proof, either in a proof box or covered with plastic wrap, for about 40 minutes, or until about 50 percent thicker (see page 302). Stretch open the slits with a finger to keep them from closing up in the oven. Bake in a 450°F oven for about 25 minutes.

SPLIT LOAVES (PAIN FENDU)

These classic loaves have a split or crease down the middle. You can make *pain fendu* using any of the basic dough recipes. Knead the dough and let it ferment until it has doubled in volume. Punch down and divide the dough in half to shape into two stubby loaves that taper only slightly—each should be about 9 inches long and about 5 inches wide at the widest point. Sprinkle the loaves with flour, then press a wooden spoon handle or thin dowel into the dough along the length of each loaf. Turn the loaves over onto a sheet pan so the split is on the bottom, then reinforce the split by pressing again, now on the top, with the wooden spoon handle. Let proof until almost doubled in volume, about an hour (see page 302). Preheat the oven to 450°F and bake the loaves for about 25 minutes, until they are golden brown.

3. Stretch open the slits with a finger to keep them from closing up in the oven.

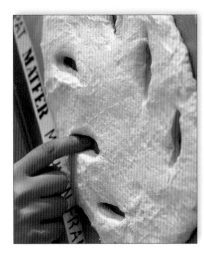

2. Make six 2-inch slits in the dough, cutting at a diagonal to the center of the loaf. Let the loaf proof.

SHAPING A FOUGASSE

1. Punch down the dough and shape it into an oval 12 inches long and 9 inches wide.

3. Let proof until doubled in size, then bake.

2. Turn the loaves over onto a sheet pan so the split is now on the bottom, then reinforce the split by pressing again, now on the top, with the wooden spoon handle.

SHAPING SPLIT LOAVES (PAIN FENDU)

1. When you've shaped the loaves, press a wooden spoon handle into the dough along the length of each loaf.

BAKING

Proofing

Once the dough has been shaped, it is ready for its final rising, called "proofing." Just like its fermentation before shaping, proofing can take place at room temperature, in the refrigerator, or in a proofing box (see below). Again, the dough will develop more flavor the more slowly it's allowed to rise. But flavor development during proofing is less crucial than during the first fermentation—most of the flavor should by now be developed—so it makes sense to proof in whatever way fits into your baking schedule. It is often convenient to shape the dough and leave it at room temperature long enough to get everything going—30 minutes to an hour—and then stick it in the refrigerator until the next morning. Then it needs only about 1 hour to come to room temperature before going into the oven. If you're in a hurry or it is just more convenient to bake the bread sooner, let it proof at room temperature for about 1½ to 2 hours, or in a proofing box for 30 to 90 minutes, until slightly less than doubled in size.

When proofing shaped dough, it is important to keep the surface of the dough from drying out and forming a crust, which will keep the dough from expanding. The easiest approach is to cover the shaped dough with plastic wrap that has been brushed or sprayed with a very thin layer of oil. The plastic wrap must not be tucked in, which would inhibit the rise. Most of the time, kitchen room temperature—about 70°F—is fine for proofing. If your kitchen is cold and/or you're averse to using plastic wrap (it can stick to very wet dough), you may want to improvise a proofing box. This method solves the humidity and temperature problems.

Don't be tempted to let your dough rise in a distinctly warm place—over 85°F—or it may develop odd or unpleasant flavors and aromas. If the dough, such as brioche, contains a lot of butter, the butter will ooze out if allowed to go over 80°F.

SCORING

Many loaves of bread are scored with a razor blade before baking. Professionals use one with a little handle called a *lame* (French for blade), but a single-edged razor blade works well. The purpose of scoring is not only decorative: It allows the bread to expand and prevents cracking in a random and unsightly way. If the dough is slightly underproofed—it hasn't quite doubled in volume—it will quickly expand, especially in the cracks, soon after it goes into the oven. Bakers refer to this as "oven spring."

When scoring your bread, do your best to make each cut in a single slashing movement with no hesitation. If you hesitate, the blade will stick to the dough and pull on it, possibly ruining its appearance. Bread is usually scored about ½ inch deep. Some round loaves and rolls are scored with scissors (see page 298), or with a serrated knife for a rustic look.

GLAZING

Bread is sometimes brushed with water or egg wash immediately before it goes into the oven. The water helps prevent a crust from forming prematurely on the loaf. Water can also be used to make seeds, oats, or other garnishes adhere. Unlike egg wash, water does not affect browning. Richer breads, such as brioche or challah, are usually brushed with egg wash just before they go into the oven to help create a shiny golden crust. Take care to brush gently—too vigorous a brushing can cause even slightly overproofed dough to collapse.

Improvising Your Own Proofing Box

Place the dough on a sheet pan, *bânneton*, or other surface, then put the container with the dough in it in a covered box large enough to hold it along with a loaf pan. Place the loaf pan, one-third full of hot tap water (boiling water is too hot), next to the container in the box. Replace the cover.

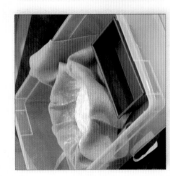

A boule is being proofed in a *bânneton* (see page 297 for shaping a *boule*), which is in turn placed in a homemade proofing box.

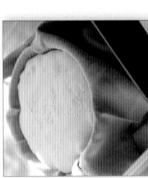

Proofed *boule*.

Scoring a bâtard-*shaped loaf. Score with a rapid, single movement with the blade inserted about ¹/₂ inch into the dough.*

Scoring a boule *with scissors.*

Scoring a rustic boule *with a bread knife.*

BAKING

As home bakers, we're at a disadvantage. Professional bakers have heavy-duty ovens that retain heat even if the door is opened frequently and have steam injectors that ensure a humid environment that allows the dough to expand fully as it cooks. You can maintain a more even temperature with a home oven by preheating to 500°F and placing a baking stone on the floor or bottom rack of the oven. Baking stones take a long time to get hot (and, of course, to cool, hence their value in keeping the oven temperature constant), so be sure to put the stone in the oven before you turn it on and preheat for at least 30 minutes. Many bakers bake bread directly on the stone by placing the dough on a peel—a flat wooden tool (half shovel, half paddle) with a long handle—and quickly sliding the dough onto the stone with a quick, confident jerk. Because in home ovens this sometimes causes the bottom of the bread to burn, I suggest sliding the bread onto a sheet pan on the lowest rack of the oven, a couple of inches above the stone. When you put the bread in the oven, turn down the heat to the baking temperature called for in the recipe.

Keeping a home oven humid is a bit trickier. The goal is to keep producing steam in the oven without opening the door so often that the oven cools off too much. Place a sheet pan or a heavy-duty roasting pan on the bottom shelf or the floor (on top of the stone if you are using one) of the oven. Just before you slide in your loaf, pour hot, but not boiling, water into the pan so the water is at least ¹/₃ inch deep—stand back, it spatters. Slide the dough onto a shelf above the water

and close the door. Grab a spray bottle of water and crack the oven door open just far enough to let you spray the inside walls while avoiding getting too much water on the bread. After the first spray, wait for 30 seconds and spray again; wait another 30 seconds and spray once more. (Be careful not to spray the oven window—cold water on hot glass can cause it to crack.)

COOLING

Let bread cool on a cake rack. This lets air circulate around the bread so any moisture that is released evaporates. If the bread is placed on a flat surface, moisture accumulates on the bottom and interferes with the development of the crust. Resist the temptation to tear into the bread before it's cool—it is continuing to cook.

Judging When Bread Is Done

To check whether a loaf of bread is fully cooked, most bakers recommend tapping the loaf to see if it sounds hollow. But few of us are able to discern what fully cooked bread sounds like. It is more reliable to slide an instant-read thermometer into the center of the loaf, through the bottom so the hole doesn't show. Most bread will measure about 205°F when it's done; very rich breads that contain eggs are ready at a somewhat lower temperature, about 185°F.

BASIC DOUGHS: THE STRAIGHT DOUGH METHOD

Most basic yeasted breads are made from only water, yeast, salt, and flour. All variations in flavor, texture, and appearance come about by using different amounts of these ingredients and different techniques for incorporating them.

The simplest method of making yeasted bread is the straight dough method. This simply means that the ingredients for the bread are all combined at the beginning. So-called indirect methods involve making a sponge or other starter with some of the flour, water, and yeast and then adding the risen starter to the remaining ingredients (see page 306).

White Bread (Straight Dough)

This loaf, a very basic white bread made using the straight dough method, uses a relatively large amount of yeast to get it to rise quickly. If you want a slower rise and more flavorful bread, use less yeast and/or refrigerate the dough for part of the rise (see sidebar at right).

MAKES ONE 8-CUP LOAF, 2 BAGUETTES, 1 BOULE, 1 BÂTARD, OR 10 ROLLS

4 cups flour

1½ cups barely warm water

1½ teaspoons active dry yeast (see sidebar, right)

1 teaspoon salt

Before beginning, review the steps for bread making on page 286.

Put the flour in a large bowl, the bowl of a stand mixer, or the work bowl of a food processor and make a well in the middle with the back of your fist. Pour in the water, which should feel neither warm nor cool. Sprinkle the yeast over the water and let it sit for 10 minutes. Mix the ingredients, add the salt, and mix some more.

Kneading by hand: Mix for 3 minutes and let rest for 20 minutes, covered with a bowl or plastic wrap. Knead for about 15 minutes more, or until the dough is smooth and passes the windowpane test (see page 289).

Kneading with a stand mixer: Fit the mixer with the dough hook. Mix for 2 minutes to moisten the flour. Cover with a moist towel or plastic wrap and let sit for 20 minutes. Knead the dough on medium speed for about 7 minutes, or until the dough is smooth and passes the windowpane test (see page 289). Turn the mixer to high speed if needed to get the dough to slap against the sides of the bowl.

Kneading with a food processor: Process for 10 seconds, cover with a moist towel or plastic wrap, and let rest for 20 minutes. Process for 1 minute, or until the dough has formed pellets. You'll notice that the dough will come together in a smooth single mass when you pick it up and knead it for a few seconds.

Fermentation: Cover the dough with plastic wrap or a moist towel. Leave the dough for about 2 hours at warm room temperature for the fastest rise, or first for 30 minutes at room temperature, then overnight in the refrigerator for the slowest.

Shaping: Punch down the dough and shape it into a loaf or loaves or rolls (see page 295).

Proofing: Cover with oiled plastic or a moist towel and let rise in a warm place—perhaps a proofing box (see page 302)—for 1 to 3 hours, until doubled in volume.

Baking: Preheat the oven to 425°F. Place a sheet pan on the floor of the oven or on the bottom rack and pour in enough hot water to come about ⅓ inch up the side of the sheet pan. Slide the loaf onto an oven rack over the pan of water and immediately spray the oven walls with water (see page 303); wait for 30 seconds, then spray again. Bake to an internal temperature of 205°F. Let the bread cool on a cake rack.

Judging Yeast Amounts and Rising Times

For a quick rise, about 90 minutes, use ½ teaspoon yeast per 1 cup flour. For a 4- to 6-hour rise, use half that amount. You can even experiment with smaller amounts and longer rising times.

The straight dough method is a simple combining of the yeast, water, salt, and flour.

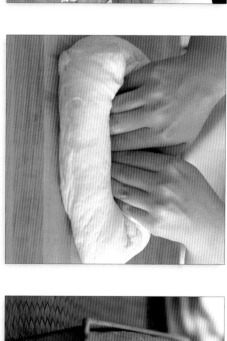

Kneading dough by hand (see page 289).

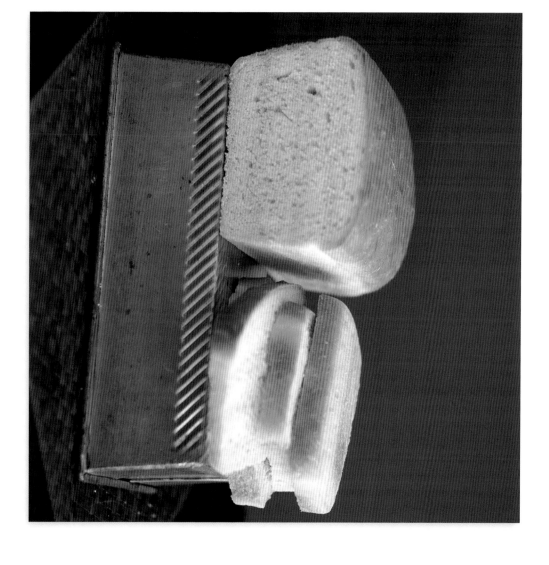

BASIC DOUGHS: INDIRECT METHODS

The breads in this section are made with sponges or starters, wherein portions of the water, flour, and yeast are combined in advance and allowed to rise before being added to the rest of the ingredients. This process maximizes the bread's flavor.

Sponge Starter

Combine about one-fourth of the flour called for in the recipe with half of the water and all of the yeast (proof the yeast in a little water first; see page 286). Cover with a moist towel or with plastic wrap and let rise until doubled or even tripled in volume. Mix with the rest of the ingredients and then follow the directions for kneading, fermentation, and shaping.

MAKING A SPONGE STARTER

1. Pour the warm liquids over the flour and stir with a whisk to combine.

2. Sprinkle all the yeast over the flour mixture.

3. The level of the sponge starter is marked on the container.

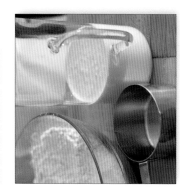

4. The sponge starter is ready to use when doubled in volume.

5. Combine the starter with the rest of the bread ingredients.

White Bread (Sponge Starter)

This bread using a sponge starter is the second quickest dough (after the straight dough method). The sponge starter is a very easy method to incorporate into your baking. Because this recipe contains milk, the loaf ends up with a softer crust than breads made with water only. If you prefer a more brittle crust, substitute water for the milk.

MAKES ONE 8-CUP LOAF, 2 BAGUETTES, 1 BOULE, OR 1 BÂTARD

4 cups flour

³/₄ cup plus 1 tablespoon barely warm water

²/₃ cup barely warm milk

1¹/₂ teaspoons active dry yeast (see sidebar, page 304)

1 teaspoon sugar

³/₄ teaspoon salt

Oil for the pan

Before beginning, review the steps for bread making on page 286.

Making the starter: Put 1¹/₂ cups of the flour, the water, and milk in a bowl. Stir to combine with a whisk and sprinkle the yeast over. Wait for about 3 minutes, for the yeast to moisten, and stir again until the mixture has the consistency of a thick batter. Cover the starter with plastic wrap and let rise for 1 to 2 hours, until doubled or even tripled in volume.

Mixing: Combine the remaining 2¹/₂ cups flour and the sugar with the sponge. Cut off one-fifth of the dough to reserve for the next batch (see sidebar, opposite). You can save this for up to 3 days in the refrigerator or up to 1 month in the freezer. The next time you make bread, knead this reserved piece into the milk/flour mixture just after you add the milk.

Kneading: Mix the dough by hand for 3 minutes or with a mixer fitted with the dough hook on medium speed for 2 minutes. If you're using a food processor, process the dough for 10 seconds. Cover the dough with a moist towel or with plastic wrap and let rest for 20 minutes. Add the salt to the dough and knead again by hand or with the mixer on medium speed for about 7 minutes, or until the dough is smooth and passes the windowpane test (see page 289). Turn the mixer to high speed if needed to get the dough to slap against the sides of the bowl. If you're using a food processor, process for 1 minute and then knead by hand for 1 minute, which should cause the broken-up dough to come together into a cohesive mass.

Fermentation: Cover the dough with plastic wrap or a moist towel. Leave the dough for about 2 hours at warm room temperature for the fastest rise, or for 30 minutes at room temperature, then overnight in the refrigerator for the slowest.

Shaping: Punch down the dough. Shape the dough as a loaf (see page 295) and place it in an oiled 8-cup loaf pan.

Proofing: Cover with plastic wrap and let rise for about 2 hours at room temperature, or until about twice its original volume.

Baking: Preheat the oven to 425°F. Place a sheet pan on the floor of the oven or on the bottom rack and pour in enough hot water to cover the bottom of the sheet pan. Slide the loaf onto an oven rack over the pan of water and immediately spray the oven walls with water; wait for 30 seconds, then spray again (see page 303). Bake for 50 minutes, or until the bread sounds hollow when you tap it. Let sit for 5 minutes, then turn out onto a cake rack to cool.

White Bread (Mature Starter)

....

This dough is typical of the dough used in France to make baguettes. Because the starter—called a pâte fermentée—is fermented relatively slowly, it has time to develop a complex flavor that comes through in the bread. The starter used here is very stiff, not like the sponge or poolish starters on pages 306 and 309. Because it's made ahead of time and is allowed to ferment twice, it is similar to using leftover dough from a previous batch.

MAKES ONE 8-CUP LOAF, 2 BAGUETTES, 1 BOULE, 1 BÂTARD, OR 1 BAGUETTE WITH LEFTOVER DOUGH FOR THE NEXT BATCH

4 cups flour or more as needed

1 teaspoon salt

1 1/2 cups barely warm water or more as needed

1 1/2 teaspoons active dry yeast proofed in 1 tablespoon barely warm water for 10 minutes

Before beginning, review the steps for bread making on page 286.

Making the starter: The day before you plan on baking the bread, thoroughly combine 1 cup of the flour with 1/4 teaspoon of the salt (this amount of salt won't hurt the yeast, just slow it down a little) and 1/2 cup of the water. Add the yeast and combine thoroughly. Let sit for 3 minutes. Knead just until the flour is moistened and there is no dry flour on the work surface. Put

Using Leftover Dough

If you make bread regularly, you can use an old trick popular with artisan bakers: Set a piece of fermented dough aside to incorporate into your next batch of bread. The leftover dough acts as a starter. Most of the time, you will need to add yeast in addition to the leftover bread dough to get your dough to rise. But if you incorporate leftover dough into your bread, your bread will have more flavor. When using leftover dough, cut the amount of yeast you would normally use (1 1/2 teaspoons per 4 cups flour) by one-third (1/2 teaspoon per 4 cups flour).

the dough in a bowl, cover it with plastic wrap, and let rise until doubled or tripled in volume. Punch it down, put it back in the bowl, cover with plastic wrap, and keep in the refrigerator overnight or for up to 3 days. It should double in volume a second time. You can also freeze the dough for up to 1 month.

Mixing: Combine the starter with the remaining 3 cups flour and 1 cup water on a work surface, in the bowl of a stand mixer, or in the work bowl of a food processor. Mix by hand for 2 minutes, with the stand mixer on medium to high speed for 2 minutes, or in a food processor for 10 seconds. Cover with a moist towel or plastic wrap and let rest for 20 minutes.

Kneading: Add the remaining 3/4 teaspoon salt and knead by hand for about 7 minutes, or in a stand mixer fitted with the dough hook on medium to high speed for about 5 minutes. Turn the mixer to high speed if needed to get the dough to slap against the sides of the bowl. If you're using a food processor, process for 1 minute (see sidebar, page 308), until the dough forms little pellets. Work these together by hand for 1 minute. The dough should be smooth and pass the windowpane test (see page 289).

Fermentation: Cover the dough with a moist towel or plastic wrap and let it rise at room temperature for 2 to 4 hours, until doubled in volume. Punch down the dough by stirring it.

Shaping: Shape the dough into the form you want (see page 295).

Proofing: Allow the dough to rise for 1 to 2 hours, until approximately doubled in volume. Ideally the bread should be proofed in a humid proofing box (see page 302), but short of that, cover the dough with a moist towel.

continued

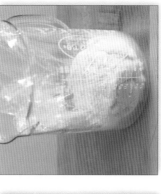

1. Combine 1 cup flour and 1/4 teaspoon salt in a bowl and pour over 1/2 cup water. Add the yeast.

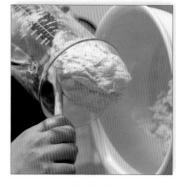

2. Stir.

3. Dump the mixture out on the counter and knead just long enough to moisten all the flour.

4. Put the starter in a container and cover with plastic wrap.

5. Let rise until at least doubled in volume.

6. Combine the remaining dough ingredients and stir in the starter.

White Bread (Mature Starter), continued

Baking: Preheat the oven to 425°F. Put a sheet pan on the floor or bottom rack of the oven. When the oven is hot and you're ready to bake, pour enough water into the sheet pan to cover its surface. Immediately slide your loaf or loaves onto a middle rack over the pan of water. Close the oven door, but a minute later crack it open and spray inside with a sprayer (see page 305). Do this a couple of times during the first 10 minutes of baking to prevent too thick a crust from forming too early—such a crust keeps the bread from rising. Bake for about 50 minutes, or until the bread sounds hollow when you tap on it or a thermometer inserted into the bottom of one of the loaves reads 205°F. Let the bread cool on a cake rack.

Kneading in a Food Processor

There's nothing wrong with making bread in a food processor, but there is one caveat. Because they're so powerful and work at such high speeds, food processors generate a lot of friction and thus heat. When making bread, knead for 30 seconds and then feel the dough with the back of your hand. If it feels distinctly hot, put the work bowl, along with the dough, in the freezer for 15 minutes to cool it down before kneading anymore. If you know you're going to be making dough in the food processor, use ice water and chill the flour in the freezer beforehand.

Ciabatta

A ciabatta, "slipper" in Italian, is rather flat and full of holes. The trick to creating the holes is to use a very wet starter, called a poolish (see page 285), which allows for a very slow fermentation, and to avoid punching down the dough after its first rise. Because of its wetness, ciabatta dough will spread over any surface you bake it on. Baking the dough in a cake pan or baking dish will hold its shape in the oven. While not as picturesque as the classic slipper shape, the bread fills with holes and rises beautifully. This version contains olive oil, which softens the crust somewhat—important when using a home oven, in which it is hard to generate the necessary humidity. Because ciabatta dough is so loose, it is easier to make in a mixer than by hand. Ciabatta dough is too wet to knead in a food processor.

MAKES ONE 8-CUP CIABATTA

3 cups flour
1¼ cups plus 2 tablespoons barely warm water
1½ teaspoons active dry yeast (see sidebar, page 304)
¼ cup extra virgin olive oil
¾ teaspoon salt
Room temperature butter for the baking dish

Calculating the Amount of Liquid in a Bread Recipe

A typical dough has about slightly more than one-third as much water by volume as flour. In other words, if you have 3 cups flour, you need to add 1 cup and 2 tablespoons water or other liquid to make a dough with the right consistency. When you add starter to a dough, you have to keep in mind that the starter is made with equal parts by volume of flour and water, which is to say much more water than regular dough. When adding starter to a dough, subtract ¼ cup plus 3 tablespoons liquid from the recipe per cup of starter. For instance, if you have a recipe based on 5 cups flour and 1½ cups water and you decide to use 2 cups starter, you need to subtract ¾ cup plus 2 tablespoons from the amount of water, leaving you with ½ cup plus 2 tablespoons water to add to your 5 cups flour.

Before beginning, review the steps for bread making on page 286.

Making the starter: Put ¾ cup of the flour and ¾ cup of the water in a bowl. Stir to combine with a whisk and sprinkle the yeast over. Wait for about 3 minutes, for the yeast to moisten, and stir again until the mixture has the consistency of a thick batter. Cover the sponge with plastic wrap and let rise for 1 to 2 hours, until doubled or even tripled in volume.

Mixing: Combine the starter with the remaining flour and water, and the oil. Mix with a stand mixer fitted with the dough hook for about 2 minutes, or by hand for about 2 minutes. Cover with a moist towel or plastic wrap and let rest for 20 minutes.

Kneading: Add the salt and knead with a stand mixer on medium speed for about 7 minutes, or by hand for about 10 minutes, or until the dough is smooth and passes the windowpane test (see page 289). Turn the mixer to high speed if needed to get the dough to slap against the sides of the bowl.

Fermentation: Cover the dough with plastic wrap or a moist towel. Leave the dough for about 2 hours at warm room temperature for the fastest rise, or for 30 minutes at room temperature then overnight in the refrigerator for the slowest.

Shaping: Because it is so wet, ciabatta dough is very difficult to shape. Bake it in an oiled 11-inch cake pan (as shown here), or use any kind of baking dish you like. Transfer the dough gently—don't punch it down—to the baking dish.

Proofing: Cover with plastic wrap and let rise at room temperature for about 2 hours, or about twice its original volume.

Baking: Preheat the oven to 450°F. Place a sheet pan on the floor of the oven or on the bottom rack and pour in enough hot water to cover the bottom of the sheet pan. Slide the loaf onto a rack over the pan of water and immediately spray the oven walls with water; wait for 30 seconds, and spray again (see page 303). Turn down the oven to 425°F. Bake for about 35 minutes, or until the loaf sounds hollow when tapped or a thermometer stuck into the bottom reads 205°F. Let cool for 5 minutes before turning the ciabatta out onto a cake rack.

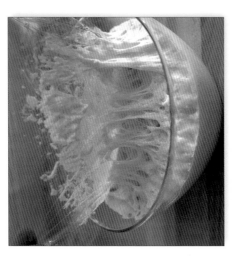

3. Let rise until at least doubled in volume.

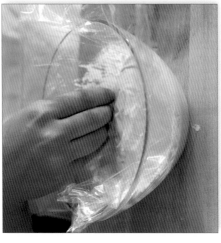

1. To make the starter, combine 3/4 cup flour with 3/4 cup warm water. Sprinkle the yeast over the flour mixture and let soften for 3 minutes. Stir with a whisk to combine.

6. Transfer the dough gently into an oiled cake pan and cover with plastic wrap.

2. Cover with plastic wrap.

5. Cover and let rest, then add salt and knead until smooth.

4. Put the starter, remaining flour and water, and the oil in the mixer bowl and combine on slow speed until the flour is moistened.

8. Bake until golden brown.

7. Let rise until between doubled and tripled in thickness.

BAKING

Making a Natural Starter

Making a natural starter, which can be more or less sour, allows you to extract more flavor from the flour than any other method of making breads. Natural (and hence sourdough) starter is made in 2 stages: the first, most time-consuming stage is making the basic culture from wild yeasts, while the second stage "expands" the basic culture by combining it with a significant amount of flour and water. The first stage takes several days, but once you have the starter on hand, it will keep indefinitely at room temperature provided you feed it every day. It will keep in the refrigerator as long as you feed it 3 times a week, and for up to 2 weeks in the freezer, although freezing will weaken it somewhat. Only 2 ingredients are used to make sourdough starter, flour and water; it contains no commercial yeast.

When you first mix flour (specifically, organic rye or whole wheat flour) and water, several different processes occur simultaneously. Since the only yeast present is what is contained in the flour and because these yeasts start out weaker than commercial yeast, you need to use natural selection to develop a strain that is hardy enough to make your bread rise and to survive in an acidic environment. By repeatedly fermenting a small amount of flour and water and letting the yeasts tire themselves out, weaker strains are gradually eliminated as more vital strains take over. At the same time, beneficial bacteria that ferment flour and yeast by-products (especially alcohol) into lactic and acetic acids are allowed to coexist with the yeasts. These acids are responsible for the characteristic tang of sourdough bread.

Most recipes for sourdough seed cultures start out with needlessly large amounts of flour—flour that is eventually discarded as the starter is fed and there's just too much of it. Here, the basic culture begins with only 1 teaspoon flour and 1 teaspoon water and the amounts are doubled each day of the feeding. Because sourdough seed culture should always be fed with at least the same amount of flour and water already in it, on day 2, add 1 teaspoon flour and 1 teaspoon water; on day 3, add 2 teaspoons flour and 2 teaspoons water; on day 4, add 4 teaspoons flour and 4 teaspoons water; and so on. Continue in this way until you have the amount of culture you need—this recipe makes 2 cups—to make the final batch of culture for the bread. To maintain the culture, keep it in the refrigerator and every 2 days pour half of it out and add 1 cup flour and 1 cup water. You can also keep it at room temperature, but it will require daily feedings.

How Sour Is Sour?

The tartness and acidity of sourdough bread starter can be controlled by timing the basic culture feedings to favor either yeast or bacteria. Because yeast reproduces more quickly than bacteria, you can tilt the flavor balance toward the less acidic by feeding the starter as soon as it rises, before the bacterial fermentation has time to catch up. For a more sour starter, wait longer between feedings so the yeast mostly dies off—and what yeast remains is acid resistant—and the bacteria have time to take over. To make a basic culture less sour, two or three days before you're planning to use it, replace three-fourths of it with four times the flour and water in the remaining starter instead of just matching or doubling the amounts. If the basic culture is at room temperature, you will need to feed it twice a day to further diminish its acidity. The extra flour and water allow the yeast to become vigorous and lively before the bacteria have time to catch up; if you want a more sour starter, just double the amounts in the usual way at each feeding.

Day 1: Combine 1 teaspoon organic rye or whole wheat flour and 1 teaspoon water in a small bowl and cover with plastic wrap. Leave at room temperature for 24 hours.

Day 2 (24 to 36 hours later): Often the starter does nothing for the first 24 hours but then suddenly froths up and is usually ready for the second feeding after about 36 hours. When the starter has frothed up, stir in 1 teaspoon organic rye or whole wheat flour and 1 teaspoon water. Cover with plastic wrap and set aside at room temperature.

Day 3 (24 hours later): Stir in 2 teaspoons organic rye or whole wheat flour and 2 teaspoons water. Cover with plastic wrap and set aside at room temperature.

Day 4 (24 hours later): Stir in 4 tablespoons flour—at this stage it doesn't have to be organic flour—and 4 tablespoons water. Cover with plastic wrap and set aside at room temperature. You now have about 6 tablespoons of culture.

Day 5 (24 hours later): Stir in 8 tablespoons flour and 8 tablespoons water. Cover with plastic wrap and set aside at room temperature.

MAINTAINING THE STARTER

Once you have about 2 cups of starter, you need to maintain it with regular feedings. About 24 hours before you're ready to use it to bake bread, you need to expand it by working some of it with a relatively large amount of flour and water.

Day 6 (24 hours later): Stir ¾ cup flour and ¾ cup water into the culture. You now have 3 cups of culture that you can maintain by throwing half of it out each day and replacing what you threw out with 1 cup flour and 1 cup water. You can cut the feedings to every 2 days if you refrigerate the culture.

EXPANDING THE STARTER

A day before baking, when you anticipate making sourdough bread, begin by building the natural starter into a finished sourdough starter by adding flour and water. If your starter isn't as vigorous as you'd like—it takes longer than 8 hours to double in volume—consider adding a small amount of yeast to hurry things along. This method of combining yeast with a natural starter is called the "mixed method."

Day 7 or 24 hours before you're ready to make bread: Combine 1 cup starter—don't use it all, you want to maintain some for future projects—with 1 cup flour and 1 cup water and allow it to rise at cool room temperature for 24 hours. If you don't have a cool place for the rising, let rise at room temperature for 4 hours and then transfer to the refrigerator for 20 more hours.

Day 8: You are ready to make bread.

MAKING AND MAINTAINING A NATURAL STARTER

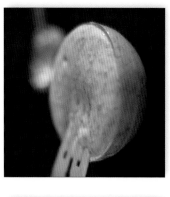

1. Combine 1 teaspoon flour and 1 teaspoon water in a small bowl and cover with plastic wrap (day 1).

2. After 24 hours or so, the starter suddenly froths up.

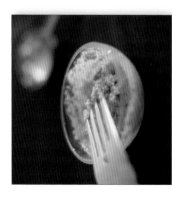

3. Feed the starter with another teaspoon of flour and another teaspoon of water, and cover with plastic (day 2).

4. The starter will froth up again (day 3); add 2 teaspoons flour and 2 teaspoons water (remove to a larger bowl if necessary). Cover with plastic.

5. Next day (day 4) stir in 4 tablespoons flour and 4 tablespoons water.

6. On day 5, stir in 8 tablespoons flour and 8 tablespoons water.

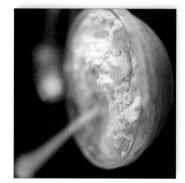

7. From day 6 onward, maintain (or "feed") the starter by throwing away half of it every day and adding 1 cup flour and 1 cup water (feed every 3 days if you are refrigerating the starter).

Sourdough Bread

This recipe gives you the option of using the mixed method—both a sourdough starter and commercial yeast. The sourdough starter provides flavor, while the yeast provides plenty of rise. If you prefer, you can just use the starter

MAKES ONE 8-CUP LOAF, 2 BAGUETTES, 1 BOULE, OR 1 BÂTARD

5 cups flour

1½ cups water

2 cups expanded sourdough starter (opposite page)

¼ teaspoon active dry yeast proofed in 1 tablespoon barely warm water and 1 tablespoon flour, if using mixed method

1 teaspoon salt

In a bowl, mix the flour, water, and sourdough starter. If using the mixed method, add the yeast and combine. Cover the dough with plastic wrap or a moist towel and let rest for 20 minutes. Add the salt and knead by hand for about 12 minutes or with a stand mixer fitted with the dough hook on medium speed for about 7 minutes, or until the dough is smooth and passes the windowpane test (see page 289). Turn the mixer to high speed if needed to get the dough to slap against the sides of the bowl. Cover with plastic wrap and allow to rise at room temperature for 4 to 8 hours, until doubled in volume.

Shape the dough (see page 295) and allow to proof, covered with plastic wrap at room temperature or uncovered in a proofing box (see page 302), for 2 to 4 hours, until doubled in size.

Preheat the oven to 450°F. Slide a sheet pan on the floor or bottom rack of the oven and allow to heat for 10 minutes. Pour enough hot water to just cover the bottom of the sheet pan. Immediately spray water in the oven (see page 303) and close the door. Wait for 30 seconds, crack open the door, and spray again; repeat once more after 30 seconds. Turn down the oven to 425°F. Bake for about 45 minutes, or until golden brown and a thermometer stuck into the bottom reads at least 205°F. Let cool on a cake rack.

1. Add the starter to the flour.

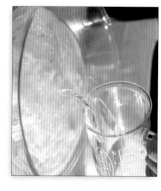

2. Pour the water over the mixture.

3. (Mixed method only) Add the proofed yeast to the mixture.

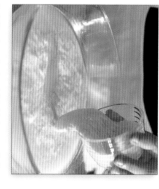

4. Mix the ingredients until all the flour is moistened. Cover with a moist towel or plastic wrap and let rest for 20 minutes.

5. Knead by hand for about 12 minutes or with a stand mixer for about 7 minutes, or until the dough passes the windowpane test.

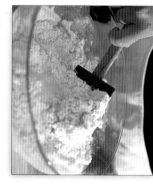

6. Cover the dough with plastic wrap and let rise at room temperature for about 8 hours, depending on the strength of the starter, or until doubled in volume. Shape the dough. Proof and bake until golden brown.

Rye Bread

Rye bread made with a natural starter or even with yeast and organic rye flour will likely taste like nothing you've ever experienced. The full complex flavor of rye, unaltered by the presence of caraway seeds (a pernicious habit that obscures the more subtle flavor of the rye), is so striking that you're likely to declare it the best bread you've ever tasted.

This recipe produces a deep rye flavor and is designed to conform to your schedule and level of enthusiasm. The quickest and easiest approach—double in an afternoon—is to make a sponge out of some of the flour, water, and yeast and let it rise at room temperature. The longer method—double in 2 days—is made with a sourdough starter.

MAKES 2 BAGUETTES, 1 BOULE, OR 1 BÂTARD

2½ cups organic rye flour
2½ cups all-purpose flour

One-day method

2 cups plus 1 tablespoon barely warm water
1 teaspoon active dry yeast (see sidebar, page 304)
1 teaspoon salt

Two-day method

1½ cups barely warm water
2 cups expanded sourdough starter (see page 312)
1 teaspoon salt

Before beginning, review the steps for bread making on page 286.

One-day (sponge) method: Put 1¼ cups of the all-purpose flour and 1¼ cups of the rye flour in a bowl. Pour the water over the flour. Sprinkle over the yeast, wait 3 minutes, and mix together with a wooden spoon. Cover with plastic wrap. If you're in a hurry, let the sponge rise at room temperature for about 1 hour, or until doubled in volume. If you're not in a hurry, leave the sponge at room temperature for 30 minutes and then refrigerate for about 4 hours, or until doubled in volume. In another bowl, combine the remaining flour, the salt, and the sponge. Cover the dough with plastic wrap and let rest at room temperature for 1 hour. Knead by hand for about 12 minutes or in a stand mixer fitted with the dough hook on medium speed for about 7 minutes, or until the dough is smooth and passes the windowpane test (see page 289). Turn the mixer to high speed if needed to get the dough to slap against the sides of the bowl. Cover the dough with a moist towel and let rise at room temperature until doubled in volume, 2 to 3 hours.

Two-day (sourdough starter) method: In a bowl, mix the rye flour, all-purpose flour, water, sourdough starter, and salt. Cover the dough with plastic wrap or a moist towel and let rest for 20 minutes. Knead by hand for about 12 minutes or with a stand mixer fitted with the dough hook on medium speed for about 7 minutes, or until the dough is smooth and passes the windowpane test (see page 289). Turn the mixer to high speed if needed to get the dough to slap against the sides of the bowl. Cover with plastic wrap and allow to rise at room temperature for 4 to 8 hours, until double in volume.

Both methods: Shape the dough (see page 295) and allow to proof, covered with plastic wrap at room temperature or uncovered in a proofing box (see page 302), for 1 to 4 hours, until doubled in size. Score as shown here or on page 303 and sprinkle the loaf with flour, if you like.

Preheat the oven to 450°F. Slide a sheet pan on the floor or bottom rack of the oven and allow to heat for 10 minutes. Put the bread on a rack just above the sheet pan. Pour enough hot water to just cover the bottom of the sheet pan. Immediately spray water in the oven (see page 303) and close the door. Wait for 30 seconds, crack open the door, and spray again; repeat once more after 30 seconds. Turn down the oven to 425°F. Bake for about 45 minutes, or until golden brown and a thermometer stuck into the bottom reads at least 205°F. Let cool on a cake rack.

1. Add the sponge to the dough. Combine for 2 minutes to moisten the flour.

2. Knead the dough until smooth, by hand as shown here or in a mixer (see page 290). Cover with plastic wrap and allow to double in volume.

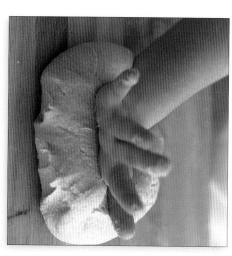

3. Punch down and shape. Here the dough is shaped into a *boule*.

4. Place the dough on a floured sheet pan. Sprinkle the top with flour (optional).

5. Score the dough with a series of lines about 1½ inches apart and ½ inch deep.

6. Bake until golden brown and hollow sounding when tapped. Spray inside the oven with water during the first stage of baking.

Sourdough Whole Wheat Bread

Much like rye bread, recipes for whole wheat bread often include some bread flour to provide extra gluten. Because whole wheat flour contains the bran, these minute pieces of the broken-up seed coats of the grain cut through the gluten structure and weaken it. The added bread flour helps keep the gluten strong. Whole wheat flour also contains the fat from the wheat germ so it turns rancid very quickly. Many people don't recognize the smell of rancid flour and assume it's a strong odor like the smell of rancid butter. It smells like old vegetable oil or stale nuts—you'll soon learn to recognize the smell and flavor. Buy your flour from a supplier who has a high turnover and takes flour seriously.

Commercial whole wheat flour is ground quickly in a machine that overheats it, compromising its flavor and nutritional value. Buy stone-ground flour, which is made in a traditional way that doesn't change the flavor or remove the nutrients. Whole wheat bread can be made using any starter. This recipe uses a sourdough starter for maximum flavor.

MAKES TWO 6-CUP LOAVES, 1 BOULE, OR 24 ROLLS

2¼ cups stone-ground whole wheat flour

2¼ cups bread flour

1½ cups barely warm water

2 cups expanded sourdough starter (see page 312)

1 teaspoon salt

Oil for the loaf pans

Before beginning, review the steps for bread making on page 286.

In a bowl, combine the whole wheat flour and bread flour with the water and add the starter. Mix for 1 minute and then add the salt. Knead the dough with a stand mixer fitted with the dough hook on medium speed for about 7 minutes, or by hand for about 12 minutes, or until the dough is smooth and passes the windowpane test (see page 289). Turn the mixer to high speed if needed to get the dough to slap against the sides of the bowl. Allow to rise, covered with plastic wrap or a moist towel, at room temperature for about 6 hours or in the refrigerator for about 15 hours, or until doubled in volume.

Form 2 loaves and put into 2 oiled 6-cup loaf pans or shape the loaf into a *boule* (see page 297). Allow to proof, covered with plastic wrap at room temperature or uncovered in a proofing box (see page 302) for about 3 hours, or until doubled in size. Score as shown here or on page 303.

Preheat the oven to 500°F. Slide a sheet pan on the floor or bottom rack of the oven and allow to heat for 5 minutes. Pour in enough hot water to just cover the bottom of the sheet pan. Place the loaf in the oven above the water in the pan and immediately close the oven door. Crack open the door and spray water into the oven (see page 303). Wait for 30 seconds, crack open the door, and spray again; repeat once more after 30 seconds. Turn down the oven to 425°F. Bake for about 45 minutes, or until the bread is golden brown and a thermometer stuck into the bottom reads at least 205°F. Let cool on a cake rack.

VARIATION

SOURDOUGH WHOLE WHEAT RAISIN BREAD: Knead 1 cup coarsely chopped walnut halves and ½ cup raisins into the dough and allow to rise for about 4 hours, or until doubled in volume. Oil six 2-cup loaf pans. Punch down the dough, shape into 6 small loaves, and put into the prepared pans. Allow to proof for 1 to 4 hours, until almost doubled in volume. Bake at 450°F for about 25 minutes, or until golden brown. Let cool on a rack.

1. Combine all the ingredients except the starter.

2. Measure out 2 cups of sourdough starter.

3. Add the starter to the mixture of ingredients.

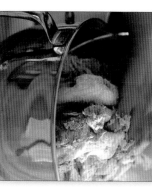

4. Place the mixture in a mixer bowl. Knead until smooth.

5. Cover the dough with plastic wrap and let rise until at least doubled in volume.

6. Shape the dough into loaves or a *boule*. Proof, score, and bake.

1. Knead the dough with the walnuts and raisins, allow to ferment at room temperature covered with plastic wrap or a moist towel. Punch down.

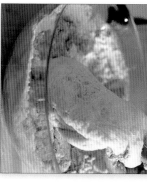

2. Shape the dough by folding the sides into the center and pressing the dough firmly with your fingertips so that the dough from the sides is drawn into the center of the loaf.

3. Continue shaping the dough into a cylinder.

4. Divide the dough into 6 parts.

5. Place the dough in oiled loaf pans and proof until almost doubled in volume.

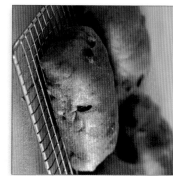

6. Bake until golden brown.

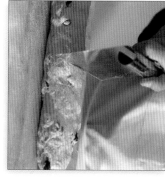

Pumpernickel Bread

If you want the pumpernickel to be dark brown instead of gray, add some cocoa powder to the dough during kneading. This recipe can be made with a natural starter or with yeast.

MAKES TWO 6-CUP OR THREE 4-CUP LOAVES

3 cups pumpernickel flour

2 cups all-purpose flour

Caramel syrup made with 1 cup sugar and ³/4 cup water (page 356)

1¹/2 cups barely warm water

2 cups sourdough starter (page 311), or 1¹/2 teaspoons active dry yeast proofed in ³/4 cup barely warm water

1¹/4 teaspoons salt

¹/2 cup unsweetened cocoa powder (optional)

Oil for loaf pans

Before beginning, review the steps for bread making on page 286.

In a bowl, combine the pumpernickel flour, all-purpose flour, and the caramel syrup and pour over ¹/2 cup plus 2 tablespoons water. Add the remaining water and the sourdough starter or the yeast proof. Cover the dough with plastic wrap or a moist towel and let rest for 20 minutes. Add the salt and knead the mixture with a stand mixer fitted with the dough hook on medium speed for about 7 minutes, or until the dough is smooth and passes the windowpane test (see page 289). Turn the mixer to high speed if needed to get the dough to slap against the sides of the bowl. Let the dough rise for 1 to 4 hours, until doubled in volume. Punch it down. If you like pumpernickel bread dark, knead in the cocoa powder during kneading.

Transfer the dough to oiled loaf pans, cover with plastic wrap, and let rise at room temperature for about 3 hours, or in the refrigerator for about 12 hours, or until doubled in volume.

7. Fold the sides of the loaves in toward the center until they have a cylindrical shape the size of your loaf pans.

8. Put the dough in the oiled loaf pans. Let proof until doubled in volume. Bake.

MAKING PUMPERNICKEL BREAD

1. Start by making the caramel: Stir sugar in a heavy bottom saucepan until melted and deep brown.

2. Pour in ³/4 cup water; stand back. Boil for about 1 minute to dissolve the caramel.

3. Pour the caramel mixture and ¹/2 cup plus 2 tablespoons water over the two kinds of flour.

4. Add the salt, then work in the starter or yeast and the remaining water.

5. Knead until smooth and let double in volume. Punch down the dough.

6. Knead in the optional cocoa powder either by hand or in the mixer.

Preheat the oven to 450°F. Slide a sheet pan on the floor or bottom rack of the oven and allow to heat for 10 minutes. Pour enough hot water to just cover the bottom of the sheet pan. Immediately slide your loaves onto a middle rack over the pan of water. Close the oven door, but a minute later crack it open and spray inside with water (see page 303). Wait for 30 seconds and spray a second time. Bake for about 30 minutes for small loaves, 40 minutes for large loaves, or until a thermometer stuck through the bottom of one of the loaves reads 205°F. Let the loaves cool on a cake rack.

Pizza Dough

You can make pizza using any of the basic white bread doughs, including the straight dough on page 304, the sponge dough on page 306, and even sourdough (page 313), provided the dough isn't too wet and sticky to work with. This basic dough contains olive oil, making it perfect for pizza dough. The olive oil provides flavor and softens the crust. The dough is quite sticky; if it's hard to manage, sprinkle a little extra flour over it, but avoid this if you can.

MAKES 1½ POUNDS DOUGH, ENOUGH FOR
TWO 11-INCH THIN PIZZA CRUSTS

3 cups flour

3/4 cup barely warm water

1/2 teaspoon active dry yeast proofed in 1 tablespoon barely warm water

3/4 teaspoon salt

6 tablespoons extra virgin olive oil

Before beginning, review the steps for bread making on page 286.

Mix the flour, water, and yeast in a bowl. Add the salt and mix, then add the oil. Knead the dough with a stand mixer fitted with the dough hook on medium speed for about 7 minutes, or until the dough is smooth and passes the windowpane test (see page 289). Turn the mixer to high speed if needed to get the dough to slap against the sides of the bowl. You may also, during this time, pull the dough off the hook a couple of times so that the dough is mixed evenly. Put the dough in a bowl and cover with plastic wrap. Allow to double in volume, at room temperature for about 4 hours, or at room temperature for 1 hour and then overnight in the refrigerator.

MAKING PIZZA DOUGH

1. Combine the flour, water, and activated yeast. Mix the dough on slow speed until the ingredients are well combined and cling to the paddle in a single mass.

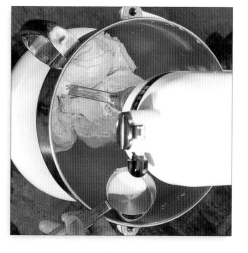

2. Continue kneading until the dough pulls away from the sides and bottom of the bowl. Mix in the salt, then the oil. This immediately liquefies the dough so that it again clings to the walls of the mixer bowl.

3. Continue kneading the dough on medium speed until it stops clinging to the walls of the bowl and instead clings to the paddle.

Pizza Margherita

Much of the trick to making pizza is shaping the dough. While most of us can't send the dough twirling toward the ceiling, everyone can roll it out with a rolling pin or stretch it with their fingers. This dough is dry enough to roll out, but if you're using a sticky dough, it's easier to pull it into a round with your fingers. You can also alternate between stretching the dough and rolling it with a pin.

Once you've made the dough, topping possibilities are limitless. Here are recipes for two pizzas: the classic pizza Margherita found everywhere in Italy and, in the variation, a French pizza made with Roquefort cheese and walnuts.

MAKES TWO 11-INCH PIZZAS

Extra virgin olive oil for brushing

1½ pounds pizza dough (page 319)

4 medium tomatoes, sliced

12 ounces mozzarella cheese, sliced

6 large basil leaves (optional)

Brush two 11-inch pizza pans with olive oil. Divide the dough in half and form each half into a ball, shaping the dough with your fingers, pressing and turning, until the dough is at least somewhat round. Put one ball on each of the pizza pans. Put the pans in the refrigerator for 15 minutes. Shape the dough by pressing on it and stretching it with your fingers or with a rolling pin until it covers the pizza pan. You may have to press and stretch the dough 2 or 3 times, with a 15-minute rest between each time to get the dough to cover the pizza pans. Press up against the edges of the round from the inside to form a border. Brush the dough with olive oil.

Preheat the oven to 500°F. Coat the basil leaves with olive oil, roll them up, and slice the roll so you end up with thin strips. Arrange the tomato slices and cheese slices on the pizza. Bake for about 15 minutes, or until the crust is brown. Just before the pizza is done, sprinkle the basil strips over the top, and bake until done.

VARIATION

ROQUEFORT AND WALNUT PIZZA: Follow the recipe for pizza Margherita, replacing the tomatoes and mozzarella cheese with Roquefort cheese and walnuts. Crumble 8 ounces Roquefort cheese on top of the dough, then sprinkle over 1 cup coarsely chopped walnuts. Bake for about 15 minutes, or until the crust is brown.

1. Divide the dough in two and round both pieces of dough.

2. Start stretching the dough with your fingers, working around the dough, pulling as you go.

3. Start rolling the dough, flouring as you go, to prevent sticking.

4. Stretch the dough with your fingers.

5. You may need to stretch the dough more than once, letting it rest in between.

6. Form a border by pushing along the outside rim of the dough with your fingers so excess dough accumulates and forms a rounded edge.

7. Check the size of the dough with the pizza pan.

8. Roll the dough up on the rolling pin and then over the oiled pan. Press the dough around the edges inward to help form the mounded border.

9. Trim the dough by rolling over it with a rolling pin—if the pan has a rim—and cut away the excess on the edge. If your pan doesn't have a rim, cut around it with a knife. Leave the border you've made inside the pan so it isn't cut off.

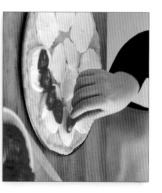

10. Press the dough into the edges of the pan, forming a border as you go. Brush excess flour off the dough and brush the dough with olive oil.

11. To make pizza margherita, prepare the ingredients and arrange them on the pizza dough.

12. Coat the basil leaves with olive oil so they don't turn dark when you slice them.

13. When the pizza is almost done, cut the basil leaves into thin strips and sprinkle over the pizza.

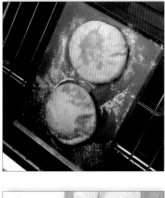

1. Quarter the dough. Roll each quarter into a ball so it's easier to cut in half.

2. Cut each of the quarters in half. Shape the balls by pressing them together at the base with the flats of your hands.

3. Roll each of the balls into 6-inch disks. Flour as needed to prevent sticking.

4. Put the floured sheet pans in the oven for 5 minutes. Put the disks, two at a time, directly on the heated sheet pan. Bake until lightly brown. Let cool.

Pita Bread

While most of us can find pita bread at the supermarket, storebought versions will never have the flavor and texture of freshly baked.

MAKES EIGHT 6-INCH PITA BREADS

3 cups flour

³/₄ **cup barely warm water**

³/₄ **teaspoon active dry yeast proofed in 1 tablespoon barely warm water with 1 tablespoon flour**

³/₄ **teaspoon salt**

¹/₄ **cup plus 2 tablespoons extra virgin olive oil plus more as needed**

Before beginning, review the steps for bread making on page 286.

Mix the flour, water, and yeast in a bowl. Add the salt and mix in, then add the oil. Knead the mixture with a stand mixer fitted with the dough hook on medium speed for about 7 minutes, or by hand for about 12 minutes, or until the dough is smooth and passes the windowpane test (see page 289). Turn the mixer to high speed if needed to get the dough to slap against the sides of the bowl. Brush a bowl with oil and place the dough in it. Cover with plastic wrap and let rise for about 3 hours at room temperature, or until tripled in volume.

Press down the dough. Use a bench scraper to divide the dough into quarters, then cut each quarter in half. Roll each of these pieces into a ball. Roll out the balls into 6-inch disks, flouring as needed to prevent sticking. Because the dough is elastic, you may have to let the disks rest once or twice while you are rolling them out to get them to hold their shape.

Place a pizza stone on the floor of the oven and preheat the oven to 500°F. Flour 2 sheet pans. Arrange the disks on the sheet pans, two per pan, and slide the pans into the oven, two at a time, and cook for about 10 minutes, or until the breads are lightly browned. Turn them over and bake for 2 minutes on the other side. Repeat with the remaining disks.

Bread Sticks (Grissini)

We all want to know how to make those crispy little bread sticks served at the beginning of a meal in some Italian restaurants. Most of those we encounter aren't of very good quality, so you'll be delighted with this homemade version. One of the great things about making these bread sticks is how many you can make with just a small amount of dough. The dough used here is relatively stiff and is flavored with Parmigiano-Reggiano cheese. The rising time is slow because of the salt in the dough and in the cheese. You can also include herbs such as thyme or rosemary.

MAKES SIXTEEN 12-INCH BREAD STICKS

4 cups flour

1 cup barely warm water

3/4 teaspoon active dry yeast (see sidebar, page 304)

1/2 teaspoon salt

4 ounces Parmigiano-Reggiano cheese, finely grated

1/2 cup extra virgin olive oil

Before beginning, review the steps for bread making on page 286.

Put the flour in a bowl and make a well in the middle with the back of your fist. Pour in the water. Sprinkle the yeast over the water and let it sit for 10 minutes. Mix the ingredients, add the salt, and mix for 3 minutes more. Add the cheese and oil and combine. Knead the mixture with a stand mixer fitted with the dough hook on medium speed for about 7 minutes or by hand for about 12 minutes, or until the dough is smooth and passes the windowpane test (see page 289). Turn the mixer to high speed if needed to get the dough to slap against the sides of the bowl. Brush a bowl with oil and place the dough in it. Cover with oiled plastic wrap and let rise for 4 to 6 hours at room temperature, until tripled in volume.

Press down the dough. Preheat the oven to 450°F. Use a bench scraper to divide the dough into quarters, and then divide each quarter into quarters. Roll them with both hands starting from the middle and working outward until the sticks are about 12 inches long. Arrange the sticks on floured sheet pans. Bake the *grissini* for 15 to 20 minutes, until pale brown and crispy—bite into one if you're not sure they are done. Let cool on racks.

1. Put the dough in the oiled bowl and cover with a piece of oiled plastic wrap. Let rise until tripled in volume.

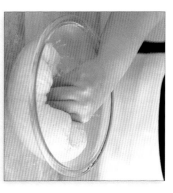

2. Punch down the dough.

3. Cut the dough into quarters and quarter each quarter or use a scale and cut the dough into 2-ounce pieces.

4. Roll the pieces with the flats of your hands. Spread your fingers apart as you roll to stretch the dough from end to end. Place on floured sheet pans. Bake until pale brown.

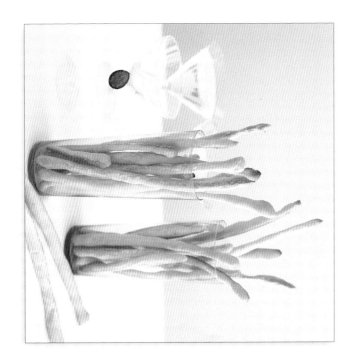

Focaccia

This topping is made by combining Moroccan olives and onions slowly sweated in olive oil, but, like pizza, you can make focaccia with just about anything you like. Using a mixed method, I make the focaccia dough with "leftover dough," which is really just a piece of dough made ahead of time and then combined with the rest of the ingredients before the final rising (see page 285).

MAKES ONE 13 BY 17-INCH FOCACCIA

3 cups flour

1 cup barely warm water

1/2 teaspoon yeast proofed in 1 tablespoon barely warm water for 3 minutes

3/4 teaspoon salt

1/4 cup plus 3 tablespoons extra virgin olive oil plus more as needed

2 pounds red or white onions, sliced very thin

1 cup Moroccan or other dark olives, pitted and halved

Coarse salt for sprinkling

Before beginning, review the steps for bread making on page 286. Make the leftover dough by mixing 1 cup of the flour, 1/2 cup of the water, and the yeast in a bowl. Add 1/4 teaspoon of the salt and mix it in. Let this mixture triple in volume and punch it down.

Put the remaining 2 cups flour, 1/2 cup water, and 1/2 teaspoon salt in the bowl of a stand mixer fitted with the dough hook. Add 1/4 cup of the olive oil and the leftover dough. Mix on slow speed for 2 minutes. Cover the dough with a moist towel or plastic wrap and let rest for 20 minutes. Knead the dough for about 7 minutes, or until the dough is smooth and passes the windowpane test (see page 289). Turn the mixer to high speed if needed to get the dough to slap against the sides of the bowl. Cover the dough with plastic wrap and let rise at room temperature for about 2 hours, or until doubled in volume.

Heat the remaining 3 tablespoons olive oil in a heavy-bottomed pan over medium heat. Add the onions and cook for about 30 minutes, stirring frequently, until the onions soften and turn pale brown. Cover with plastic wrap (to prevent them from turning gray).

Brush a 13 by 17-inch sheet pan with olive oil. Depending on the stickiness of the dough, you can either roll it or press it into shape. You may have to work in 2 or 3 stages, letting the dough rest for 10 minutes in between, to get it into the rectangular shape of the sheet pan. Press along the edges of the dough to form a border and press on the dough with your fingers to make dimples. Cover with plastic wrap and let rest at room temperature for about 1 hour, or until at least twice as thick.

Preheat the oven to 450°F. Spread the onions and olives over the dough, leaving a 1-inch border, drizzle with olive oil, and sprinkle with coarse salt. Don't press on the dough. Bake for about 25 minutes, or until the edges of the focaccia are golden brown. If the focaccia browns unevenly, turn the pan around halfway through the baking. Let cool before serving.

1. Slice the onions and cook them gently for about 30 minutes, or until they release all their moisture and become soft.

2. When the dough has doubled in volume, take it out of the bowl. Punch it down and bring it together on the work surface.

3. Roll the dough into a rectangle, roll it up on the rolling pin, and unroll it over the sheet pan. If it's too sticky, press it into the sheet pan with your fingers.

4. Press the dough into the corners of the sheet pan. There should be a little extra dough all around the focaccia to form the border.

5. Press down the dough with your fingertips to deflate. Cover the dough with plastic wrap and let rise until twice as thick.

6. Spread the onions over the dough. Arrange the olive halves over the onions, leaving a 1-inch border. Drizzle with olive oil and sprinkle with coarse salt.

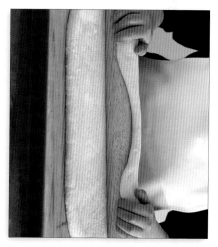

7. Bake until golden brown.

2. Butter each of the molds with a thick layer of room-temperature butter, as shown here for a large mold.

4. Place the pieces of brioche in the buttered molds with the smaller section on top.

6. Place the brioches in a warm place (but not warmer than 86°F) for 1 to 4 hours depending on the temperature of the rising area, until they double in volume. Brush with egg wash and bake until golden brown.

1. Cut the brioche dough into 8 equal pieces, about 3 ounces each. Flatten out each piece of dough slightly with the heel of your hand, then roll into a ball.

3. Dip the side of your hand into flour and roll the balls, one at a time, back and forth with your hand two-thirds from the end of the ball to cause one-third of the dough to partially separate from the bottom two-thirds.

5. Use the ends of 2 fingers to push down to the bottom round of brioche. Work around the mold, pressing firmly so your fingers go all the way to the bottom of the mold.

2. Mix with the dough hook on low to medium speed for about 3 minutes, or until smooth; cover with a moist towel or plastic wrap and let rest for 20 minutes.

1. Stir the salt into the flour to distribute it evenly. (The salt mustn't touch the yeast before it has been evenly distributed in the flour.) Add the egg-yeast mixture to the flour mixture and place in a mixer bowl.

4. Continue mixing until all of the butter is absorbed.

3. Add the butter by handfuls and continue to mix on low to medium speed.

6. Continue mixing for a total of about 10 minutes from the time you added the butter until the dough pulls away from the sides of the bowl.

5. If the dough creeps up to the top of the dough hook, push it down into the bowl with a rubber spatula.

7. Wrap the dough in plastic wrap or put it in a bowl covered with plastic wrap. Let rise until increased in size by 50 percent. Refrigerate until doubled in volume.

Brioche is made with eggs instead of water and once kneaded into a cohesive dough, cold butter is worked in bit by bit. The result is a rich, delicate, soft texture that is simply wonderful served for breakfast with jam and butter. Brioche makes marvelous toast. Recipes for brioche vary in the amount of butter they contain—anywhere from one-fifth the weight of the flour to an equal amount—but this recipe is in the middle. One caveat when making brioche: If the room is hot, the dough will seem too runny when you've added all the butter and you may be tempted to add extra flour; resist the temptation as the dough will firm up once it's chilled.

MAKES 1 BRIOCHE LOAF OR 8 INDIVIDUAL BRIOCHES

3 cups plus 3 tablespoons flour

5 eggs

1½ teaspoons active dry yeast proofed in 1 tablespoon barely warm water and 1 teaspoon flour

½ teaspoon salt

1 cup butter, cut into ½-inch slices, plus room-temperature butter for the mold(s)

Egg wash (see sidebar, page 146)

Before beginning, review the steps for bread making on page 286.

Mix the flour, eggs, and yeast in the bowl of a stand mixer fitted with the dough hook. Mix on medium speed for about 3 minutes, or until well combined. Cover the bowl with a moist towel or plastic wrap and let the dough rest for 20 minutes. Add the salt and knead the dough on medium speed for about 7 minutes, or until the dough is smooth and passes the windowpane test (see page 289). Turn the mixer to high speed if needed to get the dough to slap against the sides of the bowl. Add the butter, a handful at a time, waiting for each batch to be absorbed before adding more. Put the dough in a bowl, cover with plastic wrap, and let rise at room temperature for about 3 hours, or until increased in volume by 50 percent. Refrigerate the dough, without punching down, and let rise until double the original volume. This last cool rising will make the dough firmer and easier to work with.

To make a brioche loaf, brush a 6-cup nonstick loaf pan with room-temperature butter. Divide the dough into 8 equal pieces, about 3 ounces each. Roll each piece into a ball. Arrange the balls in the buttered loaf pan in 2 rows of 4. Cover the loaf pan with oiled plastic wrap and let the brioche rise at room temperature for 2 to 5 hours depending on the temperature, until more than doubled but not quite tripled in volume—up to the rim of the pan.

Preheat the oven to 325°F. Brush with egg wash and bake for about 50 minutes, or until golden brown and hollow sounding when tapped.

To make individual brioches, brush eight 3½-inch (the diameter at the top) fluted molds with room-temperature butter and divide the dough into 8 equal pieces, about 3 ounces each. Round the pieces and then roll them using the side of your hand to form the head. Place the side of your hand two-thirds of the way from one end of the cylinder and roll while pressing down gently. Don't go all the way through the cylinder. Place the cylinder, with the smaller end up, in a mold. Press around the small end—the head—with your fingertips to make the head (tête) poke above the rest of the dough. Repeat with the rest of the dough. Cover with plastic wrap and let rise at room temperature for about 2 hours, or until doubled in volume. Large têtes are made the same way, but with a larger amount of dough.

Preheat the oven to 425°F. Brush the brioches with egg wash and bake for about 35 minutes, or until golden brown and hollow sounding when tapped. You can also insert a thermometer in the bottom of the loaf, which should read 185°F.

MAKING A BRIOCHE LOAF

1. Butter a nonstick loaf pan thickly with room-temperature butter. Roll the dough into 8 equal balls. Arrange the balls in 2 rows in the prepared loaf pan. Let rise.

2. Bake until golden brown. If you are unsure whether the loaf is done, turn it out of the pan and tap it on the bottom. It should have a hollow sound.

Panettone

. . . .

Panettone is a traditional Italian bread usually served at Christmastime. Like brioche and challah, it gets much of its flavor from butter. It also gets flavor from the candied fruits it contains.

MAKES 1 PANETTONE

2 1/3 cups flour

3/4 cup plus 2 tablespoons milk, barely warmed

2 tablespoons sugar

1 teaspoon active dry yeast

1 egg

1/2 teaspoon salt

1/2 cup cold butter, sliced

1 tablespoon grated orange zest (see page 194)

1/4 cup diced dried apricots, steeped in just enough water to cover

1/4 cup dark raisins, steeped in just enough water to cover

1/4 cup golden raisins, steeped in just enough water to cover

1/4 cup diced candied orange peel (see below)

Before beginning, review the steps for bread making on page 286.

Combine the flour, milk, and sugar in a bowl. Sprinkle the yeast over the mixture and let soften for 3 minutes. Add the egg and mix, then add the salt. Mix for 3 minutes, cover with an upturned bowl or plastic wrap, and let rest for 20 minutes. Add the butter and the orange zest. Knead the dough by hand for about 7 minutes or with a standup mixer fitted with the dough hook on medium speed for about 5 minutes, or until all the butter has been absorbed and the dough is smooth and passes the windowpane test (see page 289). Turn the mixer to high speed if needed to get the dough to slap against the sides of the bowl. Drain the dried fruits and mix them and the orange rind into the dough. Cover the dough with plastic wrap pressed against the surface of the dough. Let rise at room temperature for about 3 hours, or for about 1 hour and then overnight in the refrigerator, or until it increases in volume about 50 percent.

Press down the dough, shape it into a ball, and push in any protruding fruit to prevent it from burning. Place the dough in a paper ring so it will hold its shape. (If you can't find the

Candying Orange Peel

Lightly candied orange peel makes a delightful and intense flavoring for dessert soufflés, biscotti, panettone, and cakes. To make 1 cup, peel 3 oranges in rough strips. You're not zesting the oranges, but taking off the whole peel, including the pith, all the way down to the flesh of the orange. Put the peels in a saucepan with enough water to cover and bring to a boil. Boil for 10 minutes, drain off the water, add fresh water to cover, and boil for 10 minutes more. Drain off the water.

Add 1 cup of sugar and 2 cups water to the saucepan. Bring to a slow simmer over low heat and simmer very gently for 40 minutes. If the syrup evaporates too much and you notice that the liquid is very thick and syrupy, add 1/4 cup water and continue simmering over very low heat. The peel is done when the white pith is translucent and waxy looking. If you're unsure, bite into a piece—it should be sweet and not bitter.

Let the peel cool in the syrup. Pour peel and syrup into a clean jar, making sure all the peel is covered with syrup. You can use immediately or store for months on a kitchen shelf.

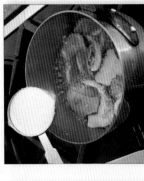

1. Peel 3 oranges in strips, cover with water, and boil for 10 minutes. Drain, cover with water, boil, and drain again.

2. Put the peels back in the saucepan with 1 cup sugar and 2 cups water.

3. Simmer very gently for 40 minutes.

4. Save the peels in their cooking liquid.

traditional paper holders, improvise one with some parchment paper and scotch tape.) Cover the dough with plastic wrap touching the surface and let rise for about 2 hours at room temperature, or until doubled in volume.

Preheat the oven to 375°F. Bake for about 1 hour, or until golden brown on top and 185°F in the center. If the top starts to brown too much before the panettone is done, cover it with aluminum foil. Let cool on racks.

1. Stretch the once fermented and punched down dough on the work surface and sprinkle over the candied orange rind, the apricots, and the raisins.

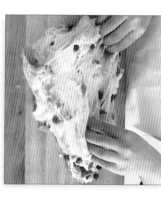

2. Knead the apricots, raisins, and orange rind into the dough, then stretch the dough out so the fruit is evenly distributed.

3. Shape the dough into a ball. Put the dough in a paper mold to rise. Cover the top of the dough with plastic wrap.

4. When the dough has doubled in size, remove the plastic and bake until golden brown.

Challah

Challah is made much like brioche—with lots of eggs—and is traditionally braided. It makes wonderful toast and French toast.

MAKES ONE 17-INCH BRAIDED LOAF

5 cups flour

1/4 cup sugar

1/2 cup milk, barely warmed

5 eggs, warmed in the shell (see page 10)

2 egg yolks

1 teaspoon active dry yeast, proofed in 1 tablespoon barely warm water with 1 teaspoon flour

1 teaspoon salt

Room-temperature butter for the pan

Egg wash (see sidebar, page 146)

Before beginning, review the steps for bread making on page 286.

In a small bowl, combine 1 cup of the flour with the sugar, milk, eggs, egg yolks, and yeast. Stir lightly with a whisk until smooth. Cover with plastic wrap and let ferment for 1 hour at room temperature. In a large bowl, combine the remaining 4 cups flour with the salt. Pour the egg mixture over the flour-salt mixture and mix for about 2 minutes, or long enough to moisten. Cover with an inverted bowl or with plastic wrap and let rest for 20 minutes.

Knead the dough by hand for about 10 minutes or with a stand mixer fitted with the dough hook on medium speed for about 7 minutes, or until smooth. Turn the mixer to high speed if needed to get the dough to slap against the sides of the bowl. Cover with plastic wrap and let rise for about 2 hours at room temperature, or until doubled in volume.

Punch down the dough and divide it into 3 equal pieces. Round the sections by pressing along the sides near the bottom with the sides of your hands. Roll and stretch each ball of dough into a rope about 24 inches long. Since the dough is very elastic, you'll need to stretch the dough in several stages, allowing it to rest for 10 minutes between each stretching and rolling. Butter a 13 by 17-inch sheet pan. Braid the ropes as shown on page 299 and place the loaf on the prepared sheet pan. Cover the loaf with plastic wrap and let it rise for 1 to 2 hours, or until almost doubled in volume.

Preheat the oven to 400°F and set a sheet pan, about one-quarter full of water, on the floor or bottom rack of the oven. Brush the loaf with egg wash. Put the pan with the loaf into the oven on a rack over the water and close the door. Crack open the door and spray with water 3 times at 30-second intervals (see page 303). Turn down the oven to 375°F. Bake for about 45 minutes, until the loaf is deep brown and the inside temperature is 185°F. If the loaf isn't done but it is already brown, cover it loosely with aluminum foil and turn down the oven to 325°F. Let cool on a rack.

1. Mix and ferment the dough, then add the rest of the flour. Knead the dough for about 2 minutes to moisten all the flour.

2. Cover the dough and let rest for 20 minutes.

3. Knead the dough by hand for about 10 minutes, until smooth. Let it rise at room temperature for about 2 hours, or until doubled in volume.

4. Divide the dough into 3 pieces and round each piece of dough into a ball.

5. Roll each ball of dough into a rope about 24 inches long and begin to braid.

6. Braid the ropes as shown on page 299.

7. Place the loaf on a buttered sheet pan. Cover the loaf with plastic wrap and let it rise until almost doubled in volume.

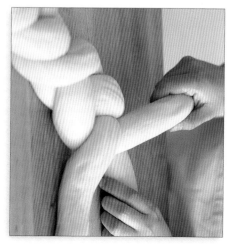

8. Remove the plastic wrap and brush the loaf with egg wash.

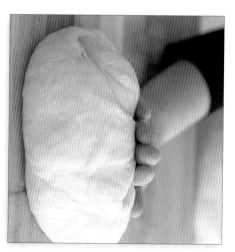

9. Bake until deep brown.

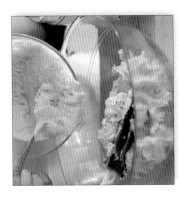

1. First, make the sponge: Stir the yeast-milk mixture into 1/2 cup flour. Cover with plastic wrap and let ferment at room temperature until doubled in volume.

2. Cream the sugar and butter, scraping down the sides of the food processor or mixer to make sure the mixture is well combined.

3. Work in the eggs and egg yolks one or two at a time and process or beat the mixture until smooth.

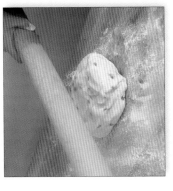

4. Stir in the sponge.

5. Add the raisins, then let the dough rest at room temperature for 1 hour.

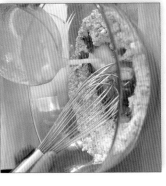

6. Prepare the streusel topping by first combining the flour and sugar, then stirring in the melted butter.

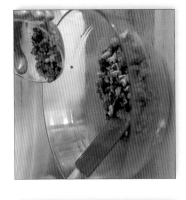

7. Stir in the walnuts.

8. Shape the dough according to the kind of pan you're baking it in (square or round).

9. Tranfer the dough to the buttered pans.

10. Press the dough into the edges of the pans.

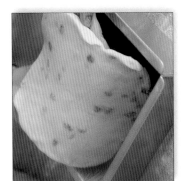

11. Sprinkle the streusel mixture over the coffee cakes and let sit for 90 minutes. Bake until a toothpick inserted comes out clean.

Coffee Cakes

Some coffee cakes are made using baking powder, like quick breads, but this yeast-risen coffee cake is a little like a cross between bread and cake. This recipe contains 3 components—a breadlike sponge mixture, a cake batter, and a streusel topping.

TWO 9-INCH SQUARE OR 10-INCH ROUND CAKES

Sponge

1/2 cup milk, barely warmed

2 teaspoons active dry yeast (see sidebar, page 304)

1/2 cup flour

Batter

3/4 cup butter, at room temperature

1/4 cup sugar

1/2 teaspoon salt

3 eggs

2 cups flour

1/2 cup raisins, soaked in just enough water to cover, drained

2 teaspoons grated lemon or orange zest (see page 194)

1 teaspoon vanilla extract

Topping

1 cup flour

2 cups firmly packed dark brown sugar

1 cup butter, melted

1/2 cup chopped walnuts

Room-temperature butter for the pans

To make the sponge, pour the milk into a bowl. Sprinkle the yeast over the milk and let steep for 3 minutes. Stir in the flour and mix until well combined. Cover with plastic wrap and let rise at room temperature for about 45 minutes, or until at least doubled in volume.

To make the batter, while the sponge is rising, cream the butter, sugar, and salt in a food processor, with a mixer, or by hand. Work in the eggs, one at a time, followed by the flour. Combine in a food processor for 5 seconds, with a stand mixer for about 30 seconds, or with a handheld mixer for about 1 minute, or just long enough to make a smooth mixture. Add the sponge to the egg mixture. Add the raisins, zest, and vanilla. Stir together, then knead for about 3 minutes, or until smooth. Cover with plastic wrap and let rise at room temperature for 1 to 1 1/2 hours, until increased in size by 50 percent.

To make the streusel topping, combine the flour and sugar, then stir in the melted butter and, finally, the walnuts. Set aside.

To finish the coffee cakes, brush two 9-inch square baking dishes or two 10-inch round cake pans with butter. Divide the dough in half and shape it with your hands or a rolling pin to the same size as the pans. Set the dough in the pans and cover with the streusel topping. Let sit at room temperature for about 90 minutes, or until increased in height by 50 percent.

Preheat the oven to 350°F. Bake for about 50 minutes, or until a toothpick comes out clean. Let cool for 10 minutes and turn out of the pans onto a cake rack.

Cinnamon Rolls

. . . .

Cinnamon rolls are made with a basic dough flavored with vanilla, orange zest, and cinnamon, covered with a sweet filling, rolled up, and then sliced to make the rolls. You can make cinnamon rolls with regular yeast or you can use a natural starter to give them more flavor. Both methods are given here.

MAKES 2 POUNDS DOUGH, ENOUGH FOR 10 CINNAMON ROLLS

Using a yeast starter

1 1/2 teaspoons active dry yeast (see sidebar, page 304)

4 cups flour

1 cup barely warm water

2/3 cup cream

1 egg

1 teaspoon salt

Using a natural starter

4 1/2 cups flour

1/2 cup cream

1 egg

1 teaspoon salt

2 cups natural starter (see page 311)

Flavorings

1 teaspoon vanilla extract

1 tablespoon grated orange zest (see page 194)

1 teaspoon ground cinnamon

Filling

1/2 cup butter

1/4 teaspoon salt

1 1/2 cups light brown sugar

Oil for the pan

Egg wash (see sidebar, page 146)

Before beginning, review the steps for bread making on page 286.

To make a yeast-leavened dough: In a bowl, combine the yeast with 1 cup of the flour and the water and leave at room temperature for about 2 hours, or until doubled in volume. Add the remaining flour, the cream, egg, salt, and the flavorings. Knead in a stand mixer fitted with the dough hook at medium speed for about 7 minutes or by hand for about 12 minutes, or until smooth. Turn the mixer to high speed if needed to get the dough to slap against the sides of the bowl. Cover with plastic wrap and let rise at room temperature for about 1 hour, or until doubled in volume.

To make the dough with a natural starter: Combine the flour, cream, egg, and salt with the natural starter and the flavorings and knead and let rise as above, except count on a rising time closer to 6 hours.

To make the filling: In a heavy-bottomed saucepan over medium heat, combine all the ingredients and stir. When the butter has melted and the mixture is bubbling, turn the heat down to low and continue stirring for about 5 minutes, or until the mixture smells like butterscotch.

To make the rolls: Punch down the dough gently and press it into a 14-inch square on a smooth oiled surface, such as a large sheet pan. If the dough is very elastic and won't hold its shape, cover it with plastic wrap and let it rest in the refrigerator for 15 minutes, then try again. Spread the filling over the dough with an offset spatula, leaving a 1/2-inch border. Pinch along one wider side, so the roll starts out tight, and roll up the dough. Trim the ends, then slice the log into 1-inch rounds by sliding a piece of dental floss under one end of the log and pulling the two ends across each other. Place the rolls on an oiled or nonstick sheet pan, leaving at least 2 inches between the rolls to allow them to expand; cover with plastic wrap. Let proof at room temperature for about 30 minutes, or until slightly puffed.

Preheat the oven to 400°F. Brush the rolls gently with egg wash, and lower the oven temperature to 350°F. Bake for about 40 minutes, or until golden brown. Let the rolls cool on a cake rack.

1. Combine the filling ingredients in a saucepan over medium heat. Cook until smooth, stirring, about 5 minutes. Let cool.

2. Roll the dough into a 14-inch square.

3. Pour the filling mixture over the dough and spread it, leaving a 1/2-inch border.

4. Start rolling the dough by folding over a tiny bit of one end and pinching it and continuing to roll it, bit by bit, as tightly as possible.

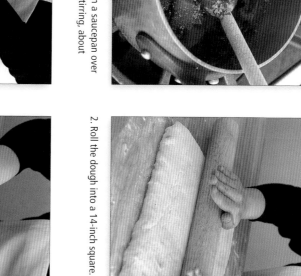

5. Roll up the dough as tightly as you can.

6. Trim off the uneven ends, then slice the roll into 1-inch-thick rolls by sliding a piece of dental floss under the roll and then pulling the ends, effectively cutting the roll into slices.

7. Arrange the slices on an oiled or nonstick sheet pan. If you want the rolls to stick together, leave no room between them; otherwise leave at least 2 inches. Glaze the cinnamon rolls with egg wash then bake until golden brown.

Sticky Buns

. . . .

These sticky buns are essentially the same as the cinnamon rolls except the filling is different and the rolled buns are baked in pans that have been lined with a sweet nut mixture. When the buns are turned out of the pans, the sticky nut mixture comes with them as their topping.

MAKES 9 SMALL STICKY BUNS

Oil for the work surface and pan

1 recipe cinnamon roll dough (page 334)

1/3 cup melted butter

1/4 cup plus 2 tablespoons brown sugar

11/4 cups chopped walnuts

Topping

1/4 cup dark brown sugar

1/2 cup butter, melted

2/3 cup chopped walnuts

To make the dough roll, on an oiled work surface, roll, stretch, and press on the dough to form an 11 by 16-inch rectangle. Brush the dough generously with the melted butter. Sprinkle over the sugar and walnuts. Roll up the dough as tightly as you can. Chill the dough for 30 minutes to make it easier to slice.

To make the topping, in a small saucepan, heat the sugar and butter over medium heat until smooth, then pour into an oiled 9-inch square baking pan. Sprinkle the chopped walnuts over the topping.

Slice the roll into 9 rounds using dental floss or a sharp knife, and arrange these in the baking pan, in 3 rows of 3 each, over the topping. Cover with plastic wrap and let sit at room temperature for about 1 hour.

Preheat the oven to 375°F. Place the baking pan on a sheet pan and slide it into the oven. Don't put the pan directly on a stone or on the bottom of the oven or the topping may burn. Bake for about 60 minutes, or until a toothpick comes out clean. While the buns are still hot, slide a knife all along the sides of the pan to detach them. Let cool for about 5 minutes before turning the sticky buns out onto a plate. Don't wait too long or the topping will congeal and cause the buns to cling to the pan. If that happens, heat the bottom of the pan gently until the buns release.

1. Combine the sugar and butter for the topping in a saucepan and stir over medium heat until smooth.

2. Pour the mixture into an oiled 9-inch square baking pan. Rotate to coat.

3. Sprinkle the mixture with the chopped walnuts for the topping (not the filling).

4. Roll the dough into a rectangle and brush it with melted butter.

5. Sprinkle with sugar and walnuts and roll up the dough.

6. Trim off the ends and slice the log into 9 rounds with dental floss.

7. Arrange the slices of rolled dough in the sugar glaze—and nut-lined pan.

8. Bake until a toothpick slid into one of the buns comes out clean. While the buns are still hot, slide a knife all along the sides of the pan to detach them.

9. Turn a plate upside down over the pan of buns. Hold the baking dish with one hand and the plate with the other and turn over. Give the pan a shake, and take it away, leaving the buns on the plate.

10. Serve the finished sticky buns so that guests can pull them apart themselves.

QUICK BREADS AND BREAD-BASED DESSERTS

Quick breads are breads made without yeast. They usually contain another leavening, such as baking powder or baking soda. This section contains some classic quick breads, such as muffins, scones, and biscuits, and a few dessert recipes that rely on biscuits or bread for a base.

Banana Nut Bread Muffins

Like apricot bread and other fruit breads, banana bread is a quick bread, made with a chemical leavening such as baking powder or baking soda instead of yeast. Banana bread batter also makes great muffins. The muffin cups shown here each hold 3 ounces of batter. You can also use larger muffin cups to make fewer muffins.

MAKES 12 MUFFINS

1/4 cup plus 2 tablespoons butter, melted, plus more for the muffin cups

2 ripe bananas

2 cups flour

1/2 teaspoon salt

1/2 teaspoon baking soda

1/2 teaspoon baking powder

2 eggs

2 egg whites

1/2 cup granulated sugar

1/2 cup brown sugar

2/3 cup toasted and coarsely chopped walnuts

Preheat the oven to 350°F. Butter the muffin cups.

Mash the bananas using a pastry cutter or potato masher.

In a large bowl, whisk together the flour, salt, baking soda, and baking powder. In a bowl, combine the butter, eggs, egg whites, granulated sugar, and brown sugar, then pour the mixture over the flour mixture. Add the nuts and bananas. Fold the mixture just long enough to moisten the dry ingredients. Scoop the mixture into the muffin cups.

Bake for about 25 minutes, or until a toothpick comes out clean. Turn the muffins out on a rack to cool.

MAKING BANANA NUT BREAD MUFFINS

1. Use a pastry cutter or potato masher to mash the bananas.

2. Whisk together the liquid ingredients, then whisk in the brown and white sugars.

3. Stir the sugar mixture into the flour mixture, then fold in the walnuts and bananas.

4. Use a 3-ounce ice cream scoop to transfer the dough into the muffin cups. Bake.

Apricot Bread

These loaves aren't bread in the classic sense—they contain no yeast—but are quick breads leavened with baking powder. But they look like bread because they are baked in loaves. You can bake the batter in 3 small loaf pans, or make a larger single loaf and bake it at 350°F. You can use this recipe as a model for a variety of fruit and nut breads by substituting other dried fruits for the apricots and adding the same volume of nuts as fruit.

MAKES THREE 2-CUP LOAVES

2 cups dried apricots, cut into ⅓-inch dice

½ cup butter, at room temperature, plus more for the loaf pans

1½ cups flour

1 teaspoon baking powder

¼ teaspoon salt

½ cup sugar

1 teaspoon vanilla extract

2 eggs, beaten

½ cup milk

Cut the dried apricots into ⅓-inch cubes and pour over just enough boiling water to barely cover. Let sit for 20 minutes and drain. Preheat the oven to 375°F. Butter three 3½ by 6-inch loaf pans.

In a bowl, whisk together the flour, baking powder, and salt. In a large bowl, cream the butter, sugar, and vanilla. Don't worry if it's a little lumpy. Add the eggs one at a time and beat until smooth. Fold in half of the flour mixture, half of the milk, the rest of the flour mixture, and the rest of the milk. Fold in the apricot cubes. Fill the loaf pans about three-quarters full. Smooth the tops with an offset spatula.

Bake for about 40 minutes for small loaves, 50 minutes for a large loaf, or until a knife slid into the loaves comes out clean.

1. Cut the dried apricots into ⅓-inch cubes and pour over just enough boiling water to barely cover. Let sit for 20 minutes and drain.

2. Combine the butter, sugar, and vanilla in a bowl. Beat the mixture until well combined. Don't worry if it's a little lumpy.

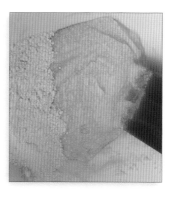

3. Add the eggs one at a time. Beat the mixture until smooth. Fold in half the flour mixture, half the milk, the rest of the flour mixture, and the rest of the milk.

4. Fold in the apricot cubes.

5. Fill the loaf pans about three-quarters full. Smooth the tops with an offset spatula.

6. Bake until a knife slid into the loaves comes out clean.

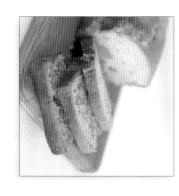

Popovers

• • • • • • • • • • • • • • • • • • • •

If you're making popovers for the first time, your first batch may surprise you because there is nothing about the raw ingredients—a liquid batter with no leavening—that hints at their eventual airiness. Though nothing could be easier to make, there is one essential trick for guaranteeing success. They must be baked in a heavy pan—the heavier the better—and not in regular muffin tins, which retain too little heat. If there is not enough heat held in the pan, the butter just sits there and bakes as you'd think it would, into a congealed little puck. A heavy pan, on the other hand, delivers intense heat for the first minute or so, the critical minute essential to causing the popovers to rise. So it makes sense to buy a popover pan that you can also use for muffins instead of the other way around. You can also use 2 muffin tins the same size nestled together. Serve popovers right out of the oven with some good butter and preserves.

MAKES 16 POPOVERS

2 cups flour

³/₄ teaspoon salt

4 eggs

2²/₃ cups milk

¹/₂ cup butter, melted

3 tablespoons vegetable oil or more as needed

Preheat the oven to 500°F. Combine the flour, salt, eggs, and enough of the milk to make a stiff batter. Smooth out the lumps with a whisk and whisk in the rest of the milk and the butter. Let the batter rest at room temperature for 30 minutes. Put the popover molds in the oven to preheat for 10 minutes, then quickly open the oven door and brush with vegetable oil. Give the oil a minute to heat up and then quickly pour in the batter—using a pitcher is easiest—to come three-quarters up the sides of the molds.

Bake for about 20 minutes, or until golden brown, turn down the oven to 300°F and bake for 10 minutes more. Serve immediately with butter or jam.

MAKING POPOVERS ——————

Pour the batter into each of the cups so it comes three-quarters up the sides. The batter will expand immediately.

Blueberry Muffins

· ·

You can use any berry you like in this basic muffin recipe. One trick: Toss the berries with flour, which keeps them from sinking in the muffin cups and all ending up on the bottom. Use muffin tins with 6-ounce cups.

MAKES TWELVE 6-OUNCE MUFFINS

1/2 cup butter, at room temperature, plus more
    for the muffin cups

1³/4 cups plus 2 tablespoons flour plus more
    for the muffin cups

1 teaspoon baking soda

1/2 teaspoon baking powder

1/2 teaspoon salt

3/4 cup granulated sugar

2 eggs

1/2 cup sour cream

1/4 cup milk

1 pint blueberries

Confectioners' sugar (optional)

Preheat the oven to 350°F. Unless you are using a nonstick pan as shown here, brush the muffin tins with butter and dust them with flour. In a bowl, whisk together the 1³/4 cups flour, the baking soda, baking powder, and salt. In a large bowl, cream the butter and granulated sugar by hand or with a handheld mixer for about 4 minutes, or until smooth. Add the eggs one by one, waiting until the first egg is absorbed before adding the second. Sift the dry ingredients over the bowl and stir in the sour cream and milk. Stir the mixture with a rubber spatula until all the liquid is absorbed and there is no loose flour in the bowl. Don't overwork the mixture. Toss the blueberries with the 2 tablespoons flour and fold them into the batter. Fill the cups of the muffin tins three-quarters full with batter.

Bake for about 25 minutes, or until golden brown and a knife or toothpick stuck into one of the muffins comes out clean. Turn out onto a cake rack and sprinkle with confectioners' sugar.

MAKING BLUEBERRY MUFFINS

1. Toss the blueberries with flour and fold them into the batter.

2. Spoon the batter into the muffin cups.

3. Sprinkle the finished muffins with confectioners' sugar (optional).

1. When the dough starts to come together, scrape it away from the sides of the bowl with a bench scraper.

2. Dump the dough onto a work surface and knead slightly to get it to come together. Pull the dough into a mound. It should barely hold together.

3. Use the heel of your hand to flatten the mound into a disk.

4. Roll the dough out into a 2/3-inch-thick disk and cut out the biscuits with a fluted cookie cutter.

5. Bake until golden brown.

Baking Powder Biscuits

While really more akin to pastry than to bread, baking powder biscuits are best served hot at a meal, perhaps a special meal, where they can accompany meats or other substantial foods. You can make these by hand in a bowl, by hand on a work surface, in a mixer, or in a food processor. Here, the biscuits are made in a bowl with a pastry cutter.

MAKES 1 1/2 POUNDS DOUGH, 12 BISCUITS

2 cups flour

1 teaspoon baking soda

1/4 teaspoon salt

1/2 cup cold butter, thinly sliced

3/4 cup buttermilk or more as needed

Preheat the oven to 400°F. In a large bowl, stir together the flour, baking soda, and salt. Place the butter over the dry ingredients so none of the pieces is clinging to another and cut through the mixture with a pastry cutter until the butter is about the size of peas. Add the buttermilk and combine the mixture with a rubber spatula just long enough to absorb the liquid and any loose flour. If you still see loose flour, add another 2 tablespoons buttermilk. Don't overwork the dough.

Dump the dough out onto a work surface and use your hands to gather it together into a mound. Flatten it into a disk. At this point, it may be necessary to knead it a little to get it to hold together. Don't knead it any more than necessary for it to hold together in a loose shaggy mass. Roll it out into a 2/3-inch-thick disk and use a 2 1/2-inch fluted cookie cutter to cut out the biscuits. Place them on a sheet pan. Gather up the scraps, roll out again, and cut more biscuits.

Turn down the oven to 375°F. Bake for about 20 minutes, or until golden brown. Serve right out of the oven.

Scones

Scones are a lot like biscuits, but the dough is lightly sweetened. This recipe can accommodate any sort of dried fruit.

MAKES 8 SCONES

3 cups flour

5 tablespoons sugar

1 tablespoon plus 1 teaspoon baking powder

½ teaspoon salt

1 cup cold butter, thinly sliced

1¼ cups milk or heavy cream plus more as needed

1 cup dried cranberries, cherries, or diced dried apricots, soaked for 30 minutes in just enough hot water to cover, drained

Preheat the oven to 375°F. In a large bowl, whisk together the flour, sugar, baking powder, and salt. Arrange the butter on top so the slices don't overlap and cut through the mixture with a pastry cutter until the butter is about the size of peas. Add the milk and stir the mixture just long enough to absorb the milk and any loose flour. If you still see loose flour, add another 2 tablespoons milk. Sprinkle the cranberries over the mixture while stirring so they are evenly distributed in the dough. Stir together the dough with a rubber spatula for about 1 minute. Don't overwork the dough.

Dump the dough out onto a work surface and use your hands to gather it together into a mound, then flatten it into a disk. At this point, it may be necessary to knead it a little to get it to hold together. Don't knead it any more than necessary for it to hold together in a loose shaggy mass. Roll it out into a ¾-inch-thick disk. Cut the disk into 8 wedges and put them on a baking sheet.

Turn down the oven to 350°F. Bake for about 30 minutes, or until the scones are pale brown.

MAKING SCONES

1. Once you have mixed the dough, you can knead it in the bowl or, as shown here, on a work surface. Bring the dough together into a mound. Don't overwork it—it should look a bit ragged.

2. Flatten the mound into a ¾-inch-thick disk with the heel of your hand or with a rolling pin. Cut the disk into wedges and bake until pale brown.

Cherry Cobblers

A cobbler is simply fruit—here, Bing cherries—baked with crumbled biscuit dough on top. The crisp dough provides a contrasting texture to the soft fruit. You can make cobblers out of just about any fruit, fresh or frozen. And unlike fruit pies and tarts for which you have to do something to absorb the liquid released by the raw fruit, for cobblers this is unimportant. In fact, a cobbler with hot runny fruit juice in the bottom of the dish is quite lovely. The ratio of fruit to dough depends on the shape of the baking dishes—the wider the dish, the more dough. You can use 5-ounce crème brulée dishes, but heatproof bowls, custard cups, ramekins, or little soufflé dishes will all work. You can also make one large cobbler and serve it at the table.

1 pound (about 4¹/₂ cups) fresh or frozen Bing or
  sour cherries, pitted and halved

¹/₄ cup sugar (twice this amount if using sour cherries)
  plus 2 tablespoons for sprinkling

2 tablespoons lemon juice (optional)

1 recipe biscuit dough (page 342)

1 teaspoon ground cinnamon (optional)

Whipped cream (page 62), ice cream, crème fraîche,
  or crème anglaise (page 54) for serving

Preheat the oven to 375°F. Toss the cherries with the ¹/₄ cup sugar and lemon juice and distribute them evenly among six 5-ounce ramekins or crème brulée dishes. Crumble the biscuit dough over the fruit. Sprinkle the cobblers with the 2 tablespoons sugar. If you like, sprinkle a little ground cinnamon over the sugar.

Bake for about 30 minutes, or until the biscuit dough is golden brown and the fruit is bubbling. If the dough is browned but the fruit isn't bubbling, turn down the oven to 300°F and bake for 10 minutes more.

Serve right out of the oven with whipped cream, ice cream, crème fraîche, or crème anglaise.

MAKING CHERRY COBBLERS

Spoon the cherry mixture into ramekins or, as shown here, crème brulée dishes. Crumble the biscuit dough over the fruit. Sprinkle the cobblers with sugar. If you like, sprinkle on a little ground cinnamon.

There are three schools of thought about making shortcakes. One, the biscuit school, insists that the dough be stiff enough to roll or at least shape with two hands. Another calls for a more liquid dough or rather a batter that can be dropped on the sheet pan with two spoons. A third uses sponge cake. The rolling and shaping method is shown here, but if you want a more batterlike mixture, add an additional 1/3 cup heavy cream and spoon the batter onto the sheet pan.

MAKES 8 SHORTCAKES

2 cups flour

1/4 cup granulated sugar

1 teaspoon baking soda

1/2 teaspoon salt

1/2 cup cold butter, thinly sliced

1 egg

3/4 cup buttermilk or more as needed

2 tablespoons turbinado or granulated sugar

1 cup whipped cream made with heavy cream or crème fraîche (page 62)

2 pints strawberries, hulled and sliced (see page 86), and tossed with 1 tablespoon sugar or more to taste

Preheat the oven to 375°F. In a large bowl, whisk together the flour, sugar, baking soda, and salt. Add the butter and cut in with a pastry cutter until the pieces are no larger than small peas. In a small bowl, combine the egg with the buttermilk and pour the mixture over the dough. Stir together the mixture with a rubber spatula until there is no uncombined flour on the bottom of the bowl. If you see a lot of loose flour, add one or two tablespoons more buttermilk and mix again.

Dump the dough out onto a work surface and use your hands to gather it together into a mound, then flatten into a disk. At this point, it may be necessary to knead it a little to get it to hold together. Don't knead it any more than necessary for it to hold together in a loose shaggy mass. Roll it out into a 3/4-inch-thick disk. Use a 3 1/4-inch cookie cutter to cut out the shortcakes and arrange them on a parchment paper–lined sheet pan. Brush each of the shortcakes with buttermilk and sprinkle over the turbinado sugar.

Bake for about 20 minutes, or until pale brown.

Just before serving, slice the shortcakes in half horizontally with a serrated knife. Arrange the strawberries over the bottom halves of the shortcakes—work directly over the serving plates so there is less transferring—and dollop the whipped cream over them. Put on the lids and serve.

MAKING STRAWBERRY SHORTCAKES

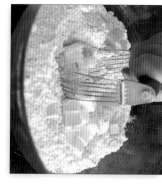

1. Mix the dry ingredients. Sprinkle the butter over the flour mixture. Use a pastry cutter to cut the butter into pieces about the size of small peas.

2. Add the egg and buttermilk. Stir the mixture together with a rubber spatula. If you see a lot of loose flour on the bottom of the bowl, add 1 or 2 tablespoons more of buttermilk and mix again.

3. Divide the dough into balls, a half-cup each, all the same size. Flatten into disks.

4. Brush the disks with buttermilk and sprinkle with turbinado sugar. Bake until pale brown.

5. Slice the shortcakes crosswise in half.

6. Put the bottom halves of the shortcakes on a platter or on individual plates and arrange sliced strawberries over each half.

7. Dollop the strawberries with whipped cream and put on the lids.

Cut the crusts off 16 slices of bread and cut each of the slices into 3 equal strips. Melt the remaining butter and use it to brush the bread strips on both sides. Press one of the strips against the side of the mold. Keep the strip vertical and make sure it touches the bottom of the mold. Crush the bread if necessary to hold it in place. Continue with more strips—each mold needs 12—overlapping them as little as possible but enough that no filling will show through. Cut rounds out of 4 remaining bread slices, 1 round per slice—make the largest cutouts the slices will allow (you can always cut them smaller)—and brush them on both sides with butter. Press the rounds into the bottoms of the molds so they press up against the bread strips. Keep in mind that they will shrink in the oven and should be as large as possible while still lying flat.

Preheat the oven to 350°F. Fill the bread-lined molds with the apples, pressing them firmly into the molds. Make sure the apples come at least 1/2 inch over the rims of the molds to make up for their shrinking in the oven. Bake for about 1 hour, or until the bread is golden brown on the sides. To see the bread, stick a small knife along the side of a charlotte and press the bread gently inward. Trim off the ends of the bread with a serrated knife. Let cool for 1 hour and refrigerate for at least 2 more hours.

To get the charlottes out of the molds, dip them in a bowl of hot water for 1 minute to melt the butter that's holding them in the molds. Hold a plate over each of the molds, turn the whole assembly over, and lift off the molds. Warm the charlottes in a microwave for 3 or 4 minutes or in a 250°F oven for 30 minutes. Don't get the charlottes too hot or they may collapse. Serve in halves or wedges with whipped cream or vanilla ice cream.

Apple Charlottes

These old-fashioned desserts, which combine the flavors of apples, butter, and vanilla, provide a warming contrast when served with whipped cream or vanilla ice cream. You can make 12-ounce charlottes in the traditional molds with heart-shaped handles—each charlotte serves 2 or more—but you can also make smaller versions in ramekins. If you're using ramekins, the overlapping of vertical bread strips may be too minute and tedious; instead, wrap a strip or two of bread, on its side, to line the sides. Cram in as long a strip or two as you can—the bread shrinks in the oven.

MAKES FOUR 12-OUNCE CHARLOTTES

8 large sweet apples, such as Golden Delicious, peeled, halved, and cored

1 cup butter

1 vanilla bean, split in half lengthwise (optional)

3/4 cup sugar

1 loaf tight-crumbed sliced white bread, such as Pepperidge Farm (at least 20 slices)

Sweetened whipped cream (see page 62) or vanilla ice cream for serving (optional)

Cut the apple halves crosswise in thirds and again in thirds lengthwise so you end up with 9 rough cubes per half. Melt 1/2 cup of the butter in a large nonstick pan and add the apples. Add the vanilla bean and sprinkle the sugar over the apples. Toss or gently stir the apples over medium heat for about 15 minutes, or until they are golden brown and soft and any liquid they release has evaporated. Remove the vanilla bean.

1. Cut each apple half crosswise in thirds and then lengthwise in thirds to make 9 pieces.

2. Gently sauté the apples in butter, with sugar and the optional vanilla bean. Cook until the apples are soft and deep brown.

3. Cut the crusts off 16 white bread slices. Cut each slice into 3 strips.

4. Cut rounds as large as possible out of 4 slices.

5. Brush the bread strips on both sides with melted butter.

6. Press the strips against the sides of the molds, overlapping just slightly. Brush the bread rounds on both sides with butter.

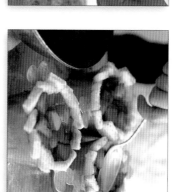

7. Press the bread rounds into the molds against the strips.

8. Spoon the cooked apples into the molds—press on them firmly—until they come at least 1/2 inch above the rim of the mold.

9. Bake until the bread is golden brown on the sides. Trim off the ends of the bread with a serrated knife.

10. Allow to cool for 1 hour and refrigerate for at least 2 hours. Dip the charlottes in hot water briefly. Turn a charlotte over a plate and lift off the mold. Serve warm or at room temperature with whipped cream or ice cream.

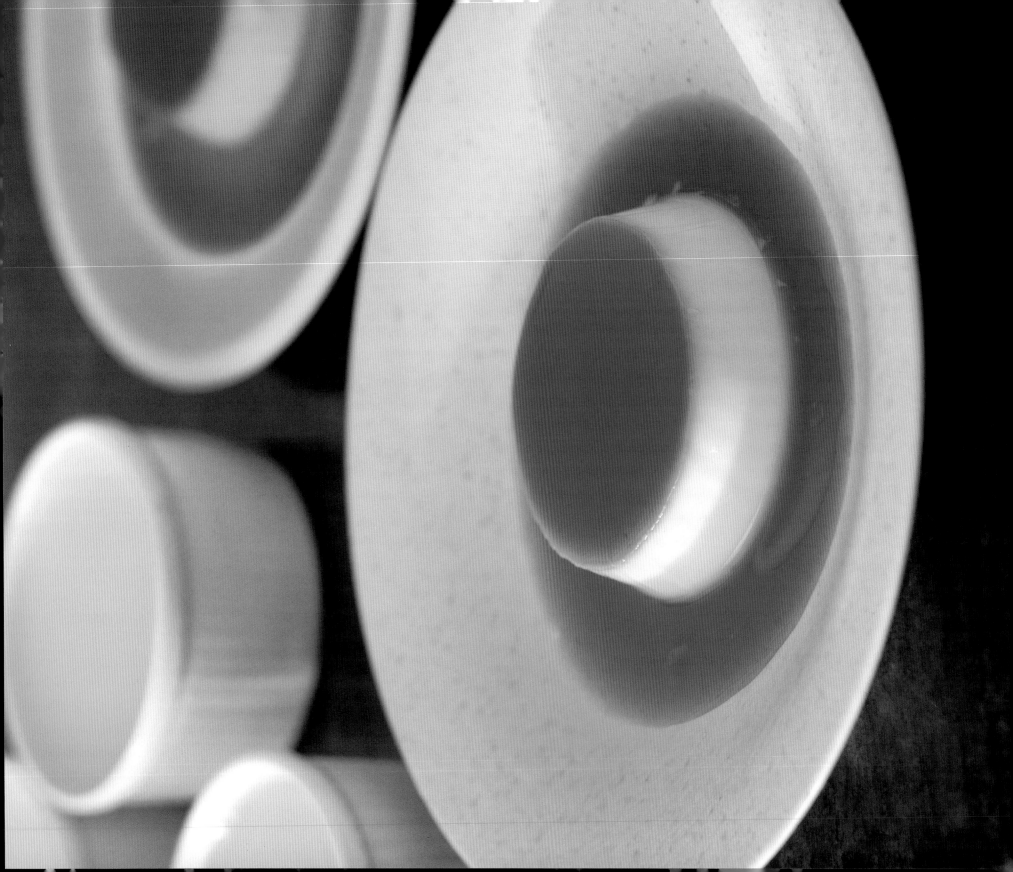

CUSTARDS, SOUFFLÉS, FRUIT CURDS, AND MOUSSES

Coffee *Pots de Crème* · 353

Crèmes Caramels · 355

Crèmes Brûlées · 357

Cheese Soufflés · 359

Grand Marnier Soufflés · 362

Lemon Curd · 364

Passion Fruit Curd · 364

Passion Fruit Mousse · 365

Classic Chocolate Mousse · 366

White Chocolate Mousse · 367

Flourless Chocolate Cake · 368

Methods and Techniques

Making Coffee Pots de Crème • 353

Making Crèmes Caramels • 354

Caramel • 356

Making Caramel and Caramel Sauce • 356

Making Crèmes Brûlées • 357

Making Cheese Soufflés • 360

Making Grand Marnier Soufflés • 363

Making Lemon Curd • 364

Making Passion Fruit Curd • 365

Repairing Chocolate Mixtures that Have Seized • 366

Making Classic Chocolate Mousse • 367

Making White Chocolate Mousse • 367

Making a Flourless Chocolate Cake • 369

CUSTARDS

This is a chapter of spoonable, even spreadable, desserts. Most are baked, but several are made on the stovetop (mousses, curds), and these typically have versatile and various uses—for example, mousses are capable of being served on their own or used as a filling for cakes, pies, or tarts.

A custard is a liquid or semiliquid mixture that is combined with eggs or egg yolks and then gently cooked until it sets—either on the stovetop in a double boiler or in the oven in a bain marie, or water-filled baking pan. Virtually any sweet or savory mixture can be combined with beaten egg—one egg sets about 2/3 cup of mixture—and baked into a custard.

While terrifying to many cooks, not too much can go wrong with a soufflé. You need only be careful with the egg whites—make sure the bowl is dry and grease free and there is not a speck of yolk anywhere—and avoid overcooking the soufflés, which causes them to fall the instant they come out of the oven.

Most of us adore chocolate mousse served alone, but many of us don't realize that mousses can be used as fillings for cakes. In French, *mousse* means froth or foam: Shaving cream and the foam on the ocean are both *mousses*. Chocolate mousse makes a beautiful filling for cakes: While deeply flavorful, it's lighter than buttercream because it contains air.

Fruit curds, especially lemon curd, are among the most popular tart fillings because they're light and sweet without being too sweet and because they provide a tangy and refreshing accent to the fruit. They can also be used as a spread on scones or other breads, or folded together with whipped cream to make a mousse.

Most familiar custards are sweet custards such as crème caramel, crème brûlée, and *pots de crème*. Custards can be made with fruit juices or purees and baked in tarts like those shown on pages 186 to 195. While the most common dessert custards are made in virtually the same way, they have varying consistencies depending on whether they're made with milk, cream, or a mixture of milk and cream and whether they've been set with whole eggs, egg yolks, or a mixture of the two. The pots de crème are made with a mixture of milk and cream set with egg yolks; the crème caramel is made with milk and whole eggs plus egg yolks; and, the richest of all, crème brûlée is made with all cream and egg yolks.

Once the ingredients for the custards have been combined, they're gently baked, usually in a bain marie, which helps the custards cook evenly and keeps them from overheating and curdling. While vanilla is the most popular sweet-custard flavoring, the possibilities are limitless. You can flavor custards with ground spices such as ginger or cinnamon; spirits such as rum, Cognac, or kirsch; fruit purees such as raspberry; chocolate; or coffee.

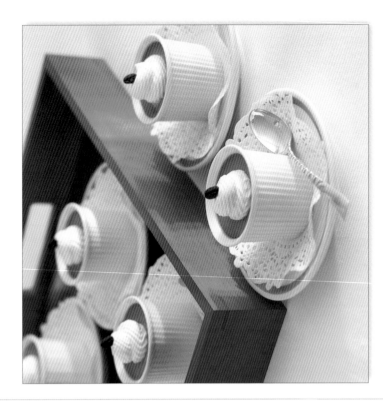

Coffee Pots de Crème

Pots de crème (pronounced *poe de krem*) get their name from the little pots with lids that are traditionally used to bake the custard. Since these are expensive and have only one use, you can use small ramekins instead. Because *pots de crème* are made with a mixture of milk and cream, they are halfway in richness between crème caramel and crème brûlée. These pots de crème are flavored with coffee, which is easiest to do by whisking some instant coffee into the hot milk and cream. However, a much deeper coffee flavor is extracted by infusing the hot milk and cream with ground coffee and then straining it out.

MAKES SIX 4-OUNCE POTS DE CRÈME

1 cup heavy cream

1 cup milk

¼ cup freshly ground dark roast coffee

½ cup sugar

7 egg yolks

Garnish (optional)

½ cup heavy cream

2 teaspoons sugar

6 espresso beans

Preheat the oven to 300°F. Combine the cream, milk, and coffee in a heavy-bottomed saucepan. Bring the mixture to a simmer over medium heat and let steep, off the heat, for 10 minutes. Strain into a bowl through a fine-mesh sieve. In a bowl, whisk the sugar and egg yolks for about 2 minutes, or until the mixture is slightly pale. Use the whisk to stir in the cream mixture. Continue stirring until there is no egg yolk clinging to the sides of the bowl. Strain again and pour the mixture into six 5- or 6-ounce ramekins or *pot de crème* cups with lids. If using ramekins, cover each of them with a small sheet of aluminum foil to prevent a crust from forming on top of the custard.

Put the custards in a baking dish with high sides and pour in enough hot water—the hottest water from the tap will do—to come about halfway up the sides of the ramekins. Bake for about 40 minutes, or until the custards have set. To check, remove the foil from two of them—choose two from different positions in the baking dish—and gently move them back and forth. When you no longer see the liquid moving, the custards have set.

Remove the custards from the baking dish. Allow to cool to room temperature. Refrigerate for at least 2 hours. Don't be tempted to stick them in the refrigerator while still warm or moisture will condense on the underside of the foil and drip down onto the custards.

To garnish, beat the cream and sugar to stiff peaks. Serve the *pots de crème* with a swirl of whipped cream and an espresso bean on top.

1. Combine the cream, milk, and ground coffee in a saucepan and bring to a simmer. Let steep for 10 minutes. Strain the cream mixture.

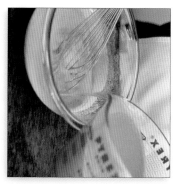

2. While the cream mixture is coming to a simmer, whisk the egg yolks with sugar for about 2 minutes, or until pale. Gently stir the hot cream mixture into the beaten egg yolk mixture.

3. Strain the mixture one more time.

4. Pour the mixture into the ramekins, then cover each of the filled ramekins with aluminum foil. Place the ramekins in a baking dish and pour in enough hot tap water to come halfway up the sides of the ramekins. Bake until set. Cool, refrigerate, and serve.

1. Line the bottoms of the ramekins with caramel.

2. Beat together the sugar, eggs, and egg yolks.

3. Bring the milk and vanilla to a simmer and pour it into the egg mixture while stirring—not beating—with a whisk. Stir until smooth and the milk is completely incorporated. If while stirring you've generated a lot of froth, skim it off with a bench scraper.

4. Strain the mixture.

5. Fill the ramekins with the egg mixture.

6. Place the ramekins in a baking pan and pour in enough hot water to come halfway up their sides. Bake until the custards have set.

7. Take the custards out of the water bath and refrigerate for at least 3 hours. Run a knife around each of the custards to loosen them.

8. Put a plate over a crème caramel and, while holding the ramekin firmly against the plate, flip the whole thing over. Give it a quick up and down shake while still holding firmly and lift off the ramekin.

Crèmes Caramels

. . . .

Crème caramel is the least rich of the sweet custards because it is made with milk and whole eggs—or whole eggs with a small number of additional yolks—but with no cream. It gets its name, of course, from the caramel used to line the rame-kins in which the custards are baked. The custards are baked in a bain marie—a shallow pan filled partway with water—to keep them from overheating.

MAKES SIX 6-OUNCE CRÈMES CARAMELS

2 cups sugar

3 cups milk

2 teaspoons vanilla extract

4 whole eggs

2 egg yolks

Preheat the oven to 325°F. Using 1 1/2 cups of the sugar, prepare the caramel (see method, page 356). Pour just enough caramel into six 6-ounce ramekins to cover the bottoms with a thin layer. Avoid getting any on the sides of the ramekins.

Bring the milk to a simmer in a heavy-bottomed saucepan. Add the vanilla. In a bowl, whisk the remaining 1/2 cup sugar with the eggs and egg yolks for about 2 minutes, or until the mixture is slightly pale. Use a whisk to stir the hot milk into the egg mixture and stir until the eggs are completely combined with the milk. If you see a lot of froth on the mixture, skim it off with a pastry scraper. If you see specks of egg in the mixture, strain it through a fine-mesh sieve.

Pour the mixture into the caramel-lined ramekins and arrange the ramekins in a baking dish with sides at least as high as the ramekins. Pour enough hot tap water into the baking dish to come halfway up the sides of the ramekins. Bake for about 50 minutes, or until the surface of the custards stay still when you wiggle them back and forth.

Allow to cool for 1 hour at room temperature and then refrigerate for at least 2 hours.

Run a knife around each of the custards to loosen them. Put a rimmed plate over a crème caramel and, holding the ramekin firmly against the plate, flip the whole thing over. Give it a quick up and down shake while still holding firmly and lift off the ramekin. Serve cold.

9. A little pool of caramel will surround the custard. Serve cold.

Caramel

Many recipes for caramel combine sugar with water before the mixture is heated. Because the water has to evaporate completely in order for the sugar to caramelize, this just wastes time. Instead, put the sugar in the pan over the heat and stir it until it turns a deep red. Caramel syrup, caramel sauce, and butterscotch sauce are easily fashioned from this basic sauce.

To make 1 cup of caramel, place 2 cups sugar in a heavy-bottomed saucepan over medium to high heat and stir continuously with a heavy wooden spoon as the sugar melts and turns color. The caramel is ready when it is smooth and deep reddish-brown in color.

Unless you're making one of the caramel sauces shown in the Variations (right), dip the bottom of the pan into a bowl of cold water for about 1 second, to stop the cooking but not so long that the caramel hardens. Use immediately.

VARIATIONS

CARAMEL SYRUP: Pour 1 cup water into 1 cup hot caramel (stand back, it spatters). Bring it back to a boil and simmer, while stirring, until all the caramel has dissolved into the syrup. Makes 2 cups.

CARAMEL SAUCE: Add 1 cup heavy cream to 1 cup hot caramel (stand back, it spatters). Stir until the sauce is smooth and evenly colored. Adjust the consistency by adding more cream to thin the sauce or by boiling the sauce down a couple of minutes to thicken the sauce. Makes 1$^2/_3$ cups.

BUTTERSCOTCH SAUCE: Add 3/4 cup butter to 1 cup hot caramel (stand back, it spatters) and stir until the butter melts and the mixture is smooth. Continue stirring over medium heat for about 1 minute, or until the mixture smells like butterscotch. Add 1 cup heavy cream and stir until smooth. Simmer the sauce until it has the consistency you like. If it's too thick, thin it with 1 to 2 tablespoons water.

MAKING CARAMEL AND CARAMEL SAUCE

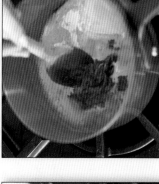

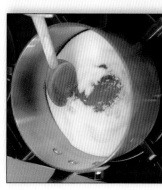

1. Put the sugar in a heavy-bottomed saucepan over medium to high heat.

2. Continuously stir the caramel with a heavy wooden spoon . . .

3. . . . until there are no lumps.

4. To make caramel sauce, pour heavy cream into the hot caramel. Stand back. Stir with a wooden spoon until smooth.

BAKING

Crèmes Brûlées

Crème brûlée is made with the same basic ingredients as pots de crème (page 353)—heavy cream and egg yolks—but is flavored with a whole vanilla bean and finished with a top layer of crunchy caramel.

MAKES SIX 5-OUNCE CRÈMES BRÛLÉES

2 cups heavy cream
1 vanilla bean, split in half lengthwise, or
2 teaspoons vanilla extract
6 egg yolks
1 cup sugar

Preheat the oven to 300°F. In a heavy-bottomed saucepan, bring the cream to a simmer with the vanilla bean or vanilla extract. If using a vanilla bean, scrape out the tiny seeds from each half and stir them into the cream.

In a bowl, whisk the egg yolks and ¹/₂ cup of the sugar for about 2 minutes, or until slightly pale. Stir the hot cream into the yolk mixture. Continue stirring until no yolk clings to the sides of the bowl.

Arrange six 5-ounce crème brûlée dishes or ramekins in a jelly roll pan or shallow roasting pan and pour in the custard mixture. Pour enough hot tap water into the pan to come halfway up the sides of the dishes. Bake for about 40 minutes, or until the custard doesn't jiggle when you gently move the dishes.

Take the custards out of the jelly roll pan and let cool at room temperature for 1 hour. Refrigerate for at least 4 hours.

Within an hour of serving, sprinkle the remaining ¹/₂ cup sugar over the custards so they are covered evenly with a thin layer. Tilt a blowtorch over each crème brûlée with the flame a couple of inches away from the top. Move the torch around until the sugar melts and forms a transparent sheet. Serve.

1. Prepare the ingredients exactly the same way as for crème caramel, but instead of whole eggs, use egg yolks; and instead of milk, use heavy cream. Fill the dishes as close to the top as you can.

2. Place the custards in a jelly roll pan or shallow baking pan and pour in enough hot tap water to come about halfway up the sides of the molds. Bake until firm when jiggled. Refrigerate for at least 4 hours.

3. Sprinkle the custards with just enough sugar to form a thin layer with no gaps in it.

4. Wave a blowtorch over the custards. Don't hold the torch too close or the surface won't caramelize evenly.

While the principles of making sweet and savory soufflés are the same—beaten egg whites are folded with a denser mixture that provides flavor and substance—savory soufflés are based on béchamel sauce and sweet soufflés are based on pastry cream or sabayon, a fluffy mixture made with egg yolks. And while soufflés have to be served as soon as they're baked, the molds can be floured or sugared and the base mixture can be made ahead of time so that the only last-minute work is beating the egg whites, folding them with the base mixture, and baking.

Though not essential, an aluminum-foil collar wrapped around the soufflé dishes before baking prevents any loose and still-runny soufflé mixture from spilling down the sides as the soufflé heats and expands. The collar itself must be buttered and floured (or sugared or coated with grated Parmesan cheese), so the soufflé mixture doesn't stick to it. Don't bother with collars if your soufflé dishes are less than full. For the most dramatic soufflés, use smaller molds so the filling actually comes up over the rims before baking and use collars to hold the filling in place.

Cheese Soufflés

A cheese soufflé is the most satisfying of all savory soufflés and also provides a model for making savory soufflés out of just about anything. The model is simple: *Make a béchamel sauce*—essentially, milk thickened with a little flour—and combine it with cheese and egg yolks. Beat egg whites to stiff peaks and fold them with the béchamel mixture while folding over additional grated cheese—ideally, a dry cheese such as Parmigiano-Reggiano that grates very fine. Spoon the mixture into individual soufflé dishes that have been buttered and coated with grated cheese or flour. If your soufflé dishes are 10 ounces or larger, there is no need to make collars. If, however, they're smaller—say 8 ounces—make 4 aluminum foil collars out of 4 sheets of aluminum foil, each about 4 times as long as the diameter of the dishes, by folding the sheets lengthwise in thirds. The strips should be wide enough to come about 2 inches over the rim of the soufflé dish. Bake the soufflés until they rise 1 to 2 inches out of the dishes. Jiggle one to see if it seems stiff or fluid—this takes some practice—and probe into the soufflé with a spoon. It should be slightly runny in the very center.

MAKES 4 INDIVIDUAL SOUFFLÉS

2 tablespoons butter, at room temperature, for dishes plus 3 tablespoons if using collars

5 tablespoons finely grated authentic Italian Parmesan or other dry cheese for dishes plus 1/2 cup if using collars

Béchamel base

3 tablespoons butter

3 tablespoons flour

3/4 cup milk

Tiny pinch or grating of nutmeg

1/4 teaspoon salt

5 grinds of pepper

4 egg yolks

5 ounces Gruyère or other firm cheese, grated (about 1 cup)

Soufflés

7 egg whites

Pinch of cream of tartar, unless using a copper bowl

2 ounces authentic Italian Parmesan or other dry cheese such as aged Gouda, grated (about 3/4 cup lightly packed)

To prepare the soufflé dishes and collars if using, brush the soufflé dishes and the collars with butter. You don't need to brush the entire strips of aluminum foil, just that part that will reach above the dishes. Coat the dishes and buttered parts of the collars with the grated cheese.

To make the béchamel base, combine the butter and flour in a heavy-bottomed saucepan over medium heat and stir for about 2 minutes, or until smooth. Add the milk and stir the mixture with a whisk for about 5 minutes, or until it boils and thickens. Whisk until smooth. Add the nutmeg, salt, and pepper. Stir the sauce for 1 minute to cool slightly. Whisk in the egg yolks. Add the Gruyère cheese and stir the sauce until smooth.

To finish the soufflés, preheat the oven to 350°F. Beat the egg whites with the cream of tartar (if using) to stiff peaks. Combine about one-fourth of the egg whites with the base to lighten it. Fold the base with the rest of the egg whites, while sprinkling over the Parmesan cheese.

Distribute the soufflé mixture among the dishes. If the soufflé mixture comes slightly over the tops of the dishes, smooth off the tops with the back of a knife. Make a small moat around each of the soufflés with your thumb to keep the filling from sticking. Wrap around the collars. Pinch the ends of the collars together where they meet to hold them in place.

Put the soufflés on a sheet pan, turn up the oven to 375°F, and bake for about 18 minutes, or until risen 1 to 2 inches above the rims of the dishes. Stick a spoon through the side into the center of one of the soufflés. The soufflé should be very slightly runny in the very middle. Pull away the collars and serve.

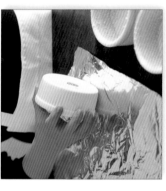

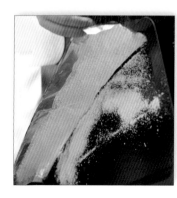

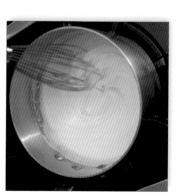

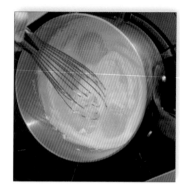

1. To prepare the molds, brush the soufflé molds with butter and coat the molds with the grated Parmesan cheese.

2. For collars: Cut four strips of aluminum foil about 4 times as long as the soufflé dishes are wide. Fold the strips in thirds lengthwise. The collars should be 1 to 2 inches wider than the soufflé dish is high.

3. Brush the collars with butter—don't butter the entire strip, just the part that will be above the dish.

4. Sprinkle the collar with the grated Parmesan.

5. Tap off the excess cheese.

6. To make the béchamel sauce, separate the eggs by moving the egg back and forth between the two halves of the broken shell while letting the white drop down into a bowl.

7. Melt the butter in a heavy-bottomed saucepan. Stir in the flour, whisk to eliminate lumps, and cook the flour for about 2 minutes.

8. Whisk the milk into the flour-butter mixture (a roux), about one-fourth at a time. Wait until the mixture thickens before adding more.

9. Continue adding milk and whisking to keep the sauce smooth and free of lumps.

10. Grate in nutmeg and add salt and pepper.

11. When the béchamel has thickened, take it off the heat and whisk it for a minute or so to cool it. Add the egg yolks and stir until smooth.

12. Whisk in the Gruyère cheese and stir until the sauce is smooth.

13. To finish the soufflés, beat the egg whites to stiff peaks (add cream of tartar, unless you are using a copper bowl).

14. Whisk about one-fourth of the beaten egg whites into the base to lighten it.

15. Add the base to the egg whites and fold together.

16. While folding together the base and egg whites, sprinkle over the Parmesan cheese.

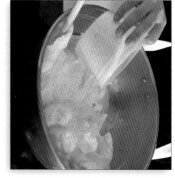

17. Fill the prepared dishes.

18. Smooth off the tops of the soufflés with the back of a knife or with a metal spatula.

19. Make a small moat around the rim of the soufflés with your thumb.

20. Wrap the collars around the soufflés.

21. Attach the collars by folding over a little bit of one end with the other.

22. Bake until the soufflés come about 2 inches above the rim of the dishes. Quickly remove the collars and serve.

Grand Marnier Soufflés

When making a Grand Marnier soufflé or, for that matter, any soufflé, the purpose is to get as much flavor as possible into the base without making the base too thin. If the base is too thin, it won't support the egg whites and the soufflé may fall. These soufflés are based on a sabayon sauce, which is essentially a mixture of egg yolks, sugar, and flavorful liquid that is beaten over heat until it thickens, but isn't allowed to get hot enough to curdle. In this recipe, a little cornstarch is added to thicken the sabayon, but not nearly as much as would be included in a classic dessert soufflé made with a pastry cream base.

These soufflés use as many ways as possible to emphasize the orange flavor. In addition to Grand Marnier, orange juice, orange zest, essential orange oil, and homemade candied orange peel macerated in additional Grand Marnier are used. The candied orange peel and the orange oil help reinforce the orange flavor, but are not essential.

Because this soufflé mixture is fairly stiff, you can make these soufflés without collars.

MAKES 6 INDIVIDUAL SOUFFLÉS

3 tablespoons butter, at room temperature, for dishes

1/4 cup superfine sugar, for dishes

Sabayon base

3 tablespoons candied orange peel (page 194; optional)

3 tablespoons Grand Marnier plus 1 tablespoon if using candied orange peel

1 tablespoon grated orange zest (see page 194)

Juice from 1 orange

1 teaspoon essential orange oil (optional)

5 egg yolks

1 teaspoon cornstarch

2 tablespoons granulated sugar

Soufflés

8 egg whites

Pinch of cream of tartar, unless using a copper bowl

1/4 cup plus 2 tablespoons superfine sugar

Preheat the oven to 400°F. To prepare the dishes, brush six 7-ounce soufflé dishes or large ramekins with the butter and coat with the superfine sugar. Refrigerate until needed.

To make the sabayon base, cut the candied orange peel into 1/4-inch dice and soak in the 1 tablespoon Grand Marnier for 30 minutes. Combine the orange zest and juice, orange oil, the 3 tablespoons Grand Marnier, the egg yolks, cornstarch, and granulated sugar in a heavy-bottomed saucepan, ideally one with sloping sides. Whisk over medium heat for about 2 minutes, or until the mixture is light and fluffy and then stiffens. Be careful to reach into the corners of the pan with the whisk so that egg doesn't accumulate in there and curdle. Don't let the mixture boil. Whisk for 2 minutes off the heat to cool the mixture and so the heat retained in the pan doesn't cause the base to curdle. Add the candied orange peel with the soaking liquid.

To finish the soufflés, beat the egg whites with the cream of tartar (if using) to medium peaks and add the superfine sugar. Beat to stiff peaks. Fold the egg whites with the base and distribute the mixture among the soufflé dishes. Smooth off the tops of the soufflés and make a small moat around the rim of each dish with your thumb to keep the filling from sticking.

Bake the soufflés for about 15 minutes, or until they rise about 1½ inches above the rims of the dishes. Reach through the side of one of the soufflés with a spoon to check the center. The very center should be loose and a tiny bit runny. If it's not, bake for 3 minutes more and check again. Serve.

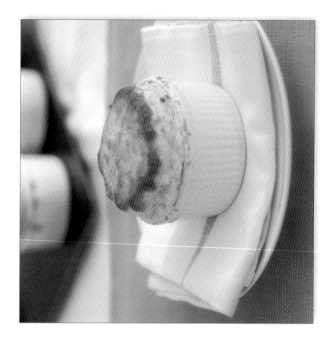

1. Brush the soufflé dishes or ramekins with butter. Coat the dishes with superfine sugar by putting the sugar in one of the dishes and rotating it over the next dish.

2. Zest the orange before you juice it.

3. Squeeze the orange over a strainer set in a saucepan, preferably one with sloping sides.

4. Cut the optional candied orange peel into ¼-inch dice. In a bowl, macerate the orange peel in the 1 tablespoon Grand Marnier.

5. Combine the orange zest, orange juice, orange oil, the 3 tablespoons Grand Marnier, egg yolks, cornstarch, and granulated sugar in a saucepan. Whisk the mixture together, off the heat, until well mixed.

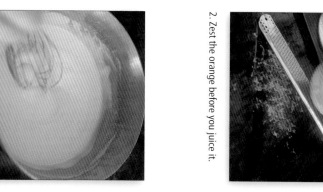

6. Whisk over medium heat until the mixture thickens; don't let it boil.

7. Whisk the mixture for 2 minutes off the heat and stir in the candied orange peel with the soaking liquid.

8. Beat the egg whites (and cream of tartar, if using) to medium peaks, add the sugar, and beat to stiff peaks. Transfer the whites to a bowl as shown here or fold in the bowl you used for beating the whites. Pour the sabayon mixture over the beaten whites.

9. Fold until well combined.

10. Use a rubber spatula to fill the soufflé dishes or ramekins. Smooth over the tops of the soufflés to even them off and make sure they're full.

11. Run your thumb around the edge of the dishes to make a small moat. Bake until the soufflés are just a tiny bit runny inside and the mixture has risen about 1½ inches over the rims of the dishes.

Eggs, sugar, and fruit juice or puree are the essential ingredients of fruit curds—though butter is often added to round out the flavor. Lemon curd is a popular filling for tarts, and it and other fruit curds can be used to fill cakes or to flavor buttercream or mousseline (see page 58). Folded together with whipped cream, fruit curds make wonderful mousses which can be served chilled on their own or used as cake fillings. They are also nice spreads for scones or other baked goods.

Lemon Curd

Lemon curd is like the filling in a lemon meringue pie but without all the starch. At its best, it's tangy and sour and creamy, which makes it perfect when juxtaposed with richer or sweeter components such as meringue. This is the most basic of lemon curds. Many recipes call for butter. While not essential, the butter softens the fruit's sharp acidity. You can also use browned butter (beurre noisette, page 196), which gives the curd an intense and delicious butterscotch flavor and makes the curd somewhat stiffer once it cools.

MAKES 1¹/₂ CUPS, ENOUGH FOR TWO 9-INCH
ROUND CAKE LAYERS

2 eggs

¹/₂ cup sugar

1 tablespoon grated lemon zest (see page 194)

¹/₃ cup lemon juice

4 tablespoons butter, cubed or sliced (optional)

Combine the eggs, sugar, zest, and juice in a heatproof bowl that fits over a saucepan. Whisk until smooth and slightly pale.

Place the bowl over a saucepan of simmering water and stir with a whisk. As the mixture warms, add the butter, a handful at a time, and continue stirring. Whisk the mixture over the heat until it thickens, taking care not to let it boil.

Spread in a cake, or let it cool, then whisk with other mixtures such as buttercream or crème mousseline.

1. Combine all of the ingredients except the butter in a heatproof bowl that fits at least partially in a saucepan. Whisk until smooth and slightly pale.

2. Put the bowl over a saucepan of simmering water and stir with a whisk.

3. As the mixture warms, add the butter and continue stirring.

4. Whisk the mixture over the heat until it thickens, but don't let it boil.

Passion Fruit Curd

Because it is so acidic, passion fruit curd is much like lemon curd. The amount of sugar needed varies depending on the sweetness of the fruit. Passion fruit puree is very tart, so this recipe calls for a lot of sugar. If you've made a curd and it is not sweet enough, you can sweeten it with corn syrup or, if the curd is the base for a mousse, by oversweetening the whipped cream. Passion fruit curd can be used as a layer in a cake, or it can be combined with buttercream or crème mousseline to add tang.

MAKES 3 CUPS, ENOUGH FOR THREE 9-INCH
ROUND CAKE LAYERS

1 cup strained passion fruit puree

4 eggs

1 cup sugar

¹/₂ cup butter, cubed or sliced (optional)

Place the puree in a nonreactive saucepan and bring it to a simmer. Set aside.

Combine the eggs and sugar in a heatproof bowl that fits over a saucepan. Whisk until smooth.

Place the bowl over a saucepan of simmering water and stir with a whisk. As the mixture warms, add the butter, a handful at a time, and continue stirring until the curd thickens slightly. It should remain liquid. Because it contains so much butter, the curd will thicken when cold. Strain the mixture while it is still warm.

Cover the mixture with plastic wrap; be sure the plastic wrap is touching the surface of the curd, or a skin will form. Use as a cake filling or combine with other mixtures such as buttercream or crème mousseline.

MAKING PASSION FRUIT CURD

1. Place the passion fruit puree in a saucepan and bring it to a simmer.

2. Whisk together the eggs and sugar in a wide bowl until smooth. Place the bowl over a saucepan of simmering water and add the butter. Stir with a whisk or rubber spatula until it thickens but remains liquid. The curd will thicken when chilled.

3. Strain the mixture while it is still warm.

4. Cover the curd with plastic wrap; be sure the plastic wrap is touching the surface of the curd, or a skin will form.

Passion Fruit Mousse

To turn a fruit curd into a fruit mousse, fold in whipped cream. If you're not using the mousse right away and serving it within a day, add gelatin as we do here to keep it from separating. Note: Whenever you combine tropical fruit with gelatin, bring the tropical fruit puree to a simmer before you add the gelatin. This kills protease enzymes that would otherwise interfere with the gelatin setting. This mousse can be used to make napoleons (page 226).

MAKES 5 CUPS, ENOUGH FOR THREE 9-INCH ROUND CAKE LAYERS

4½ teaspoons (1½ packets) powdered unflavored gelatin

¼ cup water

3 cups passion fruit curd (opposite page)

1½ cups heavy cream

3 tablespoons sugar

Put the gelatin and water in a small bowl and let sit for about 10 minutes, or until it swells, or blooms, and absorbs the water. Stir the softened gelatin with a fork to get rid of any lumps. Then put the bowl over a saucepan of simmering water until the gelatin dissolves.

Place the passion fruit curd in a nonreactive saucepan and bring it to a simmer over medium-low heat. Pour the melted gelatin into the still-hot fruit curd and mix thoroughly with a whisk. Set aside until the curd feels neither hot nor cold.

Whip the cream to medium peaks, beating in the sugar.

Fold the whipped cream into the curd mixture. Immediately place in serving dishes and chill, or use to fill a cake or pastry.

Dark chocolate mousse is made foamy with beaten eggs, egg whites, and whipped cream, either alone or in combination. Traditional mousse recipes call for beating egg yolks with melted chocolate, sometimes melted with butter, but because of egg anxieties, in modern recipes the egg yolks are cooked. Because egg whites are considered safer than egg yolks, recipes that call for cooking the yolks often include raw beaten egg whites. To avoid raw egg whites, use whipped cream or Italian meringue (page 60).

To make the simplest mousse, melt chocolate and butter with a liquid flavoring such as vanilla, coffee, liqueur, or *eau de vie*. Use at least one-fourth as much liquid as you have chocolate—any less, and the chocolate may seize and stiffen up into a grainy mess; too much liquid and the mousse may end up too runny. Once you have your chocolate base, simply fold it with sweetened beaten egg whites (raw, or cooked as Italian meringue) or whipped cream.

To use egg yolks, which give a mousse a creamy consistency and help the mousse hold its shape, combine them with the liquid flavoring and whisk them over a pot of barely simmering water until they get frothy and stiffen into what the French call a *sabayon* or the Italians, when Marsala wine is used as the flavoring, a *zabaglione*. Then, melt the chocolate directly into the sabayon or melt it separately, alone, or with butter, and stir it into the finished sabayon. The chocolate sabayon mixture is then folded with beaten egg whites, whipped cream, or both.

Chocolate mousse is easy to serve alone—pour it while still warm into wineglasses or just spoon it out onto plates—but it also makes an excellent cake filling.

Repairing Chocolate Mixtures that Have Seized

When small amounts of liquid are added to melted chocolate, the chocolate coagulates and turns granular, a condition known as "seizing." The mixture can be repaired only by adding more liquid. The higher the cocoa content of the chocolate, the more liquid is required to make it smooth when melted. While you can use water to thin out seized chocolate, it is better to use heavy cream when you are making a mousse. Use as little cream as possible to smooth out the chocolate—too much and you'll thin the mousse so it never sets; too little and it will stay grainy.

Classic Chocolate Mousse

This chocolate mousse is made by cooking egg yolks over a saucepan of barely simmering water before combining them with other ingredients. The trick is to get the egg yolks hot enough to kill any bacteria, but not so hot that they curdle. The best way to judge the temperature is with an instant-read thermometer, which should reach 150°F. In this recipe, a small amount of sugar is beaten into the egg yolks to stabilize them, so they're less likely to curdle.

MAKES 3 CUPS, ENOUGH FOR THE INSIDE LAYERS
OF A 4-LAYER 9-INCH ROUND CAKE

6 ounces bittersweet chocolate, chopped

1/4 cup plus 2 tablespoons butter, cubed or sliced

4 egg yolks

3 tablespoons sugar

1 teaspoon vanilla extract, or 2 tablespoons Cognac, rum, or kirsch

1 cup heavy cream for whipping or more as needed to thin the chocolate mixture

Combine the chocolate and butter in a heatproof bowl. Set the bowl over a saucepan of barely simmering water and stir with a wooden spoon or whisk until melted and smooth. Take the bowl off the heat, leaving the saucepan of simmering water on the stove.

Combine the egg yolks and sugar in a heatproof bowl and set it over the saucepan of barely simmering water. Whisk for about 5 minutes, or until pale and slightly stiff. Remove from the heat. Stir the chocolate mixture into the egg yolks, add the vanilla, and stir until well mixed. If at this point the mixture becomes stiff or grainy, whisk in heavy cream or water, 1/4 cup at a time, until the mixture is smooth (see sidebar, left). Stir for a few minutes to cool. Let cool to room temperature.

Whip the cream to soft peaks. Stir about one-fourth of the whipped cream into the chocolate mixture and then fold in the rest with a rubber spatula.

If you are using the mousse as a layer in a cake, you can use it right away provided you are making your cake in a springform pan or cake ring, which will hold the mousse in place; otherwise, chill the mousse for at least 1 hour before you use it. If you are serving the mousse alone, chill for at least 1 hour before serving unless you are serving it in glasses, which should be filled before chilling. When chilling mousse, cover it with plastic wrap against the surface to keep a dark crust from forming.

1. Combine the egg yolks and sugar in a metal bowl set over a saucepan of barely simmering water. Beat with a whisk until the mixture is pale and slightly stiff, adding heavy cream as necessary to make it smooth.

2. Add the melted chocolate mixture and flavoring to the egg mixture. Stir and let cool to room temperature.

3. Fold the whipped cream into the chocolate-egg mixture, adding cream or water to thin if it turns grainy.

White Chocolate Mousse

White chocolate can be substituted for dark chocolate in many mousse recipes, but because mixtures made with it are more likely to be runny, gelatin is often added to the mousse to help it set.

White chocolate mousse makes a great cake filling, as does whipped white chocolate ganache (page 51). One caveat: Some brands of white chocolate may turn grainy when you heat them. I've had continued success with Lindt brand white chocolate.

MAKES 2¹/₂ CUPS, ENOUGH FOR THE INSIDE LAYERS OF A 3-LAYER 9-INCH ROUND CAKE

1 teaspoon (¹/₃ packet) powdered unflavored gelatin

¹/₄ cup cold water

1¹/₂ cups heavy cream

7 ounces white chocolate, chopped

Put the gelatin and cold water in a small bowl and let sit for about 10 minutes, or until it swells, or blooms, and absorbs the water. Stir the softened gelatin with a fork to get rid of any lumps.

Bring ¹/₂ cup of the cream to a simmer in a small saucepan and stir in the gelatin and its soaking liquid. Off the heat, stir the mixture until the gelatin completely dissolves.

Pour the hot gelatin mixture over the white chocolate in a heatproof bowl and stir until all the chocolate melts. If it doesn't entirely melt, set the bowl over a saucepan of hot water for 30 seconds to 1 minute and stir some more. Don't let the

white chocolate get too hot; it has much less tolerance for heat than does dark chocolate and will coagulate if too hot. Remove from the heat and let cool for 5 minutes, or until no longer hot enough to melt the whipped cream but not cold enough to set. If it starts to set, heat it for a few seconds.

Beat the remaining cream to medium peaks. Pour the chocolate mixture into the bowl of whipped cream and fold until smooth with a rubber spatula. If you're assembling a cake in a cake ring, use the mousse right away while you can still pour it. If you're serving the mousse on its own, ladle or spoon it into bowls or glasses and chill in the refrigerator for at least 2 hours before serving.

MAKING WHITE CHOCOLATE MOUSSE

1. Chop the white chocolate. Pour the hot cream–gelatin mixture over the chopped chocolate to melt and stir until smooth. If the chocolate doesn't melt, set the bowl over a saucepan of simmering water for 30 seconds to 1 minute and stir until smooth.

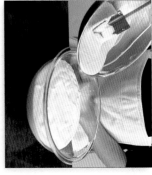

2. Whip the rest of the cream to medium peaks and fold in the white chocolate mixture.

Flourless Chocolate Cake

A flourless cake is essentially a mousse that's baked and, like a soufflé, allowed to fall in on itself after baking. Virtually all flourless cakes are made with chocolate, because the chocolate functions somewhat like flour and allows the cake to hold its shape. And like a chocolate mousse, air is incorporated by beating egg yolks with sugar, and beating the egg whites separately. Don't worry if the cake cracks—it should— or if it's a little runny in the center.

This recipe calls for frosting the cake with whipped ganache, but the cake is rich enough that a sprinkling of confectioners' sugar is enough. Flourless chocolate cake is also great glazed with hot ganache (page 50) or with chocolate glaze (page 53).

MAKES 1 ROUND LAYER CAKE (9 BY 1 INCH), OR
1 ROUND LAYER CAKE (8 BY 1½ INCHES)

Butter and flour for the pan

1/2 cup almond flour, or 2/3 cup blanched almonds

1/2 cup plus 2 tablespoons butter

3 ounces bittersweet chocolate, chopped

5 egg yolks

3/4 cup plus 2 tablespoons sugar

4 egg whites

Pinch of cream of tartar, unless using a copper bowl

2 tablespoons Cognac (optional)

Preheat the oven to 350°F. Use a round cake pan either 9 by 1 inch or 8 by 1½ inches. For a springform pan, coat it liberally with butter and flour; for a regular cake pan, line the bottom with a round of parchment paper. If using blanched almonds, grind them to a powder in a food processor; set aside.

Combine the butter and chocolate in a stainless steel bowl and set it over a saucepan of simmering water. When the mixture has almost completely melted, remove the bowl from the heat and stir until smooth.

While the chocolate is melting, beat the egg yolks in a stand mixer on high speed with ¼ cup of the sugar for about 8 minutes, or until the egg yolks become pale and quadruple in volume. Using a rubber spatula, fold the egg yolk mixture with the chocolate-butter mixture. If the mixture turns thick and grainy, repair it as explained in the sidebar on page 366.

Using a stand mixer on high speed, beat the egg whites with the cream of tartar (if using) for about 1 minute, or until soft peaks form. Add the remaining sugar and beat for about 1 minute more, or until medium peaks form. (Beating will take longer if you are using a whisk or hand mixer.)

Add the Cognac to the chocolate mixture and fold in the almond flour (or ground almonds). Stir in one-quarter of the egg whites to lighten the mixture, then fold in the remainder. Fold only long enough to make the mixture homogeneous.

Transfer the batter to the prepared cake pan, and bake for about 20 minutes. The cake is supposed to be loose in the middle, so a toothpick inserted in the center won't come out clean.

Before you take the cake out of the pan, let it cool completely. Just before unmolding, place the cake pan over a burner on high heat and move it back and forth for about 15 seconds to loosen the cake. You can frost this cake with buttercream, but a dollop of whipped cream, passed at the table, is lighter.

1. Brush the inside of a springform pan liberally with room-temperature butter. Put flour in the pan and rotate it to coat the sides. Tap the pan against the work surface to loosen any excess flour.

2. Combine the egg yolks in a bowl with 1/4 cup of the sugar. Beat for about 8 minutes, or until the mixture is pale yellow and fluffy.

3. Place a bowl with the chopped chocolate and butter over a pan of simmering water. When the mixture has almost completely melted, take the bowl off the heat and continue to stir until smooth.

4. Fold the egg yolk mixture into the chocolate mixture with a rubber spatula.

5. Beat the egg whites with the cream of tartar (if using) to soft peaks, then add the sugar and beat to medium peaks.

6. Fold Cognac (if using) into the chocolate mixture; fold in the almond flour.

7. Stir one-fourth of the egg whites into the chocolate mixture to lighten it, then fold in the rest of the egg whites. Fold just long enough to make the mixture homogeneous.

8. Transfer the mixture to the cake pan.

9. Bake until a knife comes out with crumbs attached to it—not until it is completely dry.

10. Frost the cake with chocolate buttercream, if you like (see page 45).

A

Almond flour

cream, 159

financiers, 262

frangipane, 159

linzer pastry dough, 140

macarons, 266–67

sponge cake, 20–21

Almond paste. *See also* Marzipan

buttercream, 48

sponge cake, 22–23

Almonds

cookies, Florentine, 268

cream, 159

frangipane, 159

linzertorte, 208–9

–puff pastry galette (pithiviers), 206–7

raspberry buttercream layer cake, 74–75

tartlets, 176

tuiles, 264

Alsatian apple tart, 186–87

Angel food cake, 24

Apples

charlottes, 346–47

pie, 168–69

strudel, 228–31

tart, Alsatian, 186–87

tart, classic French, 170–71

tart, crispy, 200–201

tarte tatin, 172–73

Apricots

bread, 339

frangipane tart, 175

fruit and cheese Danish purses, 222

jelly roll, 106

miniature cake petit fours, 102–3

panettone, 328–29

scones, 343

tartlets, 177

Autolyse, 289

B

Babas, 36–37

Baguettes, 296, 297

Baking powder, xiii

Baking soda, xiii

Baking stones, 303

Baklava, pistachio, 232–33

Bananas

cream pie, 196–97

nut bread muffins, 338

Barquettes, red currant, 182

Bâtards, 297

Bavarian cake, strawberry, 92–95

Bavarian creams

making, 54

strawberry, 54

Bench scrapers, xv

Berries. *See also individual berries*

frangipane tartlets, 178

–passion fruit mousse tart, 181

pies, individual deep-dish, 204

tartlets, 182

Beurre noisette, 196

Biga, 285, 287

Biscotti, 269

Biscuit (fine-crumb European sponge cake), 14–15

Blackberries

Biscuits, baking powder, 342

–lemon cream tart, 183

–peach mousseline tart, 180

Blueberries

Danish packets, 224

frangipane tart, 176

muffins, 341

pie, 164–65

turnovers, 204

Bourbon, xiii

Boules, 297

Bread-based desserts

apple charlottes, 346–47

cherry cobblers, 344

strawberry shortcakes, 345

Bread dough

dividing and rounding, 294

fermentation and, 293

kneading, 289–93, 308

leftover, as starter, 285, 307

liquid in, 309

mixing ingredients for, 288–89

proofing, 302

punching down, 293

scoring, 302, 303

shaping, 295–300

Bread machines, 293

Bread pans, xiv

Breads, quick

apricot, 339

baking powder biscuits, 342

banana nut muffins, 338

blueberry muffins, 341

popovers, 340

scones, 343

Breads, yeasted. *See also* Bread dough; Starters

artisan-style, 284

baking, 305

bread sticks (*grissini*), 323

brioche, 326–27

challah, 330–31

ciabatta, 309–10

cinnamon rolls, 334–35

coffee cakes, 332–33

Breads, yeasted, *continued*
  cooling, 303
  focaccia, 324–25
  glazing, 302
  indirect method for, 284
  judging doneness of, 303
  panettone, 328–29
  pita, 322
  pumpernickel, 318–19
  rye, 314–15
  sourdough, 313
  sourdough whole wheat, 316–17
  sourdough whole wheat raisin, 316–17
  "straight dough" method for, 284
  white, 304–8
Brioche, 326–27
Brownies, 272
Bûche de noël, 108
Buns, sticky, 336–37
Butter
  brown, 196
  unsalted vs. salted, xiii
Butter cakes
  cream and butter sheet, 29
  devil's food, 30
  fluffy light, 28
  German chocolate, 26–27
  pound, 25–26
  types of, 25
  vanilla, 31
Buttercream
  almond, 48
  amount required, for one cake, 46
  chestnut, 48
  chocolate, 48
  citrus, 48
  coffee, 48
  consistency of, 44
  decorating cakes with, 117
  flavoring, 48
  hazelnut, 48
  Italian meringue, 46
  orange, quick and easy, 46
  pistachio, 48
  professional-style, 45
  reconstituting congealed or separated, 49
  storing, 4, 44
  types of, 44
  vanilla, 48
Butterscotch sauce, 356

C

Cake decorating
  with buttercream, 117
  with cake crumbs, 115
  with caramel cages, 83, 117
  with cat's tongue cookies, 116
  with chocolate curls, 118
  with chocolate strip, 114
  with cocoa powder, 117
  with confectioners' sugar, 118
  with flowers, 116
  with fruits, 116
  with ladyfingers, 115
  with layered cake squares, 98, 117
  with marzipan leaves and berries, 111
  with marzipan roses, 111
  with meringue logs, 115
  with mirrors, 82, 93, 116
  with nuts, 115
  with paper cones, 87, 115
  with rolled cake slices, 97, 117
  with rolled fondant, 112–13
  with serrated knives, 118
Cake fillings
  chestnut cream, 64
  chocolate mousse, classic, 366–67
  crème mousseline, classic, 57
  egg white–based, 58
  fruit crème mousseline, 58
  Italian meringue, 60
  lemon curd, 364
  passion fruit curd, 364–65
  passion fruit mousse, 365
  storing, 4, 5, 44
  strawberry Bavarian cream, 56
  types of, 44
  whipped cream, stabilized, 62–63
  white chocolate mousse, 367
Cake pans
  filling, 7
  preparing, 6
  sizes of, xiv
Cake racks, xiv
Cake rings, 78, 79, 84–85
Cakes. *See also* Cake decorating; Cake fillings; Layer cakes; Rolled cakes; Sponge cakes
  almond flour sponge, 20–21
  almond paste sponge, 22–23
  amount of frosting, glaze, or syrup needed for, 69
  angel food, 24
  apricot jelly roll, 106
  basic ingredients for, 4
  bûche de noël, 108
  butter, 25–31
  butter-enriched sponge, 16–17
  carrot, 32–35
  cheese, 42–43
  chiffon, 34–35
  chocolate cherry, 84–85
  chocolate hazelnut, 72–73
  chocolate meringue, individual, 94
  chocolate mousse dome, 96–97
  chocolate soufflé, 12–13
  chocolate sponge, 12
  coating, with hot glaze, 52
  coffee, 332–33
  cream and butter sheet, 29
  custard, 42–43
  dark chocolate mousse, 80
  devil's food, 30, 70–71
  dump, 25, 31
  even rising of, 5
  fine-crumb European sponge (*biscuit*), 14–15
  flourless chocolate, 368–69
  fluffy light butter, 28
  French meringue layer, 38–39
  French sponge cake, basic (genoise), 8–9
  German chocolate, 26–27
  high-ratio, 25, 31
  mango crème mousseline, 81–82
  moist sponge, 10–11
  oil-based, 32–35

orange buttercream layer, 76–77
peach crème mousseline, 98–99
petit fours, miniature, 102–3
piping batter for, 7
pound, 25–26
raspberry buttercream layer, 74–75
rolled pistachio buttercream, 104–5
sheet, 100–101
sizes and shapes of, 4
sour cream sponge, 18–19
strawberry and white chocolate
  mousse ladyfinger, 78–79
strawberry Bavarian, 92–93
strawberry-marzipan, classic
  (fraisier), 86–89
types of, 4
vanilla butter, 31
whipped cream-covered chocolate
  chestnut, 90–91
yeast, 36–37
Cake stands, 69–70
Caramel
  butterscotch sauce, 356
  cages, 83, 117
  crèmes caramels, 354–55
  making, 356
  sauce, 356
  syrup, 356
Carrot cake, 32–33
Cat's tongue cookies (langues de chat),
  116, 263
Challah, 330–31
Chantilly cream, 62
Charlottes, apple, 346–47
Checkerboard sablée cookies, 250–51
Cheese. See also Cream cheese
  bread sticks (grissini), 323
  goat cheese filling, 162
  pizza Margherita, 320
  puffs (gougères), 235
  quiche Lorraine, 238
  Roquefort and walnut pizza, 320
  soufflés, 359–61
  straws, 236
Cheesecake, 42–43
Cherries
  biscotti, 269
  and cheese Danish purses, 222

chocolate cake, 84–85
cobblers, 344
pie, 166–67
scones, 343
tartlets, 178
Chestnuts
  buttercream, 48
  cake, whipped cream-covered
    chocolate, 90–91
  cream cake filling, 64
  puree, 64
Chiffon cake, 34–35
Chocolate
  brownies, 272
  bûche de noël, 108
  buttercream, 48
  cake, flourless, 368–69
  cake, German, 26–27
  checkerboard sablée cookies, 250–51
  cherry cake, 84–85
  chestnut cake, whipped cream-
    covered, 90–91
  chip cookies, 258–59
  croissants, 218–19
  curls, 70, 71, 118
  devil's food cake, 30, 70–71
  éclairs, 210–11
  fondant, 163
  frosting, creamy (crème d'or), 52
  ganache, dark, 50–51
  ganache tart, 179
  ganache tartlets, miniature dark, 181
  glaze, dark, 53
  hazelnut cake, 72–73
  marbled sablée cookies, 252
  meringue cakes, individual, 94
  meringue logs, 41, 115
  mousse, classic, 366–67
  mousse cake, dark, 80
  mousse dome cake, 96–97
  raspberry-ganache tart, 179
  sablée cookies, 250
  seized, 366
  soufflé cakes, 12–13
  spiral-patterned sablée cookies,
    252–53
  sponge cake, 12
  strip, wrapping cakes with, 114

Ciabatta, 309–10
Cinnamon rolls, 334–35
Citrus fruits. See also individual fruits
  buttercream, 48
  tarts, 194–95
  zest, candying, 194
  zest, grating, 194
Clafoutis, roast pear, 188–89
Cobblers, cherry, 344
Coconut
  cream pie, 199
  macaroons, 267
Coffee
  buttercream, 48
  éclairs, 210–11
  fondant, 163
  pots de crème, 353
Coffee cakes, 332–33
Cognac, xiii
Convection ovens, xiv
Cookie presses, 254
Cookies
  almond tuiles, 264
  biscotti, 269
  blood orange tuiles, lacy, 265
  brownies, 272
  cat's tongue (langues de chat), 263
  checkerboard sablée, 250–51
  chocolate chip, 258–59
  chocolate sablée, 250
  coconut macaroons, 267
  decorating, 249
  dough, basic butter, 246
  financiers, 262
  Florentine almond, 268
  holiday butter, 248
  jelly, 247
  lemon bars, 274–75
  macarons, 266–67
  madeleines, 260
  madeleines, cakey, 261
  marbled sablée, 252
  pecan fingers, 257
  sablée, 250
  shortbread, 256
  spiral-patterned sablée, 252–53

Copper bowls, xiv
Corn syrup, xiii

Cranberries
  Biscotti, 269
  scones, 343
Cream, xiii
Cream cheese
  carrot cake, 32–33
  cheesecake, 42–43
  Danish filling, 162
  Danish twirls, miniature, 223
  and fruit Danish purses, 222
  tart and pie pastry dough, 135
  tart filling, 161
Cream puffs, 213
  pastry dough (pâte à choux), 155
  pastry swans, 214–15
Crème anglaise (vanilla custard sauce), 54–55
Crème d'or (creamy chocolate frosting), 52
Crème mousselines
  about, 56
  classic, 57
  flavoring, 56
  fruit, 58
Crèmes brûlées, 357
  dishes, xiv
Crèmes caramels, 354–55
Croissants, 216–17
  chocolate, 218–19
  dough, 156–57
  size of, 219
Currants
  barquettes, 182
  biscotti, 269
Custards
  about, 186, 352
  cakes, 42–43
  coffee pots de crème, 353
  crèmes brûlées, 357
  crèmes caramels, 354–55
  pies and tarts, 186
  sauce, vanilla (crème anglaise), 54–55

D

Danish pastries
  cheese filling, 162
  dough for, 220
  packets, fruit, 224
  purses, fruit and cheese, 222
  rolled, 225
  tartlets, fruit, 220–21
  twirls, miniature cheese, 223
  types of, 220
Devil's food cake, 30, 70–71
Dobos, 18
Dump cakes, 25, 31
Duxelles (mushroom filling), 162

E

Eaux de vie, xiii
Éclairs, 210–11
Eggs
  beating whole, 8
  size of, xiii
  warming, 10
  wash, 146
Equipment, xiv–xv

F

Filo dough, 232
Financiers, 262
Florentine almond cookies, 268
Flour
  cake, 130
  folding with, 16
  for pastry dough, 129, 130
  types of, xiii
Flourless chocolate cake, 368–69
Flowers, decorating cakes with, 116
Focaccia, 324–25
Fondant
  chocolate, 163
  coffee, 163
  flavoring, 163
  liquid, 163
  rolled, 66–67, 112–13
Food processors, xiv
Fougasse, 300
Fraisier (classic strawberry-marzipan cake), 86–89
Frangipane, 159
  hazelnut, 161
French meringue layer cake, 38–39
Frostings. See also Buttercream; Glazes; Royal icing
  amount required, for one cake, 46, 69
  applying, with a spoon, 59
  chocolate, creamy (crème d'or), 52
  egg white–based, 58–59
  glazes vs., 44, 50
  seven-minute, 59
  storing, 4, 44
Fruit. See also individual fruits
  and cheese Danish purses, 222
  crème mousseline, 58
  custard pies and tarts, 186
  Danish packets, 224
  Danish tartlets, 220–21
  Danish twirls, miniature cheese, 223
  decorating cakes with, 116
  fresh vs. frozen, xiii
  glazes, 61
  -hazelnut puff pastry tartlets, 202–3
  mousses, 365
  precooking, for pies and tarts, 164
  tartlets, miniature puff pastry, 203
  tartlets, miniature raw, 182
  tarts, 179
Fruit curds
  about, 352, 364
  lemon, 364
  making, 358
  passion fruit, 364–65

G

Galette, almond–puff pastry (pithiviers), 206–7
Ganache
  dark chocolate, 50–51
  tarts and tartlets with, 179–81
  whipped, 51
  white chocolate, 51
Genoise (basic French sponge cake), 8–9
German chocolate cake, 26–27
Glazes. See also Fondant; Ganache
  amount required, for one cake, 69
  dark chocolate, 53
  frostings vs., 44, 50
  fruit, 61

hot, coating cake with, 52
lemon, 61
storing, 44
white chocolate, 44
Goat cheese filling, 55
Gougères (cheese puffs), 235
Grand Marnier soufflés, 362
Grissini (bread sticks), 323

H

Hazelnuts
biscotti, 269
buttercream, 48
cake, chocolate, 72–73
frangipane, 161
-fruit puff pastry tartlets, 202–3
meringue (dacquoise), 40
peeling, 161
praline paste, 161
tartlets, 176
High-ratio cakes, 25, 31
Holiday butter cookies, 248

I

Italian meringue, 60
buttercream, 46

J

Jalousie, mushroom, 234–35
Jelly cookies, 247
Jelly roll, apricot, 106

K

Key lime tart, 194
Kiwis
frangipane tartlets, 178
-whipped white chocolate ganache
tart, 180

L

Ladyfingers
cake, strawberry and white
chocolate mousse, 78–79
decorating cakes with, 115
making, 14–15

Langues de chat (cat's tongue cookies),
storing, 110
-strawberry cake, classic (fraisier),
86–89
Layer cakes. See also individual recipes
116, 263
American, 68
amount of frosting, glaze, or syrup
needed for, 69
assembling, in cake rings, 84–85
assembling, on cake stands, 69–70
assembling, without a cake stand, 75
with different layers, 72
European, 68
making layers for, 18
rectangular, 76
square, with marzipan topping,
88–89
with two fillings, 91
types of, 68
Lemons
bars, 274–75
-blackberry cream tart, 183
curd, 185, 364
glaze, 61
meringue pie, 184–85
-strawberry cream tart, 183
tart, 194
tart, Key, 194
Levain levure, 284
Limes
tart, 194
tart, Key, 194
Linzer pastry dough, 140
Linzertorte, 208–9

M

Macarons, 266–67
Macaroons, coconut, 267
Madeleines, 260
cakey, 261
Mango crème mousseline cake, 81–82
Marble, xiv
Marzipan
coloring, 110
covering cakes with, 110
leaves and berries, 111
making, 109
reconstituting dried-out, 110
rolling out, 110
roses, 111

Meringue
buttercream, Italian, 46
cakes, individual chocolate, 94
disks, 38
hazelnut (dacquoise), 40
Italian, 60
layer cake, French, 38–39
logs, chocolate, 41, 115
mushrooms, 109
nut-flavored, 38
pie, lemon, 184–85
tart, passion fruit, 184
types of, 38
Mirrors, decorating cakes with, 81, 93,
116
Mixers, stand, xv
Molds and ramekins
buttering, 6
coating, with cocoa powder, 6, 7
types of, xiv
Mousses
chocolate, classic, 366–67
fruit, 54
making, 366
passion fruit, 365
uses for, 352
white chocolate, 367
Muffins
banana nut bread, 338
blueberry, 341
Mushrooms
filling (duxelles), 162
jalousie, 234–35

N

Napoleons, 226–28
Nuts. See also individual nuts
decorating cakes with, 115
oils, xiii
roasting, xiii
storing, xiii

O

Oranges
buttercream, quick and easy, 46
buttercream layer cake, 76–77
Grand Marnier soufflés, 362–63
panettone, 328–29
peel, candying, 328
slices, candied, 195
tart, 194
tuiles, lacy blood, 265
Ovens, xiv
Oven spring, 302

P

Pain epis, 297
Pain fendu, 300
Palmiers, 270–71
Panettone, 328–29
Pans, xiv, xv
Paper cones, 87, 115
Parchment paper, xiv
Passion fruit
curd, 364–65
meringue tart, 184
-mixed berry mousse tart, 181
mousse, 365
tartlets or tart, 191
Pastries. *See also* Tart and pastry
fillings
almond-puff pastry galette
(pithiviers), 206–7
apple strudel, 228–31
blueberry turnovers, 204
cheese puffs (*gougères*), 235
cheese straws, 236
chocolate croissants, 218–19
cream puffs, 213
croissants, 216–17
éclairs, 210–11
fruit and cheese Danish purses, 222
fruit Danish packets, 224
miniature cheese Danish twirls, 223
mushroom *jalousie*, 234–35
napoleons, 226–28
pistachio baklava, 232–33
preheating oven for, 151
quiche Lorraine, 238

rolled Danish pastries, 225
vol-au-vents, 237
Pastry bags and tips
buying, xiv
cake batter piped with, 7
filling and using, 64–65
meringue disks piped from, 38
Pastry cream, 160–61
Pastry cutters, xv
Pastry dough
basic pie and tart (*pâte brisée*), 130–33
classic puff, 148–49
cream cheese tart and pie, 135
cream puff (*pâte à choux*), 155
croissant, 156–57
extra buttery sweet (*pâte sablée*), 134–35
flakiness of, 128
flaky pie and tart, 136–37
lining pan with, 141–44
linzer, 140
quick puff, 150–51
rolling out, 141, 144
sweet crisp (*pâte sucrée*), 138–39
sweetened basic pie and tart (*pâte brisée sucrée*), 131
tips for, 129–30
types of, 128
Pastry scrapers, xv
Pâte à choux, 155
Pâte brisée, 128, 130–33
Pâte brisée sucrée, 128, 131
Pâte fermentée, 307, 308
Pâte sablée, 128, 134–35
Peaches
-blackberry mousseline tart, 180
crème mousseline cake, 98–99
frangipane tartlets, 178
Pears
and cheese Danish purses, 222
clafoutis, roast, 188–89
frangipane tart, puff pastry, 201–2
roast, in butterscotch sauce, 188
Pecans
fingers, 257
pie, 192
roasting, 257
Persimmon tart or tartlets, 191

Petits fours, miniature cake, 102–3
Pie pans, xv
Pies. *See also* Pastry dough
apple, 168–69
banana cream, 196–97
berry, individual deep-dish, 204
blind baking shells for, 144, 145
blueberry, 164–65
cherry, 166–67
coconut cream, 199
double-crust fruit, 166, 168
fruit custard, 186
lemon meringue, 184–85
pecan, 192
precooking fruit for, 164
pumpkin, 190–91
single-crust fruit, 165
troubleshooting, 145
Pistachios
baklava, 232–33
buttercream, 48
buttercream cake, rolled, 104–5
peeling, 232
Pita bread, 322
Pithiviers (almond-puff pastry galette), 206–7
Pizzas
dough, 319
making, 321
Margherita, 320
Roquefort and walnut, 320
Plastic wrap, xv
Plums
frangipane tartlets, 178
tart, 174
Poolish, 285, 287
Popovers, 340
Pots and pans, xiv, xv
Pots de crème, coffee, 353
Pound cake, 25–26
Praline paste, 161
Proofing boxes, 302
Puff pastry
-almond galette (pithiviers), 206–7
apple tart, crispy, 200–201
berry pies, individual deep-dish, 204
blueberry turnovers, 204
cases, 152–53

cheese puffs (gougères), 235
cheese straws, 236
cream puffs, 213
dough, classic, 148–49
dough, cream (pâte à choux), 155
dough, quick, 150–51
éclairs, 210–11
fruit tartlets, miniature, 203
mushroom jalousie, 234–35
napoleons, 226–28
palmiers, 270–71
pear frangipane tart, 201–2
rectangles, 153
swans, cream, 214–15
tartlets, fruit-hazelnut, 202–3
tips for, 151, 154
trimmings, 148
vol-au-vents, 237
Pumpernickel bread, 318–19
Pumpkin pie, 190–91

Q
Quiche Lorraine, 238

R
Raisins
apple strudel, 228–31
bread, sourdough whole wheat, 316–17
coffee cakes, 332–33
panettone, 328–29
rolled Danish pastries, 225
Ramekins. See Molds and ramekins
Raspberries
buttercream layer cake, 74–75
-classic crème mousseline tart, 180
-ganache tart, 179
linzertorte, 208–9
peach crème mousseline cake, 98–99
strawberry Bavarian cake, 92–93
Rolled cakes
apricot jelly roll, 106
bûche de noël, 108
making, 104, 105
pistachio buttercream, 104–5
Rolling pins, xv

Rolls
cinnamon, 334–35
shaping, 298
Roquefort and walnut pizza, 320
Royal icing, 67, 249
Rum, xiii
Rye bread, 314–15

S
Sablée cookies, 250
checkerboard, 250–51
chocolate, 250
making, with a cookie press, 254
marbled, 252
spiral-patterned, 252–53
Salt, xiii
Sauces
butterscotch, 356
caramel, 356
dark chocolate ganache, 50–51
vanilla custard (crème anglaise), 50–51

Savarins, 54–55
Scones, 36–37
Seven-minute frosting, 59
Sheet cakes. See also individual recipes
amount of frosting, glaze, or syrup needed for, 69
making, 100–101
uses for, 100
Sheet pans, xiv
Shortbread cookies, 256
Shortcakes, strawberry, 345
Soufflé cakes, chocolate, 12–13
Soufflés
cheese, 359–61
Grand Marnier, 362–63
making, 352, 359
preheating oven for, 151
Sour cream sponge cake, 18–19
Sourdough bread, 313
controlling tartness of, 311
starter for, 285–86, 311–12
whole wheat, 316–17
whole wheat raisin, 316–17

Spatulas, rubber, xv
Spirits, xiii–xiv
Sponge cakes

almond flour, 20–21
almond paste, 22–23
angel food, 24
basic French (genoise), 8–9
butter-enriched, 16–17
chocolate, 12
fine-crumb European (biscuit), 14–15
moist, 10–11
moistening, 7
sour cream, 18–19
types of, 7
Sponge starter, 284, 287, 306
Springform pans, 78, 80, 84–85
Starters
biga, 285, 287
leftover dough as, 285
making, 286, 287
mature, 308
mixed, 286
natural (sourdough), 285–86, 311–12
poolish, 285, 287
sponge, 284, 287, 306
Sticky buns, 336–37
Strawberries
Bavarian cake, 92–93
Bavarian cream, 56
hulling and slicing, 86
-lemon cream tart, 183
-marzipan cake, classic (fraisier), 86–89
shortcakes, 345
and white chocolate mousse ladyfinger cake, 78–79
Strudel, apple, 228–31
Sugar
confectioners', decorating cakes with, 118
in pastry dough, 130
syrup, stages of, 47
types of, xiv
Syrups
amount required, for one cake, 69
caramel, 356
simple, 36
sugar, 47

T

Tart and pastry fillings
  almond cream, 159
  cheese Danish, 162
  cream cheese, 161
  frangipane, 159
  goat cheese, 162
  hazelnut frangipane, 161
  mushroom (*duxelles*), 162
  pastry cream, 160–61
  praline paste, 161
  types of, 158
Tartlets. *See also* Pastry dough; Tart and pastry fillings
  almond, 176
  apricot, 177
  berry, 182
  berry frangipane, 178
  cherry, 178
  dark chocolate ganache, miniature, 181
  fruit Danish, 220–21
  fruit-hazelnut puff pastry, 202–3
  hazelnut, 176
  kiwi frangipane, 178
  passion fruit, 191
  peach frangipane, 178
  persimmon, 191
  plum frangipane, 178
  prebaked shells for, 146–57
  puff pastry fruit, miniature, 203
  raw fruit, miniature, 182
  raw fruit, with custard filling, 159
  troubleshooting, 145
  white chocolate ganache, miniature, 181
Tart pans, xv
Tarts. *See also* Pastry dough; Tart and pastry fillings; Tartlets
  Alsatian apple, 186–87
  apple, classic French, 170–71
  apple, crispy, 200–201
  apricot frangipane, 175
  blackberry-lemon cream, 183
  blackberry–peach mousseline, 180
  blind baking shells for, 144, 145
  blueberry frangipane, 176
  fruit custard, 186
  ganache, 179
  Key lime, 194
  kiwi–whipped white chocolate ganache, 180
  lemon, 194
  lime, 194
  linzertorte, 208–9
  mixed berry–passion fruit mousse, 181
  orange, 194
  passion fruit, 191
  passion fruit meringue, 184
  persimmon, 191
  plum, 174
  precooking fruit for, 164
  puff pastry pear frangipane, 201–2
  raspberry–classic crème mousseline, 180
  raspberry-ganache, 179
  raw fruit, 179
  strawberry-lemon cream, 183
  tarte tatin, 172–73
  troubleshooting, 145
Tomatoes
  Pizza Margherita, 320
Tuiles
  almond, 264
  blood orange, lacy, 265
Turnovers, blueberry, 204

V

Vanilla
  butter cake, 31
  buttercream, 48
  custard sauce (crème anglaise), 54–55
  extract and beans, xiv
Vegetable oil, xiv
Vol-au-vents, 237

W

Walnuts
  apple strudel, 228–31
  banana nut bread muffins, 338
  brownies, 272
  carrot cake, 32–33
  cheese Danish twirls, miniature, 223
  chocolate chip cookies, 258–59
  coffee cakes, 332–33
  Danish pastries, rolled, 225
  and Roquefort pizza, 320
  sticky buns, 336–37
  toasting, 272
Wheat sheaf bread, 296, 297
Whipped cream
  Chantilly, 62
  -covered chocolate chestnut cake, 90–91
  making, 62
  squeezed, 62
  stabilized, 62–63
White bread
  mature starter, 307–8
  sponge starter, 306–7
  straight dough, 304–5
White chocolate
  ganache, 51
  ganache tart, kiwi–, 180
  ganache tartlets, miniature, 181
  glaze, 53
  mousse, 367
  mousse ladyfinger cake, strawberry and, 78–79
Whole wheat bread
  sourdough, 316–17
  sourdough raisin, 316–17
Windowpane test, 289

Y

Yeast. *See also* Breads, yeasted
  activating, 286, 289
  proofing, 286, 287
  rising times and, 286, 304
  role of, 284
  temperature and, 284, 286
  types of, 284, 286
Yeast cakes, 36–37